History of the war in the Peninsula and in the South of France From the Year 1807 to the Year 1814 Volume 5

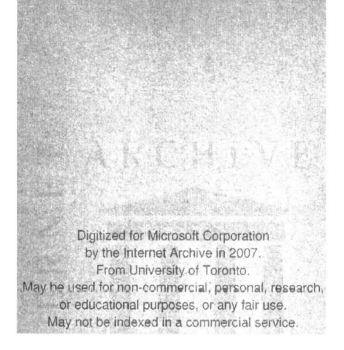

HISTORY

WAR IN THE PENINSULA

HISTORY

OF THE

WAR IN THE PENINSULA

AND IN THE

SOUTH OF FRANCE

FROM THE YEAR 1807 TO THE YEAR 1814

BY

MAJOR-GENERAL SIR W. F. P. NAPIER, K.C.B.

COLONEL 27TH REGIMENT

WITH FIFTY-FIVE MAPS AND PLANS

VOL. V.

LONDON

FREDERICK WARNE AND CO.

AND NEW YORK

TABLE OF CONTENTS.

BOOK THE TWENTIETH.

CHAPTER I.

CHAPTER II.

CHAPTER III.

CHAPTER IV.

CHAPTER V.

CHAPTER VI.

CHAPTER VII.

CHAPTER VIII.

BOOK THE TWENTY-FIRST.

CHAPTER I.

CHAPTER II.

CHAPTER III.

CHAPTER IV.

CHAPTER V.

BOOK THE TWENTY-SECOND.

CHAPTER I.

CHAPTER II.

BOOK THE TWENTY-THIRD.

CHAPTER I.

CHAPTER II.

APPENDIX.

LIST OF PLATES.

NOTICE.

1°. There are no good materials for an accurate map of the Peninsula, but the small one furnished in this volume, together with the sketches in each volume, more accurate than might be supposed, will give a clear general notion of the operations.

2°. The additional manuscript authorities consulted for this volume, are the official correspondence of lord William Bentinck; some notes by lord Hill; the journal and correspondence of sir Rufane Donkin; a journal of colonel Oglander, twenty-sixth regiment; a memoir by sir George Gipps, royal engineers; and a variety of communications by other officers. Lastly, authenticated copies of the official journals and correspondence of most of the marshals and generals who commanded armies in Spain; which were at my request supplied by the French War-Office with a prompt liberality indicative of that military frankness and just pride which ought and does characterise the officers of Napoleon's army. I have also been enabled to correct my former accounts of the assaults of Fort Gayetano at Salamanca, and those of Burgos, from the professional papers since published by the engineers.

HISTORY

OF THE

PENINSULA WAR.

BOOK THE TWENTIETH.

CHAPTER I.

WHILE the armies were striving the political affairs continued complicated and unsteady. The evils of bad government in England, Spain and Portugal, the incongruous alliance of bigoted aristocracy with awakened democracy, and the inevitable growth of national jealousies as external danger seemed to recede, were becoming so powerful, that if relief had not been obtained from extraneous events even the vigour of Wellington must have sunk under the pressure. The secret causes of disturbance shall now be laid bare, and it will then be seen that the catastrophe of Napoleon's Russian campaign was absolutely necessary to the final success of the British arms in the Peninsula. I speak not of the physical power which, if his host had not withered on the snowy wastes of Muscovy, the emperor could have poured into Spain, but of those innumerable moral diseases which corrupted the very life-blood of the contest in the Peninsula. If Russia owed her safety in some degree to that contest, the fate of the Peninsula was in return decided on the plains of Russia; for had the French veterans who there perished, returned victorious, the war could have been maintained for years in Spain with all its waste of treasures and of blood, to the absolute ruin of England even though her army had been

victorious in every battle. Yet who shall say with certainty
what termination any war will ever have? Who shall prophesy
of an art always varying, and of such intricacy that its secrets
seem beyond the reach of human intellect? What vast preparations, what astonishing combinations were involved in the
plan, what vigour and ability displayed in the execution of
Napoleon's march to Moscow! Yet when the winter came,
only four days sooner than he expected, the giant's scheme
became a theme for children's laughter!

Nevertheless the political grandeur of that expedition will
not be hereafter judged from the wild triumph of his enemies,
nor its military merits from the declamation hitherto passed
off as the history of that wondrous though unfortunate enterprise. It will not be the puerilities of Labaume, of Segur,
and their imitators, nor even that splendid military and political essay of Jomini, called the '*Life of Napoleon*,' which
posterity will accept as the measure of a general who carried
four hundred thousand soldiers across the Niemen, and a
hundred and sixty thousand to Moscow. And with such a
military providence, with such a vigilance, so disposing his
reserves, so guarding his flanks, so guiding his masses, that
while constantly victorious in front no post was lost in his
rear, no convoy failed, no courier was stopped, not even a
letter was missing: the communication with his capital was
as regular and certain as if that immense march had been but
a summer excursion of pleasure! However it failed, and its
failure was the safety of the Peninsula.

In England the retreat from Burgos was viewed with the
angry fear which always accompanies the disappointment of
high-raised public expectation; the people, taught to believe
the French weak and dispirited, saw them so strong and
daring that even victory had not enabled the allies to make a
permanent stand beyond the frontiers of Portugal. Hence a
growing distrust as to the ultimate result, which would not
have failed to overturn the war faction, if the retreat of the
French from Moscow, the defection of Prussia, and the
strange unlooked-for spectacle of Napoleon vanquished, had
not come in happy time as a counterpoise. And when the
parliament met lord Wellesley did very distinctly show, that

if the successes in the early part of the year had not been pushed to the extent expected, and had been followed by important reverses, the causes were clearly to be traced to the imbecile administration of Perceval and his coadjutors, whose policy he truly characterized as having in it '*nothing regular but confusion*.' With accurate knowledge of facts he discussed the military question, and maintained that twelve thousand infantry and three thousand cavalry added to the army in the beginning of the year, would have rendered the campaign decisive; because the Russian contest, the incapacity of Joseph and the dissensions of the French generals in Spain, had produced the most favourable crisis for striking a vital blow at the enemy's power. The cabinet he said knew this and in good time, but though there were abundance of soldiers idling at home when for the nation's welfare they should have been in the Peninsula, though the ministers had actually sent within five thousand as many men as were necessary, they had, with an imbecility marking all their proceedings, so contrived, that few or none should reach the theatre of war until the time for success had passed away. Then touching upon the financial question, with a rude hand he tore Perceval's pitiful pretexts, that the want of specie had necessarily put bounds to their efforts and that the general himself did not complain. 'No!' exclaimed lord Wellesley, 'he does not complain because it is the sacred duty of a soldier not to complain. But he does not say that with greater means he could not do greater things, and his country will not be satisfied if these means are withheld by men, who having assumed the direction of affairs in such a crisis have only incapacity to plead in extenuation of their failures.'

This stern accuser, fresh from the ministry, versed in state matters and of unquestionable talent, was well acquainted with the actual resources and difficulties of the moment and sincere in his opinions, because he had abandoned office rather than be a party to such a miserable mismanagement of England's power. He was no mean authority against his former colleagues even though the facts had not so clearly borne out his views, yet they did to the letter. That England possessed the troops and that they were wanted by

Wellington is undeniable. Even in September there were still between fifty and sixty thousand soldiers present under arms at home, and additional forces could certainly have been fed in Portugal, because the reserve magazines contained provisions for one hundred thousand men for nine months. The only question was the procuring specie to purchase supplies which could not be had on credit. Wellington had made the campaign almost without specie, and a small additional force would not have overwhelmed his resources; but what efforts, what ability, what order, what arrangements were made by the government to overcome the difficulties of the time? Was there less extravagance in public offices, public works, public salaries, public contracts? The snuff-boxes and services of plate given to diplomatists, the gorgeous furniture of palaces, the gaudy trappings wasted on Whittingham's, Roche's, and Downie's divisions, would almost have furnished the wants of the additional troops. Where were the millions lavished in subsidies to the Spaniards? where the millions which South America had transmitted to Cadiz? where the sums spent by the soldiers during the war? Real money had nearly disappeared from England and a base paper had usurped its place; but gold had not disappeared from the world and an able ministry would have found it. Those men only knew how to squander.

The subsidy granted to Portugal was paid by the commercial speculations of lord Wellington and Mr. Stuart, speculations which also fed the army, saved the whole population of Portugal from famine, and prevented the war from stopping in 1811; and so little could the ministers comprehend, much less make such arrangements, that they now rebuked their general for having adopted them, and after their own imbecile manner insisted upon a new mode of providing supplies. On every side they gave proof of incapacity. Lord William Bentinck was allowed to plan an invasion of Italy when additional troops were wanted in Portugal; and suffered to bid in the money-market against Wellington and sweep away four millions of dollars at an exorbitant premium for a chimera, when the war

Wellington, MSS.

Mr. Stuart, MSS

in the Peninsula was nearly stopped in default of that very
money which Wellington could have otherwise procured—
nay, had actually been promised at a reasonable cost. Nor
was this the full measure of their folly.

Lord Wellesley affirmed, and they were unable to deny the
fact, that dollars might have been obtained from South
America to any amount, if the government would have consented to pay the market-price for them; they would not do
it, and yet afterwards sought to purchase the same dollars at
a higher rate in the European markets! He told them and
they could not deny it, that they had empowered five different
agents to purchase dollars for five different services without
any controlling head; that they were bidding against each
other in every money-market, and the restrictions as to the
price were exactly in the inverse proportion to the importance of the service: the agent for the troops in Malta was
permitted to offer the highest price, lord Wellington was
restricted to the lowest! And besides this folly he showed
that they had, under their licensing system, permitted French
vessels to bring French goods, silks and gloves, to England,
and to carry bullion away in return. Napoleon thus paid
his army in Spain with the very coin which should have subsisted the English troops.

But incapable as the ministers were of making the simplest
arrangements and neglecting the most obvious means of
supplying the army; incapable even of sending out a few
bales of clothing and arms for the Spaniards without producing the utmost confusion, they were heedless of their general's counsels, prompt to listen to every intriguing adviser,
and to plunge into absurd complicated measures to relieve
that distress which their own imbecility had produced.
When the war with the United States broke out, a war provoked by themselves, they suffered the Admiralty, contrary
to the wishes of Mr. Stuart, to reduce the naval   Mr. Stuart's
force at Lisbon and neglect Wellington's express   Correspond-
recommendations for the protection of the mer-   ence, MSS.
chantmen bringing flour and stores to Portugal.   Then the
American privateers being unmolested run down the coast
of Africa, intercepted the provision trade from the Brazils,

one of the principal resources of the army, and emboldened
by impunity infested the coast of Portugal, captured fourteen
ships loaded with flour off the Douro, and a large vessel in
the very mouth of the Tagus. These things happened when
the ministers were censuring and interfering with the general's
commercial transactions, and seeking to throw the feeding of
his soldiers into the hands of British speculators; as if the
supply of an army was like that of a common market! never
considering that it would be the merchant's interest to starve
the troops for the increase of profit; never considering that
the commerce they would stop had paid the Portuguese
subsidy for them, and had furnished the military chest with
specie when their administrative capacity was unequal to the
task.

Never was a government better served than the British
government was by lord Wellington and Mr. Stuart. With
abilities vigilance and industry seldom equalled, they had
made themselves masters of the Portuguese policy, foreign,
domestic, military, civil, and judicial; they knew all the
causes of mischief and faithfully represented them to the
Portuguese and British governments, and had devised effectual remedies. By the former they were met with vexatious
opposition; the latter, neglecting their advice, lent themselves
to those foolish financial schemes before touched upon as
emanating from Villiers, Vansittart and the count of Funchal;
the first deficient as an ambassador and statesman, the second
universally derided as a financier, the third from his long
residence in London knowing little of Portugal, deriving that
little from his brother the restless principal, and in all his
schemes having reference to his own intrigues in the Brazils.
Their plans were necessarily absurd. Funchal revived the
old project of an English loan, and in concert with his coadjutors desired to establish a bank after the English manner;
advancing several minor details and propositions, most of
them suggested before by principal Souza but rejected by
Wellington, and all designed to evade not to remedy the evils.
Finally they devised, and the English cabinet actually entertained the plan, of selling the crown and church property of
Portugal; and this spoliation of the catholic church was to be

effected by commissioners, one of them to be
Mr. Sydenham, an Englishman and a protes-
tant! Thinking however that the pope would not
readily yield consent, they resolved to apply to his
nuncio, who being in their power they expected to find more
pliable.

Mr. Syden-
ham.
Mr. Stuart,
MSS.

Having thus provided in their way for financial difficulties,
the ministers concocted for the supply of the army, what they
called a modified system of requisitions after the manner of
the French! Their speeches, their manifestoes, their whole
scheme of policy, which in the working had nearly crushed
the liberties of England and had plunged the whole world
into war; that policy whose aim and scope was, they said, to
support established religion the rights of monarchs and the
independence of nations was thus cast aside.   Yea! these
men, to remove difficulties caused by their own incapacity and
negligence, were ready to adopt all they had before condemned
and reviled in the French; they were eager to meddle in the
most offensive manner with the catholic religion, by getting
from the nuncio who was in their power what they could
not get from the pope voluntarily; they were ready to interfere with the rights of the Portuguese crown by selling its
property, and desired to adopt the very system of requisitions
which they had so often denounced as rendering the name of
France abhorrent to the world!

All these schemes were duly transmitted to Wellington and
Mr. Stuart, and the former had in the field to unravel the
intricacies, detect the fallacies, and combat the wild speculations of men who were giving a loose to their imaginations
on such complicated questions of state.   It was while preparing to fight Marmont he had to expose the futility of a
loan,—it was on the heights of San Christoval, on the field
of battle itself, that he demonstrated the absurdity of attempting to form a Portuguese bank,—it was in the trenches of
Burgos he dissected Funchal's and Villiers's schemes of finance,
and exposed the folly of attempting the sale of church property,
—it was at the termination of the retreat that with a mixture of
rebuke and reasoning he quelled the proposal to live by forced
requisitions—and on each occasion he showed himself as well

acquainted with these subjects as he was with the mechanism of armies. Reform abuses, raise your actual taxes with vigour and impartiality, pay your present debt before you contract a new one, was his constant reply to the propositions for loans. And when the English ministers pressed the other plans, which, besides the bank, included a re-coinage of dollars into cruzados, in other words the depreciation of the silver standard, he with an unsparing hand laid their folly bare. The military and political state of Portugal he said was such that no man in his senses, native or foreigner, would place his capital where he could not withdraw it at a moment's notice. When Massena invaded that country unreasonable despondency had prevailed amongst the ministers, now they seemed to have a confidence as wild as their former fear; but he who knew the real state of affairs; he who knew the persons that were expected to advance money; he who knew the relative forces of the contending armies, the advantages and disadvantages attending each; he who knew the absolute weakness of the Portuguese frontier as a line of defence, could only laugh at the notion that the capitalists would take gold out of their own chests to lodge it in the chests of the bank and eventually in those of the Portuguese treasury, a treasury deservedly without credit. The French armies opposed to him in the field (he was then on San Christoval) were just double his own strength, and a serious accident to Ballesteros, a rash general with a bad army, would compel the Anglo-Portuguese force to retire into Portugal and the prospects of the campaign would vanish; and this argument left out of the question any accident which might happen to himself or general Hill. Portugal would he hoped be saved, but its security was not such as these visionaries would represent it.

They had proposed also a British security in jewels for the capital of their bank, and their reasonings on this head were equally fallacious. This security was to be strengthened by collecting the duties on wines exported from Portugal to England, and they had not even ascertained whether those duties were conformable to the treaty with England. Then came the former question. Would Great Britain guarantee the capital of the subscribers whether Portugal was lost or saved?

If the country should be lost the new possessors would
understand the levying of duties upon wines as well as the
old; would England make her port drinkers pay two duties,
one for the benefit of the bank capitalists, another for the
benefit of French conquerors? If all these difficulties could
be got over a bank would be the most efficacious mode in
which England could use her credit for the benefit of Portugal; but all the other plans proposed were mere spendthrift
schemes to defray the expenses of the war, and if the English
government could descend to entertain them they would fail,
because the real obstacle, scarcity of specie, would remain.

A nation desirous of establishing public credit should begin,
he said, by acquiring a revenue equal to its fixed expenditure,
and must manifest an inclination to be honest by performing
its engagements with respect to public debts. This maxim
he had constantly enforced to the Portuguese government,
and had they minded it instead of trusting to the fallacious
hope of getting loans in England, the deficiency of their
revenue would have been made up without imposing new
taxes, and even with the repeal of many which were oppressive and unjust. The fair and honest collection of taxes
which ought to exist would have been sufficient. For after
protracted and unsparing exertions, and by refusing to accept
their paper money on any other condition in his commissariat
transactions, he had at last forced the Portuguese authorities
to pay the interest of that paper and of their exchequer bills,
called ' Apolicies grandes;' and the effect had been to increase
the resources of the government though the government had
even in the execution evinced its corruption. Then showing
in detail how this benefit had been produced he traced the
mischief created by men whom he called the sharks of Lisbon
and other great towns, meaning speculators, principally Englishmen, whose nefarious cupidity led them to cry down the
credit of the army-bills and then purchase them, to the
injury of the public and of the poor people who furnished the
supplies.

A plan to re-coin Spanish dollars and gain eight in the
hundred of pure silver, which they contained above the Portuguese cruzado, he treated as a useless fraud. In Lisbon,

where the cruzado was current, some gain might perhaps be
made; but it was not certain, and foreigners, Englishmen
and Americans from whom the great supplies were purchased,
would immediately add to their prices as the coin deteriorated.
The operations and expenditure of the army were not confined
to Lisbon, nor even to Portugal, and the cruzado would not
pass for its nominal value in Spain; thus the greatest inconvenience would result from a scheme at the best unworthy of
the British government. In fine the reform of abuses, the
discontinuance of useless expenses, economy and energy were
the only remedies.

Such was his reasoning, yet it had little effect on his perse-
cutors; for when his best men were falling by hundreds, his
brightest visions of glory fading on the smoky walls of
Burgos, he was again forced to examine and refute anew
voluminous plans of Portuguese finance, concocted by Funchal
and Villiers with notes by Vansittart. And these projects
were accompanied with complaints that frauds had been practised on the custom-house and violence used towards the inhabitants by the British commissaries, whose misconduct was the
real cause of the financial distresses of Portugal. The patient
industry of genius was never more severely taxed!

Wellington repelled the charge of exactions and frauds as
applied to the army; he showed that to reform the custom-
house so as to prevent frauds had been his unceasing recommendation to the Portuguese government; that he had in detail
taught that government how to remedy the evils they complained of, how to increase their customs, how to levy their
taxes, and arrange their whole financial system in a manner
to render their revenues equal to their expenses, without that
oppression and injustice which they were in the habit of
practising: for the extortions and violence complained of,
were perpetrated by the Portuguese commissariat, and yet the
troops of that nation were starving. Having exposed Funchal's ignorance of financial facts in detail, and challenged him
to prove his charges against the British army, he discussed
the great question of selling the crown and church lands,
proposed as a substitute for that economy and reform of
abuses which he so long, so often, and so vainly had pressed

upon the regency. The proposal was not quite new. 'I have already,' he observed, 'had before me a proposition for the sale or rather transfer of crown lands to the creditors of the Junta de Viveres; but these were the uncultivated lands in Alemtejo, and I pointed out the improbability that any-body would take such lands in payment, and the injury to the public credit by making the scheme public if not likely to be successful. My opinion is that there is nobody in Portugal possessed of capital who entertains, or who ought to enter-tain such an opinion of the state of affairs in the Peninsula as to lay out his money in the purchase of crown lands. The loss of a battle, not in the Peninsula even but elsewhere, would expose his estate to confiscation, or at all events to ruin by a fresh incursion of the enemy. Even if any man could believe that Portugal is secure against the invasion of the enemy, and his estate and person against the 'violence, exac-tions and frauds' (these were Funchal's words respecting the allied army) of the enemy, he is not during the existence of the war, according to the conde de Funchal's notion, exempt from those evils from his own countrymen and their allies. Try this experiment, offer the estates of the crown for sale, and it will be seen whether I have formed a correct judgment on this subject.' Then running with a rapid hand over many minor though intricate fallacies for raising the value of the Portuguese paper-money, he thus treated the great question of the church lands.

First, as in the case of crown lands, there would be no purchasers; nothing could render it palatable to the clergy, and the influence of the church would be exerted against the allies, instead of being as hitherto strongly exerted in their favour. It would be useless if the experiment of the crown lands succeeded, and if that failed this sale could not succeed; but the attempt would alienate a powerful party in Spain as well as in Portugal. Moreover if it should succeed and be honestly carried into execution, it would entail a burthen on the finances of five in the hundred on the purchase-money for the support of the ecclesiastical owners of the estates. The best mode of obtaining for the state eventually the benefit of the church property would be to prevent the monasteries and nunneries from receiving novices, because, in course of time, the pope might consent to the sale of the estates, or the nation might assume possession when the ecclesiastical corporations became extinct. It was no disadvantage to Spain or Portugal that large portions of land should be held by the church. The bishops and monks were the only proprietors who lived on their estates and spent the revenues amongst the labourers; until the habits of the new landed proprietors changed, the transfer of landed property from the clergy to the laymen would be a misfortune.

This memoir, sent from the trenches of Burgos, quashed Funchal's projects; but that intriguer's object was to get rid of his brother's opponents in the regency by exciting powerful interests against them; wherefore, failing in this proposal, he ordered Redondo, now marquis of Borba and minister of finance, to repair to the Brazils, intending to supply his place with one of his own faction. Wellington and Stuart were at this time doggedly opposed by Borba, but as the credit of the Portuguese treasury was supported by his character for probity, they forbade him to obey the order, and represented the matter so forcibly to the prince regent that Funchal was severely reprimanded for his audacity. And it was amidst these vexations that Wellington retreated, and in Correspondence with Mr. Stuart, MSS. such destitution that he declared all former distress for money had been slight in comparison of his present misery! British naval stores had been trucked for corn in Egypt; and the English ministers, finding Russia was gathering specie from all quarters, desired Mr. Stuart to prevent English and American merchant captains carrying coin away from Lisbon; a remedial measure, indicating their total ignorance of the nature of commerce. It was not attempted to be enforced; but then it was they transmitted their plan of supplying the army by requisitions the particulars of which may be best gathered from the answers to it.

Mr. Stuart, firm in opposition, shortly observed that it was by avoiding and reprobating such a system, although pursued alike by the natives and by the enemy, that the British character and credit had been established so firmly as to be of the greatest use in the operations of the war. Wellington entered more deeply into the subject.

Nothing he said could be procured from the country in the mode proposed by the ministers' memoir, unless resort was also had to the French mode of enforcing their requisitions. The proceedings of the French armies were misunderstood. It was not true that the French never paid for supplies. They levied contributions where money was to be had, and with this paid for provisions in other parts; and when requisitions for money or clothing were made they were taken on account of the regular contributions due to the government. Heavier indeed they were than even an usurping government was entitled to demand; yet it was a regular government account, and the British could not adopt a similar plan without depriving their allies of their own legitimate resources. Requisitions were enforced by terror. A magistrate was ordered to provide for the troops, who would, in case of failure take the provisions and punish the village or district in a variety of ways. Were it expedient to follow this mode of requisition there must be two armies, one to fight the enemy, one to enforce the requisitions; for the Spaniards would never submit quietly to such proceedings. The conscription gave the French a more moral description of soldiers, and if this second army was provided the British troops could not be trusted to inflict an exact measure of punishment on a disobedient village; they would plunder it as well as the others, but their principal object would be to get at and drink as much liquor as they could, and then destroy all property falling in their way; the objects of their mission, the bringing supplies to the army and inflicting an exact measure of punishment on the magistrates or district, would not be accomplished at all. Moreover the holders of supplies in Spain, being unused to commercial habits would regard payment for these requisitions by bills of any description to be rather worse than the mode of contribution followed by the French, and would resist it as forcibly. And upon such a nice point did the contest hang, that if they accepted the bills and discovered how to get cash for them by discounting high, it would be the most fatal blow possible to

the credit and resources of the British army in the Peninsula.
The war would then soon cease.

The memoir asserted, that though sir John Moore had been
well furnished with money the Spaniards would not give him
provisions; and this was urged as an argument for enforcing
requisitions. But to say Moore was furnished with money,
itself the index to the ministers' incapacity, Wellington told
them was not true. 'Moore had been even worse furnished
than himself. That general had borrowed a little a very
little money at Salamanca, but had no regular supply for the
military chest until the army had nearly reached Coruña;
and the Spaniards were not very wrong in their reluctance to
meet his wants, for the debts of his army were still unpaid in
the latter end of 1812.' In fine, supplies could only be
procured from the country by payment on the spot or soon
after the transaction, unless the Spanish government would
yield a part of the government contributions and the revenues
of the royal domains, to be received from the people in kind
at a reasonable rate. This he had obtained in the province
of Salamanca, and the system might be extended to other
provinces as the legitimate government was re-established.
But this only partially met the evil, it would give some supplies cheaper than they could otherwise be procured, but
they must afterwards be paid for at Cadiz in specie and less
money would come into the military chest, which, as before
noticed, was only supported by mercantile speculations.

Such were the discussions forced upon Wellington when
all his faculties were wanted on the field of battle, and such
was the hardiness of his intellect to sustain the additional
labour: such also were the men, calling themselves statesmen,
who then wielded the vast resources of Great Britain. The
expenditure of that country for the year 1812 was above one
hundred millions, the ministers who controlled it were yet
so ignorant of the elementary principles of finance, as to
throw upon their general amidst the clangor and tumult of
battle the task of exposing such fallacies. And to reduce
these persons from the magnitude of statesmen to their
natural smallness of intriguing debaters is called political pre-
judice! But though power may enable men to trample upon

reason for a time they cannot escape ultimate retribution, she re-assumes her sway and history delivers them to the justice of posterity. Perverse however as the English ministers were, the Portuguese and Spanish governments were more so; and the temper of the Spanish rulers was at this time of even greater importance, because of Napoleon's misfortunes. The opportunity given to strike a decisive blow at his power in the Peninsula demanded an early and vigorous campaign, and the experience of 1812 had taught Wellington no aid could be had from Spain unless a change was made in the military system. Hence when assured the French armies had taken winter-quarters, he resolved in person to urge the Cortes to give him the real as well as nominal command of their troops.

During the past campaign and especially after Abispal had resigned, the weakness of the Spanish government became more deplorable; nothing was done to ameliorate the military system, an extreme jealousy actuated the Cortes and the regency; and when the former offered Wellington the command of their armies Mr. Wellesley advised him to accept it, were it only to give a point upon which Spaniards true to the English alliance and the aristocratic cause might rally in case of reverse. The disobedience of Ballesteros had been indeed promptly punished, but the vigour of the Cortes was the result of offended pride, not of sound policy, and the retreat of the allies was the signal for a renewal of those dangerous intrigues which the battle of Salamanca had arrested without crushing.

Lord Wellington reached Cadiz the 24th of December. He was received without enthusiasm, yet with honour, and his presence seemed agreeable to the Cortes and the people; party passions subsided, and his ascendancy of mind procured patient hearing, even when in private he urged the leading men to turn their attention to the war, to place in abeyance their factious disputes, and above all things to uphold the inquisition, lest they should drive the church party into the arms of the enemy. His exhortations had no effect save to encourage the serviles to look more to England; yet they did not prevent the Cortes yielding to him the entire control of

fifty thousand men to be paid from the English subsidy, with
an engagement that he should have power of dismissal and
the right to recommend for promotion; that no general should
be appointed without his knowledge and consent, and that all
orders and reports should pass through him.

At his recommendation also the Spanish forces were re-
organized in four numbered active armies and two reserves.
The Catalans were to form the first army. Elio's troops including the divisions of Sarsfield, Duran, Bassecour, the Empecinado, Roche, and Villa Campa, received the name of the
second army. The forces in the Morena, formerly under
Ballesteros, constituted the third army under Del Parque.
The troops of Estremadura, Leon, Gallicia and the Asturias,
including Morillo's, Penne Villemur's, Downie's and Carlos
d'España's separate divisions, were called the fourth army and
given to Castaños, whose appointment to Catalonia was can-
celled and his former dignity of captain-general in Estremadura and Gallicia restored. The partidas of Longa, Mina,
Porlier and the other chiefs in the northern provinces were
afterwards united to this army as separate divisions.

Abispal, made captain-general of Andalusia, commanded
the first reserve, and Lacy, replaced in Catalonia by Copons,
was ordered to form a second reserve in the neighbourhood of
San Roque. Such were the new dispositions; but when
Wellington had completed this important negotiation some
inactivity was for the first time discovered in his own proceedings. His stay was prolonged without apparent reason,
and it was whispered that if he resembled Cæsar, Cadiz had provided him with a Cleopatra; yet he soon returned to the army
by Lisbon, where he was greeted with very great honours
and the most unbounded enthusiasm, especially by the people.
His departure from Cadiz revived all the political dissensions.
The liberals and serviles became more rancorous, and the
executive was always on the side of the latter, the majority of
the Cortes on the side of the former; neither enjoyed the
confidence of the people nor of the allies, and the intrigues
of Carlotta advanced: a desire to make her sole regent was
manifested, and sir Henry Wellesley, tired of fruitless opposition, remained neuter. One cause of this feeling was her

vehemence against the insurgents of Buenos Ayres, another
the disgust given to the merchants of Cadiz by the diplomatic proceedings, or rather intrigues of lord Strangford,
with that revolted state.   The princess denounced England as
pursuing a smuggling policy, and not without truth, for
Wellington's counsels had been unheeded.   Lord Castlereagh
offered indeed a new mediation, the old commission being to
proceed under the restriction of not touching at Mexico;
whither a new mission composed entirely of Spaniards was to
proceed accompanied by an English agent without an osten-
sible character.   This proposal ended as the others had done
and jealousy of England increased.

Early in 1813, Carlotta, diligently served by Pedro Souza,
had gained adherents amongst the liberals in the Cortes, for
she was ready to sacrifice even the rights of her posterity;
and as she promised to maintain all ancient abuses the clergy
and serviles were not averse to her.   The decree to abolish
the inquisition, now the test of political party, passed on the
7th of March and the regency were ordered to have it read
in the churches.   The clergy of Cadiz resisted the order.
They intimated their refusal through the medium of a public
letter, and the regency encouraged them by removing the
governor of Cadiz, admiral Valdez, a known liberal and opponent of the inquisition, appointing in his stead Alos a warm
advocate for that horrid institution.   But in the vindication
of official power the Spaniards are prompt and decided.
Augustin Arguelles moved and it was instantly carried, that
the sessions of the extraordinary Cortes should be declared
permanent, with a view to measures worthy of the nation
and to prevent the evils with which the state was menaced by
the opposition of the regency and the clergy to the Cortes.
A decree was then proposed for suppressing the actual
regency and replacing it with a provisional government, to be
composed of the three eldest councillors of state.   This being
conformable to the constitution was carried by a majority of
eighty-six to fifty-eight, while another proposition, that two
members of the Cortes publicly elected should be added to
the regency, was rejected as an innovation by seventy-two
against sixty-six.   The councillors Pedro Agar, Gabriel Ciscar,

and the cardinal Bourbon, archbishop of Toledo, were then installed as regents.

A committee, appointed to consider how a government felt by all parties to be imperfect could be improved, now recommended that the cardinal-archbishop who was of the blood-royal should be president of the regency, leaving Carlotta's claims unnoticed; and as Ciscar and Agar had been formerly removed from the regency for incapacity, it was generally supposed the intention was virtually to make the archbishop sole regent. Soon however Carlotta's influence was again felt; for a dispute arising in the Cortes between what were called the Americans and the liberals about the annual Acapulco-ship, twenty of the former joined her party, and it was resolved that Ruiez Pedron, a distinguished opponent of the inquisition, should propose her as the head of the regency. When almost sure of a majority the scheme was detected, and the people, who liked her not, became so furious that her partisans were silenced. The opposite side proposed on the instant that the provisional regency should be made permanent, which was carried; and thus, chance rather than choice ruling, an old prelate and two imbecile councillors were entrusted with the government, and factious intrigues and rancour exploded more frequently as the pressure from above became slight.

More than all others the clergy were violent and daring, yet the Cortes was not to be frightened. Four canons of cathedrals were arrested in May, and orders were issued to arrest the archbishop of St. Jago and many bishops, because of a pastoral letter published against the abolition of the inquisition; for according to the habits of their craft of all sects, they deemed religion trampled under foot when the power of levying money and spilling blood was denied to ministers professing the faith of Christ. Nor did the English influence fail to suffer; the democratic spirit advanced hastily, the Cadiz press teemed with writings to excite the people against the designs of the English cabinet, and to raise a hatred of the British general and his troops. They were not all falsehoods, nor unsuccessful, because the desire to preserve the inquisition displayed by Wellington and his brother,

although arising from military considerations, accorded too
much with the known tendency of the English cabinet's
policy not to excite the suspicions of the whole liberal party.
The bishops of Logroño, Mondonedo, Astorga, Lugo and
Salamanca, and the archbishop of St. Jago were arrested;
several other bishops fled to Portugal and were there protected as martyrs in the cause of legitimacy and despotism.
The bishop of Orense and the ex-regent Lardizabal had
before this escaped to Algarve and the Tras os Montes, and
from the latter the prelate kept up an active intercourse with
Gallicia, where the Cortes were far from popular; indeed the
flight of the bishops created general anger, for the liberal
party was stronger in the Isla than in other parts, and by a
curious anomaly the military were generally their partisans
while the people were partisans of the clergy. Nevertheless
the seeds of freedom, though carelessly sown by the French
on one side and the Cortes on the other, took deep root, and
have since sprung up into strong plants in due time to
burgeon and bear fruit.

When the bishops fled from Spain, Gravina, the pope's
nuncio, assumed such a tone that the good offices of sir
Henry Wellesley could only for a time screen him from the
vengeance of the Cortes, and finally the latter, encouraged by
the English newspapers, dismissed him and sequestered his
benefices. He also took refuge in Portugal and with the
expelled clergy sought to render the Cortes odious in Spain.
He formed a strict alliance with the Portuguese nuncio,
Vicente Machiechi, and they interfered, not with the concerns
of Spain only but with the catholics in the British army,
and even extended their intrigues to Ireland; whereupon, as
justice was never the English policy towards that country,
alarm pervaded the cabinet, and the nuncio, protected when
opposed to the Cortes, was considered troublesome and indiscreet regarding the Irish.

This state of feud led to a crisis of a formidable and decisive nature. Many persons in the Cortes held secret intercourse with Joseph, being desirous to acknowledge his
dynasty if he would accede to the general policy of the Cortes
in civil government. He had as already shown organized a

large native force, and the coasts of Spain and Portugal swarmed with French privateers manned with Spanish seamen; the victory at Salamanca withered these resources for the moment, but Wellington's failure at Burgos and retreat revived them and gave a heavy shock to public confidence in the power of England; a shock which the misfortunes of Napoleon in Russia only could have prevented from being fatal. That wonderful man had indeed, with the activity and energy which made him the foremost hero of the world, raised a fresh army to march into the heart of Germany; but for this he was forced to withdraw so many old soldiers from Spain that the French could no longer act on the offensive. This stayed the Peninsula cause on the brink of a precipice, for in that curious and authentic work, called '*Bourrienne and his errors*,' it appears that early in 1813, the ever-factious conde de Montijo, then a general in Elio's army, secretly made proposals to pass over with his forces to the king; and soon afterwards the whole army of Del Parque, then advancing into La Mancha, made offers of a like nature.

They were negotiating with Joseph when the emperor's orders compelled him take up the line of the Duero; but being thus advertised of French weakness feared to continue their negotiations; Wellington then advanced, and as this feeling for the intrusive monarch was not general, resistance revived with the British successes. But if Napoleon, victorious in Russia, had strengthened his army, this defection would have taken place and have been followed by others; the king at the head of a Spanish army would have reconquered Andalusia, Wellington would have been confined to the defence of Portugal, and England would not have purchased the independence of that country with her own permanent ruin. This conspiracy is not however related with entire confidence, because no trace of it is to be found in the king's papers taken at Vitoria. Nevertheless there are abundant proofs that the work called '*Bourrienne and his errors*,' inasmuch as it relates to Joseph's transactions in Spain, was compiled from his correspondence; many documents also taken at Vitoria were lost at the time, and in a case involving lives would probably have destroyed the proofs of a treason which had failed. Napoleon in his memoirs speaks of secret negotiations with the Cortes about this time, and he is corroborated by the correspondence of the British embassy at Cadiz and by the intrigues against British influence.

CHAPTER II.

In Portugal the English general desired to apply all resources
to the war; but he had to run counter to the habits of the
people and the government, to detect the intrigues of subordinates and of higher powers, to oppose factious men in the
local government, to stimulate the sluggish apathy and combat
the often honest obstinacy of those who were not factious.
And all this without power of recompensing or chastising,
and even while forced to support those who merited rebuke
against the more formidable intriguers of the court of Brazil;
for the best men of Portugal were in the local government, and
he was not foiled so much by them as by the sluggish national
system, dull for good purposes but vivacious for mischief.
And at Rio Janeiro the personal intrigues fostered by the
peculiarly scheming disposition of the English envoy lord
Strangford,—the weak yet dogged habits of the prince,—and
the meddling nature and violence of Carlotta, stifled all great
national views.   There also the Souzas, a family deficient
neither in activity nor talent, were predominant, and the
object of all was to stimulate the government in Portugal
against the general's military policy. To this had been opposed
the influence of the English government, but that resource
was dangerous and only to be resorted to in extremities.
When to all these things is added a continual struggle with
the knavery of merchants of all nations, his difficulties must
be admitted, his indomitable vigour his patience and his
extraordinary mental resources admired.   An instructive
lesson in the study of nations is thus presented.   Wellington was not simply a general who with greater or less means
was to plan military operations, leaving to others the set-
tling of political difficulties. He had also to regenerate
a people and force them against the current of their preju-

dices and usages in a dangerous and painful course; to teach
at once the populace and the government; to infuse spirit and
order without the aid of rewards or punishments, and to
excite enthusiasm through the medium of corrupt oppressive
institutions while he suppressed all tendency towards revolution. Thus only could he maintain the war, and as it was
beyond the power of man to continue such a struggle for any
length of time, he was more than ever anxious to gather
strength for a decisive blow, which the enemy's situation now
rendered possible. It may indeed be wondered at that he so
long supported the pressure, and more than once he was like
to yield and would have yielded if fortune had not offered
him certain happy military chances, yet such as few but himself could have profited from. In 1810, on the Busaco
mountain and in the lines, the military success was rather
over the Portuguese government than the enemy,—at Santa-
rem in 1811 the glory of arms scarcely compensated for the
destitution of the troops,—at Fuentes Onoro and on the
Caya, after the second unsuccessful siege of Badajos, the Portuguese army had nearly dissolved; and the astonishing sieges
of Ciudad Rodrigo and Badajos in 1812 were necessary to
save the cause from dying of inanition. Even then the early
deliverance of Andalusia was frustrated, and time, more valuable than gold or life in war, was lost; the enemy became the
strongest in the field, and despite the victory of Salamanca
the political evils were felt in the repulse from Burgos and
the double retreat from that place and Madrid. Accumulated
mischiefs were now to be encountered in Portugal.

It has been shown how obstinately the regency opposed the
plans of financial reform; for thinking Portugal out of danger
and tired of their British allies they had no desire
to aid, nor indeed any wish to see Spain delivered
from her difficulties. To harass the English
general and drive him away or force him, and through him
his government, to grant them loans or new subsidies was
their object. But Wellington knew that Portugal could, and
was resolved it should find resources within itself. Wherefore, after the battle of Salamanca when a fresh subsidy
was demanded he would not listen; and when that scheme

Mr. Stuart's
Correspond-
ence, MSS.

already exposed, of feeding or rather starving their troops through the medium of a treaty with the Spanish government, was proposed, he checked the shameful and absurd plan by applying a part of the money in the chest of aids intended for the civil service to the relief of the Portuguese troops. Yet the regency did not entirely fail in their aim, many persons dependent upon the subsidy were thus deprived of their payments, their complaints hurt the British credit, and the British influence with the people, · whose faithful attachment to the alliance no intrigues had hitherto been able to shake, was reduced.

Mr. Stuart's Correspondence, MSS.

Into every branch of government the regency then infused their own captious spirit. They complained falsely that general Campbell had insulted the nation by turning some Portuguese residents publicly out of Gibraltar in company with Jews and Moors; they refused the wheat delivered to them in lieu of their subsidy, saying it was not fit for food though the English troops were then living on the same grain, though their own troops were glad to get it, and no other was to be had. When a wooden jetty was to be thrown in the Tagus for the convenience of landing stores, they supported one Caldas, a rich proprietor, in his refusal to permit the trees wanted to be felled, alleging the rights of property, although he was to be paid largely and they had themselves then and always disregarded the rights of property,—especially when poor men were concerned—seizing upon whatever was required for the public service or the support of their own irregularities, without payment and in shameful violation of law, and humanity.

Wellington's Correspondence, MSS.

The commercial treaty and the proceedings of the Oporto wine company, an oppressive corporation unfair in all its dealings, irresponsible, established in violation of that treaty and supported without regard either to the interests of the prince regent or his British allies, furnished them also with continual subjects for disputes, and nothing was too absurd or too gross for their interference. Under the management of Mr. Stuart, who had vigorously enforced Wellington's plans, their paper money had obtained a reasonable and increasing circulation, their custom-house resources had increased, the expenses of their navy and arsenal had been reduced, and it was evident that an extensive vigorous application of the same principles would overcome all financial difficulties; but there were too many personal interests, too much shameful profit made to permit such a reform.   The naval establishment instead of being entirely transferred to the Brazils was continued in the Tagus, and with it the arsenal as its natural appendage; and though the infamous Junta de Viveres had been suppressed by the prince regent, the government, under pretext of paying its debts, still disbursed ten thousand pounds a month in salaries to men whose offices had been formally abolished.

About this time also the opening of the Spanish ports in those provinces from whence the enemy had been driven, deprived Lisbon of a monopoly of trade enjoyed for the last three years.   Then the regency feeling the consequent diminution of revenue, with inexpressible effrontery insisted that the grain imported by Wellington, which had saved their army and nation from famine and furnished their own subsidy, should enter the public warehouses under specific regulations and pay duty for so doing.   And so tenacious were they that he was forced to menace a formal appeal to the English cabinet; for he knew the subordinate officers, knavish in the extreme, would have sold the secrets of the army magazines to the speculators. And the latter, in whose hands the furnishing of the army would under the new plan of the English ministers be placed, being thus accurately instructed of its resources would have regulated their supplies with great nicety, so as to have famished the soldiers and paralysed the operations at the greatest possible expense.   But the supply of the army under any system was now extremely precarious; for besides the activity of the American privateers, English ships of war used to capture vessels secretly employed in bringing provision under licences from Mr. Stuart and Mr. Forster.   The captain of a Scotch merchant vessel, engaged in the same trade and having no letter of marque, had the piratical insolence to seize in the very mouth of the Tagus an American vessel sailing under a licence from Mr. Forster; thus violating at

Mr. Stuart,.
MSS.
once the licence of the English minister, the independence of Portugal, and the general law of nations. The American traders were dismayed, the Portuguese government justly indignant, and the matter altogether embarrassing, because no measure of punishment could be inflicted without exposing the secret system which had been the principal support of the army. Congress however soon passed an act forbidding neutrals to ship flour in the American ports; and this blow, chiefly aimed at the Portuguese ships, following upon the non-importation act and coupled with the illegal violence of the English vessels, nearly dried up this source of supply and threw the army principally upon the Brazil trade; which by the negligence of the Admiralty was, as before noticed, exposed to the enterprise of the United States' privateers.

During Wellington's campaign in Spain the military administration of Portugal was in the hands of the regency and all the ancient abuses revived. The army in the field received no succours, the field artillery disappeared, the cavalry was in the worst condition, the infantry reduced in numbers, the equipments scarcely fit for service, the spirit of the men waning to despondency; there was no money in the military chest, no recruits in the depôts, and the transport service was neglected altogether. Beresford's severity did not stop desertion, because want, the parent of crimes, had proved too strong for fear; the country swarmed with robbers, no fault was punished by the regency and everywhere knaves triumphed. All persons whose indolence or timidity led them to fly from the defence of their country to the Brazils, were there received and cherished as martyrs to their personal affections for the prince; they were lauded and called victims to the injustice of Beresford and the encroachments of the English officers. The prince also permitted officers possessing family interest to retire from service retaining their pay and rank; thus offering a premium for bad men to enter the army with intent to quit it in this disgraceful manner. Multitudes did so, promotion came too quickly, and the nobility, whose influence over the poor classes was great and might have been beneficially employed to keep up the zeal of the men, disappeared rapidly from the regiments: the foul stream of knaves and cowards thus continually pouring through the military ranks destroyed all cohesion and tainted everything as it passed.

Interests of the same nature polluted the civil administration. Rich people, especially those of great cities, evaded taxes and disobeyed regulations for the military service, and during Wellington's absence, English under-commissaries and that retinue of villains which invariably gather on the rear of armies, being in some measure freed from the dread of his vigilance and vigour, violated orders in a daring manner. The husbandmen were cruelly oppressed, their farming animals were carried off to supply food for the army, and agriculture was thus stricken at the root; the breeds of horned cattle and of horses rapidly and alarmingly decreased, and butcher's meat was scarcely to be procured even for the troops who remained in Portugal.

These irregularities, joined to the gross misconduct of the military detachments and convoys of sick men on all the lines of communication, produced great irritation and enabled factious persons to declaim with effect: writings and stories were circulated against the troops, the real outrages were exaggerated, others were invented, and the drift of all was to render the English odious to the nation at large. Nor was this confined to Portugal. Agents were busy to the same purpose in London, and when the enthusiasm which Wellington's presence at Lisbon had created amongst the people was known at Cadiz the press there teemed with abuse. Divers agents of the democratic party in Spain came to Lisbon to aid the Portuguese malcontents, libels accusing Wellington of a design to subjugate the Peninsula for his own ambitious views were published; and as consistency is never regarded on such occasions, it was insinuated that he encouraged the excesses of his troops out of personal hatred to the Portuguese people: the old baseness of sending virulent anonymous letters to him was also revived. In fine the republican spirit had got beyond Spain, and the Portuguese regency, terrified at its approach, appealed to Mr. Stuart for the assistance of England to check its formidable progress. They forbade Portuguese newspapers to admit observations on the political events in

Spain, they checked the introduction of Spanish democratic publications, they ordered their diplomatists at Cadiz to encou-rage writings of an opposite tendency, and support the elec-tion of deputies known for their love of despotism. This last measure was however baffled by the motion of Arguelles, which rendered the old Cortes permanent. And Mr. Stuart, judging the time unfavourable, advised reserve in the exertion of power against democrats until military successes, which the state of the continent and the weakness of the French troops in Spain promised, should enable the victors to put down such doctrines with effect: advice which was not unmeaning as shall be hereafter shown.

All these malignant efforts Wellington viewed with indif-ference. 'Every leading man,' he said, 'was sure to be accused of criminal personal ambition, and if he was conscious of the charge being false it did no harm.' His position was however rendered more difficult, and other mischiefs existed of long standing, and springing from a different source, but of a more serious character; for the spirit of captious discontent had reached the inferior magistracy, who endeavoured to excite the people against the military generally. Complaints came in from all quarters of outrages on the part of the troops, some too true, many false or frivolous; and when courts-martial for the trial of the accused were assembled the magistrates refused to attend as witnesses; because Portuguese custom rendered such an attendance degrading, and by Portu-guese law a magistrate's written testimony was efficient in courts-martial. In vain they were told English law would not punish men upon such testimony; in vain it was pointed out that the country would be ravaged if the soldiers disco-vered they might do evil with impunity. It was offered to send in each case lists of Portuguese witnesses to be sum-moned by the native authorities; but the magistrates answered that this method was insolent, and with sullen malignity con-tinued to accumulate charges against the troops, to refuse attendance in the courts, and to call the soldiers, their own as well as the British, 'licensed spoliators of the community.'

For a time the generous nature of the poor people resisted these combining causes of discontent; neither real injuries

nor exaggerations, nor the falsehood of those who attempted
to stir up wrath, produced any visible effect upon the great
bulk of the population; yet by degrees affection for the
British cooled, and Wellington expressed his fears that a civil
war would commence between the Portuguese people on the
one hand, and the troops of both nations on the other.
Wherefore his activity was redoubled to draw while he could
still control affairs all the military strength to a head, and
make such an irruption into Spain as would establish a new
base of operations beyond the power of fatal dissensions. But
what made him tremble was the course which the misconduct
of the Portuguese government and the incapacity of the English cabinet forced upon the native furnishers of supplies.

Those persons, coming in winter to Lisbon to have bills
paid, could get no money and in their distress sold the
bills to speculators; the Portuguese holders at a discount of
fifteen, the Spanish holders at a discount of forty in the hundred. The credit of the chest immediately fell, prices rose in
proportion, and as no military enterprise could carry the army
beyond the flight of this harpy, and no revenues could satisfy
its craving, the contest must have ceased if Mr. Stuart had
not found a momentary partial remedy, by publicly guaran-
teeing the payment of the bills and granting interest until
they could be taken up. The expense was thus augmented,
yet the increase fell short of the enhanced cost of supplies
which this restricted practice of the bill-holders caused, and of
two evils the least was chosen. It may seem strange that
such transactions should belong to the history of the military
operations in the Peninsula, that it should be the general's
instead of the minister's task to encounter such evils, and
to find the remedy. It was so however, and no adequate
notion of Wellington's herculean labours can be formed
without an intimate knowledge of his financial and political
difficulties.

The Portuguese military disorders had brought Beresford to
Lisbon while the siege of Burgos was still in progress, and
now, under Wellington's direction, he strained every nerve to
restore the army to its former efficient state. To recruit the
regiments of the line he disbanded all the militia-men fit for

service, replacing them with fathers of families; to restore the
field artillery, he embodied all the garrison artillerymen,
calling out the ordenança gunners to man the fortresses and
coast-batteries; the worst cavalry regiments he reduced to
render the best more efficient, but-this arm never attained any
excellence in Portugal. Lord Wellington and Mr. Stuart at
the same time grappled with the civil administration and their
efforts produced a considerable increase of revenue. The
regency could not deny this beneficial effect, nor the existence
of the evils they were urged to remedy; they admitted that their
custom-house system was incomplete, that their useless navy
consumed large sums wanted for the army; and that the
taxes, especially the '*Decima*,' were partially collected and
unproductive because the rich people in the great towns, who
had benefited largely by the war, escaped the imposts which
the poor people in the country, who had suffered most from
the war, paid. They acknowledged also that while the soldiers'
hire was in arrears, the transport service neglected, and all
persons having just claims upon the government suffered severe
privations, the tax-gatherers were allowed to keep a month's
tribute in their hands even in the districts close to the enemy;
but they would not alter their system, and Borba, the minister
of finance, combated Wellington's plans in detail with such
unusual obstinacy that it became evident nothing could be
obtained save by external pressure. Wherefore, as the season
for military operations approached, Mr. Stuart called upon
lord Castlereagh to bring the power of England to bear at
once upon the court of Rio Janeiro; and Wellington, driven
to extremity, sent the Portuguese prince-regent one of those
clear powerful and nervous statements, which left those to
whom they were addressed no alternative but submission, or
an acknowledgment that sense and justice were to be disregarded.

' I call your highness's attention,' he said, ' to the state of
your troops and of all your establishments; the army of operations has been unpaid since September, the garrisons since
June, the militia since February, 1812. The transport service
has never been regularly paid and has received nothing since
June. To these evils I have in vain called the attention of

the local government, and I am now going to open a new
campaign with troops to whom greater arrears of pay are due
than when the last campaign terminated, although the subsidy
from Great Britain, granted especially for the maintenance of
those troops, has been regularly and exactly furnished; and
although it has been proved that the revenue for the last three
months has exceeded by a third any former quarter. The
honour of your highness's arms and the cause of your allies
are thus seriously affected; the uniform refusal of the governors of the kingdom to attend to any one of the measures
which I have recommended, either for permanent or temporal
relief, has at last obliged me to go as a complainant into your
royal highness's presence, for here I cannot prevail against the
influence of the chief of the treasury.

'I have recommended the entire reform of the customs
system, and it has only been partially carried into effect. I
have advised a method of really collecting the taxes, and of
making the rich merchants and capitalists pay the tenth of
their annual profits as an extraordinary contribution for the
war. I declare that no person knows better than I do the
sacrifices and the sufferings of your people, for there is no one
for the last four years has lived so much amongst those people;
but it is a fact, sir, that the great cities and even some of the
smallest places have gained by the war, and the mercantile
class has enriched itself; there are divers persons in Lisbon
and Oporto who have amassed immense sums. Now your
government is, both from remote and recent circumstances,
unable to draw resources from the capitalists by loans; it can
only draw upon them by taxes. It is not denied that the
regular tributes nor the extraordinary imposts on the mercantile profits are evaded; it is not denied that the measures I
have proposed, vigorously carried into execution, would furnish the government with pecuniary resources; and it remains
for that government to inform your highness why they have
neither enforced my plans, nor any others which the necessity
of the times calls for. They fear to become unpopular, but
such is the knowledge I have of the people's good sense and
loyalty, such my zeal for the cause, that I have offered to
become responsible for the happy issue, and to take upon

myself all the odium of enforcing my own measures.   I have offered in vain!

'Never was a sovereign in the world so ill served as your highness has been by the Junta de Viveres, and I zealously forwarded your interests when I obtained its abolition; and yet, under a false pretext of debt, the government still disburse fifty millions of reis monthly on account of that board. It has left a debt undoubtedly and it is of importance to pay it, although not at this moment; but let the government state in detail how these fifty millions granted monthly have been applied; let them say if all the accounts have been called in and liquidated? who has enforced the operation? to what does the debt amount? has it been classified? how much is really still due to those who have received instalments? finally, have these millions been applied to the payment of salaries instead of debt?   But were it convenient now to pay the debt, it cannot be denied that to pay the army which is to defend the country, to protect it from the sweeping destructive hand of the enemy, is of more pressing importance: the troops will be neither able nor willing to fight if they are not paid.'

Then touching upon the abuse of permitting the taxgatherers to hold a month's taxes in their hands, and upon the opposition he met with from the regency, he continued,

'I assure your royal highness I give my advice to the governor of the kingdom, actuated solely by an earnest zeal for your service without any personal interest.   I can have none relative to Portugal, and none with regard to individuals, for I have no private relation with and scarcely am acquainted with those who direct or would wish to direct your affairs.   Those reforms recommended by me and which have at last been partially effected in the custom-house and the arsenal, in the navy, the payment of the interest of the national debt and the formation of a military chest, have succeeded, and I may therefore say that the other measures I propose would have similar results.   I am ready to allow that I may deceive myself on this point, but certainly they are suggested by a desire for the good of your service; hence in the most earnest and decided manner I express my ardent wish, and it is common to all your faithful servants, that you will return to the kingdom and take charge yourself of the government.'

These vigorous measures to bring the regency to terms succeeded only partially. In May they promulgated a new system for the collection of taxes which relieved the financial pressure on the army for the moment, but did not content Wellington, because it was made to square with old habits and prejudices, and thus left the roots of all the evils alive and vigorous. Every moment furnished new proofs of the hopelessness of regenerating a nation through the medium of a corrupted government; and a variety of circumstances more or less serious continued to embarrass the march of public affairs. In the Madeiras the authorities vexatiously prevented the English money agents from exporting specie, and their conduct was approved of at Rio Janeiro. At Bisao, in Africa, the troops mutinied for want of pay, and in the Cape de Verde Islands disturbances arose from the over-exaction of taxes; for when the people were weak the regency was vigorous, pliant only to the powerful. These commotions were trifling and soon ended, yet expeditions were sent against the offenders in both places, and the troops thus employed immediately committed far worse excesses and did more mischief than that which they were sent to suppress. At the same time several French frigates finding the coast of Africa unguarded, cruized successfully against the Brazil trade, and aided the American privateers to contract the already too-straitened resources of the army.

Notwithstanding these difficulties the exertions of the British officers had restored the numbers, discipline and spirit of the Portuguese army. Twenty-seven thousand excellent soldiers were again under arms and ready to commence the campaign, although the national discontent was daily increasing; and indeed the very feeling of security created by the appearance of such an army rendered the citizens at large less willing to bear the inconveniences of the war. Distant danger never affects the multitude, and the billeting of troops, who from long habits of war little regarded the rights of the citizens in comparison with their own neces-

sities, being combined with requisitions and with a recruiting
system becoming every year more irksome, formed an aggre-
gate of inconveniences intolerable to men who desired ease,
and no longer dreaded to find an enemy on their hearth-
stones. The powerful were more affected than the poorer
classes, because of their indolent habits; but their impatience
was aggravated by being debarred of the highest situations,
or supplanted by British interference; and, unlike those of
Spain, the Portuguese nobles had lost little of their hereditary
influence. Discontent was thus extended widely, dread of
French power was gone, unlimited confidence in the strength
and resources of England had succeeded; and this confidence,
to use the words of Mr. Stuart, 'being opposed to the irregularities which have been practised by individuals, and to the
difference of manners and of religion, placed the British in
the singular position of a class whose exertions were necessary for the country, but who for the above reasons were in
every other respect as distinct from the natives as persons
with whom, from some criminal cause, it was necessary to
suspend communication.'—Hence he judged that the return
of the prince-regent would be a proper epoch for the British
to retire from all situations in Portugal not strictly military;
for if anything should delay that event, the time was approaching when the success of the army and the tranquillity of the
country would render it necessary to yield to the first mani-
festations of national feeling. In fine, notwithstanding the
great benefits conferred upon the Portuguese by the British,
the latter were, and it will always be so on the like occasions,
regarded by the upper classes as a captain regards galley-
slaves, their strength was required to speed the vessel, but
they were feared and hated.

To Portugal the prince would not return, but Carlotta
being resolute to come, her apartments were finished and
her valuable effects actually arrived. Ill health was the
pretext, the real object to be near Spain; for indefatigable,
and of a violence approaching insanity, she had sold even her
plate and jewels to raise money wherewith to corrupt the
leading members of the Cortes; and if that should not promise success she proposed to distribute the money amongst

the Spanish partidas to obtain military support for her schemes. Fortunately the prince, dreading the intriguing advisers of his wife, would not suffer her to quit Rio Janeiro until the wish of the British cabinet upon the subject was known; and that was so decidedly adverse, it was thought better to do without the prince himself than to have him accompanied by Carlotta: so both remained in the Brazils and this formidable cloud passed away, yet left no sunshine on the land.

It was at this period that the offer of a Russian auxiliary force, before alluded to, was made to Wellington by admiral Grieg, and accepted by him to the amount of fifteen thousand men; yet it led to no result, because the Russian ambassador in London declared the emperor knew nothing of it! Alexander then proposed to mediate in the dispute between Great Britain and America, but the English ministers, while lauding him as a paragon of magnanimity and justice in regard to the war against Napoleon, remembered the armed neutrality and quadruple alliance, and wisely declined trusting England's maritime pretensions to his faithless grasping policy. Neither would they listen to Austria, who at this time, probably as a cloke, desired to mediate a general peace. Amidst this political confusion the progress of the military preparations was visible; and contemporary with the Portuguese, the Spanish troops under Wellington's influence and providence acquired more consistence than they had ever before possessed: a mighty power was in arms. But the flood of war which the English general finally poured into Spain, and the channels by which he directed the overwhelming torrent, cannot be described until the political situation of Joseph and that secondary warfare which occupied the French armies while Wellington was re-organizing his power are related.

CHAPTER III.

IN war it is not so much positive strength as relative situations which gives the victory. Joseph's position thus judged was weak, he could not combine the materials at his disposal, nor wield them when combined by others. France had been suddenly thrown into a new and embarrassing attitude, more embarrassing even than it appeared to her enemies, or than her robust warlike proportions nourished by twelve years of victory· indicated. Napoleon, the most indefatigable and active of mankind, turned his enemy's ignorance on this head to profit; for scarcely was it known that he had reached Paris by that wise that rapid journey from Smorghoni, which baffled his enemies hopes and left them only the power of foolish abuse—scarcely was his arrival at Paris known to the world, when a new and enormous army, the constituent parts of which he had with his usual foresight created while yet in the midst of victory, was in march from all parts to unite in the heart of Germany. On this magical rapidity he rested his hopes to support the tottering fabric of his empire, but his design was, while presenting a menacing front on every side, so to conduct his operations, that if he failed in his first stroke he might still contract his system without violent concussion. His military power was rather broken and divided than lessened, for the number of men employed **Imperial muster rolls.** in 1813 was greater than in 1812; in the latter four hundred thousand, in the former more than seven hundred thousand, and twelve hundred field-pieces, were engaged on different points, exclusive of the armies in Spain. On the Vistula, the Oder, the Elbe, he had powerful fortresses, and garrisons or rather armies, of strength and goodness to re-establish his ascendancy in Europe, if he could re-unite them in one system by placing a new host in the centre of Germany: thus also he could retain those allies who felt the attraction of his enemy's success

But this was a gigantic contest, for his adversaries deceiving their subjects with false promises of liberty had brought whole nations against him. More than eight hundred thousand men were in arms in Germany alone; secret societies were in activity all over the continent; and in France a conspiracy was commenced by men who desired rather to see their country a prey to foreigners and degraded with a Bourbon king, than independent and glorious under Napoleon. Wherefore that great monarch had now to make application on an immense scale, of the maxim which prescribes a skilful offensive as the best defence, and he had to sustain two warfares; the one depending principally upon moral force to hold the vast fabric of his former policy together; the other to meet material exigencies. The first, infinitely the most important, was to influence Germany and France, and the Peninsula contest sunk at once into an accessory. In this state he required constant rapid intelligence from Spain, because the ascendancy he yet maintained over the world by his astounding genius, might have been broken in a moment, if Wellington suddenly abandoned the Peninsula to throw his army or a part of it into France. For then would have been deranged all the emperor's calculations; then would the defection of all his allies have ensued; then would he have been compelled to concentrate both his new forces and his Spanish troops for defence, abandoning all his fortresses and his still large though scattered veteran armies in Germany and Poland. It would have been destructive of his moral power to have commotions raised on his own threshold when he was assuming the front of a conqueror in Germany.

To obviate this danger or to meet it, alike required that his armies in the Peninsula should adopt a new and vigorous system, under which, relinquishing all real offensive movements, they should yet appear daring and enterprising while preparing to abandon their former conquests. But the emperor wanted to fortify his young levies with veterans from Spain and therefore recalled the young guard, and with it many thousand men and officers of the line most remarkable for courage and conduct. In lieu the reserve at Bayonne entered Spain, being replaced with another, again to be replaced in May by further levies; and twenty thousand conscripts were appropriated for immediate service. Thus weakened in numbers, considerably so during the transit, the armies were also in quality deteriorated at a critical moment; for Wellington was being powerfully reinforced, and the partidas, augmented by English supplies liberally and now usefully dealt out, were in the northern parts acting in concert with the naval squadrons; during the operations of the French on the Tormes they had revived insurrection in Navarre and Biscay, where recent gross abuses of military authority had been perpetrated by some of the local commanders.

The French troops were indeed only relieved from the crushing pressure of Wellington's operations to struggle in the meshes of the guerilla and insurrectional warfare. Nor was its importance now to be measured by former efforts. The chiefs, more docile to the suggestions of the British chief, possessed fortified posts and harbours, their bands were swelling to the size of armies, their military knowledge of the country and of the French system of invasion was more matured, their dépôts better hidden, and they could at times bear the shock of battle on nearly equal terms. New and large bands of a far more respectable and influential kind were also formed or forming in Navarre and Biscay; where insurrectional juntas were organized of men from the best families voluntarily enrolled and not obnoxious like the partidas for rapine and violence. In Biscay alone several battalions, each mustering a thousand men, were in the field, and the communication with France was so intercepted, that the minister of war only heard of Joseph receiving his despatches of the 4th of January on the 18th of March, and then through the medium of Suchet! The contributions could no longer be collected, the magazines could not be filled, the fortresses were endangered, the armies had no base of operations, the insurrection was spreading through Aragon, and the bands of the interior were also increasing in numbers and activity.

Duke of Feltre's official Correspondence, MSS

The troops, sorely pressed for provisions, were widely dis-
seminated and everywhere occupied, and each general was
averse to concentrate his own forces or aid his neighbour.
In fine the problem was become extremely complicated, and
Napoleon only seems to have seized the true solution.

When informed by Caffarelli of the state of affairs in the
north, he thus wrote to the king, 'Hold Madrid only as a
point of observation; fix your quarters, not as monarch but as
general of the French forces, at Valladolid; concentrate the
armies of the south, of the centre, and of Portugal; the
allies will not and indeed cannot make any serious offensive
movement for several months,—wherefore it is your business
to profit from their forced inactivity, to put down the insurrection in the northern provinces, to free the communication
with France, and re-establish a good base of operations before
the commencement of another campaign, that the French
army may be in condition to fight the allies if the latter
advance towards France.' Very important indeed did Napoleon deem this object, and so earnest was he to have constant
and rapid intelligence that couriers and their escorts were
to be despatched twice a week, travelling day and night at
the rate of a league an hour. Caffarelli also was to be reinforced even by the whole army of Portugal if it was necessary to effect the immediate pacification of Biscay and
Navarre; and while this pacification was in progress Joseph
was to hold the rest of his forces in a position offensive
towards Portugal, making Wellington feel that his whole
power was required on the frontier; that neither his main
body nor any considerable detachment could safely embark
to disturb France, and that he must cover Lisbon strongly on
the frontier, or expect to see the French army menacing that
capital. These instructions, well understood and vigorously
executed, would certainly have put down the insurrection in
the rear of the king's position. And the spring would then
have seen that monarch at the head of ninety thousand men,
having their retreat upon France clear of all impediments,
and consequently free to fight the allies on the Tormes, the
Duero, the Pisuerga, and the Ebro.

Joseph unable to view the matter thus, would not make

his kingly notions subservient to military science, nor his
military movements to an enlarged policy. Neither did he
perceive that his beneficent notions of government were mis-
placed amidst the din of arms. Napoleon's orders were
imperative, but the principle of them escaped Joseph; he
was not even acquainted with the true state of the northern
provinces, nor would he at first credit it when
told to him; hence while his thoughts were intent
upon his Spanish political projects and the secret
negotiations with Del Parque's army, the partidas and insurgents became masters of all his lines of communication in
the north. The emperor's orders despatched early in January,
and reiterated week after week, only arrived the end of
February, and their execution did not take place until the end
of March, and then imperfectly; the time thus lost was
irreparable; and yet, as Napoleon reproachfully observed, the
bulletin which revealed the extent of his disasters in Russia
might alone have taught the king what to do. But Joseph
was nearly as immovable in his resolutions as Napoleon;
the firmness of the one being however founded upon extraordinary sagacity, while the other's rested on the want of that
quality; regarding opposition as a disloyal malevolence, he
judged the refractory generals to be enemies to the emperor
and to himself. Reille, Caffarelli, Suchet, alike incurred his
displeasure, and the minister of war also, because of a letter
in which he rebuked the king for having removed Souham
from command.

King's Correspondence, MSS.

Feltre's style, as towards a monarch, was offensive. Joseph
attributed it to the influence of Soult, and complaining to the
emperor, said—'The duke of Dalmatia or himself must quit
Spain. At Valencia he had forgotten his injuries, suppressed
his just indignation, and instead of sending Soult to France
had given him the direction of the operations, hoping shame
for the past, combined with his avidity for glory, would urge
him to extraordinary exertions; nothing of the kind had happened. Soult was not to be trusted. Restless, intriguing,
ambitious, he would sacrifice everything to his own advance-
ment, and possessed that sort of talent which would lead him
to mount a scaffold when he thought he was ascending a

throne, because he would want courage to strike when the crisis arrived.' Then, with a coarse sarcasm, he acquitted him 'of treachery at the passage of the Tormes because there fear alone operated to prevent him from bringing the allies to a decisive action; but he was treacherous and probably connected with the conspiracy of Malet at Paris.'

It was with such language Joseph assailed one of the greatest commanders and most faithful servants of his brother; and thus greeted that brother on his arrival at Paris after the disasters of Russia. In the most calm and prosperous state these charges might have excited jealous wrath in the strongest mind; but when the emperor had just lost his great army and found the smoking embers of an extinguished conspiracy at his palace-gates; when his friends were failing, his enemies accumulating, it seemed scarcely possible these accusations should not have ruined Soult; yet they did not even ruffle the temper of Napoleon. Magnanimous as sagacious he smiled at Joseph's anger, removing Soult from Spain because thus at feud with the king he could not act beneficially; but he made him commander of the imperial guard, and afterwards selected him from all his generals to retrieve affairs when Joseph was driven from the Peninsula.

It has been shown that when Wellington took winter-quarters, the French occupied a line stretching from Valencia to the foot of the Gallician mountains. Suchet on the extreme left was opposed by the allies at Alicant. Soult, commanding the centre, had his head-quarters at Toledo, having a detachment near the Sierra Morena watching Del Parque and two others in the valley of the Tagus. Of these last one was at Talavera, one on the Tietar; the first observed Morillo and Penne Villemur, who from Estremadura menaced the bridges on the Tagus; the second watched Hill at Coria. From the Tietar the French communicated by the Gredos mountains with Avila, where Foy's division of the army of Portugal was posted; partly for the sake of food, partly to watch Bejar and the upper Tormes, because the allies, possessing the pass of Bejar, might have suddenly united north of the mountains and breaking the French line have fallen on Madrid. On the right of Foy, Reille's army occupied Salamanca, Ledesma and

Alba on the lower Tormes—Valladolid, Toro, and Tordesillas on the Duero—Benevente, Leon and other points on the Esla. Behind the right of this great line Caffarelli's army had retaken its old positions, and the army of the centre was fixed as before in and around Madrid; its operations being bounded north of the Tagus by the mountains which invest that capital, and south of that river by the districts of Aranjuez, Tarancon and Cuenca.

Joseph issued a royal regulation marking the extent of country which each army was to forage, and ordered a certain and considerable revenue to be collected by the civil authorities for the support of his court. The subsistence of the French armies was thus made secondary to the revenue of the crown, and soldiers in a time of insurrectional war were to obey Spanish civilians; an absurdity heightened by the peculiarly active vigorous and prompt military method of the French, as contrasted with the dilatory improvident promise-breaking and visionary system of the Spaniards. Hence, scarcely was the royal regulation issued when the generals broke through it in a variety of ways, and the king as usual became involved in very acrimonious disputes. ·If he ordered one to detach troops in aid of another, he was told he should rather send additional troops to the first. If he reprimanded a general for raising contributions contrary to the regulations, he was answered that the soldiers must be fed; and always the authority of the prefects and intendants was disregarded in pursuance of Napoleon's orders. For that monarch continually reminded his brother, that as the war was carried on by the French armies their interests were paramount; that the king of Spain could have no authority over them, and must never use his military authority as lieutenant of the empire in aid of his kingly views, for with those the French soldiers could have nothing to do,—their welfare could not be confided to Spanish ministers whose capacity was by no means apparent, and whose fidelity was not certain.

King's Correspondence, MSS.

In reply Joseph again pleaded his duties towards his subjects, and his sentiments, explained with feeling and great beneficence of design, were worthy of all praise abstractedly;

but totally inapplicable, because the Spaniards were not his subjects; they were his inveterate enemies and it was impossible to unite the vigour of war with the benevolence of a paternal monarch.　All his policy was vitiated by this fundamental error, which arose from inability to view any subject largely, for his military operations had a like defect; and though he was acute, courageous and industrious in details, he never grasped the whole at once.　Men of this character, conscious of labour and good intentions, are commonly obstinate; but their qualities, useful under the direction of an able chief lead to mischief when they become chiefs themselves; for in matters of great moment, and in war especially, it is not the actual but the comparative importance of operations which should determine the choice of measures; and when all are important judgment of the highest kind is required, judgment which no man ever possessed more largely than Napoleon and which Joseph did not possess at all.　He neither comprehended his brother nor would accept advice from those whose capacity approached that of the emperor.　When every general complained of insufficient means, instead of combining their forces to press in mass against the decisive point he disputed with each, and demanded additional succours for all; at the same time repeating and urging his own schemes upon Napoleon whose intellect was so immeasurably greater than his own. The insurrection in the northern provinces he treated as a political question, attributing it to the people's anger at seeing the ancient supreme council of Navarre dismissed and some members imprisoned by a French general: a cause very inadequate to the effect.　Nor was his judgment truer with respect to time.　He proposed, if a continuation of the Russian war should prevent the emperor from sending more men to Spain, to make Burgos the royal residence, to transport there the archives and all that constituted a capital; then to have the provinces behind the Ebro, Catalonia excepted, governed by himself through the medium of his Spanish ministers and as a country at peace, while those beyond the Ebro should be given up to the generals as a country at war.

In this state his civil administration would, he said, remedy the evils inflicted by the armies, would conciliate the people by keeping all the Spanish families and authorities in safety and comfort, would draw all those who favoured his cause from all parts of Spain, and would encourage that attachment to his person which he believed many Spaniards to entertain. And while he declared the violence and injustice of the French armies to be the sole cause of the protracted resistance of the Spaniards, a declaration false in fact, that violence being only one of many causes, he continually urged the necessity of beating the English before pacifying the people. As if it were possible, off-hand, to beat Wellington and his veterans, embedded as they were in the strong country of Portugal, while British fleets with troops and succours of all kinds, hovering on both flanks of the French, were feeding and sustaining the insurrection of the Spaniards in their rear. Napoleon was willing enough to drive the English from the Peninsula and tranquillize the people by a regular government; but with profound knowledge of war, of politics, and of human nature, he judged the first could only be done by a methodical combination, in unison with that rule of art which prescribes the establishment and security of the base of operations, security which could not be obtained if the benevolent visions of the king were to supersede military vigour. He laughed in scorn when his brother assured him that the Peninsulars with all their fiery passions, their fanaticism and their ignorance, would receive an equable government as a benefit from the hands of an intrusive monarch before they had lost all hope of resistance by arms.

Joseph was not however totally devoid of grounds for his opinions. He was deeply affected by the misery which he witnessed, his Spanish ministers were earnest and importunate, and many French generals gave him too much reason to complain of their violence. The length and mutations of the war had created a large party willing enough to obtain tranquillity at the price of submission, while others were as we have seen not indisposed, if he would hold the crown on their terms, to accept his dynasty as one essentially springing from democracy, in preference to the despotic base and superstitious family which the nation was called upon to uphold. It was not unnatural therefore for him to desire to retain his capital while the negotiations with Del Parque's army were still in existence; it was not strange that he should be displeased with Soult after reading that marshal's honest but offensive letter: and certainly it was highly creditable to his character as a man and as a king, that he would not silently suffer his subjects to be oppressed by the generals.

'I am in distress for money,' he often exclaimed to Napoleon, 'such distress as no king ever endured before, my plate is sold, and on state occasions the appearance of magnificence is supported by false metal. My ministers and household are actually starving, misery is on every face, and men otherwise willing are thus deterred from joining a king so little able to support them. My revenue is seized by the generals for the supply of their troops, and I cannot as a king of Spain, without dishonour, partake of the resources thus torn by rapine from subjects whom I have sworn to protect; I cannot be king of Spain and general of the French; let me resign both and live peaceably in France. Your majesty does not know what scenes are enacted, you will shudder to hear that men formerly rich and devoted to our cause have been driven out of Zaragoza and denied even a ration of food. The marquis Cavallero, a councillor of state, minister of justice and known personally to your majesty, has been thus used. He has been seen actually begging for a piece of bread!'

If this Cavallero was the old minister of Charles the 4th, no misery was too great a punishment for his tyrannical rule under that monarch; yet it was not from the French it should have come; and Joseph's distress must have been severe, because that brave and honest man Jourdan, a marshal of France, major-general of the armies and a personal favourite of the king's, complained that the non-payment of his appointments had reduced him to absolute penury, and after borrowing until his credit was exhausted he could with difficulty procure subsistence. It is now time to continue the secondary warfare, which being spread over two-thirds of Spain and simultaneous, must be classed under two heads, namely, the operations north, and the operations south of the Tagus.

Jourdan's Correspondence, MSS.

CHAPTER IV.

OPERATIONS SOUTH OF THE TAGUS.

IN December 1812 Copons became captain-general of Catalonia instead of Eroles, but his arrival being delayed the province was not relieved from Lacy's mischievous sway until February 1813, when Eroles, taking the temporary command, re-established the head-quarters at Vich. The French, being then unmolested save by the English ships, passed an enormous convoy to France, but Eroles was not long idle.

February. Through a double spy he sent a forged letter to the governor of Taragona, desiring him to detach men with carts to transport stores from Sitjes; at the same time pretending a design to invade the Cerdaña, which brought a moveable column to that quarter, he with Manso and Villamil, by forced marches reached Torre dem barra and met the British squadron. The intention was to cut off the French detachment on its march to Villa Nueva and then to attack Taragona, but fortune rules in war; the governor received a letter from Maurice Mathieu of a different tenor from the forged letter, and with all haste regaining his fortress balked this well-contrived plan.

Sarsfield, at enmity with Eroles, was then combining his operations with Villa Campa and they menaced Alcanitz in Aragon; but Pannetier who was at Teruel to watch Villa Campa and protect Suchet's communications, immediately marched to Daroca, Severoli came from Zaragoza to the same point, and the Spaniards, alarmed by their junction, dispersed. Sarsfield then returned to Catalonia, Bassecour and the Empecinado remained near Cuenca, and Villa Campa as usual hung upon the southern skirts of the Albaracin mountain, ready to pounce on the Ebro or the Guadalquivir as advantage might

offer. Suchet was disquieted. He could not draw reinforcements from Catalonia, because Napoleon, true to his principle
of securing the base of operations, forbad him to weaken the
army there, and Montmarie's brigade was detached from
Valencia to preserve the communication between Saguntum
and Tortoza. Aragon, his place of arms and principal magazine, being infested by Mina, Duran, Villa Campa, the Empecinado and Sarsfield, was becoming daily more unquiet,
wherefore Pannetier's brigade remained between Segorbé and
Daroca to aid Severoli. Thus, although the armies of Aragon
and Catalonia mustered more than seventy thousand men, that
of Aragon alone having forty thousand with fifty field-pieces,
Suchet could not fight with more than sixteen thousand
infantry, two thousand cavalry and perhaps thirty guns beyond
the Xucar. His right flank was always liable to be turned by
Requeña, his left by the sea, and his front was menaced by
fifty thousand men, of which three thousand were cavalry with
fifty pieces of artillery.

The component parts of this force were the Anglo-Sicilian
army eighteen thousand, including Whittingham's and Roche's
divisions,—Elio's army, twelve thousand exclusive of the divisions of Bassecour, Villa Campa, and the Empecinado, which
though detached belonged to him,—Del Parque's army reinforced by new levies from Andalusia, on paper twenty
thousand. Numerically this was a formidable power if it had
been directed in mass against Suchet; but on his right Soult
from Toledo watched Del Parque, and the defection of the
latter was then being negotiated with the king. A column
from Madrid was also sent to Cuenca, which drew off Bassecour and the Empecinado, and those chiefs harassed Joseph's
positions. Early in January, Soult's brother, seeking to open
a communication with Suchet by Albacete, defeated some of
Elio's cavalry with the loss of fifty men, and pursued them
until they rallied on their main body under Freyre and offered
battle with nine hundred horsemen in front of the defile leading to Albacete. Soult, disliking their appearance, then
turned off to the right and joined a French post established in Valdepeña at the foot of the Morena, where some
skirmishes had also taken place with Del Parque's cavalry.

The elder Soult thus learned that Freyre, with two thousand
five hundred horsemen, covered all the roads leading from
La Mancha to Valencia and Murcia; that Elio's infantry was
at Tobara and Hellin, Del Parque's head-quarters at Jaen;
that the passes of the Morena were guarded, and magazines
formed at Andujar, Linares, and Cordoba, while on the other
side of La Mancha, the Empecinado had come to Hinojoso
with fifteen hundred horsemen, and the column sent from the
army of the centre was afraid to encounter him.

These dispositions and the strength of the Spaniards, not
only prevented the younger Soult from penetrating into
Murcia but delayed the march of a column under Daricau,
destined to communicate with Suchet and bring up the
detachments baggage and stores which the armies of the
south and centre had left at Valencia. The scouting parties
of both sides however met at different points, and on the
27th of January a sharp cavalry fight happened at El Corral,
in which the French commander was killed and the Spaniards
though far the most numerous were defeated. Meanwhile
Daricau, whose column had been reinforced, reached Utiel,
opened the communication with Suchet by Requeña, cut off
some small parties of the enemy, and then continuing his
march received a great convoy, consisting of two thousand
fighting men six hundred travellers and the stores and
baggage belonging to Soult's and the king's armies. This
convoy had marched for Madrid by the way of Zaragoza, but
was recalled when Daricau arrived; and under his escort,
aided by a detachment of Suchet's army placed at Yniesta,
it reached Toledo the latter end of February safely, though
Villa Campa came down to the Cabriel river to trouble the
march.

During these different operations numerous absurd reports,
principally originating in the Spanish and English newspapers,
obtained credit in the French armies; such as, that sir
Henry Wellesley and Infantado had seized the government at
Cadiz,—that Clinton had by an intrigue got possession o.
Alicant,—that Ballesteros had shown Wellington secret orders
from the Cortes not to acknowledge him as generalissimo,
or even as a grandee,—that the Cortes had removed the

regency because the latter permitted Wellington to appoint intendants and other officers to the Spanish provinces,—that Hill had devastated the frontier and retired to Lisbon though forcibly opposed by Morillo,—that a nephew of Ballesteros had raised the standard of revolt,—that Wellington was advancing, and troops had been embarked at Lisbon for a maritime expedition, with other stories of a like nature, which seem to have disturbed all the French generals save Soult, whose information as to the real state of affairs continued to be sure and accurate.   He also detected four or five of Wellington's emissaries, one a Portuguese officer on his own staff; another, called Piloti, who served and betrayed both sides; and an amazon called Francisca de la Fuerte, who, though only twenty-two years old, had already commanded a partida of sixty men with some success, and was now a spy.   But in the latter end of February he was recalled, and his command fell to Gazan, whose movements belong rather to the operations north of the Tagus.   Wherefore returning to Suchet, an exact notion of his resources and of the nature of the country shall be given.

Valencia, though nominally his stronghold was not really so.   All the defences constructed by the Spaniards were razed, and only the old walls and a small fortified post within the town, sufficient to resist a sudden attack and capable of keeping the population in awe, were preserved; the place of arms was Saguntum, and between that and Tortoza he had two fortresses, Oropesa and Peniscola.   Another line of communication, but for infantry only, was through Morella, a fortified post, to Mequinenza; and there were roads from Valencia and Saguntum, leading through Segorbé to Teruel a fortified post, and from thence to Zaragoza by Plan 2, p. 63. Daroca another fortified post: these roads were eastward of the Guadalaviar.   Westward of that river Suchet had a line from Valencia to Madrid by Requeña, which was also fortified.   Now if the whole command be looked to, the forces were very numerous, but that command was wide and in the field his army was not very numerous. Valencia was merely a point on hostile ground, maintained with a view of imposing upon the allies and drawing forth the resources of the country as long as circumstances would permit.

The proper line for covering the city and the rich country immediately around it was on the Xucar, or rather beyond it, at San Felippe de Xativa and Moxente; where a double range of mountains afforded strong defensive positions barring the principal roads leading to Valencia. There Suchet had formed an entrenched camp, much talked of at the time yet slighter than fame represented it; the real strength was in the natural formation of the ground, which was very rugged. In front of his left flank the coast road was blocked by the castle of Denia, but his right could be turned from Yecla and Almanza, through Cofrentes and Requeña; and he was forced to keep strict watch and strong detachments always towards the defile of Almanza, lest Elio's army and Del Parque's should march that way. His entrenched camp was the permanent position of defence, but he sought to keep his troops more advanced; because the country in front was full of fertile valleys, or rather coves within the hills, which run in nearly parallel ranges and are remarkably rocky and precipitous, like walls. It was of great importance to command those coves, and as the principal point in front was the flourishing town of Alcoy, he occupied it and from thence threw off smaller bodies to Biar, Castalla, Ibi, and Onii, which were on the same strong ridge as the position covering the cove of Alcoy. On his right there was another plain in which Fuente La Higuera, Villena and Yecla were delineated at opposite points of a triangle; and as this plain and the smaller valleys ministered to Suchet's wants because of his superior cavalry, the subsistence of the French troops was eased while the cantonments and foraging districts of the Sicilian army were contracted: the outposts of the allied army were in fact confined to a fourth and fifth parallel range of mountains covering the towns of Elda, Tibi, Xixona, and Villa Joyosa on the seacoast.

Plan 1. p. 57.

Suchet thus assumed an insulting superiority over an army apparently more numerous than his own. But outward appearances are deceitful in war; he was really the strongest, because want, ignorance, dissension and even treachery were

in his adversary's camps. Del Parque's army remained behind
the Morena, Elio's was at Tobarra and Hellin, and of the
Anglo-Sicilian army the British only were available in the
hour of danger. When Campbell quarrelled with Elio the
latter retired for a time towards Murcia, but after Wellington's journey to Cadiz he again came forward; his cavalry
entering La Mancha skirmished with the younger Soult, and
communicating with Bassecour and the Empecinado delayed
the progress of Daricau towards Valencia. Campbell then
remained quiet in expectation that lord William would come
with more troops; but in February fresh troubles broke out
in Sicily, and in the latter end of that month sir John Murray
assumed the command at Alicant. Thus in a few months
five chiefs with different views and prejudices had successively
arrived, and the army was still unorganized and unequipped
for vigorous service. The Sicilians, Calabrese, and French
belonging to it were eager to desert; one Italian regiment
had been broken for misconduct by Maitland, the British and
Germans were humiliated in spirit by inactivity,
and the Spaniards under Whittingham and Roche   Appendixes
were starving; for Wellington knowing how the   7, 8.
Spanish government, though receiving a subsidy, would if
permitted throw off the feeding of their troops, forbade their
being supplied from the British stores, and the Spanish
intendants neglected them.

Murray improved the equipment of the troops, and with
the aid of Elio put them in better condition. The two
armies together furnished thirty thousand effective men, of
which three thousand were cavalry, and they had thirty-seven
guns; yet very inadequately horsed, and Whittingham's and
Elio's cavalry were from want of forage nearly unfit for duty.
The transport mules were hired at the enormous rate of one
hundred and thirty thousand pounds annually;   General
and yet the supply was bad, for here as in all   Donkin's
other parts of Spain corruption and misuse of   Papers.
authority prevailed. The rich sent their fine animals to
Alicant for sanctuary and bribed the alcaldes; the mules of
the poor alone were pressed, the army was ill provided and
the country was harassed. But the troops of Whittingham and

Roche could not be relieved, save by enlarging their cantonments; wherefore Murray after some hesitation resolved to
drive the French from the mountains in his front, and following the plan of his quarter-master-general Donkin designed,
as the first step, to surprise fifteen hundred men which they
had placed in Alcoy.

Five roads led towards the French positions. 1°. On the
left the great road from Alicant passing through Monforte,
Elda, Sax, Villena, and Fuente de la Higuera, where it joins
the royal road from Valencia to Madrid, which runs through
Almanza. This way turned both the ridges occupied by the
armies. 2°. A good road leading by Tibi to Castalla, from
whence it sent off two branches on the left hand, one leading
to Sax the other through the pass of Biar to Villena; two
other branches on the right hand went, the one through Ibi
to Alcoy, the other through Onil to the same place. 3°. The
road from Alicant to Xixona, a bad road leading over a steep
rugged ridge of that name to Alcoy. At Xixona also there
was a narrow way on the right hand through the mountains
to Alcoy, which was followed by Roche when he attacked
that place in the first battle of Castalla. 4°. A carriage-road
running along the sea-coast as far as Villa Joyosa, from
whence a narrow mountain-way leads to the village of Consentayna, situated in the cove of Alcoy and behind that
town.

On the 6th of March the allied troops moved in four
columns. On the left, one moved by Elda to watch the great
Madrid road; on the right, one composed of Spanish troops
moved under colonel Campbell from Villa Joyosa to get to
Consentayna behind Alcoy; a third under lord Frederick
Bentinck, issuing by Ibi, was to turn the French right; the
fourth was to march from Xixona straight against Alcoy
and pursue the remainder of Habert's division, which was
behind that town. Lord Frederick attacked in due time
but as Campbell did not appear the surprise failed; and when
the French saw the main body winding down the Sierra in
front of Alcoy, they retired, pursued by Donkin with the
second battalion of the twenty-seventh regiment. The head
of lord Frederick's column was already engaged, the rear had

not arrived and the whole of Habert's division being concentrated a mile beyond Alcoy offered battle; Murray instead of pushing briskly forward halted; and it was not until several demands for support had reached him that he detached the fifty-eighth to the assistance of the troops engaged, who had lost about forty men, chiefly of the twenty-seventh. Habert, fearing to be cut off by Consentayna and seeing the fifty-eighth coming on, then retreated and the allies occupied Alcoy. Murray's want of vigour did not escape the notice of the troops.

After this affair the armies remained quiet until the 15th, when Whittingham forced the French posts with some loss from Albayda; and Donkin, taking two battalions and some dragoons from Ibi, drove back their outposts from Rocayrente and Alsafara, villages situated beyond the range Plan 1, p. 57. bounding the cove of Alcoy. He repassed the hills higher up with the dragoons and a company of the grenadiers of twenty-seventh under captain Waldron, and returned by the main road to Alcoy, having in his course met a French battalion through which the gallant Waldron broke with his grenadiers. Then Murray, after much vacillation, at one time resolving to advance at another to retreat, thinking it impossible to force Suchet's entrenched camp and his second line behind the Xucar, a difficult river with muddy banks; believing also that the principal French magazines were at Valencia, he conceived the idea of seizing the latter by a maritime expedition. He thought the garrison, estimated at eight hundred infantry and one thousand cavalry, would be unable to resist and that the inhabitants would rise; Suchet could not then detach men enough to quell them without exposing himself to defeat on the Xucar, and if he moved with all his force he could be closely followed by the allies and driven upon Requeña.

On the 18th Roche's division reinforced by some troops from Elio's army and a British grenadier battalion was selected for the maritime attack; the rest of the army was concentrated at Castalla, with exception of Whittingham's troops who remained at Alcoy, for Suchet was said to be advancing and Murray resolved to fight him. But to form a plan and to execute it vigorously were with Murray very different things. An able officer in the cabinet he had no quality of a general in the field. His indecision was remarkable. On the morning of the 18th he resolved to fight in front of Castalla, in the evening he assumed a weaker position behind that town, abandoning the command of a road running from Ibi in rear of Alcoy, by which Whittingham might have been cut off: when the strong remonstrances of his quarter-master-general induced him to relinquish this ground, he adopted a third position neither so strong as the first nor so defective as the last. In this manner affairs wore on until the 26th, when Roche's division and the grenadier battalion marched to Alicant to embark, with orders, if they failed at Valencia to seize and fortify Cullera at the mouth of the Xucar; and if this also failed to besiege Denia. But now the foolish ministerial arrangements about the Sicilian army worked out their natural result. Wellington, though permitted to retain the Anglo-Sicilian army in Spain beyond the period assigned by lord William, had not the full command; he was clogged with reference to the state of Sicily until the middle of March; then he became master, but this was still unknown to lord William and to Murray. Thus there were three commanding officers. Wellington for the general Murray for the particular operations; and lord William was empowered to increase or diminish the troops, and even upon emergency to withdraw the whole. And now continued dissensions in Sicily, the king having suddenly resumed the government, made him recal two thousand of the best troops, and amongst them the grenadier battalion designed to attack Valencia, wherefore that enterprise fell to the ground.

Treating of this event, Murray, or some person writing Phillipart's under his authority, makes the following observa-Military tions. 'The most careful combination could not Calendar. have selected a moment when the danger of such authority was more clearly demonstrated, more severely felt. Had these orders been received a very short time before, the allied army would not have been committed in active operations; had they reached sir John Murray a week later, there is ever reason to believe that the whole country from Alicant

to Valencia would have passed under the authority of the
allied army; and that marshal Suchet, cut off from his magazines in that province and in Aragon, would have been
compelled to retire through a mountainous and barren
country on Madrid.   But the order of lord William Bentinck
was peremptory, and the allied army which even before was
scarcely balanced, was now so inferior to the enemy that it
became an indispensable necessity to adopt a system strongly
defensive, and all hope of a brilliant commencement of the
campaign vanished.'

Upon this curious passage it is necessary to remark,
1°. That Suchet's great magazines were not at Valencia but at
Saguntum; 2°. That from the castle of Denia the fleet would
have been descried and the strong garrison of Saguntum
could have reinforced the troops in Valencia; Montmarie's
brigade also would soon have come up from Oropesa.   These
were doubtless contingencies not much to be regarded in bar
of such an enterprise; but Suchet would not have been forced
to retire by Requeña upon Madrid; he would have retired to
Liria, the road to which steered more than five miles clear of
Valencia.   He could have kept that city in check while passing, in despite of Murray; and at Liria he would have been
in his natural position, that is to say, in full command of his
principal lines of communication.   Moreover, however disagreeable to Suchet personally it might have been to be forced
back upon Madrid, that event would have been extremely
detrimental to the general cause, as tending to reinforce the
king against Wellington.   But the singular part of the passage quoted, is the assertion that the delay of a week in
lord William's order would have ensured such a noble stroke
against the French army.   Lord William only required the
troops to proceed in the first instance to Mahon.   What a
dull flagging spirit then was his, who dared not delay
obedience to such an order even for a week!

The recalled troops embarked for Sicily the 5th of April,
and Suchet alarmed at the offensive position of the allies,
which he attributed to the general state of affairs, because the
king's march to Castille permitted all the Spanish armies
of Andalusia to reinforce Elio, resolved to strike first; and

with the greater avidity, because the Spanish general Mijares
had been pushed with an advanced guard of three or four
thousand men to Yecla and was quite unsupported. This
movement had been concerted in March with Murray, who
was to occupy Villena and be prepared to fall upon the
French left if Mijares was attacked at Yecla; in return the
Spaniards were to fall on the French right if Murray was
attacked. Elio neglected to strengthen his division at Yecla with cavalry, which he had promised to do, nor did Murray occupy Villena in
force; nevertheless Mijares remained at Yecla, Elio with the
main body occupied Hellin, and the cavalry were posted on
the side of Albacete until the departure of the troops for
Sicily; Roche then joined the army at Castalla, and Elio's
main body occupied Elda and Sax to cover the main road
from Madrid to Alicant. Wherefore on the night of the
11th Suchet suddenly assembled sixteen battalions of infantry,
ten squadrons of cavalry, and twelve pieces of artillery at
Fuente la Higuera, and marched straight upon Caudete,
while Harispe's division by a cross road endeavoured to surprise the Spaniards at Yecla. The latter retired fighting
towards Jumilla by the hills, but the French artillery and
skirmishers followed close and the Spaniards were pierced in
the centre, one part broke and fled, the other part surrendered. Two hundred were killed, and fifteen hundred,
including wounded, fell into the hands of the victors, who lost
eighty men and officers.

Donkin, MSS.

Suchet's movement was known in the night of the 10th
at Castalla. All the Anglo-Sicilian army was in position,
because Whittingham had come from Alcoy, leaving only a
detachment on that side; and while Harispe was defeating
Mijares at Yecla, Suchet remained at Caudete with two divisions and the heavy cavalry in order of battle, lest Murray
should advance by Biar and Villena. The latter town, possessing an old wall and a castle, was occupied by the regiment of Velez-Malaga a thousand strong, and in the course
of the day Murray also came up with the allied cavalry and
a brigade of infantry. Here he was joined by Elio without
troops, and when towards evening, Harispe's fight being over

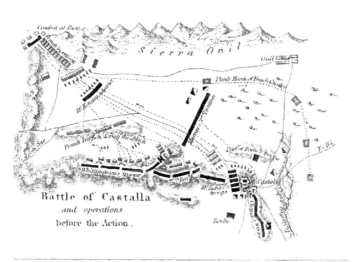

Battle of Castalla
and operations
before the Action.

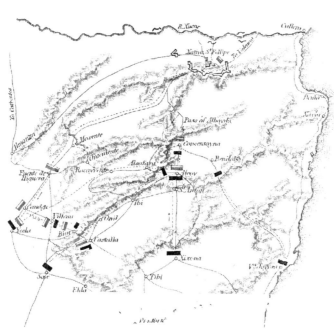

and the prisoners secured, Suchet advanced, Murray retired with the cavalry through the pass of Biar leaving his infantry under colonel Adam in front of that defile. He wished also to draw the Spanish garrison from Villena but Elio would not suffer it, and yet during the night, repenting of his obstinacy, came to Castalla entreating Murray to carry off that battalion. It was too late, Suchet had broken the gates of the town the evening before, and the castle with the best equipped and finest regiment in the Spanish army had already surrendered.

Sir John Murray's final position was about three miles from the pass of Biar. His left, entirely composed of Whittingham's Spaniards, was entrenched on a rugged sierra ending abruptly above Castalla, which, with its old castle crowning an isolated sugar-loaf hill, closed the right of that wing and was occupied in strength by general Mackenzie's division.

A space between Whittingham's troops and the town was left on the sierra for the advanced guard, then in the pass of Biar. Castalla itself, covered by the castle, was prepared for defence and the principal approaches were commanded by strong batteries, for Murray had concentrated nearly all his guns at this point. The cavalry was partly behind partly in front of the town on an extensive plain which was interspersed with olive plantations.

The right wing, composed of Clinton's division and Roche's Spaniards, was on comparatively low ground, and extended to the rear at right angles with the centre, but well covered by a 'barranco' or bed of a torrent, the precipitous sides of which were in some places one hundred feet deep.

Suchet could approach this position through the pass of Biar, or turn that defile by the way of Sax; but he supposed Elio to be on the last road, which was also uninviting because it involved a flank march along the front of Murray's position; and that general, possessing the defiles of Biar and Alcoy, might have safely pushed to the Xucar by Fuentes la Higuera or by Alcoy, seeing that Alicant was secure and that Elio could easily have escaped. The allies were far too inactive to take the initial, yet Suchet advanced cautiously, for the ground offered many means to strike a decisive blow. Murray had no such thought, his advanced guard remained on the defensive in the pass of Biar, being composed of two Italian regiments, and a battalion of the twenty-seventh, two companies of German riflemen, a troop of foreign hussars and six guns, four being mountain-pieces; it occupied strong ground, but at two o'clock in the afternoon of the 12th, the French skirmishers swarmed up the steep rocks on either flank with surprising vigour and agility, and when they had gained the summit the supporting columns advanced. The allies fought with resolution for two hours and then abandoned the pass with the loss of two guns and thirty prisoners, retreating however in good order to the main position, for they were not followed beyond the mouth of the defile. Next day, about one o'clock, the French cavalry issued cautiously from the pass extending to their left in the plain as far as Onil, and they were followed by the infantry, who immediately occupied a low ridge about a mile in front of the allies' left; the cavalry then gained ground to the front, skirted the right of the allies and menaced the road to Ibi and Alcoy.

Murray had only occupied his ground during the night, but he had previously studied and entrenched it in parts. His right wing was quite refused, and so protected by the barranco that nearly all the troops could have been employed as a reserve to the left wing; which was also strongly posted and presented a front about two miles in extent. But notwithstanding the strength of his position he shrunk from the contest, and while the head of the French column was advancing from the defile of Biar, he thrice gave Donkin orders to put the army in retreat; twice that officer remonstrated, but the last command was so peremptory that obedience must have followed, if at that moment the firing between the piquets and the French light troops had not begun.

BATTLE OF CASTALLA.

Suchet's dispositions were slowly made, as if he also was indisposed to fight; and as a crooked jut of the sierra hid all the British troops and two-thirds of the whole army, his first measure was to send a column to turn it and discover the conditions of the position. Two other heavy columns were formed opposite the left wing, and his strong cavalry gradually closed on the Baranco. The right of the allies was impregnable, and Suchet, keeping his reserve in the plain and the exploring column near Castalla to protect his left from a sally, opened his guns against the centre and right, while several columns of attack assailed their left on both sides of the jut before mentioned. Whittingham's ground being rough and steep the battle there resolved itself into a skirmish of light troops; but though the summit was entrenched and the Spaniards fought not amiss, their left was beaten from the mountain. Meanwhile on the other side of the jut the French ascended slowly, yet so firmly that it was evident good fighting only would send them down again. Their skirmishers, spreading over the mountain and here and there attaining the summit were partially driven down again, but where the main body met the second battalion of the twenty-seventh there was a terrible crash. The ground had an abrupt declination which enabled the French to form line under cover, close to the British, who were lying down in wait for the moment of charging; a grenadier officer seized the occasion to advance and challenge Waldron, also captain of grenadiers, to a duel. That agile vigorous Irishman instantly leaped forward, the hostile lines looked on, the swords of the champions glittered in the sun, the Frenchman's head was cleft in twain, and the twenty-seventh, rising up with a deafening shout, fired a deadly volley and charged with such a shock that, maugre their bravery and numbers Suchet's men were overthrown, and the side of the sierra was covered with killed and wounded. Murray erroneously attributed this brilliant exploit to colonel Adam, it was both the design and work of colonel Reeves.

When this column was overthrown, two secondary attacks were made to cover its retreat, but they also failed and the French army was thus separated in three parts; namely, the beaten troops who were in disorder, the reserve in the plains, the cavalry far on the left, fended off by the bed of the torrent, the only bridge over which was commanded by the

allies.   A vigorous sally from Castalla and a general counter-
attack would have driven the French infantry upon the defile
of Biar before their cavalry could have aided them; but Murray, who had remained during the action behind Castalla, gave
them full time to rally and retire in order; for filing by the right
through that town and there changing his front with tedious
pedantry, he formed two lines across the valley covered by
his cavalry.   Mackenzie only, breaking out by the left of Castalla with three British and one German battalion and eight
guns, followed the enemy briskly.   Meanwhile Suchet plunged
into the pass, infantry cavalry and tumbrils in one mass,
leaving only a rear-guard of three battalions with eight guns
to cover the passage.   Answering gun for gun they stood
their ground, the clatter of musketry commenced and one
vigorous charge would have dashed them upon the army
then wedged in the defile: but Mackenzie's advance had been
ordered by Donkin without Murray's knowledge, and the
latter instead of supporting it sent repeated orders to withdraw, and despite of all remonstrance compelled the troops
to come back.   Suchet thus relieved took a position across
the defile with his flanks on the heights; and though Murray
sent some companies to menace his left he retained his
ground and in the night retreated to Fuente de la Higuera,
first blowing up the castle of Villeña.   The 14th Murray
marched to Alcoy, where some of Whittingham's force had
remained to watch a French detachment holding the pass of
Albayda, by which he proposed to intercept Suchet's retreat;
but his movements were slow, his arrangements bad, the
troops got into confusion, he halted the 15th at Alcoy, and
a feeble demonstration towards Albayda terminated his operations.

In the battle the allies, including Roche's division, had
seventeen thousand combatants; the French had fifteen thousand, if a detachment left beyond Biar to watch the Spaniards

at Sax be reckoned.   Suchet says the action was
forced on by the light troops against his wish, and
that he lost only eight hundred men.   This statement is confirmed by the historian Vacani; but Murray called
it a pitched battle and said the French lost three thousand;

Suchet to the king, MSS.

the reader may choose: but in favour of Suchet's version, neither the time nor the mode of attack was conformable to his talent and experience if he had designed a pitched battle. And though the action was strongly contested at the principal point, it is scarcely possible that so many as three thousand men could have been killed and wounded. Yet eight hundred seems too few, because the loss of the victorious troops with all advantages of ground was more than six hundred. If Suchet had lost three thousand men, that is to say a fourth of his infantry, he must have been so crippled, that what with the narrow defile of Biar in the rear and the distance of his cavalry in the plain, to have escaped at all was extremely discreditable to Murray's generalship. An able commander having a superior force, and the allies were certainly the most numerous, would never have suffered the pass of Biar to be forced on the 12th; or if it were forced he would have had his army well in hand behind it, ready to fall upon the head of the French column as it issued into the low ground. But so little vigour had Murray that he resolved if the French again advanced to abandon the field and retire to Alicant!

Suchet violated several maxims of art. For without an adequate object he fought a battle, having a defile in his rear and on ground where his cavalry, in which he was superior, could not act. Neither the general state of the French affairs nor the particular circumstances invited a decisive offensive movement at the time: wherefore he should have been contented with his first successes against the Spaniards and against Colonel Adam, unless some palpable advantage had been offered to him by Murray. But the latter's position was very strong indeed, and the French army was cooped up between the pass of Biar and the allied troops. Had Elio executed a movement which Murray proposed in the night of the 12th; namely, to push troops into the mountains from Sax to strengthen Whittingham's left and menace the right flank of the enemy, Suchet's position would have been very dangerous; Elio however kept his army aloof and acted without concert though only a few miles distant. This might have been avoided if the castle and town of Villena had been in a good state of defence and the pass of Biar occupied in force behind it: the two armies would then have been secure of a junction in advance and the plain of Villena would have been commanded. To the courage of the troops therefore belongs all the merit of the success obtained, for there was no generalship, and though much blood was spilt no profit was derived from victory.

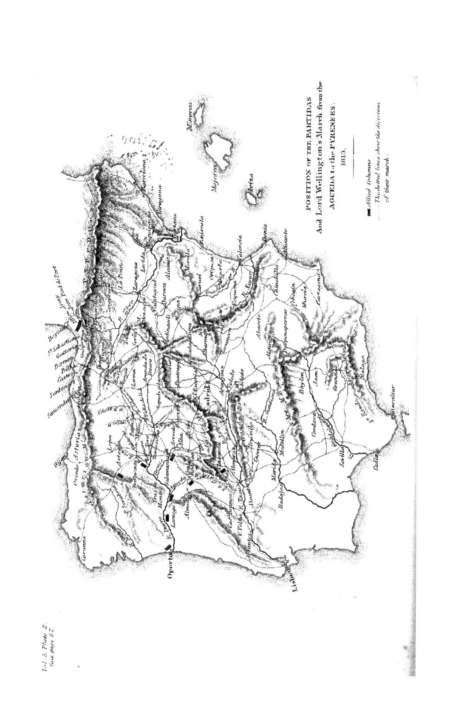

POSITION OF THE PARTIDAS
And Lord Wellington's March from the
AGUEDA to the PYRENEES.
1813.

■ Allied Columns
⋯⋯ The dotted lines shew the direction
of their march.

CHAPTER V.

OPERATIONS NORTH OF THE TAGUS.

ON this side, as in the south, one part of the French fronted Wellington's forces, while the rest warred with the partidas, watched the English fleets on the coast, and endeavoured to maintain a free intercourse with France; but the extent of country was greater, the lines of communication longer, the war altogether more difficult and the various operations more dissevered.

Four distinct bodies acted north of the Tagus.

1°. The army of Portugal, six divisions under Reille, observed the allies from behind the Tormes, the Gallicians from behind the Esla.

2°. That part of the army of the south which observed Hill from behind the Tietar, and the Spaniards of Estremadura from behind the Tagus.

3°. The army of the north under Caffarelli, whose business was to watch the English squadrons in the Bay of Biscay, to scour the great line of communication with France, and protect the fortresses of Navarre and Biscay.

4°. The army of the centre under Drouet, whose task was to fight the partidas in the central part of Spain, to cover Madrid and connect the other armies by means of moveable columns radiating from that capital. If the operations of these armies be followed in the order of their importance, and their bearing on the main action of the campaign marked, it will gradually be understood how it was, that in 1813, the French, although apparently in their full strength, were suddenly irremediably and as it were by a whirlwind swept from the Peninsula.

D'Armagnac's and Barrois' French divisions, Palombini's

Italians, Casa Palacio's Spaniards, Trielhard's dragoons, and Joseph's French guards formed the army of the centre; which, in returning from the Tormes, had one hundred and fifty men, from the rash use of alcohol, frozen to death in the Guadarama pass. Palombini had been at first detached to forage the country towards Guadalaxara, and he brought abundance of provisions to the capital; he would then have gone to Zaragoza to receive recruits and stores just arrived from Italy, but the army of the north was so pressed that he finally marched to its succour; moving however by the circuitous route of Valladolid and Burgos to scour the country. The king's guards replaced his division at Alcala, and sharp excursions were made on every side against the partidas, who being now recruited and taught by French deserters were very wary and fought obstinately.

Vacant.

On the 8th of January Espert, governor of Segovia, beat Saornil not far from Cuellar. On the 3rd of February, general Vichery, marching upon Medina Celi, routed a regiment of horse called the volunteers of Madrid, and took six hundred prisoners. The Empecinado with two thousand infantry and a thousand cavalry intercepted him on his return, but Vichery beat him with considerable slaughter and made the retreat good with a loss only of seventy men. The guerilla chief was then reinforced by Saornil and Abril in the hills about Guadalaxara; and when Drouet sent fresh troops against him, he attacked a detachment under colonel Prieur, killed twenty men, took the baggage and recovered a heavy contribution. The French were also continually harassed in the valley of the Tagus, notably so by a chief called Cuesta, who was sometimes in the Guadalupe mountains, sometimes on the Tietar, sometimes in the Vera de Placentia, and was supported at times on the side of the Guadalupe by Morillo and Penne Villemur. Hill's vicinity however disquieted them most on that side; his enterprises had made a profound impression, and the slightest change of his quarters, even the appearance of an English uniform beyond the line of cantonments, caused a concentration of troops to meet one of his sudden blows.

Nor was the army of Portugal tranquil. The Gallicians menaced it from Puebla Senabria and the gorges of the Bierzo —Silveira from the Tras os Montes,—the mountains separating Leon from the Asturias were full of bands,—Wellington was on the Agueda, and Hill, moving from Coria by the pass of Bejar, might make a sudden incursion towards Avila. Finally the communication with the army of the north was to be kept up, and on every side the partidas were enterprising, especially the horsemen in the plains of Leon: Reille however warred down these last.

Early in January Foy, returning from Astorga to relieve Leval then at Avila, killed some of Marquinez' cavalry in San Pedro and more of them at Mota la Toro; and on the 15th of that month captain Mathis killed or took four hundred of the same partida at Valderas. A convoy of guerilla stores coming from the Asturias was intercepted by Boyer's detachments; and one Florian, a celebrated Spanish partisan in the French service, destroyed the band of Garido in the Avila district. The same Florian on the 1st of February defeated the Medico and another inferior chief, and soon after passing the Tormes captured some Spanish dragoons who had come out of Ciudad Rodrigo. On the 1st of March he crushed the band of Tonto, and at the same time Mathis, acting on the side of the Carrion river, again surprised Marquinez' band at Melgar Abaxo, which was thus reduced to two hundred men and ceased to be formidable. Previous to this some Gallician troops at Castro Gonzalo on the Esla were attacked by Boyer, who beat them through Benevente with the loss of one hundred and fifty men, and then driving the Spanish garrison from Puebla Senabria raised contributions with a rigour and ferocity said to be habitual to him. His detachments afterwards penetrated into the Asturias, menaced Oviedo and vexed the country in despite of Porlier and Barceña who were in that province. Foy also, being at Avila and uneasy about Hill, endeavoured on the 20th of February to surprise Bejar with the view of ascertaining if any large body was collected behind it, but he was vigorously repulsed by the fiftieth regiment and sixth caçadores. This attack and the movements of Florian beyond the Tormes, induced Wellington to bring up another division to the

Agueda, which by a reaction made the French believe the allies were ready to advance.

As Caffarelli could not induce Reille to send him reinforcements the insurrection in the north gained strength, and the communications were entirely intercepted until Palombini, driving away Mendizabel and Longa from Burgos, enabled the great convoy and all Napoleon's despatches, which had been long accumulating there, to reach Madrid in the latter end of February. Joseph then reluctantly prepared to abandon his capital and concentrate the armies in Castille, but he neglected those essential ingredients of the emperor's plan, rapidity and boldness. By the first, Napoleon proposed to gain time for the suppression of the insurrection in the northern provinces; by the second to impose upon Wellington and keep him on the defensive. Joseph did neither, he was slow and assumed the defensive himself. He and the other French generals expected to be attacked, for they had not fathomed the English general's political difficulties; and French writers since, misconceiving the character of his warfare, have attributed to slowness in the man what was really the long-reaching policy of a great commander. The allied army was not so lithe as the French army. The latter carried on occasion ten days' provisions on the soldiers' backs, or it lived upon the country, and was in respect of its organization and customs a superior military machine; the former never carried more than three days' provisions, never lived upon the country, avoided the principle of making the war support the war, paid or promised to pay for everything, and often carried in its marches even the corn for its cavalry. The difference of this organization resulting from the difference of policy between the two nations, was a complete bar to any great and sudden excursion on the part of the British general, and must always be considered in judging his operations.

If Wellington had passed the upper Tormes with a considerable force, drawing Hill to him through Bejar and moving rapidly by Avila, he might have broken in upon the defensive system of the king and beat his armies in detail; and much the French feared such a blow, which would have been quite in the manner of Napoleon. But his views were directed by

other than mere military principles.   Thus striking, he was
not certain his blow would be decisive, his Portuguese forces
would have been ruined, his British soldiers seriously injured
by the attempt; and the resources of France would have
repaired the loss of the enemy sooner than he could have
recovered the weakness which must necessarily have followed
such an unseasonable exertion.   His plan was to bring a great
and enduring power early into the field, for like Phocion he
desired to have an army fitted for a long race, and would not
start on the short course.

Joseph conceived and dreaded such a sudden attack, but
could not conceive the spirit of his brother's plans.   It was in
vain Napoleon, while admitting the bad moral effect of abandoning the capital, pointed out the difference between flying
from it and making a forward movement at the head of an
army; the king maintained that Madrid was a better military
centre of operations than Valladolid, because it had lines of
communication by Segovia, Aranda de Duero, and Zaragoza.
Nothing could be more unmilitary than this view, unless he
was prepared to march direct upon Lisbon if the allies marched
upon the Duero.   His extreme reluctance to quit Madrid
induced slowness, and the actual position of his troops at the
moment likewise presented obstacles to the immediate execution of the emperor's orders; for as Daricau's division had not
returned from Valencia the French outposts towards the
Morena could not be withdrawn, nor could the army of the
centre march upon Valladolid until the army of the south
relieved it at Madrid.   Moreover Soult's counsels troubled the
king's judgment; for that marshal agreeing that to abandon
Madrid was to abandon Spain, endeavoured to reconcile possession of the capital with the emperor's views.

He proposed to place the army of Portugal and the army
of the south in position along the slopes of the Avila mountains and on the upper Tormes, menacing Rodrigo, while the
king with the army of the centre remained at Madrid in
reserve.   In this situation they would be an overmatch for
any force the allies could bring into the field; and the latter
could not move by the valley of the Tagus or upon the Duero
without danger of a flank attack.   Joseph, deceived by his

Spanish ministers, said that the feeding of such a force would ruin his people; but the comfortable state of the houses and the great plains of standing corn seen by the allies in their after march from the Esla to the Carrion proved that the people were not much impoverished. Soult, well acquainted with the resources of that country and a more practised master of such operations, looked to the military question rather than a conciliatory policy, and positively affirmed the armies could be subsisted; yet he does not appear to have considered how the insurrection in the northern provinces was to be suppressed, which was the principal object of Napoleon's plan. He no doubt expected the emperor would send troops for that purpose, but Napoleon knew that all the resources of France would be required in another quarter.

Hatred and suspicion would have made Joseph reject any plan suggested by Soult, and he was galled that the marshal should declare the troops could exist without money from France; yet his mind was unsettled by the proposal and the coincidence of ideas as to holding Madrid; for even when the armies were in movement he vacillated, at one time thinking
Marshal Jourdan's official Correspondence, MSS.
to stay at Madrid, at another to march with the army of the centre to Burgos instead of Valladolid. However upon the 18th of March he quitted the capital leaving the Spanish ministers Angulo and Almenara to govern there in conjunction with Gazan. The army of the south then moved in two columns, one under Conroux across the Gredos mountains to Avila, the other under Gazan upon Madrid to relieve the army of the centre, which immediately marched to Aranda de Duero and Lerma with orders to settle at Burgos. Villatte's division and all the outposts withdrawn from La Mancha remained on the Alberche, and the movements north of the Tagus were only molested by the bands. In La Mancha the retiring troops were followed by Del Parque's advanced guard under Cruz Murgeon, but the French cavalry checked it roughly at the bridge of Algobar. Cruz Murgeon then retired, and the Empecinado was defeated on the side of Cuenca in an attempt to cut off some cavalry who were escorting the marquis of Salices to collect his rents previous to quitting Madrid. When

the stores were removed from Madrid, Villatte marched on Salamanca, Gazan entered Arevalo, and the army of the south was cantoned between the Tormes, the Duero, and the Adaja, with exception of ten thousand chosen men left to hold Madrid under Leval. His orders were to keep guards at Toledo and on the Alberche, lest the allies should suddenly turn the left; and as roads beyond the Alberche led over the Gredos mountains in rear of the French advanced posts on the upper Tormes, these last were withdrawn from Pedrahita and Puente Congosto.

Reille now gradually reinforced Caffarelli, and concentrated his remaining force about Medina de Rio Seco with cavalry posts on the Esla; but the men recalled by the emperor were then in march, the French were in confusion, and the people instigated by Wellington's emissaries and expecting great events withheld provisions. The partida warfare also became as lively in the interior as on the coast, but with worse fortune. Captain Giordano, a Spaniard of Joseph's guard, killed one hundred and fifty of Saornil's people near Arevalo, and the indefatigable Florian, defeating Morale's band, seized a dépôt in the valley of the Tietar and beat the Medico; then crossing the Gredos mountains he destroyed near Segovia the band of Purchas: the king's Spanish guards also crushed some smaller partidas, and Renovales with his whole staff was captured at Carvajales and carried to Valladolid. The Empecinado coming to the hills above Sepulveda joined Merino and compelled the people of the Segovia district to abandon their houses; but being menaced by the French those chiefs regained their ancient haunts and Drouet then removed his headquarters to Cuellar.

In April Leval became so uneasy that he gave several false alarms, which caused an unreasonable concentration of the troops at Valladolid, and Drouet abandoned Cuellar and Sepulveda. Del Parque and the Empecinado were said to have re-established the bridge of Aranjuez, Elio to be advancing in La Mancha, Hill to be in the valley of the Tagus advancing by Mombeltran to seize the Guadarama. All this was false. The Empecinado, Abuelo, and Del Parque, were indeed at

April.

Joseph's
Papers,
MSS.

Aranjuez; and Firmin, Cuesta, Rivero, and the Medico were collecting near Arzobispo to mask the march of the Spanish divisions from Estremadura and the reserve from Andalusia. The prince of Anglona also had entered La Mancha with his cavalry, but it was to cover the movement of Del Parque upon Murcia; and when the true state of affairs became known, Leval drove away the Empecinado, chased Firmin from the valley of the Tagus, and re-established his posts in Toledo and on the Alberche. Joseph was then only restrained from abandoning Madrid altogether by his fear of the emperor, and his hope of still getting some contributions from thence to support his court. With reluctance also he obeyed Napoleon's reiterated orders to cross the Ducro with the army of the centre, and replace the detached divisions of the army of Portugal. He wished Drouet rather than Reille to reinforce the north, and nothing could more clearly show how entirely the subtle spirit of his brother's instructions had escaped his perception. For it was essential to hold Madrid, to watch the valley of the Tagus and enable the French armies to fall back on Zaragoza if the case arose; more essential to give moral effect to the offensive front shown towards the north of Portugal. For the last reason it was proper also that Reille and not Drouet, who was still in Madrid, should reinforce Caffarelli; because the latter's march from that capital would seem a retreat and disclose its object; whereas his movement ought to mask the object and bear the appearance of an offensive one towards Portugal.

In the contracted positions now occupied the difficulty of subsisting was increased, each general was dissatisfied, disputes multiplied, and the court clashed with the army at every turn. Leval also inveighed against the Spanish ministers and minor authorities left at Madrid; and no doubt justly, since their conduct was precisely like that of the Portuguese and Spanish authorities towards the allies. Joseph's letters to his brother became daily more bitter. Napoleon's regulations for the troops' subsistence clashed with his, and though his budget showed a deficit of many millions, the emperor disregarding it reduced the French subsidy to two millions per month, and forbad its application to any purpose save the pay of the soldiers. When Joseph asked how he was then to find resources? he was, with a just sarcasm on his political and military blindness, desired to seek what he wanted in the north which was rich enough to nourish the partidas and insurrectional juntas. Thus pushed to the wall, Joseph prevailed on Gazan secretly to lend him fifty thousand francs from the military chest; but with the other generals he could not agree, and for the vigour necessary to meet the coming campaign discord was substituted.

All the movements for concentration displeased the emperor. He condemned the army of the centre for stealing out of Madrid by the road of Lerma, as only calculated to expose the real views, and draw the allies on before the communications with France were restored. The manner in which the king held the armies on the defensive in his new position discontented him still more. The allies he said were thus told they might without fear for Portugal embark troops to invade France; whereas by a confident offensive movement backed with the formation of a battering-train at Burgos, indicating the siege of Rodrigo, Wellington would have been alarmed, France secured from the danger of insult, and the measures for suppressing the insurrection in the northern provinces have been masked. To quell that insurrection was of vital importance, yet it had now existed for seven months, in five of which the king, having ninety thousand men, was unmolested by Wellington, and had only chased some inferior bands of the interior while this warfare was consolidating in his rear, and his great adversary was organizing the most powerful army which had yet taken the field in his front. It is thus kingdoms are lost. The progress of this northern insurrection shall now be shown. Neglected by the king, it was to the last misunderstood by him; for when Wellington was actually in movement, when the dispersed French armies were crowding to the rear to avoid the ponderous mass the English general was pushing forward,—even then the king, who had done everything to render defeat certain, was urging upon Napoleon the propriety of first beating the allies and afterwards reducing the insurrection by the establishment of a Spanish civil government beyond the Ebro!

NORTHERN INSURRECTION.

In the latter end of 1812 all the French littoral posts, Santona and Gueteria excepted, had been taken by the Spaniards, and Mendizabel attacked Bilbao the 6th of January; being repulsed by Rouget, he rejoined Longa and reduced the little fort of Salinas de Anara near the Ebro, and that of Cuba in the Bureba, while bands from Logroño invested Domingo Calçada in the Rioja. On the 26th of January, Caffarelli detached Vandermaesen and Dubreton to drive the Spaniards from Santander; they seized many stores there, yet neglected to make any movement in aid of Santona which was again blockaded by the partidas. Meanwhile the convoy with the emperor's despatches was stopped at Burgos until Palombini re-opened the communications. But he had not more than three thousand men, and as the detachments belonging to the different armies were then in march to the interior, and the regiments recalled to France were also in movement, together with many convoys and escorts for marshals and generals quitting the Peninsula, the army of the north was reduced as its duties increased, and the young French soldiers died fast of a peculiar malady which especially attacked them in small garrisons. The Spaniards' forces increased, and in February Mendizabel and Longa were again in the Bureba, intercepting the communication between Burgos and Bilbao, and menacing Pancorbo and Briviesca. This brought Caffarelli from Vitoria and Palombini from Burgos. The latter, although surprised by Longa near Poza de Sal and only saving himself by his courage and firmness, finally drove the Spaniards away; but then Mina, returning from Aragon after his unsuccessful action near Huesca, surprised and burned the castle of Fuenterrabia in a daring manner; after which, assembling five thousand men in Guipuscoa he obtained guns from the English fleet at Motrico, invested Villa Real within a few leagues of Vitoria, and repulsed six hundred men who came to its succour. This brought Caffarelli from Pancorbo. Mina then raised the siege and Palombini drove the partidas towards Soria. The communication with Logroño being thus re-opened the Italians marched by Vitoria towards Bilbao, where they

arrived the 21st of February; but Caffarelli returned with
gens-d'armes and imperial guards to France, leaving the
Spanish chiefs masters of Navarre and Biscay. The people
now refused war contributions in money or kind, the harvest
was not ripe and the French were sorely distressed, because
the weather enabled the English ships to hug the coast and
intercept supplies from France by sea. The communications
were all broken; in front by Longa who was again at the
defile of Pancorbo; in rear by Mina who was in the hills of
Arlaban; on the left by a collection of bands at Caroncal in
Navarre. Abbé, governor of Pampeluna, severely checked
these last, but Mina soon restored affairs; for leaving the
volunteers of Guipuscoa to watch the defiles of Arlaban he
assembled all the bands in Navarre, destroyed the bridges
leading to Taffalla from Pampeluna and from Puente la Reyna
and though Abbé twice attacked him he got stronger, and
bringing up two English guns from the coast besieged
Taffalla.

Napoleon, discontented with Caffarelli, gave Clausel the
command in the north with discretionary power to draw
troops from the army of Portugal as he judged fitting. He
was to correspond directly with the emperor to avoid loss of
time, but was to obey the king in all things not clashing with
Napoleon's orders, which contained a complete review of what
had passed and what was fitting to be done. 'The partidas,'
the emperor said, ' were strong, organized, exercised and
seconded by the exaltation of spirit which the battle of Salamanca had produced. The insurrectional juntas had been
revived, the posts on the coast, abandoned by the French and
seized by the Spaniards, gave free intercourse with the English; the bands enjoyed all the resources of the country and
the system of warfare had hitherto favoured their progress.
Instead of forestalling their enterprises the French awaited
their attacks, and were always behind the event; they obeyed
the enemy's impulsion and the troops were fatigued without
gaining their object. Clausel must attack suddenly, pursue
rapidly, and combine his movements with reference to the
features of the country. A few good strokes against the
Spaniards' magazines, hospitals or dépôts of arms would

inevitably trouble their operations; and after one or two military successes political measures would suffice to disperse the authorities, disorganize the insurrection and bring the young men who had been enrolled by force back to their homes. Block-houses were to be constructed on well-chosen points, especially where many roads met; the forests would furnish the materials cheaply, and these posts should support each other and form chains of communication. With respect to the greater fortresses, Pampeluna and Santona were the most important and the enemy knew it; for Mina was intent to famish the first and the English squadron to get hold of the second. To supply Pampeluna it needed only to clear the communications as the country around was rich and fertile. Santona required combinations. The emperor wished to supply it by sea from Bayonne and St. Sebastian, but the French marine officers would never attempt the passage even with favourable winds and when the English squadron were away, unless all the intermediate ports were occupied by the land forces.

' Six months before these ports had been French, Caffarelli had lightly abandoned them while he marched with Souham against Wellington. Since that period the English and Spaniards held them. For four months the emperor had unceasingly ordered the retaking of Bermeo and Castro; but whether from the difficulty of the operation or the necessity of answering more pressing calls, no effort had been made to obey and the fine season now permitted the English ships to aid in the defence. Castro was said to be strongly fortified by the English, no wonder, Caffarelli had given them sufficient time and they knew its value. In one month every post on the coast from the mouth of the Bidassoa to St. Ander should be again re-occupied, and St. Ander garrisoned strongly. Simultaneous with the coast operations should be Clausel's attack on Mina, and the chasing of the partidas in the interior of Biscay. The administration of the country also demanded reform, still more did the organization and discipline of the army. The north was the pith of the French power, all would fail if that failed, whereas if it were strong, its administration sound, its fortresses well furnished, its state tranquil, no irreparable misfortune could happen in other parts.'

Clausel assumed command the 22nd of February, Abbé was then confined to Pampeluna, Mina, master of Navarre, was besieging Taffalla; Pastor, Longa, Campillo, Merino and others ranged through Biscay and Castille unmolested; and the spirit of the country was so changed, that fathers sent their sons to join partidas hitherto composed of robbers and deserters. Clausel demanded twenty thousand men from Reille, but Joseph, who was then in Madrid, proposed to send Drouet with the army of the centre instead. Clausel would not accede; twenty thousand troops were, he said, wanted beyond the Ebro; two independent chiefs could not act together; and if Drouet was only to remain at Burgos he would devour the resources without aiding the operations in the north. The king might choose another commander but the troops must be sent. Joseph yielded, yet it was the end of March before Reille's divisions moved, three upon Navarre and one upon Burgos. Meanwhile Clausel repaired to Bilbao, where Rouget had eight hundred men in garrison besides Palombini's Italians.

This place was blockaded by the partidas. The Pastor with three thousand men was in the hills of Guernica and Navarnis, between Bilbao and the fort of Bermeo; and Mendizabel having eight or ten thousand men in the mountains menaced Santoña and Bilbao and protected Castro. However the French garrison in Durango was strong, new works round Bilbao were in progress, and on the 22nd Clausel moved with the Italians and a French regiment to assault Castro. Campillo and Mendizabel came to its succour and the garrison made a sally, but the former after some sharp fighting regained the high valleys in disorder. The escalade of Castro would then have ensued, if Mendizabel had not come to Trucios, only seven miles from the French camp, and the Pastor with the volunteers of Biscay and Guipuscoa menaced Bilbao. Clausel marched with his French regiments to the latter place, leaving Palombini to oppose Mendizabel, but finding Bilbao in safety he sent Rouget with two battalions to reinforce the Italians, who then drove Mendizabel from Trucios into the hills about Valmaceda.

Castro was now to be attacked in form. Palombini occupied the heights of Ojeba and Ramales, from whence he

communicated with the garrison of Santoña, introduced a
convoy of money and fresh provisions there, received ammunition in return, and directed the governor Lameth to prepare
a battering-train of six pieces for the siege. But then he
returned hastily to Bilbao which was menaced by El Pastor,
whom he thought too strong to be meddled with until
promised a reinforcement from Durango, when he gave
battle and was defeated with a loss of eighty men. Two
days after the reinforcement joined and he beat the Pastor,
whose men dispersed, some to collect again on Palombini's
rear while others went to the interior. One column however
retired by the coast on the side of St. Sebastian, and Palombini pursued it, expecting troops from the fortress to line the
Deba and bar retreat, but an English squadron carried the
Spaniards off from Lequitio. Meanwhile El Pastor, having
rallied, descended the Deba and drove the French back to St.
Sebastian ; Palombini was thus compelled to make for Bergara
on the Vitoria road, where he left his wounded men and a
garrison, and on the 9th fell on the volunteers of Guipuscoa
at Ascoytia, but was repulsed and fell back to Bergara.

Next day he took charge of an artillery convoy going from
St. Sebastian for the siege of Castro ; yet he left Bilbao in
great danger, for the Biscayan volunteers made on the 10th a
false attack at a bridge above the entrenched camp, while
Tapia, Dos Pelos, and Campillo fell on seriously from the
side of Valmaceda. However, Mendizabel who commanded
the whole made such bad dispositions that he was repulsed by
Rouget, and then Palombini, who heard the firing, hastily
deposited his convoy and returning followed the Biscayan
volunteers to Guernica driving them upon Bermeo, where
they also got on board the English ships.

During these events Clausel remained at Vitoria to arrange
the general plan, and Mina on the 1st of April defeated one of
his columns near Lerim with a loss of six hundred men ; he
was also disappointed about his reinforcements ; for though four
of Reille's divisions and some unattached regiments joined
him, they only supplied seventeen instead of twenty thousand
men ; and as the regiments merely replaced men which had
marched to rejoin their own armies in front, this succour

dwindled to thirteen thousand. Hence, notwithstanding Palombini's activity the insurrection was in April more formidable than ever; the line of correspondence from Tor= quemada to Burgos was quite unprotected for want of troops, and the line from Burgos to Irun was not so well guarded that couriers could pass without powerful escorts, nor always then. The fortifications of Burgos were to have been improved but there was no money to pay for the works; the French could not collect provisions for magazines ordered by the king, and two generals, La Martiniere and Rey, were dis‹ puting for the command. Forty thousand Spanish partisans were in action, Taffalla surrendered to Mina, and he and Duran, Amor, Tabueca and the militia of Logroño, holding both sides of the Ebro between Calahora, Logroño, and Guardia, could in one day unite eighteen thousand foot and a thousand horsemen. Mendizabel, Longa, Campillo, Herrera, El Pastor, and the volunteers of Biscay, Guipuscoa, and Alava, in all sixteen thousand, were on the coast acting in conjunction with the English squadrons; Santander, Castro, and Bermeo were still in their hands, and maritime expeditions were preparing at Coruña and in the Asturias.

This partisan war thus presented three distinct branches, that of Navarre, that of the coast, and that on the lines of communication. The last alone occupied above fifteen thousand French; namely, ten thousand from Irun to Burgos, fifteen hundred to restore the line of correspondence between Tolosa and Pampeluna, which had been destroyed; and four thousand between Mondragon and Bilbao, the garrison of the latter place included. Nearly all the army of the north was appropriated to the garrisons and lines of communication; but the divisions of Abbé and Vandermaesen could be used on the side of Pampeluna, and there were disposable, Palombini's Italians and the divisions sent by Reille. But one of these, Sarrut's, was still in march, and all the sick of the armies in Castille were now pouring into Navarre, where, from the loss of the contributions there was no money to provide for them. Clausel had however ameliorated the civil and military administrations, improved the works of Gueteria, commenced block-houses between Irun and Vitoria, and

shaken the bands about Bilbao. Now dividing his forces he
sent Palombini to besiege Castro, and directed Foy and
Sarrut to cover the operation and oppose disembarkations.

This field force and the troops in Bilbao furnished ten
thousand men, and in the middle of April Clausel beat Mina
from Taffalla and Estella and assembled at Puente de la
Reyna in Navarre the remainder of the active army, composed
of Taupin's and Barbout's divisions of the army of Portugal
Vandermaesen's and Abbé's divisions of the army of the north,
in all thirteen thousand men. He urged L'Huillier, who commanded the reserve at Bayonne, to reinforce St. Sebastian and
Gueteria and push troops of observation into the valley of
Bastan ; and he also warned the commander of Zaragoza to
watch Mina on that side. From Puente la Reyna he made
some excursions, but lost men uselessly, for the Spaniards
would only fight at advantage; and to hunt Mina without first
barring all his passages of flight was to destroy the French
soldiers by fatigue. Here the king's dilatory warfare was
seriously felt, because the winter season, when the tops of the
mountains being covered with snow the partidas could only
move along the ordinary roads, was most favourable for the
French operations and it passed away; Clausel now despaired
to effect anything, and was even going to separate his forces
and march to the coast when, in May, Mina took post in the
valley of Roncal. The French general instantly sent Abbé's
and Vandermaesen's divisions and the cavalry against him at
once by the upper and lower parts. Suddenly closing upon
the guerilla chief they killed or wounded a thousand of his
men and dispersed the rest; one part fled from the mountains
on the side of Sanguessa with the wounded, whom they dropped
at different places in care of the country people; but Chaplan-
garra, Cruchaga, and Carena, Mina's lieutenants, going off,
each with a column, in the opposite direction and by different
routes to the valley of the Aragon, passed that river at St.
Gilla and made their way towards the sacred mountain of La
Peña near Jaca. The French cavalry following them by
Villa Real, entered that town the 14th on one side while
Mina with twelve men entered it on the other; yet he escaped
to Martes where another ineffectual attempt was made to sur-

prise him. Abbé's columns then descended the smaller valleys
leading towards the upper valley of the Aragon, while Vandermaesen's infantry and the cavalry entered the lower part of
the same valley, and the former approaching Jaca sent his
wounded men there and got fresh ammunition.

Mina and the insurgent junta trying to regain Navarre by
the left of the Aragon river were like to have been taken, but
again escaped towards the valley of the Gallego, whither also
the greater part of their troops now sought refuge.   Clausel
forbore to force them over that river, lest they should remain
there and intercept the communication from Zaragoza by
Jaca, the only free line the French now possessed and too
distant to be watched.   Abbé therefore returned to Ronçal in
search of the Spanish dépôts, and Vandermaesen entered Sos
at one end as Mina, who had now one hundred and fifty horsemen and was always intent upon regaining Navarre, passed out
at the other.   The light cavalry overtook him at Sos Fuentes
and he fled to Carcastillo; but there, unexpectedly meeting some
of his own squadrons which had wandered over the mountains
after the action at Ronçal, he gave battle, was defeated with
the loss of fifty men and fled once more to Aragon, whereupon
the insurrectional junta dispersed and dissensions arose between
Mina and the minor chiefs under his command.   Clausel,
anxious to increase this discord, sent troops into all the valleys
to seek out the Spanish dépôts and attack their scattered men;
and he was well served by the Aragonese, for Suchet's wise
administration was still proof against the insurrectional juntas.

During these events four battalions left by Mina in the
Amescoas were chased by Taupin, who had remained at Estella
when the other divisions marched up the valley of Ronçal.
Soon however Mina re-assembled at Barbastro in Aragon a
strong column, crowds of deserters from the other Spanish
armies augmented his force; and so completely had he organized Navarre, that the presence of a single soldier of his in a
village sufficed to have any courier without a strong escort
stopped.   Many bands also were still in the Rioja, and two
French battalions rashly foraging towards Lerim were nearly all
destroyed.   In fine the losses were well balanced, and Clausel
demanded more troops, especially cavalry, to scour the Rioja.

Nevertheless the dispersion of Mina's troops lowered his reputation, and the French general so improved this advantage by
address, that many townships withdrew from the insurrection
and recalling their young men from the bands commenced the
formation of eight free Spanish companies to serve on the
French side.   Corps of this sort were raised with so much
facility in every part of Spain that it would seem nations as
well as individuals have an idiosyncrasy, and in these change-
able warriors we again see the Mandonius and Indibilis of
ancient days.

Joseph, urged by Clausel, now sent Maucune's division and
some light cavalry of the army of Portugal to occupy Pam-
pleiga, Burgos, and Briviesca, and to protect the great communication, which the diverging direction of the operations
had again exposed to the partidas.   But the French had not
been less successful in Biscay than in Navarre.   Foy reached
Bilbao the 24th of April, and finding all things ready for the
siege of Castro marched to Santona to hasten the preparations
at that place; he attempted also to surprise Campillo and
Herrera in the hills above Santona, but was worsted in the
combat.   The two battering-trains then endeavoured to proceed from Bilbao and Santona by sea to Castro; the English
vessels, coming to the mouth of the Durango, stopped those at
Bilbao and compelled them to proceed by land, but thus gave
an opportunity for those at Santona to make the sea-run
in safety.

SIEGE OF CASTRO.

This place, situated on a promontory, was garrisoned by
twelve hundred men under the command of Pedro
Alvarez; three English sloops of war commanded
by the captains Bloye, Bremen, and Tayler, were at hand,
some gun-boats were in the harbour, and twenty-seven guns
were mounted on the works.   An outward wall with towers
extended from sea to sea on the low neck which connected the
promontory with the mainland, and this line of defence was
strengthened by some fortified convents; then came the town,
and behind the town at the extremity of the promontory stood
the castle.

May.

On the 4th of May, Foy, Sarrut and Palombini took post at different points to cover the siege; the Italian general St. Paul invested the place; the engineer Vacani conducted the works, having twelve guns at his disposal. The defence was lively and vigorous, and captain Tayler with great labour landed a heavy ship-gun on a rocky island to the right of the town, looking from the sea, which he worked with effect against the French counter-batteries. On the 11th a second gun was mounted on this island; but that day the breaching-batteries were opened and in a few hours broke the wall, while the counter-batteries set fire to some houses with shells. The English guns were then removed from the island and the assault was ordered, but was delayed because a foraging party sent into the hills came flying back, pursued by a column of Spaniards which had passed unperceived through the positions of the French. This threw the besiegers into confusion as thinking the covering army had been beaten, yet they soon recovered and the assault and escalade took place in the night.

The attack was rapid and fierce, the walls were carried and the garrison driven through the town to the castle, which was maintained by two companies while the flying troops got on board the English vessels; finally the Italians stormed the castle, but every gun had been destroyed and the two companies safely rejoined their countrymen on board the ships. The English had ten seamen wounded, the Spaniards lost a hundred and eighty, and the remainder were immediately conveyed to Bermeo from whence they marched inland to join Longa. The besiegers lost only fifty killed and wounded, and the Italian soldiers committed great excesses, setting fire to the town in many places. Foy and Sarrut marched after the siege, the former through the district of Incartaciones to Bilbao defeating a battalion of Biscay volunteers on his route; the latter to Orduño with the design of destroying Longa; but that chief crossed the Ebro at Puente Lara, and finding the troops sent by Joseph were beginning to arrive at Burgos, recrossed the river and after a long chase escaped in the mountains of Espinosa. Sarrut, having captured a few gun-carriages and one of Longa's forest dépôts of ammunition, returned towards Bilbao, and Foy immediately marched from that place

against the two remaining battalions of Biscay volunteers,
which under their chiefs Mugartegui and Artola were at
Villaro and Guernica.

These battalions, each a thousand strong, raised by conscription and officered from the best families, were the
champions of Biscay; but though brave and well-equipped
the difficulty of crushing them and the volunteers of Guipuscoa
was not great, because neither would leave their own peculiar
provinces. The third battalion had been already dispersed in
the district of Incartaciones, and Foy, having in the night of
the 29th combined the march of several columns to surround
Villaro, fell at daybreak upon Mugartegui's battalion and dispersed it with the loss of all its baggage. Two hundred
returned to their homes, and the French general then moved
rapidly against Artola, who was at Guernica. The Italians
being still at Bilbao were directed to flank that chief on the
west by Mungia, while a French column flanked him on the
east by Marquinez. Artola fled to Lequitio, but the column
from Marquinez, coming over the mountain, fell upon his right
just as he was defiling on a narrow way along the sea coast;
he escaped himself, yet two hundred Biscayans were killed or
drowned, three hundred with twenty-seven officers taken.
A rear-guard of two companies got off in the mountains, some
few gained an English vessel, and this success which did not
cost the French a man was attributed to Guingret, the daring
officer who won the passage of the Duero at Tordesillas during
Wellington's retreat.

The volunteer battalions of Biscay being thus disposed of,
all their magazines hospitals and dépôts fell into Foy's hands,
the junta dispersed, the privateers quitted the coast for Santander, Pastor abandoned Guipuscoa, and the Italians recovered Bermeo from which the garrison fled to the English
ships. They also destroyed the works of the little island of
Isaro, which, situated three thousand yards from the shore
and having no access to the summit save by a staircase cut in
the rock, was deemed impregnable and used as a dépôt for
the English stores. This was the last memorable exploit of
Palombini's division in the north. That general himself had
already gone to Italy to join Napoleon's reserves, and his

troops being ordered to march by Aragon to join Suchet, were actually in movement when new events caused them to remain in Guipuscoa. They were reputed brave and active soldiers, but in devastating ferocity differed little from their Roman ancestors.

During these double operations of the French on the coast and in Navarre the partidas had fallen upon the line of communication with France; thus working out the third branch of the insurrectional warfare; and their success went nigh to balance all their losses on each flank. Mendizabel was with Longa's partida upon the line between Burgos and Miranda de Ebro; the volunteers of Alava and Biscay and part of Pastor's band were concentrated on the mountains of Arlaban above the defiles of Salinas and Descarga; Merino and Salazar came up from the country between the Ebro and the Duero; and the three battalions left by Mina in the Amescoas, after escaping from Taupin, re-assembled close to Vitoria. Every convoy, every courier's escort was attacked at one or other of these points, and Mendizabel also made sudden descents towards the coast. On the 25th of April, Longa, who had four thousand men and several guns, was repulsed at Armiñion between Miranda and Trevino, by some of the drafted men going to France; but on the 3rd of May he compelled a large convoy coming from Castille with an escort of eight hundred men to return to Miranda, and even cannonaded that place on the 5th. Thouvenot, commandant of the government, immediately detached twelve hundred men and three guns from Vitoria to relieve the convoy; but then Mina's battalions endeavoured to escalade Salvatierra, and they were repulsed with difficulty. The volunteers of Alava gathered above the pass of Salinas to intercept the rescued convoy, but finding the latter would not stir from Vitoria went on the 10th to aid in a fresh attack on Salvatierra; being again repulsed, they returned to Arlaban and captured a courier with a strong escort in the pass of Descarga near Villa Real. A French regiment sent to succour Salvatierra finally drove these volunteers towards Bilbao, where, as already shown, Foy routed them; but Longa continued to infest the post of Armiñion until Sarrut arriving from the siege of Castro chased him also.

Notwithstanding these successes Clausel, whose troops were worn out with fatigue, declared it would require fifty thousand men and three months' time to quell the insurrection entirely. And Napoleon more discontented than ever with the king, complained that the successes of Clausel, Foy, Sarrut, and Palombini had brought no safety to his couriers and convoys; that his orders about posts and infantry escorts had been neglected; that the reinforcements sent to the north from Castille had gone slowly and in succession instead of at once; finally that the cautious movement of concentration by the other armies was inexcusable; since the inaction of the allies, their distance, their want of transport, their ordinary and even timid circumspection, in any operation out of the ordinary course, enabled the French to act in the most convenient manner. The growing dissensions between the English and the Spaniards, the journey of Wellington to Cadiz, the changes in his army were, he said, all favourable circumstances for the French, but the king had taken no advantage of them: the insurrection continued and the object of interest was now changed.   Joseph defended himself with more vehemence than reason against these charges, but Wellington soon vindicated Napoleon's judgment and the voice of controversy was smothered by the din of battle, for the English general was again abroad in his strength and the clang of his arms resounded through the Peninsula.

CHAPTER VI.

WHILE the French power was being disorganized in the manner just related, Wellington re-organized the allied army with greater strength than before. Large reinforcements, especially of cavalry, had come out from England, the efficiency of the Portuguese was restored in a surprising manner, and discipline had been vindicated in both services with a rough but salutary hand. Rank had not screened offenders; some had been arrested, some tried, some dismissed for breach of duty; the negligent were terrified the zealous encouraged; every department was reformed, and it was full time. Confidential officers commissioned to detect abuses in the general hospitals and dépôts, those asylums for malingerers, discovered and drove so many skulkers to their duty, that the second division alone recovered six hundred bayonets in one month; and this scouring was rendered more efficient by the establishment of permanent and ambulatory regimental hospitals; a wise measure founded on a principle which cannot be too widely extended; for as the character of a battalion depends on its fitness for service, a moral force will always bear upon the execution of orders under regimental control which it is in vain to look for elsewhere.

The Douro had been rendered navigable as high as Castillo de Alva above the confluence of the Agueda; a pontoon-train of thirty-five pieces had been formed; carts of a peculiar construction had been built to repair the great loss of mules during the retreat from Burgos; and a recruit of these animals was also obtained by emissaries, who purchased them with English merchandise even at Madrid under the beard of the enemy, and when Clausel was unable for want of transport to fill the magazines of Burgos! The ponderous iron camp-kettles of the soldiers had been laid aside for lighter vessels

carried by men, the mules being destined to carry tents instead;
it is however doubtful if these tents were really useful in wet
weather, because when soaked they became too heavy for the
animal and seldom arrived in time at the end of a march:
their greatest advantage was when the soldiers halted for a few
days. Many other changes and improvements had taken place,
and the Anglo-Portuguese troops, conscious of a superior
organization, were more proudly confident than ever, while the
French were again depressed by intelligence of the defection
of the Prussians, following on the disasters in Russia. Nor
had the English general failed to amend the condition of those
Spanish troops which the Cortes had placed at his disposal.
By a strict and jealous watch over the application of the
subsidy he kept them clothed and fed during the winter, and
now had several powerful bodies fit to act in conjunction with
his own forces.

· Thus prepared he was anxious to strike, anxious to forestall
the effects of his Portuguese political difficulties as well as to
keep pace with Napoleon's efforts in Germany, and his army
was ready to take the field in April; but he could not concentrate before the green forage was fit for use and deferred the
execution of his plan until May. It was a wide plan. The
relative strength for battle was no longer in favour of the
French; their force had been reduced by losses in the secondary

Appendix 9.   warfare, and by drafts since Wellington's retreat,
from two hundred and sixty to two hundred and
thirty thousand. Of the last number thirty thousand
were in hospital, and only one hundred and ninety-seven
thousand men, including the reserve at Bayonne, were present
with the eagles. Sixty-eight thousand, including sick, were in
Aragon, Catalonia, and Valencia; the remainder, with the
exception of the ten thousand left at Madrid, were distributed
on the northern line of communication from the Tormes to
Bayonne: it has been shown how scattered and how occupied.

· Wellington was somewhat thwarted by the duke of York,
with whom he was not on very cordial terms; instead of
receiving remounts for the cavalry, four of his regiments were
withdrawn because of their loss of horses, leaving him weaker
by twelve hundred than he ought to have been. But he had

prepared two hundred thousand allied troops for the campaign; and on each flank there was a British fleet, now a very effective aid, because the French lines of retreat run parallel to and near the sea-coast on each side of Spain, and every port opened by the advance of the allies would form a dépôt for subsistence.

This mass of troops was organized in the following manner south of the Tagus.   The first army under Copons, nominally ten thousand, was in Catalonia.   The second army under Elio in Murcia twenty thousand, including the divisions of Villa Campa, Bassecour, Duran, and Empecinado.   The Anglo-Sicilian army under Murray near Alicant, sixteen thousand. The third army under Del Parque in the Morena, twelve thousand.   The first army of reserve under Abispal in Anda-, lusia, fifteen thousand.

In the north, the fourth army under Castaños included the Spanish divisions in Estremadura, Julian Sanchez' partida the Gallicians under Giron, the Asturians under Porlier and Barceña, the partidas of Longa and Mina.   It was computed at forty thousand, to which may be added minor bands and volunteers in various parts.   Then came the noble Anglo-Portuguese army, seventy thousand fighting men with ninety pieces of artillery.   And the real difference between the French and the allies was greater than it appeared.   The French returns included officers, serjeants, drummers, artillerymen, engineers, and waggoners, whereas the Anglo-Portuguese were all sabres and bayonets.   Moreover this return of the French number was dated the 15th of March; and as there were drafts made after that period, and Clausel and Foy's losses and the reserve at Bayonne are to be deducted, the number of sabres and bayonets in June was probably not more than one hundred and sixty thousand, one hundred and ten thousand being on the northern line.

The campaign of 1812 had shown how strong the French lines of defence were, especially on the Duero, which they had since entrenched in different parts, and most of the bridges over it had been destroyed in the retreat.   But it was not advisable to operate in the central provinces of Spain.   The country there was exhausted, the lines of supply would be longer and more exposed, the army further removed from the sea, the Gallicians could not be easily brought down to co-operate, the services of the northern partidas would not be so advantageous, and the ultimate result would be less decisive than operations against the great line of communication with France. Wherefore on the northern line the operations were to run, and those defences which could scarcely be forced were to be evaded. On the lower Duero, the French army could be turned by a wide move-ment across the upper Tormes, and from thence, skirting the mountains, towards the upper Duero; but that line although most consonant to the rules of art because the army would thus be kept in one mass, led through a difficult and wasted country, the direct aid of the Gallicians would be lost, and it was there the French looked for the attack. Wellington therefore resolved to operate by his left, and so disposed his troops and spread such reports, and made such false move-ments as to mask his real design. For the gathering of partidas at Arzobispo, the demonstrations in Estremadura and La Mancha, the positions of Hill at Coria and the pass of Bejar and the magazines formed there, were all of his ordering and indicated a move by the Tagus or by Avila. The greater magazines at Celorico, Visen, Penamacor, Almeida and Rodrigo in no manner belied this; but half the army widely cantoned in Portugal, apparently for health, was really on the true line of operations which was to run through the Tras of Montes.

Plan 2, p. 63.

It was also designed to pass the Duero on the Portuguese frontier, and Wellington would have done so with the whole army in mass, if the necessity of keeping his right so far advanced in Spain during the winter had not barred that measure; for a concentration on the left would have exposed the country on his right to incursions, and disclosed his real design. Wherefore with a modified project he proposed to operate with his left, ascending the right of the Duero to the Esla, crossing that river to unite with the Gallicians, while the rest of the army advancing from the Agueda should force the passage of the Tormes. By this combination, which he hoped to effect so suddenly that the king should not have time to concentrate in opposition, the front of the allies would be changed to their right, the Duero and Carrion turned and the enemy thrown in confusion over the Pisuerga. Then moving forward in mass, the English general could fight or turn any position taken by the king; gaining at each step more force by the junction of the Spanish irregulars until he reached the insurgents of Biscay; gaining also new communications with the fleet, and consequently new dépôts at every port opened.

In the first movement the army would be divided into three parts, each too weak to meet the whole French force; and the Tras os Montes operation, upon the nice execution of which the whole depended, would be in a difficult mountainous country. Hence exact and extensive combinations were essential to success, but failure would not be dangerous because each corps had a strong country to retire upon; the worst effect would be loss of time and the opening of other operations, when the harvest would allow the French to act in masses. The problem was to be solved by hiding the project and gaining time for the Tras os Montes march; and to do this, minor combinations and resources for keeping the French armies scattered and employed were to be freely used. In that view, the bridge equipage was secretly prepared in Abrantes, and the bullock carts to draw it came from Spain by Lamego. The improved navigation of the Douro seemed more conducive to subsist a movement by the right, and yet furnished large boats by which to pass the left over that river; the wide-spread cantonments permitted changes of quarters under pretence of sickness, and thus the troops were gradually closed upon the Douro without suspicion. Hill and the Spaniards in Estremadura and Andalusia always menaced the valley of the Tagus, and contributed to draw attention from the true point; but more than any other thing the vigorous excitement of and sustenance of the northern insurrection occupied the enemy, scattered his forces, and rendered the success of the project nearly certain.

Neither did Wellington fail to give ample employment to Suchet's forces; for his wings were spread for a long flight, even to the Pyrenees, and he had no desire to find that marshal's army joined with the other French forces on the Ebro. The lynx eyes of Napoleon had scanned this point o

war also, and both the king and Clauzel had received orders
to establish the shortest and most certain line of correspondence possible with Suchet, because the emperor's plan contemplated the arrival of that marshal's troops in the north;
but Wellington found another task for it.   For after the
fight of Castalla, Freyre's cavalry joined the Andalusian
reserve under Abispal, and Elio who remained near Alicant
was to be joined by Del Parque.   These and the Anglo-
Sicilian troops furnished more than fifty thousand men,
including the divisions of Duran, Villa Campa, the Empecinado and other partisans, who were always lying on Suchet's
right flank and rear.   With such a force, or even half, if of
good troops, the simplest plan would have been to turn
Suchet's right flank and bring him to action with his back to
the sea; but the Spanish armies were not efficient for such
work and their instructions were adapted to circumstances.
To win the open part of the kingdom, to obtain a permanent
footing on the coast beyond the Ebro, to force the enemy
from the lower line of that river by acting in conjunction
with the Catalans,--these were the three objects in view, and
to attain them Wellington desired Murray to sail against
Taragona.   Suchet must, he said, decrease his Valencian force
to save it; Elio and Del Parque might then seize that kingdom;
if Taragona fell it would be good, if it was too strong
Murray could return by sea and secure the country gained by
the Spanish generals.

   Elio and Del Parque were however enjoined to keep strictly
on the defensive until Murray's operations drew Suchet away;
they were not able to fight alone and their defeat would
enable the French marshal to aid the king in the north.   Ten
thousand men were judged sufficient to reduce Taragona, but
if Murray could not embark that number there was another
mode of operating.   Some Spanish battalions sent by sea
would enable Copons to hold the country between Taragona,
Lerida and Tortoza; meanwhile Murray and Elio were to
menace Suchet in front, and Del Parque in conjunction with
the partidas was to turn his right by Requeña; this operation was to be repeated until Del Parque gained a connexion
with Copons by the left, and the partidas had cut off Suchet's

intercourse with the northern provinces: either of these plans would entirely occupy that marshal and keep him in the south.

Wellington was not aware that Reille's divisions were beyond the Ebro; the spies, deceived by the multitude of detachments passing in and out of the Peninsula, supposed the troops which reinforced Clausel to be fresh conscripts from France; the arrangements for the opening of the campaign were therefore made in the expectation of meeting a very powerful force in Leon. Hence Freyre's cavalry and the Andalusian reserve received orders to march upon Almaraz, to pass the Tagus there by a pontoon-bridge established for them, and then crossing the Gredos by Bejar or Mombeltran, to march upon Valladolid while the partidas of that quarter should harass the march of Leval from Madrid. The Spanish troops in Estremadura were to join those forces on the Agueda which were destined to make the passage of the Tormes; and the Gallicians were to come down on the Esla to unite with the Tras os Montes corps. Thus seventy thousand Anglo-Portuguese, eight thousand Spaniards from Estremadura, and twelve thousand Gallicians, in all ninety thousand fighting men, would be suddenly placed on a new front and marching abreast would drive the surprised and separated masses of the enemy refluent to the Pyrennees. A grand design and grandly it was executed! For high in heart and strong of hand Wellington's veterans marched to the encounter, the glories of twelve victories played about their bayonets, and he their leader was so proud and confident, that in passing the stream which marks the frontier of Spain, he rose in his stirrups and waving his hand cried out 'Farewell Portugal!'

But while straining every nerve and eager to strike, eager also to escape Portuguese politics and keep pace with Napoleon, he was called upon to discuss again the policy of a descent on Italy, and a new ministerial project for withdrawing his German troops to act in Germany!! Lord William Bentinck had before relinquished his views with reluctance, but now, thinking affairs favourable, again proposed to land at Naples and put forward the duke of Orleans or the archduke Francis. He urged the weak state of Murat's kingdom, the favourable disposition of the inhabitants, the offer of fifteen thousand auxiliary Russians made by admiral Grieg, the shock to Napoleon's power and the effectual diversion in favour of Spain. He supported his opinion by an intercepted letter of the queen of Naples to Napoleon, and by other authentic documents; and thus at the moment of execution Wellington's vast plans were to be disarranged to meet new schemes of war, one of which he had already discussed and disapproved of; and however promising in itself it would inevitably have divided the power of England and weakened the operations in both countries.

His reply was decisive. To withdraw the Germans would only lead to mischief, and his opinion as to Sicily was not changed by Murat's letters, as that monarch evidently thought himself strong enough to invade the island. Lord William should not land in Italy with less than forty thousand men well equipped, since it must overcome all opposition before the people would join or even cease to oppose. It was stated that the people looked to be protected from the French and preferred England to Austria. No doubt of that. The Austrians would demand provisions and money and insist upon governing them in return; the English would as elsewhere, defray their own expenses and probably give a subsidy in addition. The south of Italy was possibly the best place next to the Spanish Peninsula for the operations of a British army, and it remained for the government to choose whether they would adopt an attack on the former upon such a scale as he had alluded to. But of one thing they might be certain; if it were commenced on a smaller scale, or with any other intention than to persevere to the last and by raising feeding and clothing armies of the natives, the plan would fail and the troops would re-embark with loss and disgrace. This remonstrance fixed the vacillating ministers and Wellington was allowed to proceed with his own plans.

Designing to open the campaign the beginning of May, and the green forage being well advanced the 21st of April, he directed Murray, Del Parque, Elio, and Copons to commence their operations on the eastern coast; Abispal and Freyre were expected at Almaraz the 24th; the Estremaduran divisions had reached the Coa, and the Anglo-Portuguese force was gradually closing to the front. But heavy rains broke up the roads, and the cumbrous pontoon-train being damaged on its way did not reach Sabugal before the 13th, and was not repaired before the 15th. Thus the opening of the campaign was delayed, yet the check proved of little consequence, for on the French side nothing was prepared to meet the danger. Napoleon had urged the king to send his heavy baggage and stores to the rear, to fix his hospitals and dépôts at Burgos, Vitoria, Pampeluna, Tolosa, and San Sebastian; Joseph allowed the impediments to remain with the armies, and the sick, poured along the communications, were thrown upon Clausel at the moment when that general was scarcely able to make head against the northern insurrection.

Napoleon had early and clearly fixed the king's authority as generalissimo, and forbad him to exercise his monarchical authority towards the French armies, yet Joseph was at this moment in high dispute with all his generals upon those very points.

Napoleon had directed the king to enlarge and strengthen the works of Burgos, and form magazines there and at Santona for the armies in the field. At this time no magazines had been formed at either place, and although a commencement had been made to strengthen Burgos, it was not capable of sustaining four hours' bombardment and offered no support for the armies.

Napoleon had desired a more secure and shorter line of correspondence than that by Zaragoza should be established with Suchet; for his plan embraced, though it did not prescribe, the march of that general upon Zaragoza, and he had repeatedly warned the king how dangerous it would be to have Suchet isolated and unconnected with the northern operations. Nevertheless the line of correspondence remained the same, and the allies could excise Suchet's army from the north.

Napoleon had long and earnestly urged the king to put down the northern insurrection in time to make head against the allies on the Tormes. Now, when the English general was ready to act that insurrection was in full activity; and all the army of the north and great part of the army of Portugal were employed to suppress it instead of being on the lower Duero.

Napoleon had clearly explained to the king the necessity of keeping his troops concentrated towards the Tormes in an offensive position, and desired him to hold Madrid so as that it could be abandoned in a moment. The campaign was now being opened, the French armies were scattered, Leval was encumbered at Madrid with a part of the civil administration, with large stores parcs of artillery and the care of families attached to Joseph's court; while the other generals were stretching their imaginations to devise which of the several projects open to him Wellington would adopt. Would he force the passage of the Tormes and the Duero with his whole army and thus turn the French right? Would he march straight upon Madrid either by the district of Avila or by the valley of the Tagus or by both; and would he then operate against the north or upon Zaragoza, or towards the south in co operation with the Anglo-Sicilians? Everything was vague, uncertain, confused.

All the generals complained that the king's conduct was not military, and Napoleon told him if he would command an army he must give himself up entirely to it, thinking of nothing else; but Joseph was always demanding gold when he should have trusted to iron. His skill was unequal to the arrangements and combinations for taking an initiatory and offensive position, and he could neither discover nor force his adversary to show his real design. The French being thrown upon a timid defensive system, every movement of the allies produced alarm and the dislocation of troops without an object Del Parque's march towards Alcaraz, and that of the Spanish divisions from Estremadura in the latter end of April, were viewed as the commencement. of a general movement against Madrid; because the first was covered by the advance of some cavalry into La Mancha, and the second by the concentration of the partidas in the valley of the ·Tagus; the whole French army was thus shaken by the demonstration of a few horsemen; for when Leval took the alarm, Gazan marched towards the Guadarama with three divisions, and Droue gathered the army of the centre around Segovia.

Early in May a fifth division of Reille's troops was employed on the line of communication at Pampliega, Burgos, and Briviesca, and he remained at Valladolid with only one division of infantry and his guns, his cavalry being on the Esla. Drouet was then at Segovia, Gazan at Arevalo; Conroux was at Avila, Leval at Madrid with outposts at Toledo. The king who was at Valladolid could not therefore concentrate more than thirty-five thousand infantry on the Duero. He had indeed nine thousand excellent cavalry and more than one hundred pieces of artillery; but with such dispositions, to concentrate for a battle in advance was not to be thought of, and the first decided movement of the allies was sure to roll his scattered forces back in confusion. Thus the lines of the Tormes and the Duero were effaced from the system of operations!

About the middle of May, D'Armagnac's division came to Valladolid, Villatte's divison, reinforced by some cavalry, took the line of the Tormes from Alba to Ledesma; three divisions were at Zamora, Toro and other places on both sides of the Duero, and Reille's cavalry was still on the Esla. The front of the French was therefore defined by those rivers, for the left was covered by the Tormes, the centre by the Duero, the right by the Esla. Gazan's head-quarters were at Arevalo, Drouet's at Segovia, and the point of concentration was at Valladolid; but Conroux at Avila, and Leval at Madrid, were thrown entirely out of the circle of operations. It was at this moment that Wellington entered upon what has been in England called, not very appropriately, the march to Vitoria, that march being but one portion of the action. The concentration of the army on the banks of the Duero was the commencement, the movement towards the Ebro and the passage of that river was the middle, the battle of Vitoria was the catastrophe, and the crowning of the Pyrenees the end of the splendid drama.

CHAPTER VII.

In the latter end of April the Estremaduran troops were assembled on the Tormes, Carlos d'España had moved on Miranda del Castanar, and the campaign was going to open when a formidable obstacle menacing utter ruin arose. Some specie sent from England discharged the British soldiers' arrears to November 1812; but the men whose period of service had expired and who had reinlisted, were entitled to bounty amounting to eight hundred thousand dollars, and as death was so rife they desired to have it. But far from being able to meet this demand Wellington could not pay his muleteers, on whom his operations depended, their arrears, many had deserted in consequence and it was feared others would follow. The Portuguese troops also, being still neglected by their government and seeing the English soldiers partially paid, thought a systematic difference was going to be established between them, and thousands whose term of service was expired murmured for their discharge, which could not be legally refused. Wellington instantly threatened to apply the subsidy to paying the troops, which brought the regency to rights, and then he appealed to the honour and patriotism of the Portuguese soldiers whose term had expired. Such an appeal is never made in vain to the poorer classes of any nation, and, one and all, those brave men remained with their colours notwithstanding the shameful treatment they had endured from their government. This noble emotion would prove that Beresford, whose system of military reform was chiefly founded upon severity, might have better attained his object in another manner; but harshness is the essence of the aristocratic principle of government, and the marshal only moved in the straight path marked out for him by the policy of the day.

When this dangerous affair was terminated Castaños returned to Gallicia, and the British cavalry of the left wing, which had wintered about the Mondego, crossed the Duero, some at Oporto, some near Lamego, and entered the Tras os Montes.   The Portuguese cavalry had been quartered all the winter in that province, and the enemy sup- *French Re-* posed that Silveira would as formerly advance *ports, MSS.* from Braganza to connect Gallicia with the allies. *Plan 2, p. 63.* But Silveira was then commanding an infantry division on the Agueda, and a very different power was menacing the French on the side of Braganza.   For about the middle of May the cavalry were followed by many divisions of infantry and by the pontoon equipage, thus forming with the horsemen and artillery a mass of more than forty thousand men under Graham.   The infantry and guns, rapidly placed on the right of the Duero by means of large boats assembled between Lamego and Castello de Alva, marched in several columns towards the lower Esla, one column however having with it two brigades of cavalry went by Braganza.   On the 20th Hill came to Bejar, and the 22nd Graham being well advanced, Wellington quitted Freneda and put his right wing in motion towards the Tormes.   It consisted of five divisions of Anglo-Portuguese and Spanish infantry, five brigades of cavalry, including Julian Sanchez' horsemen, presenting with the artillery a mass of thirty thousand men.   Being divided, one part under Hill moved from Bejar upon Alba de Tormes, the other under Wellington upon Salamanca.

On the 24th Villatte withdrew his detachment from Ledesma, and the 26th, at ten o'clock in the morning, the heads of the allied columns appeared with admirable concert on all the different routes leading to the Tormes.   Morillo's division and Long's cavalry menaced Alba, Hill coming from Tamames bent towards the fords above Salamanca, and Wellington coming from Matilla marched straight against that city.

Villatte, a good officer, barricaded the bridge and the streets, sent his baggage to the rear, called in his detachment from Alba, and being resolved to discover the real force of his enemy waited for their approaching masses on the heights

above the ford of Santa Marta. Too long he waited, for the
ground on the left bank enabled Wellington to conceal the
movements, and already Fane's horsemen with six guns were
passing the ford at Santa Marta in the French rear, while
Victor Alten's cavalry removed the barricades on the bridge
and pushed through the town to attack in front. Villatte
thus suddenly assailed marched towards Babila Fuente and
gained the heights of Cabrerizos before Fane got over the
river; but ere the defiles of Aldea Lengua could be reached
he was overtaken by both columns of cavalry. The guns
opened upon his squares and killed about forty men, the
horsemen charged but were repulsed; then the French infantry
again fell fast before the round shot, and nearly a hundred
died from the intolerable heat; yet with unquelled courage the
dauntless survivors won their way in the face of thirty thousand enemies! At Babila Fuente they were joined by the
troops from Alba and the pursuit was abandoned by their
admiring and applauding adversaries; but two hundred had
fallen dead in the ranks, as many more unable to keep up
were made prisoners, and one gun being overturned in the
Aldea Lengua defile retarded six others, which were captured
with their tumbrils.

On the 27th and 28th the left of the allies approached
Zamora, the right approached Toro; the latter thus covered
the line of Rodrigo, the former neared the point of the Duero
where a bridge of communication was to be thrown. Wellington then left Hill in command and went off suddenly,
being disquieted for his combination on the Esla. The 29th
he passed the Duero at Miranda in a basket slung on a rope
stretched from rock to rock, the river foaming hundreds of
feet below—the 30th he reached Carvajales, and joined Graham who had overcome many obstacles in his passage through
the Tras os Montes. His troops, extended from Carvajales to
Tabara, were on the left in communication with the Gallicians,
but the operations were disarranged by the difficulty of crossing the Esla. That river should have been passed the 29th, at
which time the right wing should have been close to Zamora
and the passage of the Duero insured; the French would thus
have been surprised, separated, and beaten in detail. They

were indeed still ignorant that an army was on the Esla; but that river was guarded by their piquets, the stream was full and rapid, the banks steep, the fords hard to find, deep and with stony footing, and the alarm had spread from the Tormes through all the cantonments.

At daybreak on the 31st, English hussars, having infantry holding by their stirrups, entered the stream at the ford of Almendra and Graham approached the right bank with all his forces. A French piquet of thirty men was surprised in the village of Villa Perdrices by the hussars, the pontoons were immediately laid down, and the columns commenced passing, but several men even of the cavalry had been drowned at the fords. Next day the head of the allies entered Zamora, which the French evacuated after destroying the bridge. They retired upon Toro, destroyed the bridge there also and again fell back, but their rear-guard was overtaken near the village of Morales by the hussar brigade under colonel Grant. Their horsemen immediately passed a bridge and swamp under a cannonade, and then facing about in two lines gave battle; whereupon major Robarts with the tenth hussars flanked by a squadron of the eighteenth under major Hughes, the rest of that regiment being in reserve, broke both the lines at one charge, pursued for two miles and made two hundred prisoners, yet the French finally rallied on their infantry.

This secured the junction of the wings, for the Duero was fordable, and Wellington, anticipating failure at one point, had prepared to throw a boat-bridge at Espadacinta below the confluence of the Esla; he could also lay his pontoons just above Toro, because Julian Sanchez had surprised a cavalry piquet and driven the outposts from the fords of Pollos. The French columns were now concentrating, it might be for battle, and the left wing of the allies halted the 3rd, to let the Gallicians come into line and to close up their own rear. The right wing passed the Duero, the artillery and baggage by a ford the infantry at the bridge of Toro, ingeniously repaired by the lieutenant of engineers Pringle, who dropped ladders at each side of the broken arch and laid planks across just above the water level. Thus the line of the Duero was mastered, and those who understand war may say if it was an effort

worthy of the man and his army. Trace the combinations,
follow Graham's columns, some of which marched a hundred
and fifty, some two hundred and fifty miles through the wild
Tras os Montes. Through those regions held to be nearly
impracticable even for small corps, forty thousand men,
infantry, cavalry, artillery, and pontoons, had been carried
and placed as if by a supernatural power upon the Esla before
the enemy knew even that they were in movement! Was it
fortune or skill that presided? Not fortune, for the difficulties
were such that Graham crossed the Esla later than Wellington
intended, and yet so soon that the enemy could make no
advantage of the delay. Had the French even been concentrated the 31st behind the Esla, the Gallicians were then
at Benevente reinforced by Penne Villemur's cavalry which
had marched with Graham; and the Asturians were at Leon
where the Esla was fordable, and the passage of that river
could have been effected by similar combinations on a smaller
scale; for the French had not numbers simultaneously to
defend the Duero against Hill, the lower Esla against Graham,
and the upper Esla against the Spaniards. Wellington had
also, as we have seen, prepared means to bring Hill over the
Duero below the confluence of the Esla: and all these surprising exertions had been made merely to gain a fair field of
battle!

But if Napoleon's instructions had been worked out by the
king during the winter, this great movement could not have
succeeded; for the insurrection in the north would have been
crushed, or so far quelled, that sixty thousand French infantry
and ten thousand cavalry with one hundred and twenty pieces
of artillery would have been disposable. Such a force held in
an offensive position on the Tormes would have compelled
Wellington to adopt a different plan of campaign. If concentrated between the Duero and the Esla it would have
baffled him on those rivers, because operations effectual against
thirty-five thousand infantry would have been powerless
against sixty thousand. Joseph said he could not put down
the insurrection, he could not feed such large armies; a thousand obstacles arose on every side which he could not overcome; in fine he could not execute his brother's instructions.

They could have been executed notwithstanding. Activity, the taking time by the forelock, would have quelled the insurrection; and for the feeding of the troops, the boundless Tierras de Campos where the armies were now operating were covered with the ripening harvest; the only difficulty was to subsist the French who were not engaged in the northern provinces during the winter. Joseph could not find the means though Soult told him they were at hand, because difficulties overpowered him; they would not have overpowered Napoleon; but the difference between a common general and a great captain is immense, the one is victorious when the other is defeated.

Now was the field clear for the shock of battle. Wellington had ninety thousand men, with more than a hundred pieces of artillery. Twelve thousand were cavalry, and the British and Portuguese present with the colours, including serjeants and drummers, above seventy thousand sabres and bayonets: the rest of the army was Spanish. But on the wings hovered the irregulars. Sanchez' horsemen, a thousand strong, were on the right beyond the Duero; Porlier, Barcena, Salazar and Manzo on the left, between the upper Esla and the Carrion. Saornil moved upon Avila, the Empecinado menaced Leval. Finally the reserve of Andalusia had crossed the Tagus at Almaraz on the 30th, and numerous minor bands swarmed around as it advanced. The French could collect nine or ten thousand horsemen and one hundred guns, but their infantry was only thirty-five thousand strong exclusive of Leval: hence the way to victory was open, and on the 4th Wellington marched forward with a conquering violence.

Joseph could not stem or evade a torrent of war the depth and violence of which he was even now ignorant of; and a slight sketch of his previous operations will show that all his dispositions were made in the dark and only calculated to bring him into trouble. Early in May *French Correspondence, MSS.* he would have marched the army of the centre to the upper Duero, when Leval's reports checked the movement. On the 15th of that month, a spy sent to Bejar by Drouet, now count D'Erlon, brought intelligence, that a great number of country carts had been collected there and at Placentia to

follow the troops in a march upon Talavera, but after two days
were sent back to their villages,—that fifty mules had been
purchased at Bejar and sent to Ciudad Rodrigo, and the first
and fourth divisions and German cavalry had moved from the
interior towards the frontier, saying they were going, the first
to Zamora, the last to Fuente Guinaldo,—that many troops
were gathered at Ciudad Rodrigo under Wellington and Castaños,—the divisions at Coria and Placentia were expected
there, the reserves of Andalusia were in movement, the pass
of Baños, before retrenched and broken up, was repaired,—
that the English soldiers were paid their arrears, and everybody said a grand movement would commence on the 12th.
All this was accurate, but, with exception of the march to
Zamora which seemed only a blind, indicated a movement
against the Tormes and threw no light upon the real design.

On the other flank, Reille's cavalry under Boyer, having
made an exploring sweep round by Astorga, La Baneza and
Benevente, brought intelligence that a Gallician expedition
was embarking for America, another was to follow, and English divisions were also embarking in Portugal. The 23rd of
May a report from the same quarter gave notice that Salazar
and Manzo were with seven hundred horsemen on the upper
Esla, that Porlier was coming from the Asturias to join them
with two thousand five hundred men, and Giron with six
thousand Gallicians had reached Astorga,—but it was uncertain if Silveira's cavalry would come from Braganza to connect the left of the English with the Gallicians as it had done
the year before.

Thus on the 24th of May the French were still ignorant of
Graham's movement, and although it was known the 26th at
Valladolid, that Wellington had troops in the country beyond
the Esla, it was not considered a decisive movement because
the head-quarters were still at Freneda. On the 29th Reille
united his cavalry at Valderas, passed the Esla, entered Benevente and sent patroles towards Tobara and Carvajales; from
their reports and other sources he understood the whole allied
army was on the Esla; and as his detachments were closely
followed by British scouting parties he recrossed the Esla and
broke the bridge of Castro Gonzalo, leaving his light horse-

men to watch it. But the delay in the passage of the Esla, after Graham had reached Carvajales, made Reille doubt both the strength of the allies and their inclination to cross that river. He expected the main attack on the Tormes, and proposed to unite with Daricau's infantry and Digeon's dragoons, then at Toro and Zamora, to defend the Duero and lower Esla, leaving the Gallicians, whose force he despised, to pass the upper Esla at their peril.

D'Armagnac's division was at Rio Seco, and Maucune's division, which had been spread along the road to Burgos, was ordered to concentrate at Palencia on the Carrion; but Gazan on the other flank was equally deceived by the allies' movements. The 7th of May he heard from the Tormes that the preparations indicated a movement towards that river. Leval wrote from Madrid that he had abandoned Toledo because fifteen thousand English and ten thousand Spaniards were to advance by the valley of the Tagus; that rations had been ordered at Escalona for Long's cavalry, and magazines were formed at Bejar: and from a third quarter came news, that three divisions would pass the Duero to join the Gallicians and march upon Valladolid.

Gazan rightly thinking the magazines at Bejar were to supply Hill and the Spaniards in their movement to join Wellington, expected at first the whole would operate by the Esla, but on the 14th fresh reports changed this opinion; he then judged Hill would advance by the Puente Congosto upon Avila, to cut Leval off while Wellington attacked Salamanca. On the 24th his doubts vanished. Villatte told him Wellington was over the Agueda, Graham over the lower Douro; and at the same time Daricau, writing from Zamora, told him Graham's cavalry was only one march from the Esla. Conroux was instantly directed to march from Avila to Arevalo, Tilly to move with the cavalry of the army of the south from Madrigal towards the Trabancos, Daricau to send a brigade to Toro, Leval to come over the Guadarama pass and join D'Erlon at Segovia.

On the 26th, Gazan, thinking Wellington slow and crediting a report that he was sick and travelling in a carriage, relapsed into doubt. He now judged the passage of the

Agueda a feint, thought the allies' operations would be in mass towards the Esla, and was positively assured by his emissaries that Hill would move by the Puente Congosto against Segovia. The 27th he heard of the passage of the Tormes and Villatte's retreat, whereupon evacuating Arevalo he fixed his head-quarters at Rueda, and directed Conroux, who was marching upon Arevalo and so hastily that he left a moveable column behind him on the upper Tormes, to come to the Trabancos.

Gazan at first designed to take post behind that river, but there was no good position, and the 28th he rallied Conroux's, Rey's and Villatte's infantry and Tilly's cavalry behind the Zapardiel. Darleau meanwhile concentrated at Toro, Digeon at Zamora; a bridge-head was commenced at Tordesillas as the point of retreat, and guards were placed at Pollos, where the fords of the Duero were very low though as yet imprac-ticable. These movements were unmolested; Hill had no desire to drive the French over the Duero and increase the number of their troops on the Esla. The 30th, Gazan, hearing that Hill was advancing and the troops on the Esla likely to attempt the passage of that river, crossed the Duero in the night and took post at Tordesillas, intending to concentrate the whole army of the south on the right of that river; but Leval, though he had quitted Madrid on the 27th, was not yet arrived; and a large artillery convoy, the ministers and Spanish families, and the pictures from the palace of Madrid were like-wise moving by the Segovia passes.

At this time the army of Portugal and D'Armagnac's division were extended from the Esla to the Carrion, the king's guards were at Valladolid, D'Erlon was in march to the Puente Duero from Segovia and Sepulveda, yet slowly and apparently not aware of the crisis. Meanwhile the passage of the Esla had been effected, and if that river had been crossed as fore-calculated by Wellington, and a push made upon Placentia and Valladolid while Hill marched upon in Rueda, the whole French army might have been caught; what Napoleon calls '*flagrante delicto*' and destroyed. And even now it would seem Wellington could have profited more by marching than halting at Toro the 3rd; for though Leval and part of D'Erlon's army were then between the Puente

Duero and Valladolid, a large division was at Tudela de Duero to protect the convoy from Madrid; another great convoy was still on the left bank of the lower Pisuerga, and Reille and Gazan's parcs were waiting on the right bank of that river until the first convoy had passed over the Carrion. Nevertheless it was prudent to gather well to a head first, and the general combinations had been so profoundly made, that the evil day for the French was only deferred.

On the 30th Joseph designed to oppose Wellington's main body with the army of the south, while the army of the centre held the rest in check; the army of Portugal being to aid either as the case might be. And such was his infatuation, that besides pressing on Napoleon the immediate establishment of a civil Spanish administration for the provinces behind the Ebro, he demanded an order to draw Clausel's troops away from the Ebro, that he might drive the allies back to the Coa, and take the long-urged offensive position towards Portugal: Napoleon being then at Dresden and Wellington on the Duero!

On the 2nd, the king, who expected the allies at Toro the 1st, disquieted that his front was unmolested, concluded, as he had received no letter from Reille, that Wellington had turned his right and was marching towards the Carrion. On the evening of the 2nd he heard from Reille, who had retired to Rio Seco and there rallied D'Armagnac's troops; but Maucune's division was still in march from different parts to concentrate at Palencia. The halt of the 3rd was therefore to the profit of the French, for during that time they received the Madrid convoy, insured the concentration of all their troops, and recovered Conroux's moveable column which joined Leval near Olmedo. They also destroyed the bridges of Tudela and Puente Duero on the Duero, those of Simancas and Cabeçon on the Pisuerga, and passed their convoys over the Carrion, directing them under escort of Casa Palacios' Spanish division upon Burgos.

Gazan now moved upon Torrelobaton and Penaflor, D'Erlon upon Duenas, Reille upon Palencia; and the spirits of all were raised by intelligence of the emperor's victory at Lutzen, and by a report that the Toulon fleet had made a successful

descent on Sicily.   It would appear that Napoleon certainly
contemplated an attack upon that island, and lord William
Bentinck thought it would be successful; it was prevented
by Murat's discontent; instead of attacking he fell off from
Napoleon and opened a negotiation with the British.

Wellington advanced on the 4th, his bridge of communication was established at Pollos, stores of ammunition were
formed at Valladolid, some had also been taken at Zamora,
and the cavalry flankers captured large magazines of grain at
Arevalo.   Towards the Carrion the march was rapid, by parallel roads and in compact order, the Gallicians on the extreme
left, Morillo and Julian Sanchez on the extreme right, and the
enemy was expected to defend the river; but the report of
prisoners and the hasty movements of the French soon showed
that they were in full retreat for Burgos.   On the 6th their
forces were over the Carrion; Reille had even reached Palencia
the 4th, and there rallied Maucune's division and a brigade of
light cavalry employed on the communications.   The king
had now fifty-five thousand fighting men, exclusive of his
Spanish division which was escorting the convoys and baggage;
but he did not judge the Carrion a good position and retired
behind the upper Pisuerga, desiring if possible to give battle
there.   He sent Jourdan to examine the state of Burgos, and
expedited fresh letters, for he had already written from Valladolid on the 27th and 30th of May, to Foy, Sarrut and
Clausel, calling them towards the plains of Burgos.   Suchet
also he directed to march upon Zaragoza, hoping he was
already on his way; but Suchet was then engaged in Catalonia,
Clausel's troops were on the borders of Aragon, Foy and
Palombini's Italians were on the coast of Guipuscoa, and
Sarrut's division was pursuing Longa in the Montaña.

Higher than seventy or eighty thousand Joseph did not
estimate the allied forces, and he was desirous of fighting
them on the elevated plains of Burgos.   But more than one
hundred thousand men were before and around him.   For all
the partidas of the Asturias and the Montaña were drawing
together on his right, Julian Sanchez and the partidas of
Castille were closing on his left, Abispal with the reserve
and Freyre's cavalry had passed the Gredos mountains and

was making for Valladolid. Nevertheless Joseph was sanguine of success if he could rally Clausel's and Foy's divisions, and his despatches to the former were frequent and urgent. Come with the infantry of the army of Portugal! Come with the army of the north and we shall drive the allies over the Duero! Such was his cry to Clausel, and again he urged his political schemes upon his brother; but he was not a statesman to advise Napoleon, nor a general to contend with Wellington; his was not the military genius, nor were his the arrangements that could recover the initiatory movement at such a crisis and against such an adversary. While still on the Pisuerga he received Jourdan's report. Burgos was untenable, there were no provisions, the new works were unfinished, they commanded the old which were unable to hold out a day: of Clausel's and Foy's divisions nothing had been heard. It was then resolved to retire beyond the Ebro. All the French outposts in the Bureba and Montaña were immediately withdrawn, and the great dépôt of Burgos was evacuated upon Vitoria, which was thus encumbered with the artillery dépôts of Madrid, of Valladolid, and of Burgos, and with the baggage and stores of so many armies and so many fugitive families; and at this moment also arrived from France a convoy of treasure which had long waited for escort at Bayonne.

Meanwhile the tide of war flowed onwards with terrible power. The allies crossed the Carrion the 7th, Joseph retired by the high road to Burgos with Gazan's and D'Erlon's troops, Reille moved by Castro Xerez. Wellington followed hard, and conducting his operations continually on the same principle, and pushing his left wing and the Gallicians along bye-roads passed the upper Pisuerga on the 8th, 9th, and 10th. Having thus turned the line of that river entirely, and outflanked Reille, he made a short journey the 11th and halted the 12th with his left wing; for he had outmarched his supplies, and had to arrange the feeding of his troops in a country wide of his line of communication. Nevertheless he pushed his right wing under Hill along the main road to Burgos, resolved to make the French yield the castle or fight for the possession; and meanwhile Julian Sanchez acting

beyond the Arlanzan cut off small posts and straggling detachments.

Reille regained the great road to Burgos the 9th, and
took ground behind the Hormaza, his right near Hormillas,
his left on the Arlanzan, barring the way to Burgos; the
other armies were in reserve behind Estepar, and in this
situation remained for three days, and were again cheered by
intelligence of Napoleon's victory at Bautzen and the consequent armistice.   But on the 12th Wellington's columns
came up.   The light division, Grant's hussars and Ponsonby's
dragoons, immediately turned the French right, while the
rest of the troops attacked the whole range of heights from
Hormillas to Estepar.   Reille, who only desired to ascertain
their numbers, seeing the horsemen in rear of his right and
his front so strongly menaced, then made for the bridge of
Baniel on the Arlanzan.   During this movement Gardiner's
horse-artillery raked his columns and captain Milles of the
fourteenth dragoons took several prisoners and a gun which
had been disabled; and it was said the 18th hussars having
outflanked a body of French cavalry might have charged
with great effect but were withheld by colonel Grant.   The
allies now pressed forward towards the bridge of Baniel,
endeavouring to cut off the retreat; yet the French repelled
the minor attacks with the utmost firmness, bore the fire of
the artillery without shrinking, and evading the more serious
attacks by their rapid yet orderly movement, finally passed
the river with a loss of only thirty men killed and a few
taken.

Being now covered by the Urbel and Arlanzan rivers, both
flooded, they could not be easily attacked, and the stores of
Burgos were removed; yet in the night Joseph again retreated along the high road by Briviesca to Pancorbo, into
which place he threw a garrison of six hundred men.   The
castle of Burgos was mined, but from hurry, or negligence,
or want of skill, the explosion was outwards at the moment a
column of infantry was defiling beneath.   Several streets
were laid in ruins, thousands of shells and other combustibles
left in the place, were ignited and driven upwards with a
horrible crash, the hills rocked above the devoted column, and

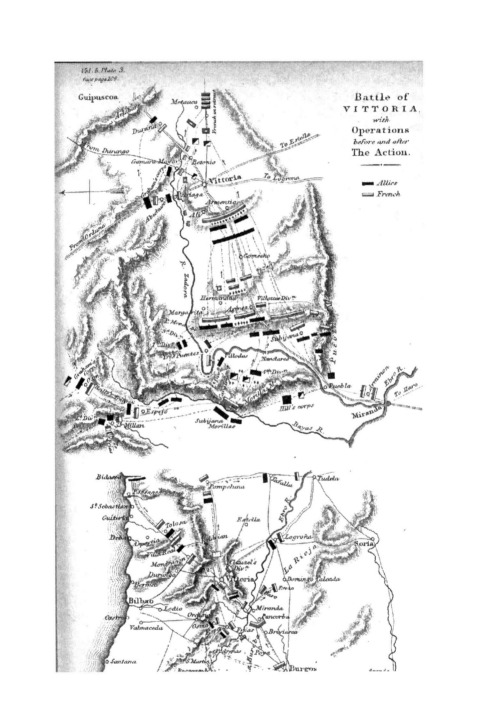

Battle of
VITTORIA,
with
Operations
before and after
The Action.

a shower of iron timber and stony fragments falling on it
in an instant destroyed more than three hundred men!
Fewer deaths might have sufficed to determine the crisis of a
great battle!

But such an art is war! So fearful is the consequence of
error, so terrible the responsibility of a general. Strongly
and wisely did Napoleon speak when he told Joseph he must
give himself up entirely to the business, labouring day and
night, thinking of nothing else. Here was a noble army
driven like sheep before prowling wolves, yet in every action
the inferior generals had been prompt and skilful, the soldiers
brave ready and daring, firm and obedient in the most trying
circumstances of battle. Infantry artillery and cavalry, all
were excellent and numerous, and the country strong and
favourable for defence; but that soul of armies, the mind of a
great commander was wanting, and the Esla, the Tormes, the
Duero, the Carrion, the Pisuerga, the Arlanzan, seemed to be
dried up, the rocks the mountains the deep ravines to be
levelled; Clausel's strong positions, Dubreton's thundering
castle had disappeared like a dream, and sixty thousand
veteran soldiers though willing to fight at every step, were
hurried with all the tumult and confusion of defeat across the
Ebro. Nor was that barrier found of more avail to mitigate
the rushing violence of their formidable enemy.

Joseph having possession of the impregnable rocks the
defile and forts of Pancorbo, now thought he could safely
await for his reinforcements, and extended his wings for the
sake of subsistence. On the 16th D'Erlon marched to Aro
on the left, leaving small posts of communication between
that place and Miranda, and sending detachments towards
Domingo Calçada to watch the road leading from Burgos to
Logroño. Gazan remained in the centre with a strong
advanced guard beyond Pancorbo; for as the king's hope
was to retake the offensive he retained the power of issuing
beyond the defiles, and his scouting parties were pushed
forward towards Briviesca in front, to Zerezo on the left, to
Poya do Sal on the right. The rest of Gazan's remaining
troops were cantoned by divisions as far as Armiñion behind
the Ebro, and Reille marched to Espejo, also behind the Ebro

and on the great road to Bilbao. Being there joined by Sarrut from Orduña he took a position, placing Maucune at Frias, Sarrut at Osma, and La Martiniere at Espejo; guarding also the Puente Lara, and sending strong scouting parties towards Medina de Pomar and Villarcayo on one side, and towards Orduña on the other.

All the encumbrances of the armies were now assembled in the basin of Vitoria, and the small garrisons of the army of the north came in; for Clausel having received the king's first letter on the 15th of June, had stopped the pursuit of Mina, and proceeded to gather up his scattered columns, intending to move by Logroño to the Ebro. He had with him Taupin's and Barbout's divisions of Reille's army; but after providing garrisons, only five thousand of his own army were disposable, and he could not bring more than fourteen thousand men to aid the king; nevertheless the latter confident in the strength of his front was still buoyant with the hope of assembling a force powerful enough to retake the offensive. His dream was short-lived.

While the echoes of the explosion at Burgos were still ringing in the hills, Wellington was in motion by his left towards the sources of the Ebro. The Gallicians moved from Aguilar de Campo high up on the Pisuerga, Graham moved from Villa Diego and in one march passed the Ebro at the bridges of Rocamunde and San Martin. The centre of the army followed on the 15th, and the same day the right wing under Hill marched through the Bureba and crossed at the Puente Arenas. This general movement was masked by the cavalry and the Spanish irregulars, who infested the French rear on the roads to Briviesca and Domingo Calçada; the allies were thus suddenly placed between the sources of the Ebro and the great mountains of Reynosa, and cut the French entirely off from the sea-coast. All the ports except Santona and Bilbao were immediately evacuated by the enemy; Santona was invested by Mendizabel, Porlier, Barcena, and Campillo; and English vessels entered Santander, where a dépôt and hospital station were established, because the royal road from thence through Reynosa to Burgos furnished a free communication with the forces. This single blow severed the long connexion of the English troops with Portugal, which was thus cast off by the army as a heavy tender is cast from its towing rope: all the British military establishments were broken up and transferred by sea to the coast of Biscay.

Now the English general could march bodily down the left bank of the Ebro, and fall upon the enemy wherever he met with them; or, still turning the king's right, place the army in Guipuscoa on the great communication with France, while the fleet keeping pace with this movement furnished fresh dépôts at Bilbao and other ports. The first plan was a delicate and uncertain operation, because narrow and dangerous defiles were to be passed; the second, scarcely to be contravened, was secure even if the first should fail; both were compatible to a certain point, inasmuch as to gain the great road leading from Burgos by Orduña to Bilbao was a good step for either; and failing in that the road leading by Valmaceda to Bilbao was still in reserve. Wherefore with an eagle's sweep Wellington brought his left wing round, and pouring his numerous columns through all the deep valleys and defiles descended towards the great road of Bilbao between Frias and Orduña. At Modina de Pomar, a central point, he left the sixth division to guard his stores and supplies, but the march of the other divisions was unmitigated; neither the winter gullies nor the ravines, nor the precipitate passes amongst the rocks, retarded even the march of the artillery; where horses could not draw men hauled, when the wheels would not roll the guns were let down or lifted up with ropes; and strongly did the rough veteran infantry work their way through those wild but beautiful regions; six days they toiled unceasingly; on the seventh, swelled by the junction of Longa's division and all the smaller bands which came trickling from the mountains, they burst like raging streams from every defile and went foaming into the basin of Vitoria.

Many reports reached the French, some absurdly exaggerated, as that Wellington had one hundred and ninety thousand men; but all indicating more or less distinctly the true line and direction of his march. As early as the 15th Jourdan warned Joseph that the allies would probably turn his right; and as Maucune's scouts told of the presence of the English troops that day on the side of Puenet

General Thouvenot, MSS.

Marshal Jourdan, MSS.

Arenas, he pressed the king to send Reille to Valmaceda and close the other armies towards the same quarter. Joseph yielded so far that Reille was ordered to concentrate his troops at Osma on the morning of the 18th, with the view of gaining Valmaceda by Ordula if it was still possible; if not he was to descend rapidly from Lodio upon Bilbao and rally Foy's division and the garrisons of Biscay. Gazan was directed to send a division of infantry and a regiment of dragoons to relieve Reille at Puente Lara and Espejo, but no decided dispositions were made.

Reille ordered Maucune to quit Frias and join him at Osma, but having some fears for his safety gave him the choice of coming by the direct road across the hills, or the circuitous route of Puente Lara. Maucune started late in the night of the 17th by the direct road, and when Reille reached Osma with La Martinicre's and Sarrut's divisions on the morning of the 18th, he found a strong English column issuing from the defiles in his front, and the head of it was already at Barbarcena on the high road to Orduña. This was Graham with the first third and fifth divisions, and a considerable body of cavalry. Reille, who had eight thousand infantry and fourteen guns, made a demonstration in the view of forcing the British to show their whole force, and a sharp skirmish and heavy cannonade ensued, wherein fifty men fell on the side of the allies, a hundred on that of the enemy. But at half-past two o'clock Maucune had not arrived, and beyond the mountains, on the left of the French, the sound of a battle arose which seemed to advance along the valley of Boveda into the rear of Osma. Reille, suspecting what had happened, instantly retired fighting towards Espejo where the mouths of the valleys opened on each other, and there suddenly from Bovedo and the hills on the left Maucune's troops rushed forth, begrimed with dust and powder, breathless and broken into confused masses.

Official Journal of General Boyer, chief of the staff, MSS.

Proverbially daring, he had marched over the Araçena ridge instead of going by the Puente Lara, and his leading brigade, after clearing the defiles, halted on the bank of a rivulet near the village of San Millan in the valley of Boveda. There, without planting piquets, they waited for their other brigade

and the baggage, when suddenly the light division, moving on
a line parallel with Graham's march, appeared on some rising
ground in their front; the surprise was equal on both sides,
but the British riflemen dashed down the hill with loud cries
and a bickering fire, the fifty-second followed in support and
the French retreated fighting as they best could.　The rest of
the English were in reserve and watching this combat, thinking all their enemies were before them, when the second French
brigade, followed by its baggage, came hastily out from a
narrow cleft in some perpendicular rocks on the right hand.
A confused action ensued, for the reserve scrambled over some
rough intervening ground to attack this new enemy, and the
French to avoid them made for a hill a little way in their
front; whereupon the fifty-second, whose rear was thus menaced,
wheeled round and running at full speed up the hill met
them on the summit.　However, the French soldiers, without
losing their presence of mind, threw off their packs and half-
flying, half-fighting, escaped along the side of the mountains
towards Miranda, while the first brigade, still retreating on the
road towards Espejo, were pursued by the riflemen.　Meanwhile
the sumpter animals run wildly about the rocks with a wonderful clamour; and though the escort huddled together and fought
desperately, all the baggage became the spoil of the victors,
and four hundred of the French fell or were taken; the rest,
thanks to their unyielding resolution and activity, escaped,
though pursued through the mountains by some Spanish irregulars.　Reille being still pressed by Graham then retreated
behind Salinas de Añara.

A knowledge of these events reached the king that night,
yet neither Reille nor the few prisoners he had made could
account for more than six Anglo-Portuguese divisions at the
defiles.　No troops had been felt on the great road from
Burgos, and Hill was judged to be marching with the others
by Valmeceda into Guipuscoa.　It was however clear that six
divisions were concentrated on the right and rear of the
French, and no time was to be lost; wherefore Gazan and
D'Erlon marched in the night to unite at Armiñon, a central
point behind the Zadora river, up the left bank of which it
was necessary to file in order to gain the basin of Vitoria.

But it could only be entered at that side through the pass of Puebla de Arganzan, which was two miles long and so narrow as scarcely to furnish room for the road. To cover this dangerous movement Reille fell back in the night to the Bayas river, where he was to dispute the ground vigorously; for by that line Wellington could enter the basin before Gazan and D'Erlon could thread the pass of Puebla; he could also send a corps from Frias to attack their rear on the Miranda side while they were engaged in the defile. And one of these things he should have endeavoured to accomplish, but the troops had made very long marches on the 18th, and it was dark before the fourth division reached Espejo. D'Erlon and Gazan therefore united at Armiñon without difficulty about ten o'clock in the morning of the 19th, and immediately commenced the passage of the defile of Puebla; the head of their column appeared on the other side at the moment when Wellington was driving Reille back upon the Zadora.

Reaching Bayas before mid-day the 19th, the allies, if they could have forced the passage at once would have cut off D'Erlon and Gazan from Vitoria; but Reille was strongly posted, his front covered by the river, his right by Subijana de Morillas which was occupied as a bridge-head, the left secured by very rugged heights opposite the village of Pobes. This position was however turned by the light division while the fourth division attacked it in front, and after a skirmish in which eighty of the French fell, Reille was forced over the Zadora; but D'Erlon had then passed the defile of Puebla and was in position, Gazan was coming rapidly into second line, the crises had passed, the combat ceased and the allies pitched their tents on the Bayas. The French armies now formed three lines behind the Zadora, and the king hearing that Clausel was at Logroño, eleven leagues distant, expedited orders to him to march upon Vitoria; Foy also, who was in march for Bilbao, was directed to halt at Durango, to rally the garrisons of Biscay and Guipuscoa and come down on Vitoria. All these orders were received too late.

CHAPTER VIII.

THE basin into which all the French troops parcs convoys and
encumbrances were thus poured, was about eight miles broad
by ten in length, Vitoria being at the further end.   The river
Zadora, narrow and with rugged banks, after passing very
near that town runs towards the Ebro with many windings
and divides the basin unequally, the largest portion being on
the right bank.   A traveller coming from Miranda by the
royal Madrid road, would enter the basin by the pass of
Puebla, through which the Zadora flows between two very
high and rough mountain ridges, the one on his right called
the heights of Puebla, that on his left the heights of Morillas.
The road leads up the left bank of the Zadora, and on emerging
from the pass, six miles to the left would be seen the village
of Subijana de Morillas, furnishing that opening into the basin
which Reille defended while the other armies passed the
defile of Puebla.   The spires of Vitoria would appear eight
miles distant; and from that town the road to Logroño goes
off on the right hand, the road to Bilbao by Murgia and
Orduña on the left hand, crossing the Zadora at a bridge near
the village of Ariaga; further on, the roads to Estella and to
Pampeluna branch off on the right, a road to Durango on the
left; and between them the royal causeway leads over the
great Arlaban ridge into the mountains of Guipuscoa by the
formidable defiles of Salinas.   But of all these roads, though
several were practicable for guns, especially that to Pampeluna,
the royal causeway alone could suffice for the retreat of such
an encumbered army.   And as the allies were behind the hills
edging the basin on the right of the Zadora, their line was
parallel to the great causeway, and by prolonging their
left they could infallibly cut off the French from that
route.

I 2

Joseph felt the danger, and first thought to march by
Salinas to Durango, with a view to cover his communications
with France and join Foy and the garrisons.   But in that
rough country neither his artillery nor his cavalry, on which
he greatly depended though the cavalry and artillery of the
allies were scarcely less powerful, could act or subsist; he
would have had to send them into France; then pressed in
front and surrounded by bands in a mountainous region he
could not long have remained in Spain.   Another project was,
if forced from the basin of Vitoria, to retire by Salvatierra to
Pampeluna and bring Suchet's army up to Zaragoza; but
Joseph feared thus to lose the great communication with
France; because the Spanish regular army and the bands
could seize Tolosa while Wellington operated against him on
the side of Navarre.   It was replied that troops detached
from Clausel's and Reille's armies might oppose them; the
king however hesitated; for though the road to Pampeluna
was practicable for wheels, it required something more for the
enormous mass of guns and carriages of all kinds now heaped
around Vitoria.   One large convoy had marched on the 19th
by the royal causeway for France, another, still larger, was to
move the 21st under escort of Maucune's division; the fighting
men in front of the enemy were thus diminished; yet the plain
was still covered with artillery parcs and equipages of all
kinds, and Joseph, infirm of purpose, continued to waste time
in vain conjectures about his adversary's movements.

On the 19th nothing was done, but the 20th some of
Reille's troops passed the Zadora to feel for the allies towards
Murguia, and being encountered by Longa's Spaniards at the
distance of six miles, after some successful skirmishing recrossed the Zadora.   The 21st at three o'clock in the morning
Maucune's division, three thousand good soldiers, marched
with the second convoy, and the king took up a new line of
battle.   Reille, then reinforced by a Franco-Spanish brigade of
infantry and Digeon's dragoons, formed the extreme right,
having to defend the Zadora where the Bilbao and Durango
roads crossed it by the bridges of Gamara Mayor and Ariaga.
The French division defended the bridge, the Franco Spanish

brigade was pushed to Durana on the royal road, Plan 3, p. 109. and supported by a French battalion and a brigade of light horsemen; Digeon's dragoons and a second brigade of light cavalry were in reserve near Zuazo de Alava and Hermandad. The king's centre, distant six or eight miles from Gamara following the course of the Zadora, was on another front, because the stream, turning suddenly to the left round the heights of Margarita descends to the defile of Puebla nearly at right angles with its previous course. Here covered by the river and on an easy range of heights, Gazan's right extended from the royal road to an isolated hill in front of the village of Margarita. His centre was astride the royal road in front of the village of Arinez; his left occupied rugged ground behind Subijana de Alava on the roots of the Puebla mountain facing the defile; and to cover this wing Maransin was posted with a brigade on the mountain. D'Erlon's army was in second line. The principal mass of the cavalry with many guns and the king's guards formed a reserve behind the centre near the village of Gomecha; and fifty pieces of artillery were massed in front, pointing to the bridges of Mendoza, Tres Puentes, Villodas, and Nanclares.

While the king was making conjectures, Wellington made dispositions for the different operations which might occur. He knew the Andalusian reserve would be at Burgos in a few days, and thinking Joseph would not fight on the Zadora, detached Giron with the Gallicians on the 19th to seize Orduña. Graham's corps was destined to follow Giron, but finally penetrated through difficult mountain ways to Murguia, thus cutting the enemy off from Bilbao and menacing his communications with France. However the rear of the army had been so much scattered that Wellington halted the 20th to rally his columns, and taking that opportunity to examine the position of the French armies observed that they seemed steadfast to fight; whereupon changing his own dispositions, he gave Graham fresh orders and hastily recalled Giron from Orduña.

The long-expected battle was now at hand, and on neither side were the numbers and courage of the troops of mean account. The allies had lost two hundred killed and wounded

in the previous operations; the sixth division, six thousand
five hundred strong, was left at Medina de Pomar; and only
sixty thousand Anglo-Portuguese sabres and bayonets, with
ninety pieces of cannon, were actually in the field.   The
Spanish auxiliaries were above twenty thousand, and the
whole army, including serjeants and artillerymen, exceeded
eighty thousand combatants.   The French muster-roll of
troops was lost with the battle and an approximation to
their strength must suffice.   The number killed and taken in
different combats was about two thousand men, and some five
thousand had marched to France with the two convoys; but
Sarrut's division, the garrison of Vitoria, and many smaller
posts had joined, and hence, by comparison with former
returns about seventy thousand men were present.   Wherefore deducting the officers, artillerymen, sappers, miners, and
non-combatants, always borne on the French muster-rolls,
the sabres and bayonets would scarcely reach sixty thousand,
but in the number and size of their guns the French had the
advantage.

All the defects in the king's position were apparent.   His
best line of retreat was on the prolongation of his right flank,
which being at Gamara Mayor was too distant to be supported
by the main body of the army; yet the safety of the latter
depended upon that point.   Many thousand carriages and
impediments of all kinds were heaped about Vitoria, blocking
all the roads and creating confusion amongst the artillery
parcs; and Maransin, placed on the Puebla mountain, was isolated and weak to hold that ground.   The centre indeed occupied an easy range of hills, its front was open with a slope to
the river, and powerful batteries seemed to bar all access by
the bridges; but many of the guns, being pushed with an
advanced post into a deep loop of the Zadora, were within
musket-shot of a wood on the right bank which was steep and
rugged, giving the allies good cover close to the river.   There
were seven bridges within the scheme of the operations,
namely, the bridge of La Puebla on the French left beyond
the defile; the bridge of Nanclares, facing Subijana de Alava
and the French end of the defile of Puebla; and three other
bridges placed around the deep loop before mentioned opened

upon the right of the French centre, that of Mendoza being highest up the stream, Vellodas lowest, Tres Puentes in the centre: lastly the bridges of Gamara Mayor and Ariaga on the upper Zadora, guarded by Reille, completed the number, and none of the seven were either broken or entrenched.

Wellington observing these things formed his army for three distinct battles.

Graham, advancing from Murguia by the Bilbao road, was to fall on Reille and attempt the passage at Gamara Mayor and Ariaga; by this movement the French would be completely turned and great part shut up between the Puebla mountain on one side and the Zadora on the other. The first and fifth Anglo-Portuguese divisions, Bradford's and Pack's independent Portuguese brigades, Longa's Spanish division, and Anson's and Bock's cavalry, in all twenty thousand men with eighteen pieces of cannon, were destined for this attack, and Giron's Gallicians came up by a forced march in support.

Hill was to attack the enemy's left. His corps, twenty thousand strong, was composed of Morillo's Spaniards, Silveira's Portuguese and the second British division, with some cavalry and guns. Collected on the southern slope of the Morillas between the Bayas and lower Zadora, and pointing to the village of Puebla, it was destined to force a passage at that point, to assail Maransin, thread the defile of La Puebla and so enter the basin of Vitoria, turning and menacing all the French left and securing the passage of the Zadora at the bridge of Nanclares.

In the centre Wellington personally directed the third, fourth, seventh, and light divisions of infantry, the great mass of the artillery, the heavy cavalry and D'Urban's Portuguese horsemen, in all thirty thousand combatants. Encamped along the Bayas from Subijana Morillas to Ulivarre, they had only to march across the ridges which formed the basin of Vitoria on that side, to come down to their different points of attack on the Zadora at the bridges of Mendoza, Tres Puentes, Villodas and Nanclares. But so rugged was the country and the communications between the different columns so difficult, that no exact concert could be expected and each general of division was in some degree master of his movements.

BATTLE OF VITORIA.

At daybreak the 21st, the weather being rainy with a thick vapour, the troops moved from their camps on the Bayas, and the centre of the army advancing by columns from the right and left of the line passed the ridges in front and slowly approached the Zadora. The left column pointed to Mendoza, the right column skirted the Morillas ridge, on the other side of which Hill was marching. That general seized the village of Puebla about ten o'clock and commenced the passage. Morillo leading with his first brigade on a bye-way assailed the mountain of La Puebla, where the ascent was so steep the soldiers seemed to climb rather than walk, and the second brigade, being to connect the first with the British troops below, only ascended half way. No opposition was made until the first brigade was near the summit, but then a sharp skirmishing commenced, Morillo was wounded, his second brigade joined, and the French feeling the importance of the height reinforced Maransin with a fresh regiment. Hill succoured Morillo with the seventy-first regiment and a battalion of light infantry, both under colonel Cadogan; yet the fight was doubtful, for though the British secured the summit and gained ground along the side of the mountain, Cadogan a brave officer and of high promise fell, and Gazan sent Villatte's division to succour his side. Strongly did these troops fight and the battle remained stationary, the allies being scarcely able to hold their ground. Hill however sent fresh troops, and with the remainder of his corps, threading the long defile of Puebla, fiercely issued forth on the other side and won the village of Subijana de Alava in front of Gazan's line: he thus connected his own right with the troops on the mountain, and maintained this forward position in despite of the enemy.

Wellington had meanwhile brought the fourth and light divisions, the heavy cavalry, the hussars and D'Urban's Portuguese horsemen, from Subijana Morillas and Montevite, down by Olabarre to the Zadora. The fourth division was placed opposite the bridge of Nanclares, the light division opposite that of Villodas; both were covered by rugged

ground and woods, and the light division was so close to the
water that their skirmishers could with ease have killed the
French gunners in the loop of the river at Villodas.   The day
was now clear, and when Hill's battle began the riflemen of
the light division spread along the bank and exchanged a
biting fire with the enemy's skirmishers.   No serious effort
was at first made, because the third and seventh divisions
having rough ground to traverse were not up; and to have
pushed the fourth division and the cavalry over the bridge of
Nanclares, would have imprudently crowded the space in front
of the Puebla defile before the other divisions were ready to
attack.   But while thus waiting, a Spanish peasant told Wellington the bridge of Tres Puentes on the left of the light
division was unguarded, and offered to guide the troops over
it.   Kempt's brigade was instantly directed towards this point,
and being concealed by some rocks from the French and well
led by the brave peasant, they passed the narrow bridge at a
running pace, mounted a steep curving rise of ground and
halted close under the crest on the enemy's side of the river;
being then actually behind the king's advanced post and
within a few hundred yards of his line of battle.   Some
French cavalry now approached and two round shots were
fired by the enemy, one of which killed the poor peasant to
whose courage and intelligence the allies were so much
indebted; but as no movement of attack was made, Kempt
called the fifteenth hussars over the river; and they came at a
gallop, crossing the narrow bridge one by one, horseman after
horseman, yet still the French remained torpid: there was an
army there, but no general.

   It was now one o'clock, Hill's assault on the village of
Subijana de Alava was developed, and a curling smoke, faintly
seen far up the Zadora on the enemy's extreme right and
followed by the dull sound of distant guns showed that
Graham was at work.   Then the king finding his flanks in
danger caused the reserve about Gomecha to file off towards
Vitoria, and gave Gazan orders to retire by successive masses.
But at that moment the third and seventh divisions being
descried in rapid movement towards the bridge of Mendoza,
the French guns opened upon them, a body of cavalry drew

near the bridge, and the numerous light troops commenced a vigorous musketry. Some British guns replied to the French cannon from the opposite bank, and the value of Kempt's forward position was instantly made manifest; for Andrew Barnard, springing forward, led the riflemen of the light division in the most daring manner between the French cavalry and the river, taking their light troops and gunners in flank, and engaging them so closely that the English artillery-men, thinking his darkly clothed troops were enemies, played upon both alike. This singular attack enabled a brigade of the third division to pass the bridge of Mendoza without opposition; the other brigade forded the river higher up, and the seventh division and Vandeleur's brigade of the light division followed; the French then abandoned the ground in front of Villodas, and the battle which had before somewhat slackened revived with extreme violence. Hill pressed the enemy harder, the fourth division passed the bridge of Nan-clares, the smoke and sound of Graham's attack became more distinct, and the banks of the Zadora presented a continuous line of fire. The French, weakened in the centre by the absence of Villatte and dispirited by the order to retreat, were perplexed, and no regular retrograde movement could be made, the allies were too close.

Now also the seventh division and Colville's brigade of the third division forded the river on the left, and were imme-diately and severely engaged with the French right in front of Margarita and Hermandad; and almost at the same time Wellington, seeing the hill in front of Arinez nearly denuded of troops by the withdrawal of Villatte's troops, carried Picton and the rest of the third division in close columns of regiments at a running pace diagonally across the front of both armies towards that central point. This attack was headed by Bar-nard's riflemen and followed by the remainder of Kempt's brigade and the hussars, but the other brigade of the light division acted in support of the seventh division. Cole advanced from the bridge of Nanclares, and the heavy cavalry, a splendid body, passing the river galloped up, squadron after squadron, into the plain ground between Cole's right and Hill's left. The French thus caught in the midst of their dis-

positions for retreat, threw out a prodigious number of skirmishers, while fifty pieces of artillery played with astonishing
activity; this fire was answered by many British guns, and
both sides were shrouded by a dense cloud of smoke and dust,
under cover of which the French retired by degrees to the
range of heights in front of Gomecha on which their reserve
had been posted.   They however continued to hold the village
of Arinez on the main road, and Picton's troops, still headed
by Barnard's riflemen, plunged into the streets amidst a heavy
fire; in an instant three guns were captured, but the post
was important, more French troops came in, and for a time
the smoke and dust and clamour, the flashing of fire-arms and
the shouts and cries of the combatants mixed with the
thundering of the guns were terrible; yet finally the British
troops issued forth victorious on the further side.   During this
conflict the seventh division, reinforced by Vandeleur's brigade,
was heavily raked by a battery at the village of Margarita,
until the fifty-second regiment, led by colonel Gibbs, with an
impetuous charge drove the French guns away and carried
the village: at the same time the eighty-seventh under colonel
Gough won the village of Hermandad.   Then all on Picton's
left advanced fighting, and on his right the fourth division
also made way, though more slowly because of the rugged
ground.

When Picton and Kempt's brigades had carried the village
of Arinez and gained the main road, the French troops near
Subijana de Alava were turned; and being hard-pressed on
their front and left flank by Hill and the troops on the Puebla
mountain, fell back for two miles in a disordered mass, striving
to regain the great line of retreat to Vitoria.   Some cavalry
launched at the moment would have totally disorganized the
French battle and secured several thousand prisoners, but it
was not tried, and the confused multitude shot ahead of
the British lines and recovered order.   The ground was
exceedingly diversified, in some places wooded in others open,
here covered with high corn, there broken by ditches vine-
yards and hamlets, and the action resolved itself into a running
fight and cannonade for six miles, the dust and smoke and
tumult of which filled all the basin, passing onwards towards

Vitoria as the allies advanced taking gun after gun in their victorious progress.

At six o'clock the French reached the last defensible height one mile in front of Vitoria. Behind them was the plain in which the city stood, and beyond the city thousands of carriages and animals and non-combatants, men women and children, were crowding together in all the madness of terror; and as the English shot went booming over head the vast crowd started and swerved with a convulsive movement while a dull and horrid sound of distress arose, but there was no hope, no stay for army or multitude; it was the wreck of a nation! Still the courage of the French soldier was unquelled. Reille, on whom everything now depended, maintained the upper Zadora, and the armies of the south and centre drawing up on their last heights, between the villages of Ali and Armentia, made their muskets flash like lightning, while more than eighty pieces of artillery, massed together, pealed with such a horrid uproar that the hills laboured and shook and streamed with fire and smoke, amidst which the dark figures of the French gunners were seen bounding with frantic energy. This terrible cannonade and musketry kept the allies in check, and scarcely could the third division, which bore the brunt of this storm, maintain its advanced position. Again the battle became stationary, and the French endeavoured to draw off their infantry in succession from the right wing; but suddenly the fourth division rushing forward carried a hill on their left and the heights were at once abandoned. Joseph, finding the royal road so completely blocked by carriages that the artillery could not pass, then indicated the road of Salvatierra as the line of retreat, and the army went off in a confused yet compact body on that side, leaving Vitoria on its left; the British infantry followed hard, and the light cavalry galloped through the town to intercept the new line of retreat which was through a marsh and the road also was choked with carriages and fugitive people, while on each side there were deep drains. Thus all became disorder and mischief, the guns were left on the edge of the marsh, the artillerymen and drivers fled with the horses, and the vanquished infantry breaking through the miserable multitude went off by Metauco towards Salvatierra:

the cavalry however still covered the retreat, and many of the generous horsemen were seen taking up children and women to carry off from the dreadful scene.

Reille, of whose battle it is time to treat, was now in great danger. Sarrut, posted by him at the village of Aranguis, had also occupied a height which covered the bridges of Ariaga and Gamara Mayor, but he had been driven from village and height a little after twelve o'clock by general Oswald, who commanded the fifth division Longa's Spaniards and Pack's Portuguese. Longa then seized Gamara Menor on the Durango road, while another detachment gained the royal causeway still further on the left, and forced the Franco-Spaniards to retire from Durana. Thus the first blow on this side deprived the king of his best line of retreat and confined him to the road of Pampeluna. However Sarrut recrossed the river in good order and a new disposition was made by Reille. One of Sarrut's brigades defended the bridge of Ariaga and the village of Abechuco beyond it; the other was in reserve supporting the first and also La Martiniere, who defended the bridge of Gamara Mayor and the village of that name beyond the river. Digeon's dragoons were behind the village of Ariaga, and Reille's own dragoons took post behind the bridge of Gamara; a brigade of light cavalry on the extreme right sustained the Franco-Spanish troops, which were now on the upper Zadora in front of Betonio; the remainder of the light cavalry under Curto was on the French left extending down the Zadora between Ariaga and Govea.

Oswald attacked Gamara with some guns and Robinson's brigade of the fifth division. Longa's Spaniards were to have led, and at an early hour when Gamara was feebly occupied, but they did not stir and the village was reinforced. Robinson's brigade formed in three columns then made the assault at a running pace, yet the fire of artillery and musketry was so heavy the troops stopped and commenced firing; then the columns got intermixed, but encouraged by their officers and the example of general Robinson, an inexperienced man but of a high and daring spirit, they renewed the charge, broke through the village and even crossed the bridge. One gun

was captured and the passage seemed to be won, when Reille
turned twelve pieces upon the village, and La Martiniere,
rallying his division under cover of this cannonade, retook
the bridge, and it was with difficulty the allied troops could
hold the village. However a second British brigade came
down and the bridge was again carried and again lost, and
thus the passage remained forbidden. Graham attacked the
village of Abechuco which covered the bridge of Ariaga, and
it was carried at once by Halket's Germans, supported by
Bradford's Portuguese and by the fire of twelve guns; yet
here as at Gamara the French maintained the bridge itself;
and at both places the troops on each side remained stationary
under a reciprocal fire of artillery and small arms.

Reille, though inferior in numbers, continued to interdict
the passage of the river until the tumult of Wellington's
battle, coming up the Zadora, reached Vitoria itself and a
part of the British horsemen rode out of that city upon
Sarrut's rear. Digeon's dragoons kept this cavalry in check
for the moment, and Reille had previously formed a reserve
of infantry under general Fririon at Betonia which now
proved his safety. For Sarrut was killed at the bridge of
Ariaga, and Menne the next in command could scarcely
draw off his troops while Digeon's dragoons held the British
cavalry at point; yet with the aid of Fririon's reserve Reille
finally secured the movement and rallied all his troops at
Betonio. He had now to make head on several sides, because
the allies were coming down from Ariaga, from Durana, and
from Vitoria; yet he fought his way to Metauco on the Salvatierra road covering the general retreat with some degree of
order. Vehemently and closely did the British pursue, and
neither the resolute demeanour of the French cavalry, which
was strengthened on the flanks by light troops and made
several vigorous charges, nor the night, which now fell, could
stop their victorious career until the flying masses of the
enemy had cleared all obstacles and passing Metauco got
beyond the reach of further injury. Then the battle ended.
The French escaped with comparatively little loss of men;
but to use Gazan's words, 'they lost all their equipages, all
their guns, all their treasure, all their stores, all their papers;

so that no man could prove even how much pay was due to him, generals and subordinate officers alike were reduced to the clothes on their backs, and most of them were barefooted.'

Never was an army more hardly used by its commander, for the soldiers were not half beaten, and yet never was a victory more complete. The trophies were innumerable. The French carried off but two pieces of artillery from the battle. Jourdan's baton of command, a stand of colours, one hundred and forty-three brass pieces, two-thirds of which had been used in the fight, all the parcs and dépôts from Madrid, Valladolid, and Burgos, carriages, ammunition, treasure, everything fell into the hands of the victors. The loss in men did not however exceed six thousand, including some hundreds of prisoners; the loss of the allies was nearly as great, the gross numbers being five thousand one hundred and seventy-six killed wounded and missing. Of these one thousand and fifty-nine were Portuguese and five hundred and fifty Spanish; hence the loss of the English was more than double that of the Portuguese and Spaniards together; and yet both fought well, and especially the Portuguese, but British troops are the soldiers of battle. The spoil was immense, and to such extent was plunder carried, principally by the followers and non-combatants, for with some exceptions the fighting troops may be said to have marched upon gold and silver without stooping to pick it up, that of five millions and a half of dollars indicated by the French accounts to be in the money-chests, a fiftieth part only came to the public. Wellington sent fifteen officers with power to stop and examine all loaded animals passing the Ebro and the Duero in hopes to recover the sums so shamefully carried off; and this disgraceful conduct was not confined to ignorant and vulgar people, some officers were seen mixed up with the mob contending for the disgraceful gain.

On the 22nd Giron and Longa entered Guipuscoa by the royal road, in pursuit of the convoy which had moved under Maucune on the morning of the battle; the heavy cavalry and D'Urban's Portuguese remained at Vitoria; but Pakenham with the sixth division came up from Medina Pomar and the remainder of the army followed Joseph towards Pampeluna, for he had continued his retreat up the Borundia and Araquil valleys all night. The weather was rainy, the roads heavy, and the French rear-guard unable to destroy the bridges set fire to the villages behind them to delay the pursuit. At five o'clock in the morning of that day Reille rallied his two divisions and all his cavalry in front of Salvatierra, halting until assured that all the French had passed, when he marched to Huerta in the valley of Araquil, thirty miles from the field of battle. Joseph reached Yrursun, a town situated behind one of the sources of the Arga from which good roads branched off to Pampeluna on one side, and to Tolosa and St. Esteban on the other. At this place he remained the 23rd, sending orders to different points on the French frontier to prepare provisions and succours for his suffering army; he also directed Reille to proceed rapidly to the Bidassoa with his infantry six hundred select cavalry, his artillerymen and their horses. Gazan and D'Erlon marched upon Pampeluna intending to cross the frontier at St. Jean Pied de Port. Joseph having reached Pampeluna the 24th, the army bivouacked on the glacis of the fortress in such a state of destitution and insubordination that the governor would not suffer them to enter the town; for his magazines were reduced by Mina's long blockade, and some writers say it was proposed to blow up the works and abandon the place: however by great exertions additional provisions were obtained from the vicinity, the garrison was augmented to three thousand, and the army marched towards France leaving a rear-guard at a strong pass about two leagues off.

Wellington having detached Graham with a corps to Guipuscoa by the pass of Adrian, left the fifth division at Salvatierra and pursued the king with the rest of the army the 23rd. On the 24th the light division and Victor Alten's cavalry came up with the French rear-guard, when two battalions of riflemen pushed their infantry through the pass, while Ross's horse artillery galloping forward, killed several men, and dismounted one of the only two pieces of cannon carried off from Vitoria. Next day the French, covered by the fortress of Pampeluna went up the valley of Roncevalles, followed by the light division which turned the town as far as Vilalba, and they were harassed by the Spanish irregular troops who swarmed on every side.

Foy and Clausel were now in very difficult positions.   The former had reached Bergara the 21st, and the garrison of Bilbao and the Italian division of St. Paul, formerly Palombini's, had reached Durango; the first convoy from Vitoria was that day at Bergara, Maucune was with the second at Montdragon.   The 22nd the garrison of Castro went off to Santona, and the fugitives from the battle spread such an alarm through the country that the forts of Arlaban, Montdragon and Salinas, commanding the passes into Guipuscoa, were abandoned, and Longa and Giron penetrated them without hindrance.   Foy had only one battalion in hand, but he rallied the fugitive garrisons, and marching upon Montdragon, made some prisoners and acquired exact intelligence of the battle.   Then he ordered the convoy to move day and night, the troops at Durango to march upon Bergara, and those from all the other posts to unite at Tolosa, to which place the artillery, baggage and sick men were now hastening from every side.   To cover their concentration, he, having been joined by Maucune, gave battle to Giron and Longa at Montdragon; but the Spaniards, thrice his numbers, had the advantage and he fell back fighting to Bergara with a loss of two hundred and fifty men and six guns.

The 23rd he marched to Villa Real de Guipuscoa, but that evening the head of Graham's column, which had crossed the Mutiol mountain by the pass of Adrian, descended upon Segura and was then as near to Tolosa as Foy was.   Yet the difficulties of passing the mountain were so great, it was late on the 24th ere Graham, who had then only collected Anson's light cavalry two Portuguese brigades of infantry and Halket's Germans, could move towards Villa Franca. The Italians and Maucune's divisions, composing the French rear, were just entering that town as the allies came in sight, and to cover it they took post at the village of Veasaya on the right bank of the Orio river.   Halket's Germans, aided by Pack's Portuguese, drove Maucune's people from the village with the loss of two hundred men, and Bradford's

Boyer's
official
Journal,
MSS.   Portuguese engaged the Italians; but the latter claimed the advantage, and the whole position was so strong that Graham had recourse to flank operations, whereupon Foy retired to Tolosa. Giron and Longa now came up by the great road, and Mendizabel, having quitted the blockade of Santona, arrived at Aspeytia on the Deba.

On the 25th Foy again offered battle in front of Tolosa, but Graham turned his left with Longa's division, and Mendizabel turned his right from Aspeytia. While they were in march, colonel Williams, having the grenadiers of the first regiment and three companies of Pack's Portuguese, dislodged him from an advantageous hill in front and purposely prolonged the fight until six o'clock in the evening, when the Spaniards having reached their destination on the flanks a general attack was made on all sides. The French, cannonaded at the causeway and strongly pushed in front while Longa drove their left from the heights, were forced beyond Tolosa on the flanks; but that town was strongly entrenched as a field-post, and they maintained it until Graham brought up his guns and bursting one of the gates opened a passage for his troops. Foy however, profiting from the darkness, made his retreat good with a loss of only four hundred men killed and wounded, and some prisoners who were taken by Mendizabel and Longa. These actions were very severe; the loss of the Spaniards was not known, but the Anglo-Portuguese had more than four hundred killed and wounded in the two days' operations, and Graham himself was hurt.

He halted the 26th and 27th to hear of Wellington's progress, and the enemy's convoys thus reached France; but Foy occupied a position between Tolosa and Ernani behind the Anezo, his force being increased by the successive arrival of the smaller garrisons to sixteen thousand bayonets, four hundred sabres, and ten pieces of artillery. The 28th he threw a garrison of two thousand six hundred good troops into St. Sebastian and passed the Urumia; the 29th he passed the Oyarsun and halted the 30th, leaving a small garrison at Passages, which however surrendered the next day to Longa.

On the 1st of July the garrison of Gueteria escaped by sea

to St. Sebastian and Foy passed the Bidassoa, his rear-guard fighting with Giron's Gallicians; but Reille's troops were now at Vera and Viriatu, they had received ammunition and artillery from Bayonne, and thus twenty-five thousand men occupied a defensive line from Vera to the bridge of Behobie, which was covered by a block-house. Graham immediately invested St. Sebastian, and Giron concentrating the fire of his own artillery and a British battery upon the block-house of Behobie, compelled the French to blow it up and destroy the bridge.

Clausel was in more imminent danger than Foy. On the evening of the 22nd he had approached the field of battle at the head of fourteen thousand men, by a way which falls into the Estella road at Aracete, not far from Salvatierra. Pakenham with the sixth division was then at Vitoria, and the French general, learning the state of affairs, retired to Logroño and halted until the evening of the 25th. This delay was like to have proved fatal. Wellington, who thought Clausel was at Tudela, thus discovered his real position, and leaving Hill to invest Pampeluna marched by Tafalla with two brigades of light cavalry and the third, fourth, seventh, and light divisions of infantry. The fifth and sixth divisions, the heavy cavalry and D'Urban's Portuguese marched at the same time from Salvatierra and Vitoria upon Logroño; and Mina also, who had now collected all his scattered battalions near Estella, and was there joined by Julian Sanchez' cavalry, followed hard on Clausel's rear. The latter moving by Calahorra reached Tudela on the evening of the 27th, and thinking this forced march of sixty miles in forty hours with scarcely a halt had outstripped all pursuers, would have made for France by Olite and Tafalla. Wellington was however in possession of those places expecting him, when an alcalde gave him notice of the danger; whereupon recrossing the Ebro he marched upon Zaragoza, and arriving the 1st of July took post on the Gallego, giving out he would there wait until Suchet or the king, if the latter retook the offensive, should come up. Wellington immediately made a flank movement to his own left as far as Caseda, and could still with an exertion have intercepted Clausel by the route of

Plan 3, p. 109.

K 2

Jaca, but he feared to drive him back upon Suchet and contented himself with letting Mina press him. That chief, acting with great ability, took three hundred prisoners and announcing that the whole allied army was at hand, so imposed on Clausel that he destroyed some of his artillery and heavy baggage, left the rest at Zaragoza and retired to Jaca.

Joseph, not being pressed, had sent Gazan again into Spain to take possession of the valley of Bastan, which was fertile and full of strong positions. But O'Donnel, count of Abispal, had now reduced the forts at Pancorbo with the Andalusian reserve, partly by capitulation partly by force, and was marching towards Pampeluna; wherefore Hill, without abandoning the siege of that place, was enabled to move two British and two Portuguese brigades into the valley of Bastan, and on the 4th, 5th, 6th, and 7th drove Gazan from all his positions, and cleared the valley with a loss of only one hundred and twenty men. The whole line of the Spanish frontier, from Roncevalles to the mouth of the Bidassoa river, was thus occupied by the victorious allies, and Pampeluna and St. Sebastian were invested. Joseph's reign was over, the crown had fallen from his head, and after years of toils and combats which had been rather admired than understood, the English general, emerging from the chaos of the Peninsula struggle stood on the summit of the Pyrenees a recognised conqueror. From those lofty pinnacles the clangour of his trumpets pealed clear and loud, and the splendour of his genius appeared as a flaming beacon to warring nations.

OBSERVATIONS.

1°. In this campaign of six weeks, Wellington marched with one hundred thousand men six hundred miles, passed six great rivers, gained one decisive battle, invested two fortresses, and drove a hundred and twenty thousand veteran troops from Spain. This immense result could not have been attained if Joseph had followed Napoleon's instructions, Wellington could not then have turned the line of the Duero. It could not have been attained if Joseph had acted with ordinary skill after the line of the Duero was passed. Time was to him most precious, yet when contrary to his expectations he had concentrated his scattered armies behind the Carrion, he made no effort to delay his enemy on that river; he judged it an unfit position, that is, unfit for a great battle; but he could have made Wellington lose a day, perhaps two or three, and behind the upper Pisuerga he might have saved a day or two more. Reille who was with the army of Portugal on the right of the king, complained that no officers of that army knew the Pisuerga sufficiently to place the troops in position; the king then had King's Correspondence, MSS cause to remember Napoleon's dictum, namely, that ' to command an army well a general must think of nothing else.' For why was the course of the Pisuerga unknown when the king's head-quarters had been for several months within a day's journey of it?

2°. The Carrion and the Pisuerga being given up, the country about the Hormaza was occupied and the three French armies were in mass between that stream and Burgos; yet Wellington's right wing only, that is to say, twenty-three thousand infantry and five brigades of cavalry, drove Reille's troops over the Arlanzan and the castle of Burgos was abandoned. This was on the 12th, the three French armies, not less than fifty thousand fighting men, had been in position since the 9th, and the king's letters prove that he desired to fight in that country, which was favourable for all arms. Nothing then could be more opportune than Wellington's advance on the 12th, because a retrograde defensive system is unsuited to French soldiers, whose impatient courage leads them always to attack; and the news of Napoleon's victory at Bautzen had just arrived to excite their ardour. Wherefore Joseph should have retaken the offensive when Wellington approached the Hormaza; and as the left and centre of the allies were at Villa Diego and Castroxerez, the greatest part at the former, that is to say one march distant, the twenty-six thousand men immediately in front would probably have been forced back over the Pisuerga, and the king have gained time for Sarrut, Foy and Clausel to join him.. Did the English general then owe his success to fortune, to his adversary's fault, rather than to his own skill? Not so. He had judged the king's military capacity, he had seen his haste, his confusion, his trouble; and knowing well the moral power of rapidity and boldness in such circumstances had acted daringly indeed but wisely, for such daring is wisdom, it is the highest part of war.

3°. Wellington's mode of turning the line of the Ebro was a fine strategic illustration. It was by no means certain, yet failure would have still left great advantages. It was certain he would gain Santander and fix a new base of operations on the coast; and he would still have had the power of continually turning the king's right by operating between him and the coast: the errors of his adversary only gave him additional advantages which he seized. But if Joseph, instead of spreading his army from Espejo on his right to the Logroño road on his left, had kept only cavalry on the latter route and on the main road in front of Pancorbo,—if he had massed his army to his right, pivoting upon Miranda or Frias, scouring all the roads towards the sources of the Ebro, the allies could never have passed the defiles and descended upon Vitoria. They would have marched then by Valmaceda upon Bilbao; but Joseph could by the road of Orduña have met them there, and with a force increased by Foy's and Sarrut's divisions and the Italians: meanwhile Clausel would have come to Vitoria and the heaped convoys have gained France in safety.

4°. When the king resolved to fight at Vitoria, he should, on the 19th and 20th, have broken some of the bridges on the Zadora and covered others with field-works to enable him to sally forth upon the attacking army; he should have entrenched the defile of Puebla and occupied the heights above in strength; his position on the lower Zadora would then have been formidable. But his great fault was the line of operation. His reasons for avoiding Guipuscoa were valid, his true line was down the Ebro; but Zarogoza should have been his base, since Aragon was fertile and more friendly than any other province of Spain. It is true he would thus have abandoned Foy; yet that general, reinforced with the reserve from Bayonne, would have had twenty thousand men and the fortress of St. Sebastian, and a strong corps must have remained to watch him. The king first reinforced by Clausel and ultimately by Suchet, would have had one hundred thousand men to oppose the allies, weakened as they would then be by the detachment watching Foy. And there were political reasons to be told hereafter, for the reader must not imagine Wellington had got thus far without trammels, which would have probably rendered this plan so efficacious as to compel the British army to abandon Spain· altogether. Then new combinations would have been made all over Europe.

5°. In the battle the French operations, with exception of Reille's fight, were a series of errors; the most extraordinary being the suffering Kempt's brigade and the hussars to pass the bridge of Tres Puentes, and establish themselves close to the line of battle, flanking the troops at the bridges of Mendoza and Villodas. This alone proves Joseph meant to retreat when Graham's attack commenced, and his position was therefore in his own view untenable. He should have occupied the Puebla mountain strongly, and have placed the infantry by corps in succession, the right refused, towards Vitoria, while the cavalry and guns watched the bridges and the mouth of the Puebla defile. He could then have succoured Reille, or marched to his own front according to circumstances, and his retreat would have been secure.

6°. The enormous fault of heaping up the baggage and convoys and parcs behind Vitoria requires no comment; but the king added a more extraordinary error, namely, remaining to the last moment undecided as to his line of retreat. Nothing but misfortunes could attend upon such bad dispositions; and that the catastrophe was not more terrible is owing entirely to an error which Wellington and Graham seem alike to have fallen into; namely, that Reille had two divisions in reserve behind the bridges on the upper Zadora. Not knowing that Maucune's division had marched with the convoy, they thought Clausel had only one division of the army of Portugal with him, whereas he had two, Taupin's and Barbout's; and Reille's reserves were composed, not of divisions but of brigades drawn from La Martiniere's and Sarrut's divisions, which were defending the bridges: his whole force, including the Franco-Spaniards who were driven back from Durana, did not exceed ten thousand infantry and

two thousand five hundred cavalry. Graham had, exclusive
of Giron's Gallicians, nearly twenty thousand of all arms, and
it is said the river might have been passed both above and
below the points of attack; it is certain also that Longa's
delay gave the French time to occupy Gamara Mayor in force,
which was not the case at first. Had the passage been won in
time very few of the French army could have escaped from
the field, but the truth is Reille fought most vigorously.

7°. As the third and seventh divisions did not come to the
point of attack in time, the battle was not fought after the
original conception; it is likely the real project was to force
the passage of the bridges, break the right centre of the enemy
from Arinez to Margarita, and then envelope the left centre
with the second, fourth, and light divisions and the cavalry,
while the third and seventh divisions pursued the others. But
notwithstanding the unavoidable delay, which gave the French
time to commence their retreat, it is not easy to understand
how Gazan's left escaped from Subijana de Alava; seeing that
when Picton broke the centre at Arinez, he was considerably
nearer to Vitoria than the French left, which was cut off from
the main road and assailed in front by Hill and Cole. The
having no cavalry in hand to launch at this time and point of
the battle has been already noticed; Wellington says, that the
country was generally unfavourable for the action of that arm;
neither side indeed used it with much effect at any period of the
battle; nevertheless there are always some suitable openings,
some happy moments to make a charge, and this seems to
have been a neglected one.

8°. Picton's sudden rush from the bridge of Tres Puentes to
the village of Arinez has been much praised, and nothing
could be more prompt and daring; but the merit of the conception belongs to the general in chief who directed it in
person. It was suggested to him by the denuded state of the
hill in front of that village, and viewed as a stroke for the
occasion it is to be admired. Yet it had its disadvantages.
For the brigade, thus crossing the front of both armies, not
only drew a flank fire from the enemy, but was exposed if the
French cavalry had been prompt and daring to a charge; it
also prevented the advance of other troops in their proper

arrangement, and thus crowded the centre for the rest of the action. However these sudden movements cannot be judged by rules, they are good or bad according to the result. This was entirely successful, and the hill thus carried was called the Englishmen's hill; not, as some recent writers have supposed, in commemoration of a victory gained by the Black Prince, but because of a disaster which there befel a part of his army. His battle was fought between Navarrette and Najera, many leagues from Vitoria and beyond the Ebro; but on this hill the two gallant knights sir Thomas and sir William Felton took post with two hundred companions, and being surrounded by Don Tello with six thousand were all killed or taken after a long and heroic resistance.

9°.- It has been observed by French writers, and the opinion has been also entertained by many English officers, that after the battle Wellington should have passed the frontier in mass, and marched upon Bayonne instead of chasing Clausel and Foy on the right and left; and if, as the same authors assert, Bayonne was then indefensible, the criticism is just; because the fugitive French army, having lost all its guns and being without musket ammunition, could not have checked its pursuers for a moment. But if Bayonne had resisted, and it was impossible for Wellington to suspect its real condition, much mischief might have accrued from such a hasty advance. Foy and Clausel coming down upon the field of Vitoria would have driven away if they did not destroy the sixth division; they would have recovered all the trophies; the king's army, returning by Jaca into Aragon, would have re-organized itself from Suchet's dépôts, and that marshal was actually coming up with his army from Valencia. Little would then have been gained by the battle. This question can however be more profitably discussed when the great events which followed the battle of Vitoria have been described.

BOOK THE TWENTY-FIRST.

CHAPTER I.

ALTHOUGH the fate of Spain was virtually decided at Vitoria, the British warfare was still fierce, dangerous, and uncertain; because on the fields of Lutzen and Bautzen Napoleon's genius had restored the general balance of success, and the negotiations which followed strongly influenced the operations in the Peninsula. Wellington's first intention was to reduce Pampeluna, and the sudden fall of the Pancorbo forts, which opened the great Madrid road was favourable for that project. But Portugal being relinquished as a place of arms, a new base was required, lest a change of fortune should force the allies to return there when the great military establishments were broken up, the opposition of the native government rancorous and the public sentiment averse to English supremacy. The western Pyrenees, in conjunction with the ocean, offered such a base; but the harbours were few, and one convenient for the army was required. Wherefore to reduce San Sebastian was of more immediate importance than to reduce Pampeluna; and it was essential to effect this in the fine season, because the coast was iron-bound and very dangerous in winter.

Pampeluna was strong. It would have taken three weeks to bring up the ordnance stores and a six weeks' attack which required twenty thousand good soldiers. An investment could be maintained with fewer and worse troops, Spaniards and Portuguese; and the magazines were likely to fail sooner under a blockade than the walls were to crumble under fire. Moreover sir John Murray had just failed at Taragona, had lost the honoured battering-train entrusted to him, and his artillery equipage was supposed to be entirely ruined; hence,

as he could make no siege, and could not act seriously without
having a place of arms, Suchet who had numerous fortresses
was free to march on Zaragoza, unite with Clausel and Paris,
and menace the right flank of the allies.   The blockade of
Pampeluna and siege of San Sebastian were therefore determined upon by Wellington; the troops returning from the pursuit of Clausel were disposed to   July.
form a covering army for both, and peasants were hired to
raise the works of investment for the first, which was entrusted
to Abispal's Andalusian reserve.   Confidently did the English
general look for the immediate fall of San Sebastian, and he
was intent to have it before the negotiations for the armistice
in Germany should terminate; but mighty pains and difficulties awaited him, and ere these can be treated of, the progress
of the war in other parts must be noticed.

CONTINUATION OF THE OPERATIONS ON THE EASTERN COAST.

It will be remembered that Del Parque in conjunction with
Elio was to act on the Xucar, while Murray sailed   Book XXII.
to attack Taragona.   Del Parque received his
orders the 24th of April, he had long known of the project
and his march was only one of twelve days, yet he did not
join Elio until the end of May.   This delay resulted partly
from the state of his army, partly from his own procrastination,
partly from Elio's conduct which created doubts of his fidelity.
It has been shown how he withdrew his cavalry when Mijares
was at Yecla, whence sprung that general's misfortune—how he
placed the regiment of Velez Malaga in Villeña, a helpless
prey for Suchet—how he left the Anglo-Sicilian army to fight
the battle of Castalla unaided.   He now persuaded Del Parque
to move towards Utiel, and send a detachment to Requeña;
thereby threatening Suchet's right, but exposing the Spanish
army to a sudden blow, and disobeying his instructions which
prescribed a march by Almanza.

This false movement Elio represented as Del Parque's own,
but the latter, when Murray remonstrated, quickly approached
Castalla by Jumilla, declaring his earnest desire to obey Wellington's orders.   The divergence had however already placed

him in danger; his left flank was so exposed while coming by
Jumilla, that Murray postponed his own embarkation to concert with Elio a combined operation, from Biar and Sax,
against Fuente de la Higuera where Suchet's troops were lying
in wait. Previous to this epoch Elio had urged Murray to
disregard Del Parque and embark at once for Taragona,
undertaking himself to secure the junction with his fellow-
commander. Now, after agreeing to co-operate with Murray,
he secretly withdrew his cavalry from Sax, sent Whittingham
in a false direction, placed Roche without support at Alcoy,
retired himself to the city of Murcia, and at the same time one
of his regiments quartered at Alicant fired upon a British
guard. Roche was attacked and lost eighty men, and Del
Parque's flank was menaced from Fuente de la Higuera; but
the British cavalry, assembling at Biar, secured his communi-
tion with Murray on the 25th, and the 27th the Anglo-
Sicilians broke up from their quarters to embark at Alicant.

Suchet was now very strong. Unmolested for forty days
after the battle of Castalla, he had improved his defensive
works, chased the bands from his rear, called up his reinforcements, re-horsed his cavalry and artillery, and foraged all the
fertile districts in front of the Xucar. On the other hand,
lord William Bentinck, alarmed by intelligence of an intended
descent upon Sicily, had recalled more British troops; and as
Whittingham's cavalry and Roche's entire division were left at
Alicant, the force actually embarked to attack Taragona,
including a fresh English regiment from Carthagena, scarcely
Appendix 1.   exceeded fourteen thousand present under arms.
Vol. VI.   Less than eight thousand were British and German, and the horsemen only seven hundred. Yet the armament was formidable, for the battering-train was complete and
powerful, the materials for gabions and fascines previously
collected at Ivica, and the naval squadron under admiral
Hallowel consisted of several line-of-battle ships, frigates,
bomb-vessels and gun-boats, besides the transports. There
was however no cordiality between generals Clinton and
Murray, nor between the latter and his quarter-master-general
Donkin, nor between Donkin and the admiral; subordinate
officers also, in both services, adopting false notions, some from

vanity some from hearsay, added to the uneasy feeling which prevailed amongst the chiefs. Neither admiral nor general seemed to have had sanguine hopes of success even at the moment of embarkation; and there was in no quarter a clear understanding of Wellington's able plan for the operations.

While Del Parque was yet in march, Suchet, if he had no secret understanding with Elio or any of his officers, must have been doubtful of the allies' intentions, although the strength of the battering-train at Alicant indicated some siege of importance. He however recalled Pannetier's brigade from the frontier of Aragon, and placed it on the road to Tortoza; and knowing Clausel was then warring down the partidas in Navarre, he judged Aragon safe and drew Severoli's Italian brigade from thence, leaving only the garrisons and a few thousand men under Paris as a reserve at Zaragoza: this was the reason the army of Aragon did not co-operate to crush Mina after his defeat by Clausel in the   Book XXII. valley of Ronçal. Decaen also sent some reinforcements, wherefore, after completing his garrisons, Suchet could furnish the drafts required by Napoleon, and yet bring twenty thousand men into the field. He was however disquieted, and notwithstanding Clausel's operations feared for his troops in Aragon, where Paris had been attacked by Goyan even in Zaragoza; moreover now, for the first time since its subjugation, an unfriendly feeling was perceptible in Valencia.

On the 31st of May Murray sailed. Suchet immediately ordered Pannetier's brigade to close towards Tortoza, but kept his own positions in front of Valencia until the fleet was seen to pass the Grāo with a fair wind. Then feeling assured the expedition aimed at Catalonia, he prepared to aid that principality; but the column of succour being drawn principally from the camp of Xativa, forty miles from Valencia, he could not quit the latter before the 7th of June. Then however he took with him nine thousand select men, leaving Harispe on the Yucar with seven thousand infantry and cavalry, exclusive of Severoli's troops which were in full march from Teruel. But Murray's armament, having very favourable weather, anchored on the evening of the 2nd in the bay of Tarragona, whence five ships of war under captain Adam, and two battalions of infantry with some guns under colonel Prevot, were detached to attack San Felippe de Balaguer. This important fort, garrisoned by a hundred men, was only sixty feet square; but the site was a steep isolated rock, standing in the very gorge of a pass and blocking the only carriage-way from Tortoza to Taragona. The mountains on either hand, although commanding the fort, were nearly inaccessible themselves, and great labour was required to form the batteries. Prevot however, being joined by a brigade of Copon's army and acting in concert with the navy, placed two six-pounders on the heights south of the pass, from whence at six or seven hundred yards distance they threw shrapnel-shells.

On the 4th two twelve-pounders and a howitzer, brought to the same point by the sailors, opened their fire; and at night the seamen with extraordinary exertions dragged up five twenty-four-pounders and their stores. The troops then constructed a battery for two howitzers on the slope of the grand ridge, northward of the pass; and a second for four heavy guns on the fort rock, at a distance of one hundred and fifty yards. Earth was carried from below; everything else, even water, was brought from the ships, though the landing-place was more than a mile-and-a-half off; and as time was valuable favourable terms were offered to the garrison, but the offer was refused. The 5th the fire was continued, yet with slight success, the howitzer-battery on the great ridge was relinquished, and at night a very violent storm retarded the construction of the breaching-batteries.

Previous to this, Prevot had warned Murray that his means were insufficient and a second Spanish brigade was sent to him, yet the breaching-batteries were still incomplete on the 6th, and out of three guns already mounted one was disabled by a shot from the fort. Meanwhile Suchet, who was making forced marches to Tortoza, had ordered the governor of that place to succour San Felippe; and that officer would undoubtedly have succeeded, if captain Peyton of the Thames frigate had not obtained two eight-inch mortars, which, being worked by Mr. James of the marine artillery, exploded a small magazine in the fort and caused an early surrender. The besiegers who had lost about fifty men and others then occupied the place.

Sir Henry
Peyton,
MSS.

order and at best only available for small mountain-guns.

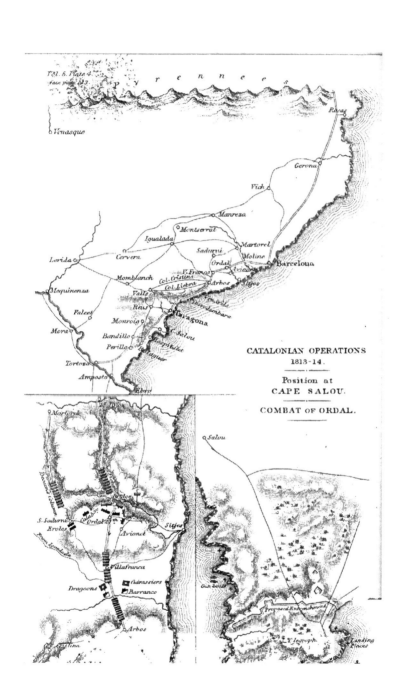

CATALONIAN OPERATIONS
1813-14.

Position at
CAPE SALOU.

COMBAT of ORDAL.

ENGLISH SIEGE OF TARAGONA.

Although the fleet cast anchor in the bay on the evening of the 2nd, the surf prevented the disembarkation of the troops until the next day. The rampart of the lower town had been destroyed by Suchet, but Fort Royal remained and though in bad condition served, together with the ruins of the San Carlos bastion, to cover the western front. The governor Bertoletti was supposed by Murray to be disaffected, yet he proved himself a loyal and energetic officer; and his garrison, sixteen hundred strong, five hundred being privateer seamen and Franco-Spaniards, served him well. The Olivo and Loretto heights were occupied the first day by Clinton's and Whittingham's infantry; the other troops remained on the low ground about the Francoli river, and the town was bombarded during the night by the navy, but the fire was sharply returned and the flotilla suffered most. Next day two batteries were commenced six hundred yards from San Carlos, and nine hundred yards from Fort Royal. They opened the 6th, and being found too distant a third was commenced six hundred yards from Fort Royal. The 8th a practicable breach was made in that outwork, yet the assault was deferred and some pieces removed to play from the Olivo; whereupon the besieged, finding the fire slacken, repaired the breach at Fort Royal and increased the defences. The subsequent proceedings cannot be understood without an accurate knowledge of the relative positions of the French and allied armies.

Taragona, though situated on one of a cluster of heights which terminate a range descending from the northward to the sea, is, with the exception of that range, surrounded by an open country called the *Campo de Taragona*, which is again environed by very rugged mountains through which the several roads descend into the plain. Westward there were only two carriage ways, one direct, by the Col de Balaguer to Taragona; the other circuitous, leading by Mora, Falcet, Momblanch and Reus. The first was blocked by the taking of San Felippe; the second, although used by Suchet for his convoys during the French siege of Taragona, was now in bad order and at best only available for small mountain-guns.

Northward there was a carriage-way leading from Lerida, which united with that from Falcet at Momblanch. Eastward there was the royal causeway, coming from Barcelona through Villa Franca, Arbos, Vendrills, and Torredembarra; this road after passing Villa Franca sends off two branches to the right, one passing through the Col de Cristina, the other through Masarbones and Col de Leibra, leading upon Braffin and Valls. It was by the latter branch M'Donald passed to Reus in 1810; he had however no guns or carriages, and his whole army laboured to make the way practicable.

Between these various roads the mountains were too rugged to permit direct cross communications; and troops coming from different sides could only unite in the Campo de Taragona now occupied by the allies. Wherefore, as Murray had fifteen thousand fighting men, and Copons, reinforced with two regiments sent by sea from Coruña, was at Reus with six thousand regulars besides Manso's division, twenty-five thousand combatants were in possession of the French point of junction.

After Lacy's departure the Catalans with the aid of captain Adam's ship had destroyed two small forts at Perillo and Ampolla, and Eroles had blockaded San Felippe de Balaguer for thirty-six days; it was then succoured by Maurice Mathieu; and the success at Perillo was more than balanced by a check which Sarsfield received on the 3rd of April from some of Pannetier's troops. The partidas had however been active in Upper Catalonia, and Copons claimed two considerable victories; one gained by himself the 17th of May at La Bispal near the Col de Cristina, where he boasted to have beaten six thousand French with half their numbers, and destroyed six hundred as they returned from succouring San Felippe. In the other, won by colonel Lander near Olot on the 7th of May, it was said twelve hundred of Lamarque's men fell. These exploits are by French writers called skirmishes; and the following description of the Catalan army, given to Murray by Cabanes, chief of Copons' staff, renders the French version the most credible.

' We do not,' said that officer, ' exceed nine or ten thousand men, extended on different points of a line running from the

neighbourhood of Reus along the high mountains to the vicinity
of Olot. The soldiers are brave but without discipline, without
subordination, without clothing, without artillery, without am-
munition, without magazines, without money and without
means of transport !'

Copons, when he came down to the Campo, frankly told
Murray, that as his troops could only fight in position he
would not join in any operation which endangered his retreat
in the high mountains. However, with exception of twelve
hundred left at Vich under Eroles, all his forces, the best
perhaps in Spain, were now at Reus and the Col de Balaguer,
ready to intercept the communications of the different French
corps, and to harass their marches if they should descend into
the Campo. Murray could only calculate upon seven or eight
hundred seamen and marines to aid him in pushing on the
works of the siege, or in a battle near the shore; and he
expected three thousand additional troops from Sicily. Sir
Edward Pellew, commanding the great Mediterranean fleet,
had promised to divert the attention of the French troops by
a descent eastward of Barcelona; and the armies of Del
Parque and Elio were to make a like diversion westward of
Tortoza. Finally, a general rising of the somatenes might
have been effected, and those mountaineers were all at Murray's disposal, to procure intelligence to give timely notice of
the enemy's approach or to impede his march by breaking
up the roads.

On the French side there was greater but more scattered
power. Suchet had marched with nine thousand men from
Valencia, and what with Pannetier's brigade and some spare
troops from Tortoza, eleven or twelve thousand men with
artillery might have come to the succour of Taragona from
that side, if the sudden fall of San Felippe de Balaguer had
not barred the only carriage way on the westward. A movement by Mora, Falcet and Momblanch, remained open, yet it
would have been tedious, and the disposable troops at Lerida
were few. To the eastward therefore the garrison looked for
the first succour. Maurice Mathieu, reinforced with a brigade
from Upper Catalonia, could bring seven thousand men with
artillery from Barcelona, Decaen could move from the Am-

purdam with an equal number, and hence twenty-five thousand
men might finally bear upon the allied army.

But Suchet, measuring from the Xucar, had more than one
hundred and sixty miles to march; Maurice Mathieu was to
collect his forces from various places and march seventy miles
after Murray had disembarked; nor could he stir at all until
Taragona was actually besieged, lest the allies should reim-
bark and attack Barcelona. Decaen had in like manner to
look to the security of the Ampurdam, and he was one hundred and thirty miles distant. Wherefore, however active the
French generals might be, the English general could calculate
upon ten days' clear operations after investment, before even
the heads of the enemy's columns could issue from the hills
bordering the Campo.

Some expectation also he might have, that Suchet would
endeavour to cripple Del Parque before he marched to the
succour of Taragona; and it was in his favour that eastward
and westward the royal causeway was in places exposed to
the fire of the naval squadron. The experience of Codrington
during the first siege of Taragona had proved indeed that an
army could not be stopped by this fire; yet it was an impe-
diment not to be left out of the calculation. Thus, the
advantage of a central position, the possession of the enemy's
point of junction, the initial movement, the good will of the
people and the aid of powerful flank diversions belonged to
Murray; superior numbers and a better army to the French;
for the allies, brave and formidable to fight in a position,
were not well constituted to move.

Taragona, if the resources for an internal defence be disregarded, was a weak place. A simple revetment three feet
and a half thick, without ditch or counterscarp, covered it on
the west; the two outworks of Fort Royal and San Carlos,
slight obstacles at best, were not armed nor even repaired
until after the investment; and the garrison, too weak for the
extent of rampart, was oppressed with labour. Here then,
time being precious to both sides, ordinary rules should have
Appendix 1.   been set aside and daring operations adopted.
Vol. VI.   Wellington had judged ten thousand men sufficient to take Taragona. Murray brought seventeen thousand,

of which fourteen thousand were effective. To do this he
had, he said, so reduced his equipments stores and means of
land transport that his army could not move from the ship-
ping; he was yet so unready for the siege, that Fort Royal
was not stormed on the 8th because the engineer was unprepared to profit from a successful assault.

This scarcity of stores was unreal; the equipments left
behind were only draft animals and commissariat field-stores;
the thing wanting was vigour in the general, and this was
made manifest in various ways.   Copons was averse to calling
out the somatenes and Murray did not press the matter.
Suchet had taken San Felippe de Balaguer by escalade;
Murray attacked in form and without sufficient means; for
if captain Peyton had not brought up the mortars, an after-
thought extraneous to the general's arrangements, the fort
could not have been reduced before succour arrived from
Tortoza: indeed the surrender was scarcely creditable to the
French commandant, for his works were uninjured and only
a small part of his powder destroyed.   It was also said, that
one of the officers employed to regulate the capitulation had
in his pocket an order from Murray to raise the siege and
embark, spiking the guns!   At Taragona, the troops on the
low ground did not approach so near by three hundred yards
as they might have done; and the outworks should have
been stormed at once, as Wellington stormed Fort Francisco
at the siege of Ciudad Rodrigo.   Francisco was a good outwork and complete; the outworks of Taragona were incomplete, ill-flanked, without palisades or casemates, and
their fall would have enabled the besiegers to form a parallel
against the body of the place as Suchet had done in the
former siege: a few hours' firing would then have brought
down the wall and a general assault might have been delivered.   The French had stormed a similar breach in that
front although defended by eight thousand Spanish troops;
and the allies, opposed by only sixteen hundred French and
Italian soldiers and seamen, were in some measure bound by
honour to follow that example, since Skerrett at the former
siege, refused to commit twelve hundred British troops in the
place, on the special ground that it was indefensible, though

so strongly garrisoned.   Murray's troops were brave, they
had been acting together for nearly a year; and, after the
fight at Castalla, had become so eager, that an Italian regiment which at Alicant was ready to go over bodily to the
enemy now volunteered to lead the assault on Fort Royal.
This confidence was not shared by their general.

Up to the 8th, Murray's proceedings were ill-judged; his
after-operations were contemptible.   As early as the 5th,
false reports had made Suchet reach Tortoza, and put two
thousand French in movement from Lerida.   Murray then
openly avowed his alarm and his regret at having left Alicant;
yet he proceeded to construct two heavy counter-batteries
near the Olivo, sent a detachment to Valls in observation of
the Lerida road, and desired Manso to watch that of Barcelona.   On the 9th his emissaries said the French were coming
from the east and from the west; and would when united
exceed twenty thousand.   Murray immediately sought an
interview with the admiral, declaring his intention to raise
the siege.   His views changed during the conference, but he
was discontented; Hallowel refused to join in a summons to
the governor and his flotilla again bombarded the place.

On the 10th the spies in Barcelona gave notice that eight
or ten thousand French with fourteen guns, would march from
that city the next day.   Copons immediately joined Manso.
But Murray, as if he now disdained his enemy, continued to
disembark stores, landed several mortars, armed the batteries
at the Olivo, and on the 11th opened their fire in concert
with that from the ships of war.   This was the first serious
attack, and the English general, professing a wish to fight the
column coming from Barcelona, sent the cavalry under lord
Frederick Bentinck to Altafulla, and in person sought a
position of battle to the eastward.   He left orders to storm
the outworks that night, yet returned before the hour
appointed, extremely disturbed by intelligence that Maurice
Mathieu was at Villa Franca with eight thousand combatants,
and Suchet closing upon the Col de Balaguer.   His infirmity
of mind was apparent to the whole army.   At eight o'clock
he repeated his order to assault the outworks, and at ten
o'clock the storming-party was in the dry bed of the Francoli

awaiting the signal when a countermand arrived; the siege
was then to be raised and the guns removed immediately
from the Olivo.   The commander of the artillery remonstrated, and the general promised to hold the batteries until
the next night; but the detachment at Valls and the cavalry
at Altafalla were called in without notice to Copons, though
he depended on their support.

All the heavy guns of the batteries on the low grounds
and the parc were removed to the beach for embarkation on
the morning of the 12th, and at twelve o'clock lord Frederick
Bentinck arrived from Altafalla with the cavalry.   It is said
he was ordered to shoot his horses, but refused to obey and
moved towards the Col de Balaguer.   The detachment from
Valls arrived next and the infantry marched to Cape Salou to
embark, but the horsemen followed lord Frederick, and were
themselves followed by fourteen pieces of artillery; each body
moved independently, and all was confused, incoherent, afflict-
ing and dishonourable to the British arms.   While the seamen
were embarking the guns, the quarter-master-general came
down to the beach with orders to abandon that business and
collect boats for the reception of troops, the enemy being supposed close at hand; and notwithstanding Murray's promise to
hold the Olivo until night-fall, fresh directions were given to
spike the guns there and burn the carriages.   Then loud
murmurs arose on every side and from both services; army
and navy were alike indignant, and so excited, that it is said
personal insult was offered to the general.   Three staff-officers
repaired in a body to Murray's quarters to offer plans and
opinions; but the admiral, who did not object to raising the
siege though opposed to the manner of doing it, would not
suffer the seamen to discontinue the embarkation of artillery;
yet he urged an attack upon the column coming from Barcelona, and opposed the order to spike the guns at the Olivo,
offering to be responsible for carrying all clear off during the
night.

Thus pressed, Murray again wavered.   Denying that he had
ordered the battering pieces to be spiked, he sent counter-
orders and directed a part of Clinton's troops to advance
towards the Gaya river. In a few hours afterwards he reverted

to his former idea, and peremptorily renewed the order for the artillery to spike the guns on the Olivo, and burn the carriages. Nor was even this unhappy action performed without confusion. The different orders received by Clinton in the course of the day had indicated the extraordinary vacillation of the commander-in-chief; and Clinton himself, forgetful of his own arrangements, with an obsolete courtesy took of his hat to salute an enemy's battery which had fired upon him; but this waving of his hat from that particular spot was also the conventional signal for the artillery to spike the guns, and they were thus spiked prematurely. The troops were however all embarked in the night of the 12th, and many of the stores and horses were shipped the 13th without the slightest interruption from the enemy; but eighteen or nineteen battering-pieces, whose carriages had been burnt, were, with all the platforms, fascines, gabions and small ammunition, in view of the fleet and army, triumphantly carried into the fortress!

Admiral Hallowel's Evidence.   Murray seemingly unaffected by this misfortune, shipped himself on the evening of the 12th and took his usual repose in bed!

While the siege was thus precipitately abandoned, the French, unable to surmount the obstacles opposed to their junction, unable even to communicate by their emissaries, were despairing of Taragona. Suchet did not reach Tortoza before the 10th, but a detachment from the garrison had on the 8th attempted to succour San Felippe, and nearly captured the naval Captain Adam, colonel Prevôt, and other officers, who were examining the country. Maurice Mathieu reached

Laffaille.   Villa Franca early on the 10th, and deceiving even his own people as to his numbers gave out that Decaen was close behind with a powerful force. To give effect to this policy, he drove Copons from Arbos the 11th, and his scouting parties entered Vendrills as if he was resolved singly to attack Murray. Pellew had however landed his marines at Rosas which arrested Decaen's march; and Maurice Mathieu alarmed at the surcease of fire about Taragona, knowing nothing of Suchet's movements and too weak to fight the allies alone, fell back in the night of the 12th to the Llobregat, his main body never having passed Villa Franca.

Suchet's operations were even less decisive. His advanced guard under Pannetier, reached Perillo the 10th. The 11th not hearing from his spies, he caused Pannetier to pass over the mountains through Valdillos to some heights which terminate abruptly on the Campo above Monroig. The 12th that officer reached the extreme verge of the hills, being then twenty-five miles from Taragona. His patroles descending into the plains met with lord Frederick Bentinck's troopers, and reported that Murray's whole army was at hand; wherefore he would not enter the Campo, but at night kindled large fires to encourage the garrison. These signals were unobserved, the country people had disappeared, no intelligence could be procured, and Suchet could not with a large force enter those wild hills where there was no water. Thus on both sides of Taragona the succouring armies were baffled at the moment chosen by Murray for flight.

Suchet now received alarming intelligence from Valencia, yet still anxious for Taragona, he pushed on the 14th along the coast-road towards Felippe de Balaguer, thinking to find Prevôt's division alone; but the head of his column was suddenly cannonaded by the Thames frigate, and he was wonderfully surprised to see the whole British fleet anchored off San Felippe and disembarking troops. Murray's operations were indeed as irregular as those of a partisan, yet without partisan vigour. Hearing in the night of the 12th, from Prevôt, of Pannetier's march to Monroig, he, to protect the cavalry and guns under lord Frederick Bentinck, sent Mackenzie's division by sea to Balaguer on the 13th, and followed with the whole army the 14th. Mackenzie drove back the French posts on both sides of the pass, the embarkation of the cavalry and artillery then commenced, and Suchet, still uncertain if Taragona had fallen, moved towards Valdillos to bring off Pannetier.

At this precise period Murray heard that Maurice Mathieu's column, which he always erroneously supposed to be under Decaen, had retired to the Llobregat, that Copons was again at Reus, and Taragona had not been reinforced. Elated by this information, he revolved various projects in his mind, at one time thinking to fall upon Suchet, at another to cut off

Pannetier; now resolving to march upon Cambrills and even to menace Taragona again by land, then to send a detachment by sea to surprise the latter; but finally he disembarked his whole force on the 15th, and being ignorant of Suchet's last movement decided to strike at Pannetier. In this view, he detached Mackenzie by a rugged valley leading from the eastward to Valdillos, and that officer reached it on the 16th; but Suchet had already carried off Pannetier's brigade, and the next day the British detachment was recalled by Murray, who had determined to re-embark.

This determination was caused by a fresh alarm from the eastward, for Maurice Mathieu, whose whole proceedings evinced both skill and vigour, hearing that the siege of Taragona was raised and the allies re-landed at the Col de Balaguer, retraced his steps and boldly entered Cambrills the 17th. On that day however Mackenzie returned and Murray's whole army was thus concentrated in the pass. Suchet was then behind Perillo, Copons at Reus, having come there at Murray's desire to attack Maurice Mathieu; and the latter would have suffered if the English general had been capable of a vigorous stroke. It was fortunate for Mackenzie that Suchet, too anxious for Valencia, disregarded his movement upon Valdillos; but taught by the disembarkation of the whole English army that the fate of Taragona whether for good or evil was decided, he had sent an emissary to Maurice Mathieu on the 16th, and then retired to Perillo and Amposta. He reached the latter place the 17th, attentive only to the movement of the fleet, and meanwhile Maurice Mathieu endeavoured to surprise the Catalans at Reus.

Copons was led into this danger by Murray, who had desired him to harass Maurice Mathieu's rear with a view to a general attack, and then changed his plan without giving any notice. However he escaped. The French moved upon Taragona, and Murray was left free to embark or to remain at the Col de Balaguer. He called a council of war, and it was concluded, as already said, to re-embark, but then Pellew's fleet appeared in the offing, and Hallowel, observing a signal announcing lord William Bentinck's arrival, answered with more promptitude than propriety, ‘*we are all delighted.*’

Murray's command having thus terminated, public discontent rendered it impossible to avoid investigation, yet the difficulty of holding a court in Spain and some disposition at home to shield him caused great delay. He was at last tried in England. Acquitted of two charges, on the third he was declared guilty of an error in judgment and sentenced to be admonished, but even that slight mortification was not inflicted. This decision does not preclude the judgment of history, nor will it sway that of posterity. The court-martial was assembled twenty months after the event, when the war being happily terminated men's minds were little disposed to treat past failures with severity. There were two distinct prosecutors, having different views; the proceedings were conducted at a distance from the scene of action, defects of memory could not be remedied by reference to localities, which opened a door for contradiction and doubt upon important points. There was no indication that the members of the court were unanimous in their verdict; they were confined to specific charges, restricted by legal rules of evidence and deprived of the testimony of all the Spanish officers, who were certainly discontented with Murray's conduct and whose absence caused the charge of abandoning Copons' army to be suppressed. Moreover the warmth of temper displayed by the principal prosecutor, admiral Hallowel, together with his signal on lord William Bentinck's arrival, whereby, to the detriment of discipline, he manifested his contempt for the general with whom he was acting, gave Murray an advantage which he improved skilfully, for he was a man sufficiently acute and prompt when not at the head of an army. He charged the admiral with deceit, factious dealings, and disregard of the service; described him as being of a passionate overweening busy disposition, troubled with excess of vanity, meddling with everything and thinking himself competent to manage both troops and ships.

Nevertheless sir John had signally failed both as an independent general and as a lieutenant acting under superior orders. On his trial indeed, blending these different capacities together with expert sophistry, he pleaded his instructions in excuse for his errors as a free commander, and his discretionary power in mitigation of his disobedience as a lieutenant; but his operations were indefensible in both capacities. Wellington's instructions, precise and founded upon the advantages offered by a command of the sea, prescribed an attack upon Taragona with a definite object, namely, to deliver Valencia.

'*You tell me,*' said he, '*that the line of the Xucar, which covers Valencia, is too strong to force; turn it then by the ocean, assail the rear of the. enemy and he will weaken his strong line to protect his communication, or, he will give you an opportunity to establish a new base of operations behind him.*'

This plan demanded promptness and energy, Murray possessed neither. The weather was so favourable, that a voyage which might have consumed nine or ten days was performed in two, the Spanish troops punctually effected their junction, the initial operations were secured, Fort Balaguer fell, the French moved from all sides to the succour of Taragona, the line of the Xucar was weakened, the diversion was complete. In the night of the 12th the bulk of the army was again afloat, a few hours would have sufficed to embark the cavalry at the Col de Balaguer, and Murray might have sailed for Valencia, while Suchet's advanced guard was still on the hills above Monroig, and himself, uncertain as to the fate of Taragona, one hundred and fifty miles from the Xucar. Murray had failed to attain the first object pointed out by Wellington's instructions, the second was within his reach; instead of grasping it he loitered about the Col de Balaguer, and gave Suchet time to reach Valencia again, in manifest dereliction of the letter and spirit of Wellington's instructions.

What was his defence? That no specific period being named for his return to Valencia he was entitled to exercise his discretion! Did he then as an independent general perform any useful or brilliant action to justify his delay? His tale was one of loss and dishonour! The improvident arrangements for the siege of San Felippe, and the unexpected fortune which saved him from the shame of abandoning his guns there also, have been noted; and when the gain of time was success he neither urged Copons to break up the roads, nor pushed the siege of Taragona with vigour.

The feeble formality of the latter operation has Philipart's been imputed to the engineer major Thac- Military kary; unjustly, because that officer had only Calendar. to furnish a plan of attack agreeable to the rules of art; it might be a cautious one, and many persons did think he treated Taragona with too much respect; but the general was to decide if the scheme of his operations required a deviation from the regular course; the untrammelled engineer could then have displayed his genius. Murray made no sign. His instructions and his ultimate views were alike withheld from his naval colleague from his second in command from his quarter-master-general; and while the last-named functionary was quite shut out from the confidence of his chief, the admiral and many others, both of the army and navy, imagined him to be the secret author of the proceedings which were hourly exciting their indignation. Murray however declared at his trial that he had rejected Donkin's advice; and indeed that officer had vainly urged him to raise the siege on the 9th and told him where four hundred draught bullocks were to be had to transport his heavy artillery. On the 12th also he opposed the spiking of the guns and urged Murray to drag them to Cape Salou, of which place he had given as early as the third day of the siege, a military plan, marking a position, strong in itself, covering several landing places, and capable of being flanked on both sides by the ships of war: it had no drawback save a scarcity of water, yet there were some springs and the fleet would have supplied the deficiency.

It is true that Donkin, unacquainted with Wellington's instructions and having at Castalla seen no reason to rely on Murray's military vigour, was averse to the enterprise against Taragona. He thought the allies should have worked Suchet out of Valencia by operating on his right flank. And so Wellington would have thought if he had only looked at their numbers and not at their quality; he had even sketched such a plan for Murray if the attack upon Taragona should be found impracticable. But he knew the Spaniards too well to like such combinations for an army, two-thirds of which were of that nation and not even under one head; an army ill-equipped and with the exception of Del Parque's troops unused to active field operations.   Wherefore, calculating their power with remarkable nicety, he preferred the sea-flank and the aid of an English fleet.   Here it may be observed, that Napoleon's plan of invasion did not embrace the coast-lines where they could be avoided.   It was an obvious disadvantage to give the British navy opportunities of acting against his communications.   He indeed seized Santona and Santander in the Bay of Biscay, because, being the only good ports on that coast the English ships were thus in a manner shut out from the north of Spain.   He likewise worked the invasion by the Catalonian and Valencian coast, because the only roads practicable for artillery run along that sea-line; but his general scheme was to hold with large masses the interior of the country, and keep the communications aloof from the danger of combined operations by sea and land.

Murray, when tried, grounded his justification on the following points.   1°. That he did not know with any certainty until the night of the 11th that Suchet was near   2°. That the fall of Taragona being the principal object and the drawing of the French from Valencia the accessory, he persisted in the siege because he expected reinforcements from Sicily and desired to profit from the accidents of war.   3° That looking only to the second object, the diversion would have been incomplete if the siege had been raised sooner or even relaxed; hence the landing of guns and stores after he despaired of success.   4°. That he dared not risk a battle to save his battering-train, because Wellington would not pardon a defeat. Now, had he adopted a vigorous plan, or persisted until the danger of losing his army was apparent and then made a quick return to Valencia, this defence would have been plausible though inconclusive.   But when every order, every movement, every expression discovered his infirmity of purpose, his pleading can only be regarded as the subtle tale of an advocate.   The admiral was right in thinking the fault was not so much in the raising of the siege as the manner of doing it, and in the feebleness of the attack.   For first, however numerous the chances of war are, fortresses expecting

succour do not surrender without being vigorously assailed;
and the arrival of reinforcements from Sicily was uncertain.
It was scarcely possible for the governor, while closely invested,
to discover that no fresh stores or guns were being landed;
still less could he judge so timeously of Murray's final intention by that fact, as to advertise Suchet that Taragona was in
no danger. Neither were the spies, if any were in the allies'
camp, more capable of drawing such conclusions, seeing that
sufficient artillery and stores for the siege were landed the
first week; and the landing of more guns could not have
deceived them, when the feeble operations of the general
and the universal discontent furnished surer guides for their
reports.

Murray designed to raise the siege as early as the 9th, and
only deferred it after seeing the admiral from his natural vacillation. It was therefore mere casuistry to say, that he first
obtained certain information of Suchet's advance on the night
of the 11th. On the 8th and 10th through various channels
he knew the French marshal was in march for Tortoza, and
his advanced guard menacing the Col de Balaguer; the
approach of Maurice Mathieu was also known; he should
therefore have been prepared to raise the siege without the loss
of guns on the 12th. Why were they lost? They could not
be saved he said without risking a battle in a bad position,
and Wellington had declared he would not pardon a defeat!
This was the after-thought of a sophister, and not warranted
by the instructions, which on that head referred only to Del
Parque and Elio: but was it necessary to fight a battle to
save the guns? all persons admitted they could have been
embarked before mid-day on the 13th. Pannetier was then at
Monroig, Suchet behind Perillo, Maurice Mathieu falling back
from Villa Franca. The French on each side were therefore
respectively thirty-six and thirty-four miles distant on the
night of the 12th, and their point of junction was Reus. Yet
how form that junction? The road from Villa Franca by the
Col de Cristina was partially broken up by Copons; the road
from Perillo to Reus was always impracticable for artillery,
and from the latter place to Taragona was six miles of very
rugged country. The allies were in possession of the point

of junction, Maurice Mathieu was retiring, not advancing. And if the French could have marched thirty-four and thirty-six miles through the mountains in one night, and been disposed to attack in the morning without artillery, they must still have ascertained the situation of Murray's army; they must have made arrangements to watch Copons, Manso, and Prevôt, who would have been on their rear and flanks; they must have formed an order of battle and decided upon the mode of attack before they advanced. . It is true that their junction at Reus would have forced Murray to suspend his embarkation to fight; but not, as he said, in a bad position with his back to the beach, where the ships' guns could not aid him and where he might expect a dangerous surf for days. The naval officers denied the surf at that season; and it was not right to destroy guns and stores when the enemy was not even in march for Reus; coolness and consideration would have enabled Murray to see there was no danger. In fact no emissaries escaped from the town, and the enemy had no spies in the camp, since no communication took place between the French columns until the 17th. On the 15th Suchet knew nothing of the fate of Taragona.

This reasoning leaves out the chance of falling with superior forces upon one of the French columns. It supposes however that accurate info.mation was possessed by the French generals; that Maurice Mathieu was as strong as he pretended to be, Suchet eager and resolute to form a junction with him. Yet in truth Suchet knew not what to do after the fall of Fort Balaguer, Maurice Mathieu had less than seven thousand men of all arms, he was not followed by Decaen, and he imagined the allies to have twenty thousand men, exclusive of the Catalans. The position at Cape Salou was only six miles distant, and Murray might with the aid of the draft bullocks discovered by Donkin have dragged all his heavy guns there, still maintaining the investment; he might have shipped his battering-train, and when the enemy approached Reus, have marched to the Col de Balaguer, where he could, as he afterwards did, embark or disembark in the presence of the enemy. The danger of a flank march, Suchet being at Reus, could not have deterred him, because he did send his cavalry and field artillery

by that very road on the 12th, and the French advanced guard
from Monroig actually skirmished with lord Frederick Bentinck.   Finally he could have embarked his main body, leaving
a small corps with some cavalry to keep the garrison in check
and bring off his guns.   Such a detachment, together with the
heavy guns, would have been afloat in a couple of   Naval evi-
hours and on board the ships in four hours; it   dence on
could have embarked on the open beach or, if   the trial.
fearful of being molested by the garrison, might have marched
to Cape Salou or to the Col de Balaguer; and if the guns had
thus been lost, the necessity would have been apparent and
the dishonour lessened.   It is clear there was no military need
to sacrifice the battering-pieces, those honoured guns which
shook the bloody ramparts of Badajos?

Wellington felt their loss keenly, Murray spoke of them
lightly. ' *They were of small value, old iron! he attached*
little importance to the sacrifice of artillery, it was his prin-
ciple; he had approved of colonel Adam losing his guns at Biar,
and he had also desired colonel Prevôt, if pressed, to abandon
his battering-train before the fort of Balaguer.' ' *Such doc-*
trine might appear strange to a British army, but it was the
rule with the continental armies and the French owed much of
their successes to the adoption of it.'

Strange indeed!   Great commanders have risked their own
lives and sacrificed their bravest men, charging desperately in
person to retrieve even a single piece of cannon in a battle.
They knew the value of moral force in war, and that of all the
various springs and levers on which it depends military honour
is the most powerful.   No! it was not to the adoption of such
a doctrine that the French owed their great successes; it was
to the care with which Napoleon fostered and cherished a
contrary feeling.   Sir John Murray's argument would have
been more pungent, more complete, if he had lost his colours
and pleaded that they were only wooden staves bearing old
pieces of silk!

CHAPTER II.

LORD WILLIAM BENTINCK arrived without troops, for having
removed the queen from Sicily he feared internal dissension;
and Napoleon had directed Murat to invade the island with
twenty thousand men, the Toulon squadron being to act in
concert; sir Edward Pellew indeed acknowledged the latter
might easily gain twenty-four hours' start of his fleet, and lord
William judged that ten thousand invaders would suffice to
conquer. Murat however opened a secret negotiation, and
thus, that monarch, Bernadotte and the emperor Francis,
united to destroy a hero connected with them by marriage
and to whom they all owed their crowns either by gift or
clemency! This early defection of Murat is cer-
Appendix 14.
tain, and his declaration that he had instructions
to invade Sicily was corroborated by a rumour, rife in the
French camps before the battle of Vitoria, that the Toulon
fleet had sailed and the descent actually made. Nevertheless
there is some obscurity about the matter. The negotiation
was never completed, Murat left Italy to command Napoleon's
cavalry, and at the battle of Dresden contributed much to the
success of that day. It is conceivable that he should mask his
plans by joining the grand army, and that his fiery spirit
should in the battle forget everything except victory; but to
disobey Napoleon as to the invasion of Sicily and dare to face
that monarch immediately after, was so unlikely as to indicate
rather a paper demonstration to alarm than a real attack.
And it would seem from the short observation of Wellington
in answer to lord William's detailed communication on this subject, namely, '*Sicily is in no danger*,' that he viewed it so, or
thought it put forward by Murat to give more value to his
defection. However it sufficed to hinder reinforcements going
to Murray.

Lord William on landing was informed that Suchet was at Tortoza with from eight to twelve thousand men, Maurice Mathieu with seven thousand at Cambrils. To drive the latter back and re-invest Taragona was easy, and the place would have fallen because the garrison had exhausted all their powder in the first siege; but this lord William did not know, and to renew the attack vigorously was impossible, because all the howitzers and platforms and fascines had been lost; and the animals and general equipment of the army were too much deteriorated by continual embarkations and disembarkations to keep the field in Catalonia. Wherefore he resolved to return to Alicant, not without hope still to fulfil Wellington's instructions by landing at Valencia between Suchet and Harispe. The re-embarkation was unmolested, the fort of Balaguer was destroyed, and one of Whittingham's regiments, destined to reinforce Copons' army, being detached to effect a landing northward of Barcelona the fleet put to sea. Misfortune still attended this unhappy armament; a violent tempest impeded the voyage, fourteen sail of transports struck upon the sands off the mouth of the Ebro, and the army was not entirely disembarked at Alicant before the 27th. Meanwhile Suchet, seeing the English fleet under sail after destroying the fort of Balaguer, marched with such extraordinary diligence as to reach Valencia from Tortoza in forty-eight hours, thus frustrating lord William's project of landing at Valencia.

During his absence Harispe had proved the weakness of the Spanish armies, and demonstrated Wellington's sagacity and prudence. That great man's warning about defeat was distinctly addressed to the Spanish generals, because the chief object of the operations was not to fight Suchet, but to keep him from aiding the French armies in the north; pitched battles were therefore to be avoided, their issue being always doubtful; the presence of a numerous and increasing force on the French front and flank was more sure to succeed. But all Spanish generals desired to fight great battles, soothing their national pride by attributing defeats to want of cavalry; it was at first doubtful if Murray could transport his horsemen to Taragona and if left behind they would have been under Elio and Del Parque, whereby those officers would have been

encouraged to fight: hence the menacing intimation pleaded
by Murray. Wellington also judged, that as Del Parque's
troops had been three years active under Ballesteros, they
must be more capable than Elio's in the dodging warfare suitable for Spaniards; Elio also best knew the country between
the Xucar and Alicant; Del Parque was therefore ordered to
turn the enemy's flank by Requeña, and Elio to menace the
front.

To trust Spanish generals was to trust the winds and clouds.
Elio persuaded Del Parque to adopt the front attack, took the
flank line himself, and detached Mijares to fall on Requeña;
and though Suchet had weakened his line the 2nd, Del Parque
was not ready until the 9th, thus giving the French a week for
the succour of Taragona and the arrival of Severoli at Liria.
Harispe had eight thousand men in front of the Xucar; the Spaniards, including Roche's and Mijares' infantry and Whittingham's cavalry, were twenty-five thousand; the Empecinado, Villa
Campa, and Frayle Nebot waited in the Cuenca and Albaracyn mountains to operate on the French rear. The disproportion
was great, yet the contest was short, and for the Spaniards
disastrous. They advanced in three columns. Elio, by the
pass of Almanza; Del Parque by Villena and Fuente de la
Higuera, menacing Moxente; Roche and the prince of Anglona
from Alcoy, by Onteniente and the pass of Albayda, menacing
San Felipe de Xativa and turning Moxente. Harispe immediately took the line of the Xucar, occupying the entrenchments in front of his bridges at Alcira and Barca del Rey near
Alberique; and during this retrograde movement Mesclop,
commanding the rear-guard, when pressed by the Spanish
horsemen wheeled round and drove them in great confusion
upon the infantry.

On the 15th Mijares took the fort of Requeña, thus turning
the line of the Xucar and securing the defiles of Cabrillas,
through which the Cuenca road leads to Valencia; Villa
Campa joined him there and so prevented Severoli from uniting
with Harispe. Del Parque advanced towards Alcira in two
columns, one moving by Cargagente, the other by Gandia.
Habert overthrew the first with one shock, took five hundred
prisoners and marched to attack the other, but it was already

routed by Gudin. After this each side held their respective
positions, while Elio joined Mijares at Requeña. Villa Campa
then descended to Chiva and Harispe's position was becoming
critical, when Suchet returned and Del Parque resumed the
position of Castalla. Thus everything turned contrary to
Wellington's designs. Elio operated by the flank Del Parque
by the front, and the latter was defeated. Murray had failed
entirely. His precipitancy at Taragona and his delays at
Balaguer were alike hurtful, and would have caused the destruction of one or both of the Spanish armies but for the
battle of Vitoria. For Suchet, detaching Musnier to recover the
fort of Requeña and drive back Villa Campa, assembled the bulk
of his forces in his old positions of San Felippe and Moxente
before the return of the Anglo-Sicilian troops; and as Elio,
unable to subsist at Utiel, had then returned towards his former
quarters the French were on the point of striking a fatal blow
against him or Del Parque, or both, when the news of Wellington's victory averted the danger.

Suchet's activity and coolness may be contrasted with the
infirmity of purpose displayed by Murray. The last always
mistimed his movements; the first doubled his force by rapidity. Suchet was isolated by Wellington's operations, his
communication with Aragon was interrupted, that province was
placed in imminent danger, and the communication between
Valencia and Catalonia was exposed to the attacks of the
Anglo-Sicilian army and the fleet;—nearly thirty thousand
Spaniards menaced him on the Xucar in front, and Villa Campa,
the Frayle and the Empecinado could bring ten thousand men
on his right flank; yet he left Harispe with only eight thousand
men to oppose the Spaniards while he relieved Taragona, and
yet returned in time to save Valencia.

When lord William Bentinck brought the Anglo-Sicilian
troops back to Alicant, his first care was to re-organize the means
of transport. This was a matter of difficulty. Murray, with a
mischievous economy, and strange disregard of Wellington's
instructions which proscribed active field operations in Valencia
if he should be forced to return from Catalonia, had discharged
six hundred mules and two hundred country carts, five-sixths
of his field equipment, before he sailed for Taragona. The

army was thus crippled while Suchet gathered strong in front, and Musnier retaking Requeña forced the Spaniards to retire from that quarter. Lord William urged Del Parque to advance from Castalla, but he had not means of carrying even one day's biscuit, and Elio, pressed by famine, went off towards Cuenca. Lord William however, commanded the Spanish armies as well as his own, and letters passed between him and Wellington relative to further operations. The latter again advised a renewed attack on Taragona or on Tortoza if the ordnance still in possession of the army would admit of such a measure; but supposing this could not be, he recommended a general advance to seize the open country of Valencia, the British keeping close to the sea and in constant communication with the fleet. Lord William's views were different. He found the Spanish soldiers robust and active, but their regimental officers bad, and their organization generally so deficient they could not stand against even a small French force. The generals pleased him at first, especially Del Parque, that is, like all Spaniards, they had fair words at command, and he thought he could undertake a grand strategic operation in conjunction with them.

To force the line of the Xucar he deemed unadvisable, inasmuch as there were only two carriage roads, both blocked by Suchet's entrenched bridges; and though the river was fordable the enemy's bank was so favourable for defence as to render the passage dangerous. The Anglo-Sicilians were unaccustomed to great tactical movements, the Spaniards altogether incapable of them. Wherefore, relinquishing a front attack he proposed to turn the enemy's right flank by Utiel and Requeña, or, by a wider march, reaching Cuenca, gain the Madrid road to Zaragoza, communicate with Wellington's army and operate down the Ebro. In either case it was necessary to cross the Albaracyn mountains, and there were no carriage roads save those of Utiel and Cuenca; but the passes near Utiel were strongly fortified by the French, and a movement on that line would necessarily lead to an attack upon Suchet which was to be avoided. The line of Cuenca was preferable though longer, and by moving in the harvest season provisions would not

Lord William Bentinck, MSS.

fail; the allies would thus force Suchet to cross the Ebro, or attack him in a position where Wellington could reinforce them if necessary, and if defeated they could retire upon his army. Wellington told him provisions would fail on the march to Cuenca even in harvest time, and without money he would get nothing; moreover by separating himself from the fleet, he would be unable to return suddenly to Sicily if that island should be really exposed to any imminent danger.

While these letters were being exchanged the Anglo-Sicilians had marched towards Villena on Del Parque's left, and Suchet was preparing to attack, when intelligence of the battle of Vitoria, reaching both parties, totally changed the aspect of affairs. The French general instantly abandoned Valencia and lord William entered that city. Clausel was at Zaragoza and Suchet knew that he desired to hold it as a point for the junction of the army of Aragon with the king, if the latter should re-enter Spain. By relinquishing all the Valencian and some of the Catalan fortresses Suchet could have concentrated thirty thousand men, and Clausel who had carried off some small garrisons had fifteen thousand; thus forty-five thousand excellent troops would have been established on Wellington's flank when he was hampered with the investment of two fortresses, and liable to be assailed in front by the re-organized and reinforced army of Vitoria. This prospect invited Suchet on one side, but on the other he wished to influence the general negotiation during the armistice in Germany by appearing strong in Spain, and therefore resolved to march on Zaragoza and keep large garrisons in Valencia: a fatal error.

He had thirty-two thousand men, six thousand were in the fortresses of Aragon, twenty-six thousand remained. From these he garrisoned Denia, Saguntum, Peniscola, Morella and Tortoza, which absorbed nearly seven thousand men, above twelve hundred being in Saguntum and five thousand in Tortoza; then destroying the bridges on the Xucar he marched himself by the coast-road on Tortoza while Musnier retired from Requeña. The Valencian people, grateful for good government, were friendly; but ere the army could reach Caspe the point of concentration, Clausel, deceived by

Mina, had fled to Jaca and the effect in Aragon was decisive. The partidas instantly united to menace Zaragoza, and Suchet sent Paris orders to abandon it and retire to Caspe, which Musnier had then reached, having picked up Severoli's brigade and the garrison of Teruel and Alcanitz in passing. On the 12th Suchet was again in military communication with Musnier, yet his army was extended along the Ebro from Caspe to Tortoza, and meanwhile, Mina having seized the Torrero, Paris evacuated Zaragoza in the night of the 9th, leaving five hundred men in the castle with much ordnance. He was encumbered with a great convoy, got entangled in the defiles of Alcubicre, was attacked, lost men guns and baggage, relinquished Caspe and fled to Huesca, where he rallied the garrison of Ayerbe; then making for Jaca he reached it on the 14th, at the moment when Clausel after another ineffectual effort to join the king had returned there. Duran then invested the castle of Zaragoza and the fort of Daroca.

This sudden and total loss of Aragon made Suchet resign that province as his field of operations, and he thereby exactly defined his own reputation. A good general not a great commander. About Tortoza, while Aragon was held by the enemy he could not feed, and the allies could land troops to seize the defiles in his rear; wherefore, fixing on the fertile country of Taragona for a base, he passed the Ebro, sent Isidore Lamarque to fetch off the garrisons of Belchite, Fuentes, Pina, and Bujarola, and moving himself by the coast road from Tortoza to Taragona, reached that place with little hurt although cannonaded by the English fleet. In this position having mined the walls for destruction he awaited lord William Bentinck. He thus established himself well for an isolated campaign, but let the great stream of war flow past unheeded. Had he continued his march on Zaragoza he would have raised the siege of the castle, saved his garrison of Daroca, perhaps have given a blow to Mina, whose orders were to retire on Tudela where Wellington designed to offer battle. But Suchet could have avoided that battle, and his appearance on Wellington's flank for a fortnight would have changed the aspect of the campaign, as shall be hereafter shown. His previous rapidity had left the Valencian allies far behind, they could not have gathered in force time enough to meddle with him; nor was their pursuit so conducted but he might have turned and defeated them.

It was not until four days after Valencia was abandoned that lord William entered it, and seven days he remained there to establish a place of arms; on the 16th moving by the coast, masking Peniscola and being in communication with the fleet, he approached the Ebro. But Suchet had that day passed that river and might have been close to Zaragoza; Del Parque's army was still near Alicant in a state of disorder; and Elio and Roche found the control of Valencia and the blockade of Saguntum and Denia more than their united forces could effect. On the 20th lord William entered Vinaros and remained there until the 26th. Suchet might then have been at Tudela or Sanguessa, and it shall be shown that Wellington could not have met him at the former place as he designed.

During this march various reports were received. *'The French had vainly endeavoured to regain France by Zaragoza.' 'Taragona was destroyed.' 'The evacuation of Spain was certain.' 'A large detachment had already quitted Catalonia.'* Lord William, who had little time to spare from Sicilian affairs then became eager; he threw a flying-bridge over the Ebro at Amposta, embarked Clinton's division with a view to seize the Col de Balaguer, and followed Suchet with the remainder of his army, which now included Whittingham's cavalry. A detachment from Tortoza menaced his bridge, but the guard was reinforced and the passage of the Ebro completed the 27th. Next day Villa Campa arrived with four thousand men and the Col de Balaguer was secured. The 29th the cavalry was threatened by infantry from Tortoza, near the Col de Alba; but the movements generally were unopposed, and the army got possession of the mountains beyond the Ebro.

Suchet was then inspecting the defences of Lerida and Mequinenza and his escort was necessarily large, because Copons was hanging on his flanks in the mountains about Manresa; yet his position about Villa Franca was exceedingly strong. Taragona and Tortoza covered the front, Barcelona the rear; the communication with Decaen was secure, and on the right flank stood Lerida, to which the small forts of Mequinenza and Monzon served as outposts. The Anglo-Sicilian troops did not exceed ten thousand effective men, and one division was on board ship from the 22nd to the 26th. Elio and Roche were at Valencia, Del Parque's army, thirteen thousand including Whittingham's infantry, was several marches in rear; it was paid from the British subsidy, but was ill-provided, and the duke was now disinclined to obedience; Villa Campa did not join until the 20th, and Copons was in the mountains above Vich. Lord William therefore remained with ten thousand men and a large train of carriages, for ten days without any position of battle behind him nearer than the hills about Saguntum; his bridge over the Ebro was thrown within ten miles of Tortoza, whence detachments could approach him unperceived through the rugged mountains, and Suchet was within two marches. That marshal however was visiting his fortresses in person, and his troops quartered for the facility of feeding were unprepared to strike a sudden blow: judging his enemy's strength in offence what it might have been rather than what it was, he awaited Decaen's force from Upper Catalonia before he offered battle.

But Decaen was himself pressed. Pellew's fleet, menacing Rosas and Palamos, had encouraged a partial insurrection of the somatenes, which was supported by the divisions of Eroles, Manso, and Villamiel. Minor combats had place on the side of Besala and Olot, Eroles invested Bañolas, and though beaten there by Lamarque the 23rd of June the insurrection spread. To quell it Decaen combined a double operation upon Vich. Designing to attack by the south himself he sent Maximilian Lamarque, with fifteen hundred French troops and some French migueletes, by the mountain paths of San Felice de Pallarols and Amias. On the 8th of July that officer gained the heights of Salud, seized the road from Olot and descended upon Roda and Manlieu, in expectation of Decaen attacking from the other side. He perceived below a heavy body in march, and heard the sound of cannon and musketry about Vich; concluding this was Decaen he advanced confidently, thinking the

Catalans were in retreat. They however fought him until dark without advantage on either side, and in the night an officer brought intelligence that Decaen's attack had been relinquished in consequence of Suchet's orders to move to the Llobregat. A previous despatch had been intercepted, all the Catalan force, six or seven thousand, was upon Lamarque's hands, and the firing heard at Vich was for Wellington's victories in Navarre. A retreat commenced, the Spaniards followed, the French got entangled in difficult ground near Salud and were forced to deliver battle; the fight lasted many hours, Lamarque's ammunition was expended, he lost four hundred men, and was upon the brink of destruction when general Beurmann came to his succour with four fresh battalions and the Catalans were finally defeated with great loss. After this Decaen marched to join Suchet, and the Catalans, moving by the mountains in separate divisions, approached lord William Bentinck.

When the allies passed the Ebro several officers conceived the siege of Tortoza would be the best operation. Nearly forty thousand men, that is to say, Villa Campa's, Copons', Del Parque's, Whittingham's, some of Elio's forces and the Anglo-Sicilians, could be united ; the defiles on the left bank of the Ebro would enable them to bar succour on that side, and force Suchet on to the circuitous route of Lerida. Wellington leaned towards this operation, but lord William resolved to push for Taragona, and even looked to assail Barcelona; a rash proceeding, for Suchet awaited his approach with an army every way superior. It does not however follow that to besiege Tortoza would have been advisable. The battering-train, larger than Murray's losses gave reason to expect, was indeed sufficient, yet the operation was a serious one; the vicinity was unhealthy, it would have been difficult to feed the Spaniards, they were inexperienced in sieges, this was sure to be a long one, not sure of success, and Suchet seeing them thus engaged might have marched to Aragon.

Lord William was at this time misled, partly by Catalan reports, partly by Wellington's successes, to believe the French were going to abandon Catalonia. He did not perceive that Suchet, judiciously posted and able to draw reinforcements

Imperial
Muster-rolls,
MSS.
from Decaen, was stronger than the allies. The
two armies of Aragon and Catalonia numbered
sixty-seven thousand men; twenty-seven thou-
sand, including Paris' division then at Jaca, were in garrison,
five thousand were sick, the remainder in the field. In Catalonia the allies were only accessories ; they were there to keep
Suchet off the flank of the allies in Navarre, and their defeat
would have been a great disaster. So entirely was this Wellington's view, that Del Parque was to make forced marches
on Tudela if Suchet should move or detach largely towards
Aragon. Lord William should therefore have secured the
defiles with his own and Villa Campa's troops, that is to say,
twenty thousand men including Whittingham's division; he
should have insulted the garrison of Tortoza, and made
gabions and fascines, which would have placed Suchet in
doubt as to his ulterior objects while he awaited the junction
of Del Parque's, Copons', and the rest of Elio's troops. Then
forty thousand men, three thousand being cavalry and attended
by a fleet, could have descended into the Campo, still leaving
a detachment to watch Tortoza. If Suchet offered battle,
the allies, superior in numbers, could have fought in a position
chosen beforehand.

It is indeed doubtful if all these corps would or could
have kept together, but lord William's actual operations were
too headlong. He had prepared platforms and fascines for
a siege in the island of Yvica, and on the 30th suddenly
invested Taragona with less than six thousand men, occupying
ground three hundred yards nearer to the walls the first day
than Murray had ever done. He thus prevented the garrison from abandoning the place, if, as was supposed, they
had that intention; yet the fortress could not be besieged
because of Suchet's vicinity and the dissemination of the
allies. The 31st the bridge at Amposta was accidentally
broken, three hundred bullocks were drowned, and the head
of Del Parque's army, being on the left of the Ebro, fell
back a day's march; however Whittingham's division and the
cavalry came up, and on the 3rd, the bridge being restored,
Del Parque also joined the investing army; Copons promised
to bring up his Catalans, Sarsfield's division did arrive, Elio

was ordered to reinforce it with three additional battalions, and Villa Campa observed Tortoza. Lord William then seeing Suchet's troops scattered, thought of surprising his posts and seizing the mountain line of the Llobregat; but Elio sent no battalions, Copons, jealous of some communications between the English general and Eroles, was slow, Villa Campa suffered the garrison of Tortoza to burn the bridge at Amposta, and Suchet suddenly returned from Barcelona and concentrated his army.

Up to this time the Spaniards, giving copious but false information to lord William and no information to Suchet, had induced faults on both sides balancing each other; a thing not uncommon in war, which demands all the faculties of the greatest minds. The Englishman thinking his enemy retreating had pressed rashly forward. The Frenchman, deeming from the other's boldness the whole of the allies were at hand, thought himself weak and awaited the arrival of Decaen, whose junction was retarded by the combined operations of the Catalans and the English fleet. In this state Suchet heard of fresh successes gained by Wellington, one of his Italian battalions was cut off at San Sadurni by Manso, and lord William took a position of battle beyond the Gaya; his left was covered by Whittingham's division which occupied Braffin, the Col de Liebra, and Col de Cristina, while his right rested on the great coast-road. These were the only carriage ways by which the enemy could approach; but they were ten miles apart, Copons held aloof, and Whittingham shrunk from defending the passes alone. Hence when Suchet, reinforced by Decaen with eight thousand sabres and bayonets, finally advanced, lord William, who had landed neither guns nor stores, decided to refuse battle. This must have been a painful decision. He had nearly thirty thousand fighting men, including a thousand marines; he had assumed the offensive, invested Taragona, where the military honour of England had suffered twice before; in fine he had provoked the action which he now declined.

Suchet had equal numbers of a better quality; the banks of the Gaya were rugged to pass in retreat, much must have been left to the general officers at different points, De)

Parque was an uneasy coadjutor, and if any part was forced
the whole line would have been irretrievably lost.   His
reluctance was however manifest, for though he expected the
enemy on the 9th, he did not send his field artillery and
baggage to the rear until the 11th, the day on which Decaen
reached Villa Franca.   Suchet dreading the fire of the fleet
endeavoured by false attacks on the coast road to draw the
allies from the defiles beyond Braffin, towards which he finally
carried his whole army; and those defiles were indeed abandoned, not as his Memoirs state because of these demonstrations, but because lord William had previously determined to
retreat.   On the 16th finding the passes unguarded he poured
through and advanced upon Valls, but the allies were then in
full retreat towards the mountains, the left wing by Reus, the
right wing by Cambrills.   Lord Frederick Bentinck with the
British and German cavalry covered the former so well that
he defeated the fourth French hussars with a loss of forty or
fifty men, and it is said that Habert or Harispe was taken but
escaped in the confusion.

Lord William now entrenched himself near the Col de
Balaguer, and Del Parque marched with his own and Sarsfield's troops to invest Tortoza, but the garrison fell on his
rear while passing the Ebro and inflicted some loss.   Nor
could lord William have long held this new position for want of
water, if lieutenant Corbyn of the Invincible, uniting intelligence with energy, had not discovered a copious spring and by
means of wooden spouts constructed with the slender pine
trees of the mountains, conducted the waters across a steep
valley and down the side of a steep mountain to the camp, a
distance of seven miles.   Suchet contrary to the wishes of his
army then returned to Taragona and destroyed the ancient
walls, which from the hardness of the Roman cement was
tedious and difficult: he afterwards resumed his positions on
the Llobregat and sent Decaen to Upper Catalonia.   The
general result of these operations had been favourable to the
allies; they had risked much but their enemy did not strike;
Suchet was kept from Navarre and had lost Taragona with
its fertile Campo.

It is strange that such a general should have suffered his

powerful army to be so paralysed. Having twenty-
seven thousand men in garrison, and thirty-two Imperial
Muster-rolls,
MSS.
thousand in hand, he was ostentatiously marching
to and fro in Catalonia while the war was being decided in
Navarre. Had he been in the latter province before the end
of July Wellington would have been overpowered. What
was to be feared? That lord William would follow or attack
one of his fortresses? Lord William could not abandon the
coast, and if the French were successful in Navarre the loss of
a fortress in Catalonia would have been a trifle, and it was
not certain that any would have fallen. Suchet pleaded
danger to France if he abandoned Catalonia. But to invade
France, guarded as she was by her great military reputation, and to do so by land, leaving behind the fortresses of
Valencia and Catalonia the latter barring all the carriage roads,
was chimerical. Success in Navarre would also have made an
invasion by sea pass as a partisan descent. Moreover France,
wanting Suchet's troops to defend her in Navarre, was ultimately invaded by Wellington and in a far more formidable
manner. This question shall be treated more largely in
another place; it is sufficient to observe here, that Clarke, the
minister of war, a man without genius or attachment to the
emperor's cause, discouraged any great combined plan of
action, and Napoleon absorbed by his own immense operations
did not interpose.

Lord William, now intent to besiege Tortoza, wished Wellington to attack Mequinenza with a detachment of his army,
but this the situation of affairs did not permit; and he soon
discovered that to assail Tortoza was beyond his own means.
Elio, when desired to assist, demanded three weeks' preparation; all the Spanish troops were in want, Roche's division,
blockading Murviedro, although so close to Valencia was on
half rations; and the siege of Tortoza was necessarily relinquished because no great or sustained operation could be
conducted in concert with such generals and such armies.
Suchet's fear was an illustration of Napoleon's maxim, that
war is an affair of discrimination. It is more essential to
know the quality than the quantity of enemies. Lord William
did not apply his mind vigorously to the campaign he was

conducting, because fresh changes injurious to the British policy in Sicily called him to that island, and his thoughts were still running upon the invasion of Italy; but as the Spaniards, deceived by the movements of escorts and convoys, reported that Suchet had marched with twelve thousand men to join Soult, he once more fixed his head-quarters at Taragona, and, following Wellington's instructions, detached Del Parque's troops by forced marches upon Tudela.

On the 5th of September the army entered Villa Franca, and the 12th, detachments of Calabrese, Swiss, German and British infantry, a squadron of cavalry and one battery, in all twelve hundred under colonel Adam, occupied the heights of Ordal. At this place, ten miles in advance of Villa Franca, being joined by three of Sarsfield's battalions and a Spanish squadron, they took position; it then appeared that very few French troops had been detached,—that Suchet had concentrated his whole force on the Llobregat—that his army was superior, because the allies, reduced by the loss of Del Parque's troops, had also left Whittingham's division at Reus and Valls to procure food. Sarsfield's division was feeding on the British supplies, and lord William again looked to a retreat, yet thinking the enemy disinclined to advance desired to preserve his forward position as long as possible.

He had only two lines to watch. One menacing his front from Molino del Rey by the main road, which Adam blocked at Ordal; the other from Martorel by San Sadurni, menacing his left; but on this route, a difficult one, he had pushed the Catalans under Eroles and Manso, reinforcing them with some Calabrese: there was indeed a third line by Avionet on his right but it was little better than a goat-path. He had designed to bring his main body up to Ordal the evening of the 12th, yet from some slight reason delayed until next day. He had however viewed the country in advance of the defile without discovering an enemy; his confidential emissaries assured him the French were not going to advance, and he returned satisfied that Adam's detachment was safe, and so expressed himself to that officer. A report of a contrary tendency was made by colonel Reeves of the twenty-seventh, on the authority of a Spanish woman who had before proved her accuracy and ability as a spy; she was now however disbelieved, and this incredulity was unfortunate.   For Suchet thus braved, and his communication with Lerida threatened by Manso on the side of Martorel, was then in march to attack Ordal with the army of Aragon, while Decaen and Maurice Mathieu, moving with the army of Catalonia from Martorel by San Sadurni, were turning the left of the allies.

COMBAT OF ORDAL.

[See Plan 4, page 143.]

Adam's position though rugged rose gradually from a magnificent bridge, by which the main road was carried over a deep impracticable ravine.   The second battalion of the twenty-seventh was posted on the right,—the Germans, De Roll's Swiss, and the artillery, defended an old Spanish fort commanding the main road,—the Spaniards were in the centre, the Calabrese on the left,—the cavalry were in reserve.   A bright moonlight facilitated the movements of the French, and a little before midnight, their leading column under Mesclop passed the bridge without let or hindrance, mounted the heights with a rapid pace and driving back the piquets gave the first alarm: the allied troops lying on their arms in order of battle were however ready, and the fight commenced.   The first effort was against the twenty-seventh, then the Germans and the Spanish battalions were vigorously assailed in succession as the French columns got free of the bridge, but the Calabrese were too far on the left to take a share in the action. The combat was fierce and obstinate.   Harispe who commanded the French constantly outflanked the right of the allies, and at the same time pressed their centre, where the Spaniards fought gallantly.   Adam was wounded early, the command devolved upon Reeves, and that officer seeing his flank turned and his men falling fast; in short, finding himself engaged with a whole army on a position of which Adam had lost the key by neglecting the bridge resolved to retreat.

He first ordered the guns to fall back, and to cover the movement charged a column of the enemy which was pressing forward on the high road, but he was severely wounded in this attack and there was no recognised commander on the spot to

succeed him. Then the affair became confused. For though
the order to retreat was given the Spaniards were fighting
desperately, the twenty-seventh thought it shame to abandon
them, the Germans and De Roll's regiment still held the old
fort, and the guns came back. Colonel Carey now brought the
Calabrese into line from the left, and menaced the right flank
of the French, but he was too late,—the Spaniards in the
centre were broken, the right was completely turned, the old
fort was lost, the enemy's skirmishers got into the allies' rear,
and at three o'clock the whole dispersed, the most part in
flight: the Spanish cavalry were then overthrown on the main
road by the French hussars and four guns were taken in the
tumult.

Captain Waldron with the twenty-seventh, reduced to
eighty men, and captain Müller with about the same number
of Germans and Swiss, broke through several small parties of
the enemy and effected their retreat in good order by the hills
on each side of the road. Colonel Carey endeavoured to gain
the road of Sadurni on the left, but meeting with Decaen's
people retraced his steps, and crossing the field of battle in
rear of Suchet's columns made for Villa Nueva de Sitjes
and embarked without loss save of a few stragglers, who fell
into the hands of a flanking battalion of French infantry
which had moved through the mountains by Begas and
Avionet. The overthrow was complete and the prisoners
were at first very numerous; yet the darkness enabled many
to escape and two thousand of them reached Manso and
Eroles.

Suchet pursuing his march came up with lord William about
eight o'clock. The latter retired skirmishing in excellent order
beyond Villa Franca; some of the French horsemen assailed
his rear-guard while others edged to their right to secure the
communication with Decaen, who was looked for by both
parties with great anxiety; but he had been delayed by the
resistance of Manso and Eroles in the rugged country between
Martorel and San Sadurni. Suchet's cavalry and artillery
continued however to infest the rear of the retreating army
until it reached a deep baranco, near the Venta de Monjos,
where the passage being dangerous and the French horsemen

importunate, that brave and honest soldier, lord Frederick
Bentinck, charged their right with the twentieth dragoons, and
fighting hand to hand with the enemy's general Meyers
wounded him and overthrew his light cavalry; they rallied
upon their heavy horsemen and advanced again, endeavouring
to turn the flank, but were stopped by the fire of two guns
which Clinton opened upon them. The cuirassiers had meantime pressed the Brunswick hussars on the allies' right and
menaced the infantry, yet were checked by the fire of the
tenth regiment. This cavalry action was vigorous, the
twentieth and the Germans fought desperately and though
few in numbers lost more than ninety men. Nevertheless
the baranco was safely passed and about three o'clock the
army having reached Arbos the pursuit ceased: the Catalans
retreated towards Igualada and the Anglo-Sicilians retired
to Taragona. It was now thought Suchet would make a
movement to carry off the garrisons of Lerida and Tortoza:
but this did not happen, and lord William went to Sicily,
leaving the command of the army to Clinton.

OBSERVATIONS.

1°. Lord William Bentinck committed errors, yet he has
been censured without discrimination. '*He advanced rashly.*'
'*He was undecided.*' '*He exposed his advanced guard without support.*' Such were the opinions expressed at the time.
Their justness may be disputed. His first object was to retain
all the French force in Catalonia; his second, to profit from
Suchet's weakness if he detached largely. He could do neither
by remaining inactive on the barren hills behind Hospitalet,
because the Spaniards would have dispersed for want of provisions and the siege of Tortoza was impracticable. It was
therefore bold and skilful to menace the enemy, if a retreat
was secure without danger or dishonour. The position at
Villa Franca fulfilled this condition. It was strong in itself
and offensive; Pellew's fleet was in movement to create diversions in Upper Catalonia, and all the emissaries and Spanish
correspondents concurred in declaring, though falsely, that the
French general had detached twelve thousand men. It is

indeed one test of a sagacious general to detect false intelligence; yet the greatest are at times deceived, and all must act
upon what appears true. Lord William's advance was founded
on erroneous data, but his position in front of Villa Franca
was well chosen; it enabled him to feed Whittingham's division about Reus and Valls; and there were short and easy
communications from Villa Franca to the sea-coast. He could
only be seriously assailed on two lines. In front by the main
road, which, though broad, was from Molino del Rey to the
heights of Ordal one continued defile. On the left by San
Sadurni, a road still more rugged and difficult than the other;
and the Catalans were launched on this side, because, without
quitting the mountains, they protected the left and menaced
the enemy's communication with Lerida. Half a march to
the rear would bring the army to Vendrills, beyond which the
enemy could not follow without getting under the fire of the
ships; neither could he forestall this movement by a march
through the Liebra and Cristina defiles, because the Catalans
falling back on Whittingham's division could hold him in
check.

2°. Ordal and San Sadurni were the keys of the position.
The last was well secured, the first not so, and there was the
real error. It was none however to push an advanced guard
of three thousand five hundred men, with cavalry and artillery,
to a distance of ten miles for a few hours. He had a right to
expect the commander would maintain his post until supported, or retreat without disaster; an officer of capacity would
have done so; but whoever relies upon the capacity of sir Frederick Adam in peace or war will surely be disappointed. In 1810
lord Wellington detached general Craufurd with two or three
thousand men to a much greater distance, not for one night
but for many weeks. And that excellent officer, though close
to Massena's immense army the very cavalry of which doubled
his whole numbers; though he had the long line of the
Agueda a fordable river to guard; though he was in an open
country and continually skirmishing, never lost so much as a
patrole, and always remained master of his movements, for his
combat on the Coa was a studied and wilful error. It was no
fault therefore to push Adam's detachment to Ordal, but it

was a fault that lord William, having determined to follow with his whole force, should have delayed for one night, or delaying, that he did not send some supporting troops forward. It was a fault not to do so because there was good reason to do it and to delay was to tempt fortune. Had lord William been at hand with his main body when the attack on Ordal commenced, the head of Suchet's force, which was kept at bay for three hours by a detachment so ill commanded, would have been driven into the ravine behind, and the victories allies would still have had time to march against Decaen by the road along which colonel Cary endeavoured to join Manso. In fine, Suchet's dispositions were vicious in principle and ought not to have succeeded. He operated on two distinct lines having no cross communications, and before an enemy in possession of a central position with good communications.

3°. It was another fault that lord William disregarded the Spanish woman's report to colonel Reeves; his observations made in front of the bridge of Ordal on the evening of the 12th accorded indeed with the reports of his own emissaries, but the safe side should always be the rule. He also, although on the spot, overlooked the unmilitary dispositions of Adam on the heights of Ordal. The summit could not be defended against superior numbers with a small corps; that officer had nevertheless extended the Calabrese so far on the left they could take no share in the action, and yet could not retreat without great difficulty. A commander who understood his business, would have blocked up the bridge in front of the heights and defended it by a strong detachment, supporting that detachment by others placed in succession on the heights behind; keeping his main body always in hand, ready to fall on the head of the enemy's column of attack or to rally the advanced troops and retreat in order. There were trees and stones to block the bridge, or its own parapet would have supplied materials; and the ravine was so deep and rugged the enemy could not have crossed it on the flanks in the dark. It is no defence to say Adam took ground in the evening after a march,—that he expected the main body up the next morning, —that lord William assured him he was safe from attack.

N 2

Every officer is responsible for the security of his post, and Adam placed no infantry piquet on the bridge, nor sent a cavalry patrole beyond it; and I have been informed by a French soldier, one of a party sent to explore the position, that they reached the crest of the heights without opposition and returned safely, whereupon Mesclop's brigade instantly crossed the bridge and attacked.

4°. Ordal must be called a surprise, yet the troops were not surprised, they were beaten and dispersed because Adam was unskilful. Suchet's victory was complete; yet he has in his Memoirs exaggerated his difficulties and the importance of his success; his private report to the emperor was more accurate. The Memoirs state that the English grenadiers defended certain works which commanded the ascent of the main road; and in the accompanying atlas a perspective view of well-conditioned redoubts with colours flying is given. The reader is thus led to imagine these were regular forts defended by select troops; but in the private report they

Appendix 19.

are correctly designated as ancient retrenchments; being the ruins of old Spanish field-works, and of no more advantage to the allies than any natural inequality of ground. Again in the Memoirs the attack of the French cavalry near Villa Franca is represented as quite successful; but the private report only says the rear was harassed by repeated charges, which is true, and moreover those charges were vigorously repulsed. The whole French loss was about three hundred men, that of the allies, heavy at Ordal, was lightened by escape of prisoners during the night, and ultimately did not exceed a thousand men including Spaniards.

ASSAULT OF ST SEBASTIAN
August 31st
1813.

CHAPTER III.

Turning from Catalonia to Navarre and Guipuscoa, we shall find Wellington's indomitable energy overcoming every difficulty. It has been shown how the Anglo-Portuguese troops were appointed to cover the siege of San Sebastian and the blockade of Pampeluna, while the Spanish divisions attacked Santona on the coast, and the castles of Daroca, Morella, and Zaragoza in the interior. These operations required many men, and Carlos d'España's division, four thousand strong, which had remained at Miranda del Castanar to improve its organization when Wellington advanced to the Ebro, was now coming up. Passages was the only port near the scene of operations suited for the supply of the army, but as it was between the covering and besieging armies, the stores and guns once landed were in danger from every movement of the enemy; the Deba river, between San Sebastian and Bilbao, was unfit for large vessels, and no permanent dépôt could be established nearer than Bilbao. At that port therefore, and at St. Ander and Coruña, the great dépôts of the army were fixed, the stores being transported to them from the establishments in Portugal. But the French held Santoña, their privateers interrupted the communication along the coast of Spain, and American privateers did the same between Lisbon and Coruña; the intercourse between San Sebastian and the ports of France was scarcely molested; and the most urgent remonstrances failed to procure a sufficient naval force on the coast of Biscay. It was in these circumstances Wellington commenced

THE SIEGE OF SAN SEBASTIAN.

This place, built on a low sandy isthmus, had the harbour on one side the river Urumea on the other. Behind it rose the Monte Orgullo, a rugged cone four hundred feet high, washed by the ocean, and its southern face, covered with batteries and overlooking the town, was cut off from the latter by defensive walls.   It was crowned by the small castle of La Mota, which was itself commanded at a distance of thirteen hundred yards by the Monte Olia which rose beyond the Urumea.   The land front was three hundred and fifty yards wide, stretching quite across the isthmus.   It consisted of a high curtain or rampart, very solid, strengthened by a lofty casemated flat bastion or cavalier placed in the centre, and by half bastions at either end.   A regular horn-work was pushed out from this front; and six hundred yards beyond the horn-work the isthmus was closed by the ridge of San Bartolomeo, at the foot of which stood the suburb of San Martin.

On the opposite side of the Urumea were certain sandy hills called the *Chofres*, through which the road from Passages passed to the wooden bridge over the river, and thence, by the suburb of Santa Catalina, along the top of a sea-wall which formed a *fausse braye* for the horn-work.   The flanks of the town were protected by simple ramparts; one washed by the water of the harbour, the other by the Urumea, which at high tide covered four of the twenty-seven feet comprised in its elevation.   This was the weak side of the fortress, for though covered by the river there was only a single wall ill-flanked by two old towers and the half-bastion of San Elmo, which was situated at the extremity of the rampart close under the Monte Orgullo.   There was no ditch, no counter-scarp, no glacis; the wall could be seen to its base from the Chofre hills, at distances varying from five hundred to a thousand yards; and when the tide was out the Urumea left a dry strand under the rampart as far as St. Elmo.   However the guns from the batteries of Monte Orgullo, especially that called the Mirador, could see this strand.   The other flank was secured by the harbour, in the mouth of which was a rocky island called Santa Clara, where the French had established a post of twenty-five men.

Before the battle of Vitoria, San Sebastian was nearly dismantled; many of the guns had been removed to form battering-trains or to arm smaller ports on the coast; there were no bomb-proofs, nor palisades, nor outworks; the wells were foul and the place supplied by a single aqueduct. Joseph's defeat restored its importance as a fortress. Emanuel Rey entered it the 22nd of June, with the escort of the convoy which quitted Vitoria the day before the battle. The town was thus filled with emigrant Spanish families, with ministers and other persons attached to the court; the population, ordinarily eight thousand, was increased to sixteen thousand and confusion prevailed. Rey, pushed by necessity, immediately forced all persons not residents to march at once to France, granting them only a guard of one hundred men; the people of quality went by sea the others by land, and fortunately all arrived, for the partidas would have given them no quarter. Foy had while retreating thrown a reinforcement into the place, and next day Mendizabel's Spaniards appeared on the hills behind the ridge of San Bartolomeo and on the Chofres. Rey then burned the wooden bridge and both the suburbs, and commenced fortifying the heights of San Bartolomeo, which the Spaniards slightly attacked the 29th and were repulsed.

Bellas' Journal of French Sieges in Spain.

On the 1st of July the governor of Gueteria abandoned that place, and with detestable ferocity secretly left a lighted train which exploded the magazine and destroyed many of the inhabitants. His troops, three hundred, entered San Sebastian, and at the same time a vessel from St. Jean de Luz arrived with fifty-six cannoneers and some workmen; the garrison was thus increased to three thousand men, and all persons not able to provide subsistence for themselves in advance were ordered to quit the place. Mendizabel then cut off the aqueduct, made approaches towards the head of the burned bridge on the right of the Urumea, and molested the workmen on the heights of Bartolomeo; and on the 3rd, the Surveillante frigate, a sloop, and some small craft blockaded the harbour; yet the French vessels from St. Jean de Luz continued to enter by night. The same day the governor made a sally with eleven hundred men to obtain news, and after some hours' skirmishing returned with a few prisoners.

Sir G. Collier's Despatch.

The 6th French vessels bringing a detachment of troops and a considerable convoy of provisions came from St. Jean de Luz. The 7th Mendizabel tried, unsuccessfully, to set fire to the convent of San Bartolomeo. The 9th Graham arrived with a corps of British and Portuguese troops, and the 13th the Spaniards marched, some to reinforce the force blockading Santona, the remainder to rejoin the fourth army on the Bidassoa. At this time Reille held the entrances to the Bastan by Vera and Echallar, but Wellington drove him thence on the 15th, and established the seventh and light divisions there to cover the passes over the Peña de Haya, by which the siege might have been interrupted.

Before Graham arrived the French had constructed a redoubt on the heights of San Bartolomeo, and connected it with the convent of that name which they also fortified. These outworks were supported by posts in the ruined houses of the suburb of San Martin behind, and by a low circular redoubt formed of casks on the main road, half-way between the convent and the horn-work. Hence to reduce the place, working along the isthmus, it was necessary to carry in succession three lines of defence covering the town and a fourth at the foot of Monte Orgullo, before the castle of La Mota could be assailed. These works had seventy-six pieces mounted, and others were afterwards obtained from France by sea.

The besieging army consisted of the fifth division under Oswald, the independent Portuguese brigades of J. Wilson and Bradford reinforced by detachments from the first division. Thus, including the artillerymen, some seamen commanded by lieutenant O'Reilly of the Surveillante, and one hundred regular sappers and miners, now for the first time used in the sieges of the Peninsula, nearly ten thousand men were employed. There was also a new battering-train, originally prepared to

Jones's Sieges.

besiege Burgos, consisting of fourteen iron twenty-four pounders, six eight-inch brass howitzers, four sixty-eight-pound iron carronades, and four iron ten-inch mortars. To these were added six twenty-four pounders lent by the ships of war, and six eighteen pounders which had moved with the army from Portugal, making altogether forty pieces commanded by colonel Dickson. The distance from the dépôt of siege at Passages to the Chofres was one mile and a half of good road, and a pontoon-bridge was laid over the Urumea river above these hills; but from thence to the height of Bartolomeo was more than five miles of very bad road.

Early in July the fortress had been twice closely examined by major Smith, the engineer who had so ably defended Tarifa. He proposed a plan of siege, founded upon the facility furnished by the Chofres to destroy the flanks rake the principal front and form a breach with the same batteries; the works being at the same time secured, except at low water, by the Urumea. Counter-batteries on the left of that river were to rake the line of defence in which the breach was to be formed; and against the castle and its outworks he relied principally upon vertical fire, instancing the reduction of Fort Bourbon in the West Indies in proof of its efficacy. This plan would probably have reduced San Sebastian in a reasonable time without any remarkable loss of men; Wellington approved of it, though he doubted the efficacy of the vertical fire, and ordered the siege to be commenced. He renewed his approval when he had examined the works in person, and all his orders were in the same spirit; but as neither the plan nor his orders were followed, the siege, which should have been an ordinary event of war, has obtained a mournful celebrity; and Wellington has been unjustly charged with contemning the maxims of the great masters. Anxious he was to save time, yet he did not urge the engineer beyond the rules. *Take the place in the quickest manner, yet do not from over speed fail to take it,* was the sense of his instructions; but Graham, one of England's best soldiers, was endowed with a genius more intuitive than reflective; and this joined to his natural modesty and a certain easiness of temper, caused him at times to abandon his own correct conceptions for the less judicious counsels of those who advised deviations from the original plan.

In the night of the 10th two batteries were commenced against the convent and redoubt of San Bartolomeo; and next night four batteries, to contain twenty of the heaviest guns and four eight-inch howitzers, were marked out on the Chofre sand-hills, at distances varying from six hundred to thirteen

hundred yards from the eastern rampart of the town. The
river was supposed to be unfordable, wherefore no parallel was
made, yet good trenches of communications, and subsequently
regular approaches were formed. Two attacks were thus
established. One on the right bank of the Urumea for the
unattached Portuguese brigades; one on the left bank for the
fifth division; but most of the troops were at first encamped
on the right bank to facilitate a junction with the covering
army in the event of a general battle.

On the 14th a French sloop entered the harbour with supplies, and the batteries of the left attack, under the direction
of the German major Hartman, opened against San Bartolomeo, throwing hot shot into that building. The besieged
responded with musketry from the redoubt, with heavy guns
from the town, and with a field-piece which they had mounted
on the belfry of the convent itself. The 15th sir Richard
Fletcher took command of the engineers, but major Smith
retained the direction of the attack from the Chofre hills and
Wellington's orders continued to pass through his hands.
This day the batteries of the left attack, aided by howitzers
from the right of the Urumea, set the convent on fire, silenced
the musketry of the besieged, and so damaged the defences,
that the Portuguese of the fifth division were ordered to feel
the enemy: they were however repulsed with great loss, the
French sallied, and the firing did not cease until nightfall.

A battery for seven additional guns to play against Bartolomeo was now commenced on the right of the Urumea, and the
original batteries set fire to the convent several times, yet the
flames were extinguished by the garrison.

In the night of the 16th Rey sounded the Urumea as high
as Santa Catalina, designing to pass over and storm the batteries on the Chofres; but the fords discovered were shifting
and the difficulty of execution deterred him from this project.
The 17th, the convent being nearly in ruins, the assault was
ordered without waiting for the effect of the new battery
raised on the other side of the Urumea. The storming party
was formed in two columns. Detachments from Wilson's
Portuguese, supported by the light company of the ninth
British regiment and three companies of the royals under

general Hay, were destined to assail the redoubt; general Bradford, leading the other column, composed of Portuguese supported by three companies of the ninth British regiment under colonel Cameron, was to assail the convent.

ASSAULT OF SAN BARTOLOMEO.

At ten o'clock in the morning two heavy six-pounders opened against the redoubt, and a sharp fire of musketry from the French, who had been reinforced and occupied the suburb of San Martin, announced their resolution to fight. The allied troops were assembled behind the crest of the hill overlooking the convent and the first signal was given; but the Portuguese advanced so slowly at both attacks that the supporting companies of the ninth regiment, passing through them, fell upon the enemy with the usual impetuosity of British soldiers. Cameron leading his grenadiers down hill was exposed to a heavy cannonade from the horn-work, yet he gained the cover of a wall fifty yards from the convent and there awaited the second signal. His rapid advance, which threatened to cut off the garrison from the suburb, joined to the fire of the two six-pounders and some other field-pieces on the farther side of the Urumea, caused the French to abandon the redoubt; Cameron then jumped over the wall and assaulted both the convent and the houses of the suburb. At the latter a fierce struggle ensued and captain Woodham of the ninth was killed in the upper room of a house to which he fought his way from below; but the grenadiers carried the convent with such rapidity that the French, unable to explode some small mines, hastily joined the troops in the suburb. There the fighting continued, and the affair was becoming doubtful, when the remaining companies of the ninth regiment arrived and the suburb with much fighting was won. At the right attack the company of the ninth, although retarded by a ravine, a thick hedge, the slowness of the Portuguese and a heavy fire, entered the abandoned redoubt with little loss; but all the troops were then, contrary to Oswald's orders, rashly led against the cask redoubt, and were beaten back by the enemy.

Of the French two hundred and forty men fell. On the British side, the companies of the ninth under Cameron alone lost seven officers and sixty men killed or wounded, and the whole operation although successful was an error. The battery on the right of the Urumea was not opened, wherefore, either the assault was precipitated or the battery was not necessary; but the loss justified the conception of the battery.

When the action ceased the engineers made a lodgment in the redoubt, and commenced two batteries for eight pieces to rake the horn-work and the eastern rampart of the place. Two other batteries, to contain four sixty-eight pound carronades and four ten-inch mortars, were also commenced on the right bank of the Urumea. The besieged then threw up traverses on the land front to meet the raking fire of the besiegers, and the latter dragged four pieces up the Monte Olia to plunge into the Mirador and other batteries on the Monte Orgullo. In the night a lodgment was made on the ruins of San Martin, the batteries at the right attack were armed, and two additional mortars dragged up the Monte Olia; on the 19th all the batteries at both attacks were armed, and in the night two approaches were commenced from the suburb of San Martin towards the cask redoubt, from whence the French were driven. On the 20th the whole of the batteries opened their fire, the greatest part being directed to form the breach.

Smith's plan was similar to that followed by marshal Berwick a century before. He proposed a lodgment on the horn-work before the breach should be assailed; but he had not then read the description of that siege, and therefore unknowingly fixed the breaching-point precisely where the wall had been most strongly rebuilt after Berwick's attack. This was the first fault, yet a slight one, because the wall did not resist the batteries very long; it was a more serious matter that Graham, at the suggestion of the commander of the artillery, began his operations by breaching. Smith was opposed to it, but Fletcher acquiesced reluctantly, on the understanding that the ruining of the defences was only postponed, an understanding afterwards forgotten.

Notes of the Siege by sir C. Smith, MSS.

The result of the first day's battery was not satisfactory. The weather was bad, the guns mounted on ship carriages failed, one twenty-four pounder was rendered unserviceable by the enemy, another useless by an accident, a captain of engineers was killed and the besiegers' shot had little effect upon the solid wall. In the night however the ship-guns were mounted on better carriages, and a parallel across the isthmus was projected; but the greatest part of the workmen, to avoid a tempest sought shelter in the suburb of San Martin, and when day broke only one-third of the work was performed.

On the 21st the place was summoned, but the governor refused to receive the letter, and the firing was resumed. The main wall still resisted, yet the parapets and embrasures crumbled away, and the batteries on Monte Olia plunged into the horn-work, with such effect, although at sixteen hundred yards distance, that the besieged having no bomb-proofs were forced to dig trenches to protect themselves. The counter-fire, directed solely against the breaching-batteries, was feeble, but at midnight a shell thrown from the castle into the bay gave the signal for a sally, and during the firing which ensued several French vessels with supplies entered the harbour. This night also the besieged isolated the breach by cuts in the rampart and other defences. On the other hand the besiegers' parallel across the isthmus was completed, and in its progress laid bare the mouth of a drain, four feet high and three feet wide, containing the pipe of the aqueduct cut off by the Spaniards. Through this narrow opening lieutenant Reid of the engineers, a young and zealous officer, crept even to the counterscarp of the horn-work, and finding the passage there closed by a door returned without an accident. Thirty barrels of powder were then placed in the drain, and eight feet was stopped with sand-bags, thus forming a globe of compression designed to blow, as through a tube, so much rubbish over the counterscarp as might fill the narrow ditch of the horn-work.

On the 22nd the fire from the batteries, unexampled from its rapidity and accuracy, opened what appeared to the besiegers a very practicable breach in the eastern flank wall, between the towers of Los Hornos and Las Mesquitas. The counter-fire of the besieged then slackened, yet the descent into the town from the breach was more than twelve feet perpendicular; and the garrison were seen from Monte Olia diligently working at the interior defences to receive the assault: they added also another gun to the battery of St. Elmo, just under the Mirador battery, to flank the front attack. On the other hand the besiegers had placed four sixty-eight pound carronades in battery to play on the defences of the breach, yet the general fire slackened because the guns were greatly enlarged at the vents with constant practice.

On the 23rd, the sea blockade being null, the French vessels returned to France with the badly wounded men; and that day the besiegers, judging the breach between the towers quite practicable, turned the guns, at the suggestion of Oswald, to break the wall on the right of the main breach. Smith opposed this, urging, that no advantage would be gained by making a second opening to get at which the troops must first pass the great breach; that time would be lost to the besiegers, and there was a manifest objection on account of the tide and depth of water at the new point attacked. His counsel was overruled, and in the course of the day, the wall being thin the stroke heavy and quick, a second breach thirty feet wide was rendered practicable. Then the fire of the besieged being much diminished, the ten-inch mortars and sixty-eight pound carronades were turned upon the defences of the great breach; and upon a stockade which separated the high curtain on the land front from the lower works of the flank against which the attack was conducted. The nearest houses were soon in flames, which spreading rapidly destroyed some of the defences of the besieged and menaced the whole town with destruction, and the assault was ordered for the next morning; but when the troops assembled, the burning houses appeared so formidable that the attack was deferred. The batteries then played again, partly on the second breach, partly on the defences, partly to break the wall in a third place between the half bastion of St. John on the land front and the main breach.

During the night the vigilant governor mounted two field-pieces on the cavalier in the centre of the land front, which being fifteen feet above the other defences commanded the high curtain; and he still had on the horn-work a light piece, and two casemated guns on the flank of the cavalier. Two other field-pieces were mounted on an entrenchment, which, crossing the ditch of the land front, bore on the approaches to the main breach, and a twenty-four pounder looked from the tower of Las Mesquitas between the main breach and where the third opening was being made, flanking both; two four-pounders were in the tower of Hornos, two heavy guns were on the flank of St. Elmo, and two others, placed on the right of the Mirador, could play Bellas. upon the breaches within the fortified line of Monte Orgullo. Thus fourteen pieces were still available for defence, the retaining sea-wall, or *fausse braye*, which strengthened the Urumea flank of the horn-work and between which and the river the storming parties must necessarily advance, was covered with live shells to roll over on the columns, and behind the flaming houses near the breach other edifices were loop-holed and filled with musketeers. However the fire, extending rapidly and fiercely, greatly injured the defences, the French withdrew their guns until the moment of attack, and as the British artillery officers declared they could in daylight silence the enemy's fire and keep the parapet clear of men, Graham renewed the order for

THE ASSAULT.

In the night of the 24th two thousand men of the fifth division filed into the trenches on the isthmus. This force was composed of the third battalion of the royals under major Frazer, destined to storm the great breach; the thirty-eighth regiment under colonel Greville, designed to assail the lesser and most distant breach; the ninth regiment under colonel Cameron, appointed to support the royals. A detachment selected from the light companies of all those battalions was placed in the centre of the royals, under the command of lieutenant Campbell of the ninth regiment; he was accompanied by the engineer Machel and a ladder party, and was to sweep the high curtain after the breach should be won.

From the trenches to the points of attack was more than three hundred yards along the contracted space between the retaining wall of the horn-work and the river—the ground was strewed with rocks covered by slippery sea-weeds,—the tide had left large and deep pools of water,—the parapet of the horn-work was entire as well as the retaining wall--the parapets of the other works and the two towers, which closely flanked the breach, although injured were far from being ruined, and every place was thickly garnished with musketeers. The difficulties of the attack were obvious, and some Portuguese, placed in a trench beyond the parallel on the isthmus and within sixty yards of the ramparts, were ordered to quell if possible the fire of the horn-work.

While it was still dark the storming columns moved out of the trenches, and the globe of compression in the drain was exploded with great effect against the counterscarp and glacis of the horn-work. The garrison astonished by this unlooked-for event abandoned the flanking parapet, and the allies rushed onwards, the stormers for the main breach leading and suffering more from the fire of the batteries on the right of the Urumea than from the enemy. Major Frazer and the engineer Harry Jones first reached the breach; and as the enemy had fallen back in confusion behind the ruins of the burning houses, those brave officers rushed up expecting that their troops would follow,—but not many followed, for it was extremely dark, and the natural difficulties of the way had contracted the front and disordered the column in its whole length; the soldiers, straggling and out of wind, arrived in small disconnected parties at the foot of the breach. The foremost gathered near their gallant leaders, yet the depth of the descent into the town and the volumes of flames and smoke with still issued from the burning houses behind awed the stoutest, and more than two-thirds of the column, irritated by the destructive flank fire, had broken off at the demi-bastion to commence a musketry battle with the enemy on the rampart.

Meanwhile the shells from the Monte Orgullo fell rapidly, the French rallied, and with a smashing musketry from the ruins and loopholed houses smote the head of the stormers, while the men in the towers smote them on the flanks; and from every quarter came showers of grape and hand-grenades tearing the ranks in a dreadful manner.   Frazer was killed on the flaming ruins, the intrepid Jones stood there awhile longer amidst a few heroic soldiers hoping for aid, but none came, and he and those with him were struck down; the engineer Machel was killed early, and the men bearing ladders fell or were dispersed.   Thus the rear of the column had got into confusion before the head was beaten, and it was in vain Greville of the thirty-eighth, Cameron of the ninth, captain Archimbeau of the royals, and many other regimental officers attempted to rally their discomfited troops and refill the breach; it was in vain that lieutenant Campbell, breaking through the tumultuous crowd with the survivors of his chosen detachment, mounted the ruins—twice he ascended, twice he was wounded, and all around him died   The royals endeavouring to retire, got intermixed with the thirty-eighth and with some of the ninth who had unsuccessfully endeavoured to pass them and get to the lesser breach.   Then swayed by different impulses, pent up in the narrow way between the horn-work and the river, the mass reeling to and fro could neither advance nor go back until the shells and musketry, constantly plied both in front and flank, had thinned the concourse and the trenches were regained in confusion.   At daylight a truce was agreed to for an hour, during which the French, who had already removed the gallant Jones and some of the wounded men from the breach, now carried off the more distant sufferers lest they should be drowned by the rising of the tide; but during the contest some grenadiers, rushing out on the breach, with an infamous barbarity stabbed several wounded soldiers lying there. *Narrative of his captivity by colonel Harry Jones.*

Five officers of engineers including sir Richard Fletcher, and forty-four officers of the line with five hundred and twenty men, had been killed wounded or made prisoners in this assault, the failure of which was signal, yet the causes were obvious and may be classed thus.

1°. Deviation from the original project of siege and from Wellington's instructions.

2°. Bad arrangements of detail.

3°. Want of vigour in the execution.

Wellington having visited the Chofre trenches on the 22nd had confirmed his first approval of Smith's plan, and gave that officer final directions for the attack finishing thus, '*Fair daylight must be taken for the assault.*' These instructions and their emphatic termination were repeated by Smith in the proper quarter, and were not followed; no lodgment was made on the horn-work, the defences were nearly entire both in front and flank, and the assault was given in darkness. Smith had ascertained by calculation and consultations with the fishermen, that the ebb of tide would serve exactly at day-break on the 24th; yet the assault was only made the 25th, and before daylight, when the high water, contracting the ground, increased the obstacles and forced the assaulting column to march on a narrow front and a long line, making an uneasy progress and trickling onwards instead of dashing with a broad surge against the breach. The rules of art being thus neglected and no extraordinary resource substituted the operation failed.

The troops filed out of the long narrow trenches in the night, a tedious operation, and were immediately exposed to a fire of grape from their own batteries on the Chofres: this fire should have ceased when the globe of compression was sprung; but what with darkness and noise it was neither seen nor heard; and though the explosion drove the enemy from the horn-work and the Portuguese advanced to the ditch, when a vigorous escalade would probably have succeeded, they had no ladders. The stormers of the great breach marched first, filling up the way and rendering the second breach, as Smith had foretold, useless, and the ladder-bearers never got to their destination. In fine the assault was ill digested.

Sir C. Smith, MSS.

There was also a neglect of moral influence followed by its natural consequence, want of vigour in execution. Deferring the assault from the 24th to the 25th, expressly because the breach was too difficult, rendered the troops uneasy; they suspected hidden danger, and in this mood emerging from the trenches were struck by the fire of their own batteries; then wading through deep pools of water, or staggering in the dark over slippery rocks and close under the enemy's flanking works whence every shot told with fatal effect, how could they manifest their natural conquering energy? A second and more vigorous assault on the great breach might have been effected by a recognised leader; but no general or staff officer went out of the trenches, and the isolated exertions of regimental officers failed. Nor were there wanting other sinister influences. Oswald had in council earnestly and justly urged the dangers arising from the irregular mode of attack; but this anticipation of ill success, in which other officers of rank joined, was also freely expressed out of council, and it is said even in the hearing of the troops, abating that daring confidence which victory loves.

Wellington repaired immediately to St. Sebastian. The causes of failure were apparent and he would have renewed the attack, but was compelled from want of ammunition to defer it, until powder and additional ordnance, for which he had written to England as early as the 26th of June, should arrive. Next day other events caused him to resort to a blockade, and the battering-train was transported to Passages, two guns and two howitzers only being retained on the Chofres and Monte Olio. This operation was completed in the night of the 26th, but at daybreak the garrison made a sally from the horn-work, surprised the trenches and swept off two hundred Portuguese and thirty British soldiers. To avoid a repetition of this disaster the guards of the trenches were concentrated in the left parallel, and patroles only were sent out, yet one of those also was cut off on the first of August. Thus terminated the first part of the siege of San Sebastian in which the allies lost thirteen hundred soldiers and seamen, exclusive of Spaniards during Mendizabel's blockade.

CHAPTER IV.

TEN days after the battle of Vitoria, marshal Soult, under a decree issued from Dresden, succeeded the king as lieutenant to Napoleon, who thus showed how little he had been biassed by Joseph's accusations. Travelling with surprising expedition, he was enabled on the 12th of July to assume the command of the three beaten armies, now re-organized in one under the title of the '*army of Spain;*' and he had secret orders to put Joseph forcibly aside if necessary, but that monarch willingly retired. At this period general Paris was still at Jaca, but Clausel had entered France, and Soult, reinforced from the interior, had nine divisions of infantry, a reserve, and two divisions of cavalry besides light horsemen attached to the infantry. Including garrisons, and twelve Italian and Spanish
Appendix 3. battalions not included in the organization, he
§ 8. Vol. VI. had one hundred and fourteen thousand men ; and, as the armies of Aragon and Catalonia had above sixty-six thousand, one hundred and eighty thousand men and twenty-six thousand horses were still menacing Spain. One hundred and fifty-six thousand were present under arms: and in Germany and Poland seven hundred thousand French troops were employed!

Such masses directed by Napoleon seemed sufficient to defy the world; but moral power, defined by himself as three-fourths of military strength; that power which puny essayists, declaiming for their hour against the genius of warriors, are unable to comprehend although the most important part of the art they decry, was wanting. One-half of this force, organized in peace and setting forth in hope at the beginning of a war, would have enabled Napoleon to conquer; now, near the close of a terrible struggle, with a declining fate and the national confidence shaken although his genius was never

more surpassingly displayed, his military power was a vast
but unsound machine. The public mind was bewildered by
combinations the full scope of which he alone could see
clearly; generals and ministers doubted and feared when they
should have supported him, neglecting their duty or coldly
executing when their zeal should have redoubled. The unity
of impulse so essential to success was thus lost, and the numerous armies carried not with them proportionate strength.
To have struggled with hope under such astounding difficulties
was scarcely to be expected from the greatest minds. But like
the emperor to calculate and combine the most stupendous
efforts with calmness and accuracy; to seize every favourable
chance with unerring rapidity; to sustain every reverse with undisturbed constancy; never urged to rashness by despair yet enterprising to the utmost verge of daring consistent with reason,
was a display of intellectual greatness so surpassing, that it is
not without justice Napoleon has been called, in reference as
well to past ages as to the present, the foremost of mankind.

Sudden and wide was the destruction caused by the snows
of Russia; it shattered the emperor's military and political
system, and the fragments of the former were useless until he
could again bind them together. To effect that he rushed
with a raw army into the midst of Germany; for his hope
was to obtain by celerity a rallying point for those veterans,
who, having survived the Russian winter and the succeeding
pestilence, were dispersed all over the continent. His first
effort was successful, but without good cavalry victory cannot
be pushed far, and the practised horsemen of France had
nearly disappeared: their successors, badly mounted and less
skilful, were too few and too weak, and thus extraordinary
exertion was required from soldiers whose youth and inex-
perience rendered them unfit even for the ordinary hardships
of war. The measure of Wellington's campaign is thus
attained; for if Joseph had opposed him with only moderate
ability, and avoided a great battle, not less than fifty thousand
veterans could have reinforced the young soldiers in Germany.
On the side of Spain those veterans were still numerous; but
the military spirit of the French people, previously almost
worn out by victory was now abashed by defeat; and even

the generals who had acquired grandeur and riches beyond their hopes were with few exceptions averse to farther toil. Napoleon's astonishing firmness of mind was understood by few in high stations, shared by fewer; and many were the traitors to him and to France, and to the glories of both. However his power was still enormous, and wherever he led in person, his brave and faithful soldiers, fighting with the true instinct of patriotism, conquered. Where he was not their iron hardihood abated.

Soult was one of the few whose indefatigable energy rendered them worthy lieutenants of the emperor; and with singular zeal and ability he now served. His troops, nominally above one hundred thousand men, ninety-seven thousand being present under arms with eighty-six pieces of artillery, were not all available for field operations. Pampeluna, San Sebastian, Santona, Bayonne, and the foreign battalions had seventeen thousand men; but most of those battalions had orders to regain their own countries with a view to form the new levies. The permanent '*army of Spain*' furnished therefore only seventy-seven thousand five hundred men present under arms, seven thousand of which were cavalry. Its condition was not satisfactory. The people on the frontier were flying from the allies, the military administration was disorganized, the recent disasters had discouraged the soldiers and deteriorated their discipline. Soult was therefore desirous of some delay to secure his base and restore order ere he attempted to regain the offensive, but his instructions on that point were imperatively adverse.

Napoleon's system was perfectly adapted for great efforts, civil or military; yet so rapid had been Wellington's advance, so decided his operations, that the resources of France were in a certain degree paralysed, and the army still reeled and rocked from the blows it had received. Bayonne, a fortress of no great strength in itself, had been quite neglected; it was now being armed and provisioned; and the restoration of an entrenched camp, originally traced by Vauban to cover Bayonne, followed. Then the enforcement of discipline, the removal of the immense train of Spanish families, civil administrators and other wasteful followers of Joseph's court, the

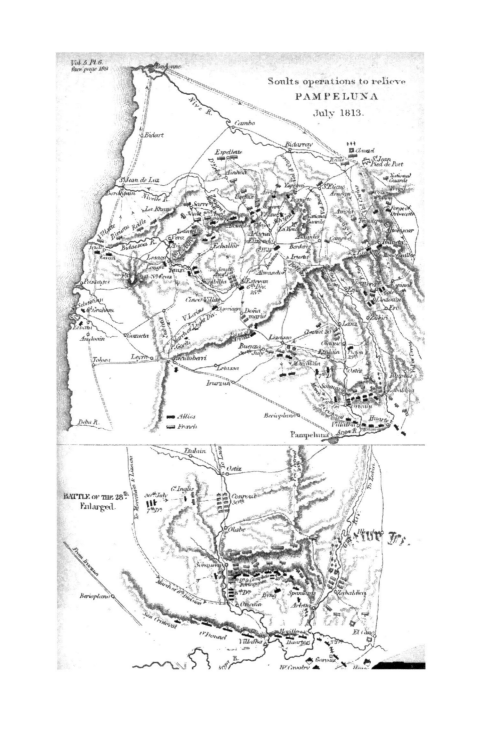

Vol.5.Pl.6.
face page 199

Soults operations to relieve
PAMPELUNA
July 1813.

Allies
French

Pampeluna

BATTLE OF THE 28ᵗʰ
Enlarged.

nistrators and other wasteful followers of Joseph's court, the

arrangement of a general system for supply of money and
provisions, aided by judicious efforts to stimulate the civil
authorities and excite the national spirit, indicated that a
great commander was in the field.   The soldiers' confidence
soon revived, and some leading merchants of Bayonne zealously
seconded the general; but the people of the south were more
inclined to avoid the burthen of defending their country than
to answer appeals to their patriotism.

On the 14th Soult examined the line of military positions,
and ordered Reille, then occupying the passes of Vera and
Echallar, to prepare pontoons for throwing two bridges over
the Bidassoa at Biriatou.   That general, as we have seen, was
driven from those passes the next day, yet he prepared his
bridges; and such was Soult's activity that on the 16th all
the combinations for a gigantic offensive movement were
digested, the means of executing it rapidly advancing, and
orders were issued for the preliminary dispositions.

The army was divided into three corps of battle and a
reserve.   Clausel had the left wing at St. Jean Pied de Port,
and was in communication by the French frontier with Paris
at Jaca.   Drouet, count D'Erlon, occupied with
the centre the heights near Espelette and Ainhoa,   Soult, MSS.
having an advanced guard near Urdax.   Reille was in position with the right on the mountains overlooking Vera from
the side of France.   The reserve under Villatte, comprising a
separate body of light horsemen and the foreign battalions,
guarded the banks of the Bidassoa from the mouth upwards
to Irun, at which place the stone bridge was destroyed.   The
two divisions of cavalry under Trielhard and Pierre Soult
were on the banks of the Nive and the Adour.

Wellington's counter-dispositions were as follows.

Byng's brigade of British infantry, detached from the
second division and reinforced by Morillo's Spaniards, was on
the extreme right.   These troops had early in June driven
the French from the village of Valcarlos in the valley of that
name, and had foraged the French territory; but, finding no
good permanent position, retreated again to the rocks in front
of the passes of Roncevalles and Ibañeta.

On the left of Byng, Campbell's brigade, detached from

Hamilton's Portuguese division, was posted in the Alduides and supported with the fourth division by Cole, who was at Viscayret in the valley of Urroz.

On the left of Campbell, Hill defended the Bastan with the remainder of the second division and Hamilton's Portuguese now commanded by Silveira. Picton, with the third division, was stationed at Olague as a reserve to those troops and to Cole.

On the left of Hill the seventh and light divisions occupied a chain of mountains running by Echallar to Vera, and behind them at the town of San Estevan, was posted the sixth division.

Longa's Spaniards continued the line of defence from Vera to Giron's position, which extended along the mountains bordering the Bidassoa to the sea, crossing the great road of Irun.

Behind Giron was the besieging army under Graham, with thirty-six pieces of field artillery; some regiments of British and Portuguese cavalry were with the right wing and centre; but the main body of cavalry and the heavy guns were behind the mountains, chiefly about Tafalla. The great hospitals were in Vitoria, the commissariat depôts on the coast, and to supply the troops in the mountains was exceedingly difficult and onerous.

O'Donnel blockaded Pampeluna with the Andalusian army of reserve, and Carlos d'España's division was on the march to join him. Mina, Julian Sanchez, Duran, Empecinado, Goyan and some smaller bands, were on the side of Zaragoza and Daroca, cutting the communication between Soult and Suchet, and the latter, as we have seen, was falling back upon Catalonia.

Wellington's army in Navarre and Guipuscoa, was above one hundred thousand men, of which the Anglo-Portuguese
Appendix 4, furnished fifty-seven thousand present under arms,
Vol. VI. seven thousand being cavalry; but the Spanish regulars under Giron, O'Donnel, and Carlos d'España, including Longa's and Mendizabel's men, scarcely
Duke of
Wellington, amounted to twenty-five thousand According to
MSS. the respective muster-rolls, the troops in line

actually under arms and facing each other were, of the allies eighty-two thousand, of the French seventy-eight thousand; but as the rolls of the latter include every man and officer of all arms belonging to the organization, and the British and Portuguese rolls so quoted would furnish between ten and twelve thousand additional combatants, the French force must be reduced, or the allies augmented in that proportion. This surplus was however compensated by the foreign battalions temporarily attached to Soult's army, and by the numerous national guards, fierce warlike mountaineers to fight and very useful as guides.   In other respects Wellington stood at a disadvantage.

His theatre of operations was a trapezoid, with sides from forty to sixty miles in length, and having Bayonne, St. Jean Pied de Port, St. Sebastian and Pampeluna, all fortresses in possession of the French, at the angles.   The interior, broken and tormented by savage mountains, narrow craggy passes, deep water-courses, precipices and forests, appeared a wilderness which no military combinations could embrace, and susceptible only of irregular and partisan operations.   But the great spinal ridge of the Pyrenees furnished a clue to the labyrinth.   Running diagonally across the quadrilateral, it separated Bayonne, St. Jean Pied de Port, and San Sebastian from Pampeluna; thus the portion of the allied army which more especially belonged to the blockade of Pampeluna was in a manner cut off from that which belonged to the siege of San Sebastian.   They were distinct armies, each having its particular object, and the only direct communication between them was the great road running behind the mountains from Toloza and Irurzun to Pampeluna.   The centre of the allies was indeed an army of succour and connexion; but of necessity very much scattered, and with lateral communications so few difficult and indirect as to prevent any unity of movement; nor could Hill move at all until an attack was decidedly pronounced against one of the extremities, lest the most direct gun-road to Pampeluna, which he covered, should be unwarily opened to the enemy.   The French general, taking the offensive, could therefore by beaten roads concentrate against any part of the English general's line, which, necessarily a passively defensive one, followed an irregular trace of more than fifty miles of mountains.

Wellington having his battering-train and stores about San Sebastian, which was also nearer and more accessible to the enemy than Pampeluna, made his army lean towards that side. His left wing, including the army of siege, was twenty-one thousand, with singularly strong positions of defence; his centre, twenty-four thousand, could in two marches unite with the left wing to cover the siege or fall upon the flanks of an enemy advancing by the high road of Irun; but three days or more were required by those troops to concentrate for the security of the blockade on the right. Soult however judged that no decisive result would attend a direct movement upon San Sebastian, because Guipuscoa was exhausted of provisions; and the centre of the allies could fall on his flank before he reached Ernani, which, his attack in front failing, would place him in a dangerous position. Moreover, by means of his sea communication he knew San Sebastian was not in extremity; but he had no communication with Pampeluna and feared its fall. Wherefore he resolved to operate by his left.

Profiting by the French roads leading to St. Jean Pied de Port, covering his movement by the Nivelle and Nive rivers and by the positions of his centre, he hoped to gather on Wellington's right quicker than that general could gather to oppose him; and thus, compensating by numbers the disadvantage of assailing mountain positions, force a way to Pampeluna. That fortress once succoured, he designed to seize the road of Irurzun, to fall upon the separated divisions of the centre as they descended from the hills, or operate on the rear of the force besieging San Sebastian while a corps of observation, which he proposed to leave on the lower Bidassoa, menaced it in front and followed it in retreat. The siege of San Sebastian, the blockade of Pampeluna, and probably that of Santona would be thus raised; the French army, united in an abundant country and its communication with Suchet secured, would be free either to co-operate with that marshal or to press its own attack.

In this view and to mislead Wellington by vexing his right

simultaneously with the construction of the bridges against his left, Soult wrote to Paris, desiring him to march when time suited, from Jaca by the higher valleys towards Aviz or Sanguessa, to drive the partisans from that side, and join the left of the army when it should have reached Pampeluna. Clausel was directed to repair the roads in his own front, and push the heads of his columns towards the passes of Roncevalles; then to send a strong detachment into the Val de Baygorry, near the lateral pass of Yspegui, to menace Hill's flank which was at that pass, and the front of Campbell's brigade in the Alduides.

On the 20th Reille's troops on the heights above Vera and Sarre, being cautiously relieved by Villatte, marched through Cambo towards St. Jean Pied de Port. They were to reach the latter early on the 22nd, and on that day also the two divisions of cavalry and the parc of artillery were to be concentrated at the same place. D'Erlon with the centre was still to hold his positions at Espelette, Ainhoüe or Ainhoa and Urdax, thus covering and masking the great movements taking place behind. Villatte who, including the foreign battalions, had fifteen thousand sabres and bayonets remained in observation on the Bidassoa. If threatened by superior forces he was to retire slowly and in mass upon the entrenched camp commenced at Bayonne; halting in succession on the positions of Bordegain in front of St. Jean de Luz, and on the heights of Bidart in rear of that town. He was especially directed to show only French troops at the advanced posts, and if the assailants made a point with a small corps to drive them vigorously over the Bidassoa again. But if the allies should in consequence of Soult's operations against their right retire, Villatte was to relieve San Sebastian and follow them briskly by Tolosa.

Rapidity was of vital importance to the French, but heavy and continued rains swelled the streams and ruined the roads in the deep country between Bayonne and the hills; the head-quarters, which should have arrived at St. Jean Pied de Port on the 20th, only reached Olhonce, a few miles short of that place, the Soult, MSS. 21st; and Reille's troops unable to make way at all by Cambo, took the longer road of Bayonne. The cavalry was retarded in like manner, and the whole army, men and horses, were worn down by the severity of the marches.   Two days were thus lost, but on the 24th more than sixty thousand fighting men, including cavalry national guards and gens-d'armes, with sixty-six pieces of artillery, were assembled to force the passes of Roncevalles and Maya.   The main road leading to the former was repaired, three hundred sets of bullocks were provided to draw the guns up the mountain, and the national guards of the frontier were ordered to assemble in the night on the heights of Yropil; where they were to be reinforced the morning of the 25th by regular troops, being to vex and turn the right of the allies, which extended to the foundry of Urbai--ceta.   Such were Soult's first dispositions, but as mountain warfare is complicated, the objects of the hostile forces and the nature of the country must be shown.

It has been said the great spine of the hills runs diagonally across the theatre of operations.   From this spine huge ridges shot out on either hand, and the communications between the valleys thus formed on both sides of the main chain passed over certain comparatively low places, called ' cols' by the French and *puertos* by the Spaniards.   The Bastan, Val Carlos, and Val de Baygorry the upper part of which is divided into the Alduides and the Val de Ayra, were on the French side of the great chain: on the Spanish side were the valleys of Ahescoa or Orbaiceta, the valley of Iscua or Roncevalles, the valley of Urros, the Val de Zubiri, and the valley of Lanz, the two latter leading down directly upon Pampeluna, which stands within two miles of the junction of their waters.   The disposition and force of the armies shall now be traced from left to right of the French, and from right to left of the allies.   But first it must be observed, that the main chain, throwing as it were a shoulder forward from Roncevalles towards St. Jean Pied de Port, placed the entrance to the Spanish valley of Ahescoa or Orbaiceta in the power of Soult; who could thus by Yropil turn the extreme right of his adversary with detach-ments, although not with an army.

Val Carlos.—Two issues led from this valley over the main chain, namely the Ibañeta and Mendichuri passes, and there was also the lateral pass of Atalosti leading into the Alduides;

all comprised within a space of two or three miles. The high road from St. Jean Pied de Port to Pampeluna, having ascended by the left-hand ridge of Val Carlos, runs along the crest until it reaches the superior ridge; and then along the summit of that also until it reaches the pass of Ibañeta, whence it descends to Roncevalles. Ibañeta may therefore be called the Spanish end of the pass; but it is also a pass in itself, because a narrow road, leading through Arnegui and the village of Val Carlos, there joins the main road.

Clausel's three divisions of infantry, all the artillery, and the cavalry, were formed in two columns in front of St. Jean Pied de Port. The head of one was placed on some heights above Arnegui, two miles from the village of Val Carlos; the head of the other at the Venta de Orrisson on the main road, two miles from the remarkable rocks of Chateau Piñon; near which one narrow way descends on the right to the village of Val Carlos, another on the left to the foundry of Orbaiceta.

On the right-hand ridge of Val Carlos, near the rock of Ayrola, Reille's divisions were concentrated with orders to ascend at daylight and march by the ridge towards a culminant point of the great chain called the Lindouz; then to push detachments through Ibañeta and Mendichuri to the villages of Roncevalles and Espinal. He was also to seize the passes of Sahorgain and Urtiaga on his right, and approach the distant passes of Renecabal and Bellate; thus closing the issues from the Alduides and menacing those from the Bastan.

Val de Ayra. The Alduides. Val de Baygorry.—The ridge of Ayrola, at the foot of which Reille's troops were posted, separates Val Carlos from the valleys named above, which were designated as the Alduides in the upper part, Val de Baygorry in the lower. The issues from the Alduides over the great chain towards Spain were the passes of Sahorgain and Urtiaga; and there was also a road running from the village of Alduides through the Atalosti pass to Ibañeta, a distance of eight miles, by which Campbell's brigade communicated with and could join Byng and Morillo.

Bastan.—This district, including the valley of Lerins and the Cinco Villas, is separated from the Val de Baygorry by the mountain of La Houssa, on which the national guards of Val de Baygorry and the Alduides were to assemble on the night of the 24th and light fires, to make it appear a great body was menacing the Bastan by that flank. The Bastan however does not belong to the same geographical system as the other valleys. Instead of opening to the French territory it is entirely enclosed with mountains; and while the waters of the Val Carlos, the Alduides, and Val de Baygorry run off northward by the Nive, those of the Bastan run off westward by the Bidassoa; the streams being separated by the Mandale, Commissari, La Rhune, Santa Barbara, Ivantelly, Atchiola and other mountains.

With reference to the French army, the entrances to the Bastan were by the passes of Vera and Echallar on the right, the Col de Maya and Arietta passes in the centre; on the left the lateral passes of Yspegui, Lorrieta, and Berderez, leading from Val de Baygorry and the Alduides. The issues over the principal chain of the Pyrenees in the direct line from the Maya entrances, were the passes of Renecabal and Bellate; the first leading into the valley of Zubiri, the second into the valley of Lanz. There was also the pass of Artesiaga leading into the Val de Zubiri, but it was nearly impracticable; and all the roads through the Bastan were crossed by strong positions dangerous to assail.

Col de Maya comprised several passages in a space of four miles, all of which were menaced by D'Erlon from Espelete and Urdax; and he had twenty-one thousand men, furnishing eighteen thousand bayonets. His communications with Soult were maintained by cavalry posts through Val de Baygorry; and his orders were, to attack the allies when the combinations in Val Carlos and on the Houssa should cause them to abandon the passes at Maya; but he was especially directed to operate by his left, and secure the lateral passes, with a view to the concentration of the whole army. Thus if Hill retreated by Bellate, D'Erlon was to move by Berderez and the Alduides; if Hill retired upon San Estevan, D'Erlon was to move by Bellate. Such being the dispositions of the French general those of the allies shall now be traced.

Byng and Morillo guarded the passes in front of Roncevalles with sixteen hundred British and three or four thousand Spaniards. Byng's brigade and two Spanish battalions occupied the rocks of Altobiscar on the high road facing Chateau Piñon; one Spanish battalion was at the foundry of Orbaiceta on their right; Morillo with the remainder occupied the heights of Iroulepe, overlooking the nearest houses of the straggling village of Val Carlos.

Plan 6, page 193.

These positions, four and five miles from the French columns at Venta de Orrisson and Arnegui, were insecure. They were indeed steep, but too extensive; moreover, although the passes behind them led into the Roncevalles that valley did not lead direct to Pampeluna; the high road after descending a few miles turned to the right and crossed two ridges and the intervening valley of Urros before it entered the valley of Zubiri, down which it was conducted to Pampeluna: wherefore after passing Ibañeta in retreat, the allies could not avoid lending their flank to Reille's divisions as far as Viscayret in the valley of Urroz. It was partly to obviate this danger, partly to support O'Donnel while Clausel's force was in the vicinity of Jaca, that the fourth division, six thousand strong, occupied Viscayret; six miles from the pass of Ibañeta, ten miles from Morillo's position, and twelve miles from Byng's position. But when Clausel retired to France, Cole was to observe the roads over the main chain from the Alduides, and form a rallying point and reserve for Campbell, Byng, and Morillo; his instructions being to maintain the Roncevalles passes against a front attack, but to avoid a desperate battle if the flanks were insecure.

On the left of Byng and Morillo, Campbell's Portuguese. two thousand, were encamped above the village of Alduides on a mountain called Mizpira. They watched the national guards of Val de Baygorry, preserved the communication between Byng and Hill, and in some measure covered the right flank of the latter. From the Alduides Campbell could retreat through the pass of Sahorgain upon Viscayret in the valley of Urroz, and through the passes of Urtiaga and Renacabal upon Eugui in the Val de Zubiri; finally by the lateral pass of Atalosti he could join Byng and the fourth division.

The communication between all these posts was maintained by Long's cavalry.

Continuing the line of positions to the left, Hill occupied the Bastan with the second British division, Silveira's Portuguese and some squadrons of horse; but Byng's and Campbell's brigades being detached, he had not more than nine thousand sabres and bayonets. His two British brigades under William Stewart guarded Col de Maya; Silveira was at Erazu on the right of Stewart, watching the passes of Arrieta, Yspegui and Elliorita; the two former being occupied by Brotherton's cavalry and the sixth caçadores. The direct line of retreat and point of concentration for all these troops was Elizondo.

From Elizondo the Pampeluna road over the great chain was by Bellate and the valley of Lanz. The latter running parallel with the valley of Zubiri is separated from it by a wooded and rugged ridge; and between them there were but three communications,—the one high up, leading from Lanz to Eugui, and prolonged from thence to Viscayret in the valley of Urroz—the other two lower down, leading from Ostiz and Olague to the village of Zubiri. At Olague the third division, four thousand three hundred bayonets under Picton, was ready to support Cole or Hill as occasion required.

Continuing the front line from the left of Stewart's position at the Col de Maya, the trace run along the mountains forming the French boundary of the Bastan. There the passes of Echallar and Vera were guarded by the seventh division under lord Dalhousie; and the light division under Charles Alten. The former, having four thousand seven hundred bayonets, communicated with Stewart by a narrow road over the Atchiola mountains; and the eighty-second regiment was encamped at its junction with the Elizondo road, three miles behind the pass of Maya. The light division, four thousand, was at Vera, guarding roads which led behind the mountains through Sumbilla and San Estevan to Elizondo. These two divisions being only watched by part of Villatte's reserve were available for the succour of either wing; and behind them, at the town of San Estevan, was the sixth division, six thousand bayonets, and now under Pack. This division, equally distant from Vera and Maya, having free communication with both and a direct line of march to Pampeluna over the main chain of the Pyrenees, by the *Puerto de Arraiz*, sometimes called the pass of *Doña Maria*, was available for any object.

Around Pampeluna, the point to which all the lines of march converged, O'Donnel's Andalusians maintained the blockade, and being afterwards reinforced by Carlos D'España at a very critical moment numbered eleven thousand, of which seven thousand could act without abandoning the blockade.

Head-quarters were at Lesaca. The line of correspondence with the left wing was over the Peña de Haya; with the right wing by San Estevan, Elizondo and the Alduides; the line between Graham and Pampeluna was by Goizueta and the high road of Irurzun.

As the French were almost in contact with the allies' positions at Roncevalles, the point of defence nearest to Pampeluna, it followed, that on the rapidity or slowness with which Soult overcame resistance in that quarter depended his success; and a comparative estimate of numbers and distances will give the measure of his chances. Clausel had sixteen thousand bayonets, besides cavalry artillery and national guards, the last menacing the valley of Orbaiceta. Byng and Morillo were therefore, with five thousand infantry to sustain the assault of sixteen thousand until Cole could reinforce them; but Cole, twelve miles off, could not come up under four or five hours. And as Reille's divisions, of equal strength with Clausel's, could before that time seize the Lindouz and turn the left, the allies must finally abandon their ground for a new field, where Picton could join them from Olague and Campbell from the Alduides. Then with seventeen or eighteen thousand bayonets and some guns they might oppose Clausel and Reille's thirty thousand. But Picton at Olague was more than a day's march from Byng at Altobiscar; their junction could only be effected in the Zubiri valley not far from Pampeluna; and they could only be reinforced there by seven thousand Spaniards from the blockade, and three thousand cavalry from the Ebro.

Hill, menaced by D'Erlon with a superior force, and having the pass of Maya, half a day's march further from Pampeluna than the passes of Roncevalles, to defend, could not give ready help.   If he retreated rapidly D'Erlon could follow as rapidly; and though Picton and Cole would thus be reinforced with ten thousand men Soult would gain eighteen thousand; but Hill could not move until he knew that Byng and Cole were driven from the Roncevalles passes: in fine he could not avoid a dilemma.   For if he held Col de Maya and affairs went wrong near Pampeluna his own situation would be imminently dangerous; if he held Irrueta, his next position, the same danger was to be dreaded; and Maya once abandoned D'Erlon, moving by his own left towards the Alduides, could join Soult in the valley of Zubiri before Hill could join Cole and Picton by the valley of Lanz.   But if Hill did not maintain the position of Irrueta, D'Erlon could follow and cut the sixth and seventh divisions off from the valley of Lanz.   The extent and power of Soult's combinations are thus evinced.   Hill, forced to await orders and hampered by D'Erlon, required, it might be three days to get into line near Pampeluna; but D'Erlon after gaining Maya could in one day and a half, by the passes of Berderez and Urtiaga, join Soult in the Val de Zubiri. Meanwhile Byng, Morillo, Cole, Campbell, and Picton would be exposed to the attack of double their own numbers; and however firm and able those generals might be, they could not, when thus suddenly brought together, be expected to seize the whole system of operations and act with that nicety of judgment which the occasion demanded.   It was clear therefore that Hill must be in some measure paralyzed at first, and finally be thrown, together with the sixth, seventh, and light divisions, upon an external line of operations while the French moved upon internal lines.

On the other hand, Byng, Morillo, Campbell, Cole, Picton and Hill were only pieces of resistance on Wellington's board; the sixth, seventh, and light divisions were those with which he meant to win his game.   There was however a great difference in their value.   The light division and the seventh, especially the former, being furthest from Pampeluna, having enemies close in front and points to guard, were, the seventh a day the light division two days behind the sixth division, which was free, and, the drag of D'Erlon's corps considered, a day nearer to Pampeluna than Hill. Upon the rapid handling of this well-placed body the fate of the allies therefore depended; if it arrived in time, thirty thousand infantry with sufficient cavalry and artillery would be established under the immediate command of Wellington, on a position of strength, checking the enemy until the rest of the army arrived. Where that position was and how the troops were gathered and there fought shall now be shown.

CHAPTER V.

BATTLES OF THE PYRENEES.

Combat of Roncevalles.—On the 23rd, Soult issued an order of the day remarkable for its force and frankness. Tracing with a rapid pen the leading events of the past campaign, he said the disasters had sprung from the incapacity of the king, not from the weakness of the soldiers, whose military virtue he justly extolled, inflaming their haughty courage by allusions to former glories. This address has been by writers, who disgrace English literature with unfounded aspersions of a courageous enemy, treated as unseemly boasting as to his intended operations; but the calumny is refuted by the following passage from his despatch to the minister at war. '*I shall move directly upon Pampeluna; if I succeed in relieving it I will operate towards my right, to embarrass the enemy's troops in Guipuscoa, Biscay, and Alava; and to enable the reserve to join me, which will relieve St. Sebastian and Santona. If this should happen I will then consider what is to be done, either to push my own attack or to help the army of Aragon, but to look so far ahead would now be temerity.*' Here he puts every point hypothetically, and though conscious of superior abilities he did not suppress the sentiment of his own worth as a commander and was too proud to depreciate brave adversaries on the eve of battle. '*Let us not,*' he said, '*defraud the enemy of the praise which is due to him. The dispositions of the general have been prompt skilful and consecutive; the valour and steadiness of his troops have been praiseworthy.*' Having thus stimulated the ardour of his troops he put himself at the head of Clausel's divisions at daylight the 25th, and led them up against the rocks of Altobiscar.

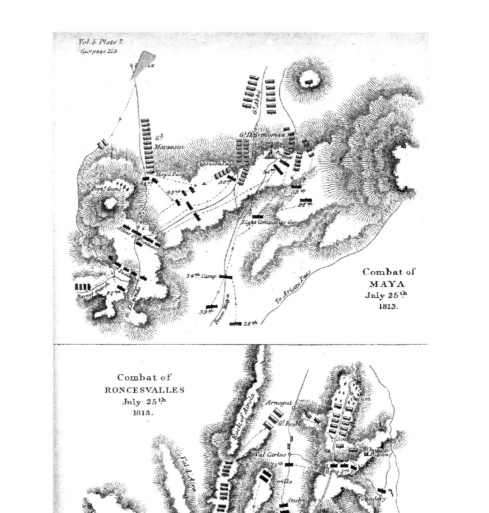

Vol. 5 Plate 7.
face page 243.

G.l Abby

Mananin

G.l D'Armagnac

Maya Pss

Port Guns

Light Company Camp

34th Camp

To Arietta Pss

Barret Church

Combat of
MAYA
July 25th
1813.

Combat of
RONCESVALLES
July 25th
1813.

Rock of Lindua

Arnegui

G.l Foyle

Val d'Aira

Val Carlos

Foundery

Campbel in res

G.l Ross

Lindua

Mendichuri Pass

Ibaneta

Orbaceita

Ansona Valley

Roncesvall

Espinal

Byng, warned the evening before that danger was near and jealous of some hostile indications towards the village of Val Carlos, had sent the fifty-seventh regiment down there, and gave notice to Cole who had meanwhile made new dispositions. Ross's brigade was now at Espinal, two miles in advance of Viscayret, six miles from the pass of Ibañeta, eleven from Byng's position, and somewhat nearer to Morillo: Anson's brigade was close behind Ross, Stubbs' Portuguese behind Anson, and the artillery was at Linzoain. In this state of affairs Soult, throwing out a multitude of skirmishers and pushing forward his supporting columns and guns as fast as the steepness of the road and difficult nature of the ground would permit, endeavoured to force Byng's position; but the latter fought strongly, the French fell fast among the rocks, and their rolling musketry pealed in vain for hours along that cloudy field of battle, elevated five thousand feet above the plains. Their numbers however continually increased in front, and the national guards from Yropil, reinforced by Clausel's detachments, skirmished with the Spanish battalions at the foundry of Orbaiceta and threatened to turn the right: Val Carlos was at the same time menaced from Arnegui, and Reille, ascending the rock of Airola, turned Morillo's left.

About mid-day Cole arrived at Altobiscar, yet his troops were still distant and the French neglected the Val Carlos to gather more thickly on Byng's front; he indeed resisted their efforts, but Reille made progress along the summit of the Airola ridge and Morillo fell back towards Ibañeta. Reille was then nearer to that pass than Byng was, when Ross's brigade, coming up the pass of Mendichuri, suddenly appeared on the Lindouz just as the French were closing up Atalosti and cutting the communication with Campbell. That officer's piquets had been attacked early in the morning by the national guards of Val de Baygorry, but he soon discovered it was only a feint and therefore moved by his right towards Atalosti when he heard the firing on that side. His march was secured by the Val d'Ayra, which separated him from the ridge of Airola along which Reille was advancing; but noting that general's strength, and seeing Ross's brigade labouring up the steeps of Mendichuri, he judged it ignorant of what was going on above. Wherefore sending advice of the enemy's proximity and strength to Cole, he offered to pass the Atalosti and join in the battle if he could be furnished with transport for his sick, and provisions on the new line of operations. But ere this reached Cole, the head of Ross's column, composed of a wing of the twentieth and a company of Brunswickers, was on the summit of the Lindouz, where most unexpectedly it encountered Reille's advanced guard. Ross, an eager hardy soldier, called aloud to charge, and captain Tovey of the twentieth running forward with his company, crossed a slight wooded hollow and full against the front of the sixth French light infantry dashed with the bayonet. Brave men fell on both sides, but numbers prevailing, these daring soldiers were pushed back again by the French. Ross however gained his object, the remainder of his brigade had come up and the pass of Atalosti was secured, yet with a loss of one hundred and forty of the twentieth and forty-one Brunswickers.

Appendix 16.

Previous to this vigorous action, Cole, seeing the French in Val Carlos and the valley of Orbaiceta, on both flanks of Byng whose front was not the less pressed, had ordered Anson to reinforce the Spaniards at the foundry, and Stubbs to enter Val Carlos in support of the fifty-seventh. He now recalled Anson to assist in defence of Lindouz, and then learning from Campbell how strong Reille was, caused Byng, with a view to a final retreat, to relinquish his advanced position at Altobiscar and take a second nearer Ibañeta. This movement uncovered the road leading down to the foundry of Orbaiceta, but it concentrated all the troops; and at the same time Campbell, although he could not enter the line of battle because Cole was unable to supply his demands, by a very skilful display of his Portuguese induced Reille to think their numbers considerable.

During these movements the skirmishing of the light troops continued; yet a thick fog coming up the valley prevented Soult from making dispositions for a general attack with his six divisions; and when night fell Cole still held the great chain of the mountains, having had only three hundred and eighty

men killed and wounded. His right was however turned by
Orbaiceta, he had but ten or eleven thousand bayonets to
oppose to thirty thousand, and his line of retreat, being for
four or five miles down hill and flanked all the way by the
Lindouz, was uneasy and unfavourable. Wherefore putting
the troops silently in march after dark he threaded the passes
and gained the valley of Urros. Anson's brigade followed as
a rear-guard in the morning, Campbell retired from the
Alduides by the pass of Urtiaga to Eugui in the valley of
Zubiri, the Spanish battalion retreated from Orbaiceta by the
narrow way of Navala and rejoined Morillo near Espinal. The
Magistral ridge was thus abandoned, yet the general result
was unsatisfactory to Soult; he acknowledged a loss of four
hundred men, he had not gained ten miles, and the distance
to Pampeluna was not less than twenty-two with strong
defensive positions in the way: and there increasing numbers
of intrepid enemies were to be expected.

His combinations, contrived for greater success, had been
thwarted partly by fortune, partly by errors of execution
which all generals expect, and the experienced are most
resigned as knowing them to be inevitable. Fortune was felt
in the fog, which rose before he could thrust forward his
heavy masses of troops entire. The failure in execution was
Reille's tardy movement; his orders were to gain with all
expedition the Lindouz, which tied together the heads of the
Alduides, Carlos, Roncevalles, and Urros valleys. There he
would have commanded the Mendichuri, Atalosti, Ibañeta
and Sahorgain passes; and by moving along the Magistral
crest could menace the Urtiaga, Renacabal, and Bellate passes,
endangering Campbell's and Hill's lines of retreat. Pellot's Cam-
But when he should have ascended the Airola he pagnes des
halted to incorporate two newly arrived conscript Pyrennées.
battalions and to issue provisions; the hours thus lost
would have sufficed to seize the Lindouz before Ross had got
through the Mendichuri. The fog would still have stopped
the spread of Soult's columns to the extent designed; but
fifteen or sixteen thousand men placed on the flank and rear
of Byng and Morillo, would have separated them from the
fourth division and forced the latter to retreat beyond

Soult's secret
Despatch,
MSS.

Viscayret. Soult thought two British divisions, besides Byng's brigade and Morillo's Spaniards, were opposed to him; he was probably misled by wounded men hastily questioned; who would declare they were of the second and fourth divisions because Byng's brigade belonged to the former; but there were, including the fourth division, only eleven thousand bayonets in the fight.

On the 26th Clausel followed Cole, and Reille was directed to move along the Magistral crest and seize the passes in Hill's rear; who would be thus crushed between him and D'Erlon, or thrown on the side of San Estevan. D'Erlon could then reach the valley of Zubiri, and Reille descending that of Lanz would prevent Picton joining Cole. This would compel those generals to retreat on separate lines, and the whole French army could issue in order of battle from the mouths of the valleys on Pampeluna. All the French columns were in movement at daybreak, but every hour brought its obstacle. The mist still hung heavily on the mountain-tops and bewildered Reille's guides, who refused to lead him along the crests; hence at ten o'clock, having no other resource, he moved down the pass of Mendichuri upon Espinal, and fell into the rear of the cavalry and artillery which followed Clausel's divisions. Soult, although retarded also by the fog and the difficulties of the ground, overtook Cole's rear-guard in front of Viscayret; and his leading troops struck hotly on some British light companies incorporated under colonel Wilson of the forty-eighth. One French squadron passing the flank fell on the rear, but Wilson faced about and beat it off, without ceasing to fight the infantry; and thus skirmishing Cole reached the heights of Linzoain one mile beyond Viscayret. There Picton came up without troops, but brought intelligence that Campbell was at Eugui, and the third division at Zubiri, having come over the ridge from Olague. The junction of all these troops was now secure, the loss of the day was less than two hundred, and nothing had been left behind. However the French continued together in front, and at four o'clock seized some heights on Cole's left; whereupon, retiring to the ridge separating the valley of Urroz from that of Zubiri he offered battle.

Disquieted by intelligence from D'Erlon, by Reille's failure, and by Campbell, who in coming from Eugui made a distant display of his Portuguese on the same ridge, Soult put off his attack until next morning, and in the night a junction of all the allies was effected. This was a great failure on the French side; Cole was unsupported for five hours, his troops had been incessantly marching and fighting for two days and a night; and every action, by augmenting the wounded and causing confusion in the rear would have increased the difficulty of retreat. Reille's false march had marred the primary combinations, the evening reports said D'Erlon had also gone wrong, and it was therefore evident that by rough fighting only could the main object be attained. Soult felt his error, and it is said his language indicated a secret anticipation of failure; he was yet too steadfast to yield, and next morning resumed his march, having renewed his orders to D'Erlon, whose operations must now be noticed.

La Pene, Campagne 1813, 1814.

That general had three divisions of infantry, furnishing eighteen thousand combatants. On the morning of the 25th he assembled two of them behind some heights near the passes of Maya, having caused the national guards of Baygorry to make previous demonstrations towards the lateral passes of Arriette, Yspeguy, and Lorietta. The disposition of Hill's force had not been changed; but Stewart, deceived by the movements of the national guards, looked towards Silveira's post on the right rather than his own front, and his division was not well posted or prepared. The ground to be defended was very strong; yet however rugged a mountain position may be, if it is too extensive and the troops are not disposed with judgment, the inequalities constituting its defensive strength favour an assailant.

There were three passes to defend. Aretesque on the right, Lessessa in the centre, Maya on the left. From these passes two roads led to Elisondo in parallel directions; one down the valley through the town of Maya, receiving in its course the Erazu road; the other along the Atchiola mountain. Pringle's brigade was charged to defend the Aretesque, and Cameron's brigade the Maya and Lessessa passes. The Col or neck, broad on the summit, was three miles wide, and on each flank

lofty rocks and ridges rose one above another; those on the
right blending with the Goramendi mountains; those on the
left with the Atchiola, near the summit of which the eighty-
second regiment belonging to the seventh division was
posted.

Cameron's brigade, encamped on the left, had a clear view
of troops coming from Urdax; but at Aretesque a great round
hill one mile in front masked the movements of an enemy
coming from Espelette. This hill was not occupied at night,
and in the daytime only by some Portuguese cavalry videttes.
The nearest guard was a piquet of eighty men, posted on the
front slope of the Col and with no immediate support; but
four light companies were encamped a mile down the reverse
slope, which was more rugged and difficult than that towards
the enemy. The rest of Pringle's brigade was disposed at
various distances from two to three miles in the rear; and the
signal for assembling on the position was to be the fire of
four Portuguese guns from the rocks above the Maya pass.
Thus, of six British regiments, furnishing more than three
thousand fighting men, half only were in line of battle and
chiefly massed on the left of a position, wide open and of an
easy ascent from the Aretesque side: they were ill-posted,
and their general, Stewart, deceived as to the real state of
affairs, was at Elisondo when the attack commenced.

COMBAT OF MAYA.
[Plan 7, page 213.]

Captain Moyle Sherer, commanding the piquet at the
Aretesque pass, was told by his predecessor that at dawn a
glimpse had been obtained of cavalry and infantry in movement along the hills in front: some peasants also announced
the approach of the French. At nine o'clock major Thorne,
a staff-officer, having patrolled round the great hill in front of
the pass discovered enough to make him order up the light
companies in support of the piquet; and they had just formed
on the neck, with their left at the rock of Aretesque, when
D'Armagnac's division coming from Espelette mounted the
great hill in front. Abbé followed, and Maransin with a third
division advanced from Ainhoa and Urdax against the Maya

pass, designing also to turn it by a narrow way leading up the Atchiola mountain. D'Armagnac's men pushing forward in several columns forced the piquet back with great loss upon the light companies, who sustained his vehement assault with infinite difficulty. The alarm guns were then heard from the Maya pass, and Pringle hastened to the front; but his regiments moving hurriedly from different camps were necessarily brought into action one after the other. The thirty-fourth came up first at a running pace, by companies, not in mass, and breathless from the length and ruggedness of the ascent; the thirty-ninth and twenty-eighth followed, yet not immediately nor together; and meanwhile D'Armagnac, closely supported by Abbé, with domineering numbers and valour combined, maugre the desperate fighting of the piquet of the light companies and of the thirty-fourth, had established his columns on the broad summit of the position.

Cameron sent the fiftieth from the left to the assistance of the over-matched troops, and that fierce and formidable old regiment charging the head of an advancing column drove it clear out of the pass of Lessessa in the centre. But the French were so many, that checked at one point they assembled with increased force at another; nor could Pringle restore the battle with the thirty-ninth and twenty-eighth regiments; they were cut off from the others, and though fighting desperately, forced back to a second and lower ridge crossing the main road to Elizondo. D'Armagnac followed them, but Abbé continued to press the fiftieth and thirty-fourth, whose natural line of retreat was towards the Atchiola road on the left, because the position trended backward from Aretesque towards that point and because Cameron's brigade was there. That officer, still holding the pass of Maya with the left wings of the seventy-first and ninety-second, then brought their right wings and the Portuguese guns into action, and thus maintained the fight; but so dreadful was the slaughter, especially of the ninety-second, that it is said the advancing enemy was actually stopped by the heaped mass of dead and dying; and then the left wing of that   Appendix 16. noble regiment, coming down from the higher ground, smote wounded friends and exulting foes alike, as mingled together they stood or crawled before its wasting fire.

It was in this state of affairs that general Stewart reached the field of battle. Lessessa and Aretesque were lost, Maya was still held by the left wing of the seventy-first; but seeing Maransin's men gathered on one side and Abbé's on the other he abandoned it to take a position on a rocky ridge covering the lateral road over Atchiola; then he called down the eighty-second from the summit of that mountain, and sent for aid to the seventh division. He was wounded, yet fought stoutly for he was a gallant man; but during this retrograde move-ment Maransin suddenly thrust the head of his division across the front of the British line and connected his left with Abbé, throwing as he passed a destructive fire into the wasted remnant of the ninety-second, which even then gave way but sullenly, for the men fell until two-thirds of the whole had gone to the ground. Still the survivors fought and the left wing of the seventy-first coming from Maya also entered into action, yet finally, one after the other, all the regiments were forced back, the first position was lost and the Portuguese guns were taken.

Abbé then followed D'Armagnac, leaving Maransin to deal with Stewart, who was pushed back, notwithstanding the strength of his new position until six o'clock, when the remnant of his force was in default of ammunition compelled to defend the highest crags with stones: he was just going to abandon the mountain when a brigade of the seventh division led by general Barnes arrived from Echallar, and charging, drove the French back to the Col de Maya. Stewart thus remained master of Atchiola, and D'Erlon, probably think-ing greater reinforcements had come up, recalled D'Armagnac and Abbé and concentrated his forces: he had lost fifteen hundred men and a general, but had taken four guns and killed or wounded fourteen hundred British soldiers.

French official Report, MSS.

British official Return.

This disastrous fight of Maya was exaggerated by French writers, and has been by an English author mis-represented as a surprise caused by the negligence of the cavalry. Stewart was surprised, his troops were not;

Southey.

and never did soldiers fight better, seldom so well; the stern valour of the ninety-second would have graced Thermopylæ. The Portuguese cavalry patroles, if any went out, which is uncertain, might have neglected their duty, and doubtless the front should have been scoured in a more military manner; but the infantry piquets and the light companies so happily ordered up by Thorne were ready; and no man wondered to see the French columns crown the great hill in front of the pass. Stewart, expecting no attack at Maya, had gone to Elisondo, leaving orders for the soldiers to cook; from his erroneous views therefore the misfortune sprung and from no other source. Having de- General Stewart's Report. ceived himself as to the point of attack he did not take military precautions; his position was only half occupied, his troops were brought into action wildly, and he caused the loss of his guns by a misdirection as to the road. He was a brave, energetic, zealous, indefatigable man, and of a magnanimous spirit; but he possessed neither the calm reflective judgment nor the intuitive genius which belongs to nature's generals.

It is difficult to understand why count D'Erlon, when he had carried the right of the position, followed two weak regiments with two divisions; leaving only one division to attack five regiments posted on the strongest ground and having hopes of succour from Echallar? Certainly if Abbé had acted with Maransin, Stewart, so hardly pressed by the latter alone, must have passed the Echallar road in retreat before Barnes's brigade arrived. Soult had directed D'Erlon to operate by his left to connect the whole army on the summit of the great chain of the Pyrenees; Soult's Despatch, MSS. he should therefore have used his whole force to crush the troops on the Atchiola before they could be succoured from Echallar,—or, leaving Maransin there, have marched by the Maya road upon Ariscun to cut Silveira's line of retreat—he remained upon the Col de Maya for twenty hours after the battle! and Hill meanwhile concentrated his whole force, now augmented by Barnes' brigade, and would have fallen upon him from the rocks of Atchiola next day, if intelligence of Cole's retreat had not come through the Alduides. This rendered the recovery of the Col de Maya useless, and Hill, withdrawing his troops during the night, posted the British brigades which had been engaged, together with one Portuguese brigade of infantry and a battery on the heights in rear of Irueta, fifteen miles from the scene of action; the other Portuguese brigade remained in front of Elizondo, and thus he covered the road of San Estevan on his left, that of Berderez on his right, and the pass of Vellate in his rear. Such was the commencement of Soult's operations to restore the fortunes of France. Three considerable actions fought on the same day had each been favourable. At St. Sebastian the allies were repulsed; at Roncevalles they abandoned the passes; at Maya they were defeated; but the decisive blow had not yet been struck.

Wellington heard of the fight at Maya on his way back from St. Sebastian after the assault, with the false addition that D'Erlon was beaten. As early as the 22nd he knew Soult was preparing a great offensive movement; yet the immoveable attitude of the French centre, the skilful disposition of their reserve, twice as strong as he at first supposed, together with the preparations made to throw bridges over the Bidassoa at Biriatou, were all calculated to mislead and did mislead him. Soult's complicated combinations to bring D'Erlon's divisions finally into line on the crest of the great chain were also impenetrable; the English general could not believe his adversary would throw himself with only thirty thousand men into the valley of the Ebro, unless sure of aid from Suchet; but that general's movements indicated a determination to remain in Catalonia. Soult thought Pampeluna in extremity and knew Sebastian was not so; Wellington knew Pampeluna was not in extremity, and previous to the assault thought Sebastian was; hence the operations against his right, their full scope not known, appeared a feint, and he judged the real effort would be to throw bridges over the Bidassoa and raise the siege of San Sebastian. In the night correct intelligence of the Maya and Roncevalles affairs arrived. Soult's project was then developed, and Graham was ordered to turn the siege into a blockade, to embark his guns and stores, and be ready to join Giron on a position of battle marked out near the Bidassoa. Cotton was ordered to move the cavalry up to Pampeluna, O'Donnel was to hold his Spanish troops in readiness, and Wellington having arranged fresh lines of correspondence proceeded to Estevan.

While the embarkation of the guns and stores was going on it was essential to hold the posts at Vera and Echallar; D'Erlon's object was not then pronounced; and once in possession of those places he could approach San Sebastian by the roads leading over the Pena de Haya, a rocky mountain behind Lesaca; or by the defiles of Zubietta and Goyzueta leading round that mountain from the valley of Lerins. Wherefore in passing through Estevan on the morning of the 26th, Wellington directed Pack to guard the bridges over the Bidassoa; but when he reached Irueta, saw the state of Stewart's division and heard that Picton had marched from Olague, he directed all the troops within his reach upon Pampeluna, indicating the valley of Lanz as the general line of movement. Of Picton's position and intentions nothing positive was known; but Wellington, supposing him to have joined Cole at Linzoain as indeed he had, judged their combined forces would be sufficient Manuscript Notes by the Duke of Wellington. to check Soult until assistance came from the centre or from Pampeluna, and he so advised Picton the evening of the 26th.

In consequence of these orders the seventh division abandoned Echallar in the night of the 26th, and the sixth division quitted San Estevan at daylight the 27th. Hill halted on the heights of Irueta until the evening of the 27th, but marched during the night through the pass of Vellate upon the town of Lanz. The light division, quitting Vera also on the 27th, retired by Lesaca to the summit of the Santa Cruz mountain, overlooking the valley of Lerins; there it halted to cover the pass of Zubieta until Longa's Spaniards blocked the roads leading over the Pena de Haya to protect the embarkation of the guns on that flank. That object effected, the division was to thread the passes, reach Lecumberri on the great road of Irurzun, and so connect Graham with the army round Pampeluna; for Wellington designed, if unable to cover that fortress, to throw his army back upon its left on a new line covering the approaches to San Sebastian. These movements sprerd fear and confusion far and wide. All the narrow valleys and roads

were crowded with baggage, commissariat stores, artillery and
fugitive families; and reports of the most alarming nature were
as usual rife; each division, ignorant of what had really happened to the other, dreaded that some of the numerous misfortunes related might be true; none knew what to expect or
where they were to meet the enemy, and one universal hubbub
filled the wild regions through which the French army was
now working its fiery path towards Pampeluna.

D'Erlon's inactivity gave great uneasiness to Soult, who
repeated the order to push forward by his left whatever might
be the force opposed, and thus stimulated, he advanced to
Elizondo on the 27th; but thinking the sixth division was
still at San Estevan, again halted. Next day, when Hill
retreated, he followed through the pass of Vellate, and his
further progress belongs to other combinations.

Picton having assumed command in the Val Zubiri the
26th, retired before dawn the 27th and without the hope or
intention of covering Pampeluna. Soult followed in the
morning, having first sent scouts towards the ridges where
Campbell's troops had appeared the evening before. Reille
marched by the left bank of the Guy river, Clausel by the
right bank, the cavalry and artillery closed the rear, the whole
in compact order: the narrow valley was thus gorged with
troops, a hasty bicker of musketry alone marking the separa-
tion of the hostile forces. The garrison of Pampeluna made
a sally, and O'Donnel in great alarm spiked some of his guns,
destroyed his magazines, and would have suffered a disaster
if Carlos d'España had not fortunately arrived at the moment
and checked the garrison. Great now was the danger. Cole,
first emerging from the valley of Zubiri, had passed Villalba,
three miles from Pampeluna, in retreat; Picton
Plan 6,
page 199. was at Huarte, and O'Donnel's Spaniards were in
confusion; in fine Soult was all but successful when
Picton suddenly turned on some steep ridges, which, under
the names of San Miguel, Mont Escava and San Christoval,
crossed the mouths of the Zubiri and Lanz valleys and
screened Pampeluna.

Posting his own division on the right of Huarte, he prolonged his line to the left with Morillo's Spaniards, called

upon O'Donnel to support him, and directed Cole to occupy
some heights between Oricain and Arletta.   But that general
having with a surer eye observed a salient hill near Zabaldica,
one mile in advance and commanding the road to Huarte,
demanded and obtained permission to occupy it instead of
the heights first appointed.   Two Spanish regiments of the
blockading troops were still there, and towards them Cole
directed his course.   Soult had also marked this hill.   A detachment issuing from the mouth of the Val de Zubiri was in
full career to seize it, and the hostile masses were rapidly
approaching the summit on either side when the Spaniards,
seeing the British so close, vindicated their own post by a
sudden charge.   This was for Soult the stroke of fate.   His
double columns, just then emerging exultant from the narrow
valley, were suddenly stopped by ten thousand men under
Cole, who crowned the summit of the mountain in his front;
and two miles further back stood Picton with a greater
number, for O'Donnel had now taken post on Morillo's left.
To advance by Villalba and Huarte was impossible, to stand
still was dangerous; the army, contracted to a span in front
and cleft in its whole length by the river Guy, was compressed
on each side by the mountains, which in that part narrowed
the valley to a quarter of a mile.   It was a moment of difficulty, but Soult, like a great and ready commander, instantly
shot the head of Clausel's columns to his right across the
ridge separating the Val de Zubiri from the Val de Lanz;
and at the same time threw one of Reille's divi-   Soult's Cor-
sions of infantry and a body of cavalry across the   respondence,
mountains on his left, beyond the Guy river, as   MSS.
far as the village of Elcano, to menace Picton's right at
Huarte.   His remaining divisions were established at Zabaldica in the Val de Zubiri, close under Cole's right, and Clausel
seized Sauroren close under that general's left.

   While Soult was thus forming his line of battle, Wellington,
who had quitted Hill's quarters in the Bastan early on the
27th, was descending the valley of Lanz, unable
to learn anything of Picton's movements or posi-   Wellington,
tion; and in this state of uncertainty he reached   MSS.
Ostiz a few miles from Sauroren, where he found Long with

the light cavalry which had furnished the posts of correspondence in the mountains. There learning that Picton had abandoned Linzoain and was moving on Huarte, he left his quarter-master-general with instructions to stop all the troops coming down the valley of Lanz until the state of affairs at Huarte should be ascertained. But at racing speed he made for Sauroren himself, and entering that village saw Clausel coming along the crest of the mountain, and knew the allied troops in the valley of Lanz were intercepted. Pulling up his horse he wrote on the parapet of the bridge of Sauroren fresh instructions to turn everything from that valley on to a road which, through Lizasso and Marcalain, led behind the hills to Oricain in rear of Cole's position: lord Fitzroy Somerset, the only staff-officer who had kept up with him, galloped with these orders out of Sauroren by one road, the French light cavalry dashed in by another, and the English general rode alone up the mountain to reach his troops. One of Campbell's Portuguese battalions first descried him and raised a joyful cry; then the shrill clamour, caught up by the next regiments, soon swelled as it run along the line into that stern appalling shout which the British soldier is wont to give upon the edge of battle, and which no enemy ever heard unmoved. Suddenly he stopped at a conspicuous point, for he desired both armies should know he was there, and a double spy who was present pointed out Soult, who was so near that his features could be distinguished. Attentively Wellington fixed his eyes upon that formidable man, and as if speaking to himself said, ' *Yonder is a great commander, but he is cautious, and will delay his attack to ascertain the cause of these cheers; that will give time for the sixth division to arrive and I shall beat him.*' And the French general made no serious attack that day!

Cole's position was the foremost ridge of a mass of mountains filling the space between the Guy and the Lanz rivers, as far back as Huarte and Villalba. Highest in the centre, it was boldly defined towards the enemy; but the trace was irregular, the right being thrown back towards the village of Arletta so as to flank the road to Huarte; which was also swept by some guns placed on a lower range, connecting the right of Cole with Picton and Morillo. Overlooking Zabaldica and the Guy, was the bulging hill vindicated by the Spaniards; it was on the right of the fourth division and distinct, but connected with the centre of the range and considerably lower. The left of the position was extremely rugged and steep, overlooking the Lanz river and the road to Villalba. Ross's brigade of the fourth division was posted on that side, having in front a Portuguese battalion whose flank rested on a small chapel. Campbell was on the right of Ross. Anson was on the highest ground, partly behind and partly on the right of Campbell. Byng was on a second mass of hills in reserve, and the Spanish hill was reinforced by a battalion of the fourth Portuguese regiment.

This front of battle being less than two miles was well filled. The Lanz and Guy torrents washed the flanks, and two miles further down broke through the crossing ridges of San Miguel and Christoval to meet behind them and form the Arga river; on the ridges thus cleft Picton's line was formed, nearly parallel to Cole's but on a more extended front. His left was at Huarte, his right strengthened with a battery, stretched to the village of Goraitz, covering more than a mile of ground on that flank; Morillo prolonged his left along the crest of San Miguel to Villalba, and O'Donnel continued the line to San Christoval. Carlos d'España's division maintained the blockade, and the British cavalry under Cotton, coming up from Tafalla and Olite, took post, the heavy brigades on some open ground behind Picton, the hussar brigade on his right: this second line entirely barred the openings of the two valleys leading down to Pampeluna.

Soult's position was also a mountain filling the space between the two rivers. It was even more rugged than the allies' mountain, and they were only separated by a narrow valley. Clausel's three divisions leaned to the right on the village of Sauroren, which was down in the valley of Lanz, close under the chapel height where the left of the fourth division was posted. His left was prolonged by two of Reille's divisions, who also occupied the village of Zabaldica in the valley of Zubiri under the right of the allies. The remaining division of this wing and a division of cavalry were, as before stated, thrown forward on the mountains at the other side of the Guy river, menacing Picton, and seeking for an opportunity to communicate with the garrison of Pampeluna. Some guns were pushed in front of Zabaldica, but the elevation required to send the shot upward rendered their fire ineffectual, and the greatest part of the artillery remained therefore in the narrow Val de Zubiri.

Combat of the 27th.—Soult's first effort was to gain the Spaniards' hill and establish himself near the centre of the allies' line of battle; this attack though vigorous had been valiantly repulsed about the time Wellington arrived, and he immediately reinforced the post with the fortieth British regiment. There was then a general skirmish along the front, under cover of which Soult carefully examined the whole position, and the firing continued on the mountain side until evening; then a terrible storm, the usual precursor of English battles in the Peninsula, brought on premature darkness and terminated the dispute. This also was the state of affairs at daybreak on the 28th, but a signal alteration took place before the great battle of that day commenced, and the movements of the wandering divisions by which this change was effected must be traced.

The Lanz covered the left of the allies and the right of the French; but the heights occupied by either army were prolonged beyond that river, the continuation of the allies' ridge sweeping forward so as to look into the rear of Sauroren; the continuation of the French heights retiring more abruptly than the forward inclination of the opposing ridge. They were both steep and high, yet lower and less rugged than the heights on which the armies stood opposed; for there rocks piled on rocks stood out like castles, difficult to approach, and so dangerous to assail that the hardened veterans of the Peninsula only would have dared the trial. Now the road by which the sixth division moved on the 27th, after threading the Doña Maria pass, sent one branch to Lanz, another by Letassa to Ostiz, a third by Lizasso to Marcalain where many ways met. The first and second fell into the road which from the Bellate pass descends the Lanz valley to Sauroren; the third, passing behind the prolongation of the hostile positions, also fell into the valley of Lanz, but near Oricain one mile behind Cole's left.

It was by Marcalain Wellington expected the sixth and seventh divisions, but the rapidity with which Soult seized Sauroren caused a delay of eighteen hours. For the sixth division, having reached Olague in the valley of Lanz at one o'clock on the 27th, halted there until four, and then, following the orders brought by lord Fitzroy Somerset, marched by Lizasso to gain the Marcalain road; but the great length of these mountain marches, and the heavy storm which terminated the action at Zabaldica, sweeping with equal violence in this direction prevented the troops from passing Lizasso that night. The march was renewed at daylight, and meanwhile Hill reached the town of Lanz, where he rallied Long's cavalry and his own artillery and moved likewise upon Lizasso. At that place he met the seventh division coming from San Estevan, and having restored Barnes's brigade to lord Dalhousie took a position on a ridge covering the road to Marcalain. The seventh division being on his right was then in military communication with the sixth division, and thus Wellington's left covered the great road leading from Pampeluna by Irurzun to Tolosa. These important movements, which were not completed until the evening of the 28th, brought six thousand men into the allies' line of battle, and fifteen thousand more into military communication with their left: yet D'Erlon remained planted in his position of observation near Elizondo without a movement!

Wellington considering the nearness of the sixth division, and the certainty of Hill's junction, imagined Soult would not venture an attack; and truly that marshal, disquieted about D'Erlon of whom he only knew that he had not followed his instructions, viewed the strong position of his adversary with uneasy anticipations. Again with anxious eyes he took cognizance of all its rugged strength, and seemed dubious and distrustful of his fortune. He could not operate with advantage by his own left beyond the Guy river, because the mountains there were too rough, and Wellington having shorter lines of movement could meet him with all arms combined; the French artillery also unable to emerge from the Val de Zubiri, would have been exposed to a counter attack. He crossed the Lanz river and ascended the prolongation of the allies' ridge, which, as he had possession of the bridge of Sauroren, was for the moment his own ground. From thence he could see the left and rear of Cole's position, and down the valley as far as Villalba; but the country beyond the ridge towards Marcalain was too broken to discern the march of the sixth division. He

Soult, MSS.

knew however from the deserters that Wellington expected four fresh divisions from that side, that is to say, the second, sixth, and seventh British, and Silveira's Portuguese division, which always marched with Hill. This knowledge and the nature of the ground determined his attack. The valley of Lanz, growing wider as it descended, offered the means of assailing the allies' left in front and rear at one moment; and the same combination would cut off the reinforcements expected from the side of Marcalain. One of Clausel's divisions occupied Sauroren, the other two were on each side of that village; that on the right hand was ordered to throw flankers on the ridge from whence Soult was taking his observations, to move in one body to a convenient distance down the valley, and then, wheeling to its left, assail the rear of the allies' left flank while the other two divisions assailed his front. Cole's left, which did not exceed five thousand men, would thus be enveloped by sixteen thousand, and Soult expected to crush it notwithstanding the strength of the ground. Reille's two divisions advancing on the side of Zabaldica, were each to send a brigade against the Spanish hill now occupied by the fortieth regiment; the right of this attack was to be connected with the left of Clausel; the remaining brigades were closely to support the assailing masses; the divisions beyond the Guy were to keep Picton in check; and Soult, having no time to lose, ordered his lieutenants to throw their troops at once into action.

First battle of Sauroren.—It was fought on the fourth anniversary of the battle of Talavera.

About mid-day the French gathered at the foot of the position, and their skirmishers spread over the face of the mountain working upward like a conflagration: but the columns of attack were not all prepared when Clausel's division, too impatient to await the general signal of battle, threw out its flankers on the ridge beyond the river and pushed down the valley of Lanz in one mass. With a rapid pace it turned Cole's left, and was preparing to wheel up on his rear, when a Portuguese brigade of the sixth division, suddenly appearing on the ridge beyond the river, drove the French flankers back and instantly descended with a rattling fire upon the right and rear of the column in the valley. Nearly at the same instant the main body of the sixth division, emerging from behind the same ridge near the village of Oricain, formed in order of battle across the front. It was the counter-stroke of Salamanca! The French while striving to encompass the left of the allies were themselves encompassed; for two brigades of the fourth division turned and smote them on their left, the Portuguese smote them on their right; and while thus scathed on both flanks with fire they were violently shocked and pushed back with a mighty force by the sixth division—not in flight however, but fighting fiercely and strewing the ground with their enemies' bodies as well as with their own.

Clausel's second division, seeing this dire conflict, with a hurried movement assailed the chapel height to draw off the fire from the troops in the valley, and gallantly did the French soldiers throng up the craggy steep; but the general unity of the attack was ruined; neither their third division nor Reille's brigades had yet received the signal, and the attacks which should have been simultaneous were made in succession, running from right to left as the necessity of giving aid became apparent. It was however a terrible battle and well fought. One column darting out of the village of Sauroren, silently, sternly, without firing a shot, worked up to the chapel under a tempest of bullets, which swept away whole ranks without abating the speed and power of the mass. The seventh caçadores shrunk abashed and that part of the position was won; but soon they rallied on Ross's brigade, and the whole mass charging the French with a loud shout dashed them down the hill. Heavily stricken they were, yet undismayed, for re-forming below they again ascended to be again broken and cast down. But the other columns of attack were now bearing upwards through the smoke and flame with which the skirmishers had covered the face of the mountain, and the tenth Portuguese regiment, fighting on the right of Ross's brigade yielded to their fury. Thus a column crowned the heights and wheeling against the exposed flank of Ross forced that gallant officer also to go back, and his ground was instantly occupied by those with whom he had been engaged in front. The fight then raged close and desperate on the crest of the position, charge succeeded charge, and each side yielded and rallied by turns; yet this astounding effort of French valour availed not. Wellington brought Byng's brigade forward at a running pace, and sent the twenty-seventh and forty-eighth British, of Anson's brigade, from the higher ground in the centre against the crowded masses, rolling them backward in disorder, and throwing them one after the other violently down the mountain side; and with no child's play, for the two British regiments fell upon the enemy three separate times with the bayonet, and lost more than half their own numbers.

During this battle on the mountain-top, the British brigades of the sixth division, strengthened by a battery of guns, gained ground in the valley of Lanz and arrived on the same front with the left of the victorious troops about the chapel. Wellington, seeing the momentary disorder of the enemy, then ordered Madden's Portuguese brigade, which had never ceased its fire against the right flank of the French column, to assail the village of Sauroren in the rear; but the state of the action in other parts and the exhaustion of the troops soon induced him to countermand this movement. Meanwhile Reille's brigades, connecting their right with the left of Clausel's third division, had environed the Spanish hill, had ascended it unchecked, and at the moment the fourth division was so hardly pressed made the regiment of El Pravia give way on the left of the fortieth. A Portuguese battalion rushing forward covered the flank of that invincible regiment, which waited in stern silence until the French set their feet upon the broad summit; but then when their glittering arms appeared over the brow of the mountain the charging cry was heard, the crowded mass was broken to pieces, and a tempest of bullets followed its flight.   Four times this assault was renewed, and the French officers were seen to pull up their tired men by the belts, so fierce and resolute they were to win; yet it was the labour of Sysiphus, the vehement shout and shock of the British soldier always prevailed; and at last, with thinned ranks, tired limbs, hearts fainting and hopeless from repeated failures, they were so abashed that three British companies sufficed to bear down a whole brigade.   And while the battle was thus being fought on the mountain, the French cavalry beyond the Guy river passed a rivulet and with a fire of carbines forced the tenth hussars to yield some rocky ground on Picton's right; yet the eighteenth hussars, having better fire-arms than the tenth renewed the combat, killed two officers and drove the French over the rivulet again.

Such were the leading events of this sanguinary struggle, which Wellington, fresh from the fight, with homely emphasis called ' *bludgeon work.*'   Two generals and eighteen hundred men had been killed or wounded on the French side, following their official reports; a number far below the estimate made at the time by the allies, whose loss amounted to two thousand six hundred.   But these discrepancies between hostile calculations ever occur, and there is little wisdom in disputing where proof is unattainable; but the numbers actually engaged were of French twenty-five thousand, of the allies twelve thousand; and if the strength of the latter's position did not save them from the greater loss their steadfast courage is to be the more admired.

On the 29th the armies rested in position without firing a shot, but the wandering divisions on both sides were now entering the line.

Hill, having sent all his baggage artillery and wounded men to Berioplano behind the Christoval ridge, still occupied his strong ground between Lizasso and Arestegui, covering the Marcalain and Irurzun roads and menacing that leading from Lizasso to Olague in rear of Soult's right: this communication with Oricain was maintained by the seventh division, and the light division was approaching his left.   On Wellington's side the crisis was over.   He had vindicated his position

with only sixteen thousand combatants; and now including
the troops of blockade he had fifty thousand, twenty thousand
being British, in close military combination: thirty thousand
were in hand, and Hill was well placed for retaking the offensive. Soult's situation was proportionably difficult. He had
sent his artillery, part of his cavalry and his wounded men
back to France immediately after the battle ; the two former
to join Villatte on the lower Bidassoa. Thus relieved he
awaited D'Erlon's arrival by the valley of Lanz, and that
general reached Ostiz a few miles above Sauroren at mid-day
on the 29th, bringing intelligence, obtained indirectly during
his march, that Graham had retired from the Bidassoa and
Villatte had crossed that river. This made Soult think his
operations had disengaged St. Sebastian, and he instantly
devised a new scheme, dangerous indeed but conformable to
the critical state of affairs. Judging it hopeless to renew the
battle, he was averse to retire when he had been reinforced
with eighteen thousand fresh men; he was yet unable to
remain, because his supplies, derived from distant magazines
by slow and small convoys, were unequal to the consumption.

Soult, MSS.

Two-thirds of the British troops the greatest
part of the Portuguese and all the Spaniards
were, he supposed, in his front under Wellington, or on his
right flank under Hill, and other reinforcements were probably on the march; wherefore he resolved to prolong his
right with D'Erlon's corps, and cautiously drawing off the rest
of his army place himself between the allies and the Bastan,
in military connexion with his reserve and closer to his frontier
magazines. Thus posted and able to combine all his troops
in one operation, he expected to relieve San Sebastian entirely,
and profit from the new state of affairs.

In this view, one division of cavalry passed over the posi-
tion from the Val de Zubiri to that of Lanz and joined
D'Erlon, who was ordered to march early on the 30th by
Etulain upon Lizasso, and to send scouting parties towards
Letassa and Irurzun, and on all the roads leading upon Pam-

Plan 6,
p. 199.

peluna. During the night the other division of
cavalry and La Martiniere's infantry, both at
Elcano on the extreme left of the French army, retired over

the mountains by Illurdos to Eugui, in the upper part of the
Val de Zubiri, having orders to cross the separating ridge
there, to enter the valley of Lanz and join D'Erlon. Reille,
marching by the crest of the position from Zabaldica to the
village of Sauroren, was gradually to relieve Clausel, who was
to assemble his troops behind Sauroren towards Ostiz, thus
following D'Erlon and to be himself followed by Reille.
Clausel, to cover these movements and maintain his connexion with D'Erlon, placed two regiments on the heights
beyond the Lanz river; but he was to hold on to Reille rather
than D'Erlon until the former had completed his dangerous
flank march across Wellington's front.

In the night Soult heard from deserters, that three divisions
were to make an offensive movement towards Lizasso on the
30th, and when daylight came he was convinced the men
spoke truly; because from a point beyond Sauroren, he dis-
cerned columns descending the ridge of Christoval and the
heights above Oricain, others in march on a wide sweep
apparently to turn Clausel's right. These were Morillo's
Spaniards, Campbell's Portuguese and the seventh division;
the former rejoining Hill to whom they belonged, the others
adapting themselves to a new line of battle which shall be
presently explained.

At six o'clock in the morning Foy's division of Reille's
corps was in march from Zabaldica towards Sauroren, where
Maucune had already relieved Conroux; the latter, belonging
to Clausel, was moving up the valley of Lanz, and Clausel,
with exception of the two flanking regiments before mentioned,
had concentrated his remaining divisions between Olabe and
Ostiz. In this state of affairs Wellington opened his batteries
from the chapel heights and sent down skirmishers against
Sauroren. Very soon this bickering of musketry spread
towards the right, becoming brisk between Cole and Foy,
while it subsided at Sauroren; but Soult relying on the great
strength of his position, ordered Reille to maintain it until
evening and went off at a gallop to join D'Erlon.   Soult's
His design was to fall with superior numbers   Report,
upon the divisions he supposed to be turning his   MSS.
right and crush them, a daring project and well conceived;

but he had to deal with a man whose rapid perception and rough stroke rendered the game dangerous.

Combat of Buenza.—Soult found D'Erlon, who had entered the Ulzema valley, making dispositions to attack Hill between Buenza and Arestegui; and the latter having only ten thousand fighting men, including Long's cavalry, occupied a very extensive mountain ridge. His right was strongly posted on rugged ground, but the left, prolonged towards Buenza, was insecure; and D'Erlon, who had not less than twenty thousand sabres and bayonets was followed by La Martiniere's division of infantry now coming from Lanz: Soult's combination was therefore extremely powerful. The light troops were already engaged when he arrived, and the same soldiers, on both sides, who had so strenuously combated at Maya the 25th were again opposed in fight. D'Armagnac was to make a false attack upon Hill's right; Abbé, emerging by Lizasso, was to turn the left and gain the summit of the ridge in the direction of Buenza; Maranzin followed Abbé, and the cavalry supported and connected the two attacks. The action was brisk at both points, but D'Armagnac, pushing his feint too far, became seriously engaged and was beaten by Da Costa and Ashworth's Portuguese, aided by a part of the twenty-eighth British regiment. Nor were the French at first more successful on the other flank, being repeatedly repulsed; Abbé however finally turned the position, gained the summit of the mountain and rendered it untenable. Hill lost four hundred men and retired to the heights of Yguaras behind Arestegui and Berasin, thus drawing towards Marcalain with his right and throwing back his left. There, uniting with Campbell and Morillo, he again offered battle, but Soult, whose principal loss was in D'Armagnac's division, had gained his main object; he had turned Hill, obtained a fresh line of retreat, and a shorter communication with Villatte by the pass of Doña Maria; and withal, the great Irurzun road to Toloza, distant only one league and

Soult's
Despatch,
MS. a half, was in his power. His first thought was to seize it and march through Lecumberri upon Toloza, or Andoain and Ernani. There was nothing to oppose him except the light division, whose movements shall be noticed hereafter; but neither he nor Hill knew of its presence; and Soult thought himself strong enough to force a way to San Sebastian, there to unite with Villatte and the artillery, which was now on the lower Bidassoa.

This project was feasible. La Martiniere's division, coming from Lanz, was not far off; Clausel's three divisions were momentarily expected, and the rest of Reille's during the night. On the 31st therefore, at least fifty thousand French would have broken into Guipuscoa, thrusting aside the light division in their march and menacing Graham in reverse while Villatte attacked him in front. The country about Lecumberri was however very strong for defence, and Wellington would have followed; yet scarcely in time; for though he foresaw the movement he was ignorant of Soult's strength; he thought D'Erlon's force to be originally two divisions of infantry, and now only reinforced with a third division; whereas it was three divisions originally, and was now reinforced by a fourth division of infantry and two of cavalry. But this error did not prevent him seizing with the rapidity of a great commander the decisive point of operation, and giving a counter-stroke which Soult, trusting to the strength of Reille's position, little expected.

When La Martiniere's division and the cavalry abandoned the mountains above Elcano, Wellington, seeing that Zabaldica was also evacuated, ordered Picton, reinforced with two squadrons of cavalry and a battery of artillery, to enter the valley of Zubiri and turn the French left, while the seventh division swept over the hills beyond the Lanz river upon their right. The march of Campbell and Morillo insured the communication with Hill; and that general was to point his columns upon Olague and Lanz, threatening the French rear, but meeting with D'Erlon was forced back to Eguaros. Cole was to assail Foy's position, yet, respecting its great strength, the attack was to be regulated by the effect produced on the flanks. Byng's brigade and the sixth division, the latter having a battery of guns and some squadrons of cavalry attached, were combined to assault Sauroren. O'Donnel's Spaniards followed the sixth division; Fane's horsemen were stationed at Berioplano with an advanced post at Irurzun;

the heavy cavalry remained behind Huarte, and Carlos d'España maintained the blockade.

Second battle of Sauroren.—These movements were begun at daylight. Picton's advance on the right was rapid; he gained the Val de Zubiri and threw his skirmishers at once on Foy's flank. At the same time general Inglis, one of those veterans who purchase every step of promotion with their blood, advancing on the left with only five hundred men of the seventh division, broke at one shock the two French regiments covering Clausel's right, and drove them down into the valley of Lanz,—he lost indeed one-third of his own men, but instantly spreading the remainder in skirmishing order along the descent opened a biting fire upon the flank of Conroux's division, then moving up the valley from Sauroren, and sorely amazed and disordered by this sudden fall of two regiments from the top of the mountain into the midst of the column. Foy was still on the crest of the position between Zabaldica and Sauroren at the moment of this attack, but too far off to give aid; his own light troops were engaged with Cole's skirmishers, and Inglis had been so sudden, that before the evil could be well perceived it was past remedy. Wellington instantly pushed the sixth division, now commanded by Pakenham, to the left of Sauroren; and he also shoved Byng's brigade headlong down from the chapel height against that village, which was defended by Maucune. Byng's assault was simultaneously enforced from the opposite direction by Madden's Portuguese; and the chapel battery sent its bullets crashing through the houses, or booming up the valley towards Conroux's column, which Inglis, closely supported by the seventh division, never ceased to vex.

The village and bridge of Sauroren and the strait beyond were now covered with a pall of smoke, the musketry pealed frequent and loud, and the tumult and affray echoing from mountain to mountain filled all the valley. Byng with hard fighting carried Sauroren, fourteen hundred prisoners were made, and the French divisions thus vehemently assailed in front and flank were entirely broken. Part retreated up the valley towards Clausel who was now beyond Ostiz; part fled up the mountain side to seek a refuge with Foy, who had remained on the summit a helpless spectator of this rout; and though he rallied the fugitives in great numbers he had soon to look to himself; for his skirmishers were driven up the mountain by Cole's men, and his left was infested by Picton's detachments. Thus pressed, he abandoned his strong position and fell back along the summit of the ridge separating the two valleys, where the woods enabled him to effect his retreat without much loss: yet he dared not descend into either valley, and thinking himself entirely cut off, sent advice of his situation to Soult and retired into the Alduides by the pass of Urtiaga.   Meanwhile Wellington, pressing up the valley of Lanz drove Clausel as far as Olague, where he was joined by La Martiniere and took a position in the evening covering the roads of Lanz and Lizasso: then the English general, whose pursuit had been damped by hearing of Hill's action, also halted near Ostiz.

The allies lost nineteen hundred men killed and wounded or taken in the two battles of this day; of these nearly twelve hundred were Portuguese, the soldiers of that nation having borne the brunt of both fights.   On the French side the loss was enormous.   Conroux's and Maucune's divisions were completely disorganized; Foy, augmented to eight thousand men by the fugitives, was entirely separated from the main body; more than two thousand men had been killed or wounded, many were dispersed in the woods and ravines, and three thousand prisoners were taken.   This blow, joined to former losses, reduced Soult's fighting men to thirty-five thousand of which the fifteen thousand under Clausel and Reille were dispirited by defeat.   Hill's force, increased to fifteen thousand by the junction of Morillo and Campbell, was in his front; thirty thousand were on his rear in the valley of Lanz or on the hills at each side; for Picton, finding no enemies in the Val de Zubiri, had crowned the heights in conjunction with Cole.

Wellington had detached some of O'Donnel's Spaniards to Marcalain when he heard of Hill's action, but he was not yet aware of the true state of affairs on that side.   His operations were founded upon the notion that Soult was in retreat towards the Bastan; and he designed to follow closely, pushing his own left forward to support Graham on the Bidassoa —yet, always underrating D'Erlon's force, he thought La Martiniere had retreated by the Roncevalles road; and as Foy's column was numerous and two divisions had been broken at Sauroren, he judged the force immediately under Soult to be weak and made dispositions accordingly. The sixth division and the thirteenth light dragoons were to march by Eugui to join Picton, who was directed upon Linzoain and Roncevalles. Cole was to descend into the valley of Lanz. Hill, supported by the Spaniards at Marcalain, was to press Soult closely, always turning the French right but directing his own march upon Lanz, from whence he was to send Campbell to the Alduides. The seventh division, which had halted on the ridges between Hill and Wellington, was to suffer the former to cross its front and then march for the pass of Doña Maria.

Wellington expecting Soult would rejoin Clausel and make for the Bastan by the pass of Vellate, intended to confine and press him closely in that district; but the French marshal was in a worse position than his adversary imagined, being too far advanced towards Buenza to return to Lanz; in fine he was between two fires and had no retreat save by the pass of Doña Maria. Wherefore calling in Clausel, and giving D'Erlon, whose divisions were in good order and undismayed, the rear-guard, he commenced his march at midnight towards the pass. Mischief was gathering around him. Graham had twenty thousand men ready to move against Villatte, and between him and Hill was the light division under Charles Alten. That general was as before said, on the Santa Cruz mountain the 27th, but had marched in the evening of the 28th to gain Lecumberri on the great Irurzun road; yet from some error or failure of orders, for the difficulty of communication was great, he commenced his descent into the valley of Lerins too late. His leading brigade got down with some difficulty and reached Leyza beyond the great chain by the pass of Zubieta; but darkness caught the other brigade and the troops were dispersed in that frightful wilderness of woods and precipices. Many made faggot torches, and thus moving about the lights served indeed to assist those who carried

them, yet misled and bewildered others who saw them at a
distance,—the heights and the ravines were alike studded with
these small fires, and the soldiers calling to each other, filled
the whole region with their clamour. Thus they continued to
rove and shout until morning showed the face of the mountain
covered with tired and scattered men and animals, who had
not gained half a league of ground beyond their starting-place;
and it was many hours ere they could be collected to join the
other brigade at Leyza.

Alten, thus isolated for three days, sent officers in all directions to obtain tidings and in the evening renewed his march
to Areysa, where he halted without suffering fires to be lighted
lest the enemy should discover him; but at night he moved
again and reached Lecumberri on the 30th. At that place
the noise of Hill's battle at Buenza was heard, and the light
division again found itself within the system of operations
directed by Wellington in person; if Soult-had continued his
movement on Irurzun it would have been in great danger; but
now, he being in retreat to Doña Maria, the light division
was a new and terrible power placed in his adversary's
hands.

It has been shown how Foy was cut off and driven to the
Alduides, how he French artillery and part of their cavalry
were again on the Bidassoa; whence Villatte had not moved
though he had skirmished with Longa on the heights of
Lesaca. Soult was thus isolated, without other resources than
his own firmness and ability. His retreat by Doña Maria was
however open as far as San Estevan, and from thence he could
ascend the Bidassoa to Elizondo and gain France by the Col
de Maya; or go down the river towards Vera by Sumbilla and
Yanzi, from which roads led over the mountains to the passes
of Echallar: there was also a third mountain-road leading
direct from Estevan to Zagaramurdi and Urdax, but too
rugged for wounded men and baggage. The road to Elizondo
was good; that down the Bidassoa was a terrible defile, so
contracted about the bridges of Yanzi and Sumbilla that a few
men only could march abreast. Soult had therefore to dread,
that Wellington would by Villate reach Elizondo before him
and block the passage there,—that Graham seizing the rocks

at Yanzi, would bar that passage and by detachments cut off
the line of Echallar.   Then, confined to the narrow mountain-
way from San Estevan to Zagaramurdi, he would be followed
hard by Hill, assailed in rear and flank during the march,
and perhaps be headed at Urdax by troops moving through
Vellate, Elizondo and the Col de Maya.

His first object being to gain Doña Maria, he, as before
stated, moved in the night of the 30th, while Wellington, not
knowing the real state of affairs, halted in the valley of Lanz
to let Hill pass his front and re-enter the Bastan, upon
which valley Byng had already moved.   When Soult's real
strength became known, the seventh division was sent to aid
Hill, but Wellington followed Byng by the pass of Vellate;
and thinking Alten might be at Zubieta, directed him to head
the French if possible at San Estevan, at Sumbilla, at any
point he could attain.   Longa was also ordered to come down
to Yanzi in aid of Alten, Graham was warned to hold his
corps in hand, and both Picton and Pakenham had their
routes changed for a time.

Combat of Doña Maria.—At ten o'clock in the morning
Hill overtook Soult's rear-guard, between Lizasso and the
Puerto.   The seventh division, coming from the hills above
Olague, was already ascending the mountain on his right, and
the French only gained a wood on the summit of the pass
under the fire of Hill's guns: there however they turned and
throwing out skirmishers made strong battle.   Stewart, leading
the second division and now for the third time engaged with
D'Erlon's troops, was again wounded and his first brigade
was repulsed; Pringle succeeding to the command renewed
the fight with the second brigade and broke the enemy; the
seventh division did the same on the right and some prisoners
were taken: but a thick fog prevented further pursuit and
the loss of the French in the action is unknown, probably less
than that of the allies, which was short of four hundred men.

The seventh division remained on the mountain, Hill fell
back to Lizasso, and then, following his orders, moved by a
short rugged way between the passes of Doña Maria and
Vellate, over the great chain to Almandoz to join Wellington,
who had now descended into the Bastan by Vellate.   Byng

had previously reached Elizondo, and captured a convoy of
provisions and ammunition left there by D'Erlon under guard
of a battalion, which he sharply engaged, took several hundred
prisoners, and then pushed for the Col de Maya. Wellington
now occupied the hills through which the road leads from
Elizondo to San Estevan, and was full of hope to strike a terrible blow; for Soult, after passing Doña Maria, had halted in
San Estevan, although by his scouts he knew the convoy had
been taken at Elizondo.   He was in a deep narrow valley,—
three British and one Spanish division were behind the
mountains overlooking the town,—the seventh division was at
Doña Maria,—the light division and Graham's Spaniards
were marching to block the Vera and Echallar exits from the
valley,—Byng was at Maya,—Hill was moving by Almandoz.
A few hours gained and the French must surrender or disperse.
Wellington gave strict orders to prevent the lighting of fires,
the straggling of soldiers, or any other indication of the presence
of troops; and he placed himself amongst some rocks at a
commanding point, from whence he could observe every movement of the enemy.   Soult seemed tranquil and four of his
gens-d'armes were seen to ride up the valley in a careless
manner.   Some of the staff proposed to cut them off; the
English general anxious to hide his own presence
forbad this, but the next moment three marauding   Notes by the
English soldiers entered the valley and were   Duke of
                                                    Wellington,
instantly carried off by the *gens d'armes;* half an MSS.
hour afterwards the French drums beat to arms and their
columns began to move out of San Estevan towards Sumbilla.
Thus the disobedience of three plundering knaves, unworthy
of the name of soldiers, deprived one consummate commander
of the most splendid success, and saved another from the most
terrible disaster.

Soult walked from the prison, but his chains still hung
about him.   The way was narrow, wounded men borne on
their comrades' shoulders and followed by baggage, filed in long
procession; Clausel had the rear-guard, but on the
morning of the 1st he was still near San   August.
Estevan when Cole's skirmishers and O'Donnell's Spaniards,
thronging on the heights along his flank, opened a fire which

he could not return. Then troops and baggage got inter-
mingled, many men fled up the hills, and the commanding
energy of Soult, whose personal exertions were conspicuous, could
scarcely prevent a general dispersion; baggage fell at every step
into the hands of the pursuers, the boldest were dismayed, and
worse would have awaited them in front, if Wellington had
been on other points well seconded by his generals.

Instead of taking the first road leading from Sumbilla to
Echallar, the head of the French passed onward towards that
leading from the bridge near Yanzi; the valley narrowed to a
mere cleft in the rocks as they advanced, the Bidassoa was on
their left, there was a tributary torrent to cross, and the bridge
was defended by a Spanish caçadore battalion, detached from
the heights of Vera by general Barceñas. The front was thus
as much disordered as the rear, and had Longa or Barceñas
reinforced the caçadores, those only of the French who being
near Sumbilla could take the road to Echallar would have
escaped; but the Spanish generals kept aloof and D'Erlon
won the defile. Reille's divisions were still to pass, and when
they came up a new enemy had appeared. This was the light
division. The order to intercept the French being received
the evening of the 31st, Alten, repassing the defiles of Zubieta,
again descended into the deep valley of Lerins and reached
Elgoriaga about mid-day the 1st of August. He had then
marched twenty-four miles, was little more than a league from
Estevan, about the same distance from Sumbilla, and the
French movement along the Bidassoa was discovered; but
instead of marching on Sumbilla he clambered up the great
mountain of Santa Cruz and made for the bridge of Yanzi.
Very sultry was the weather, the mountain steep and hard to
overcome, many men fell and died convulsed and frothing at
the mouth, while others, whose spirit and strength had never
before been quelled, leaned on their muskets and muttered in
sullen tones that they yielded for the first time.

Towards evening, after marching nineteen consecutive hours
and over forty miles of mountain roads, the head of the column
reached the edge of a precipice near the bridge of Yanzi.
Below, within pistol-shot, Reille's divisions were seen hurrying
forward along the horrid defile and a fire of musketry com-

menced, slightly from the British on the high rock, more vigorously from some low ground near the bridge of Yanzi, where the
riflemen had ensconced themselves in the brushwood: but the
scene which followed shall be described by an eye-witness.
'We overlooked the enemy at stone's throw,
and from the summit of a tremendous preci-   Cooke's
                                                Memoirs.
pice.   The river separated us, but the French
were wedged in a narrow road with inaccessible rocks on
one side and the river on the other.   Confusion impossible
to describe followed, the wounded were thrown down in
the rush and trampled upon, the cavalry drew their swords
and endeavoured to charge up the pass of Echallar, but
the infantry beat them back, and several, horses and all, were
precipitated into the river; some fired vertically at us while
the wounded called out for quarter, and others pointed to them,
supported as they were on branches of trees, on which were
suspended great coats clotted with gore and blood-stained
sheets taken from different habitations to aid the sufferers.'

On these miserable supplicants brave men could not fire;
and so piteous was the spectacle that it was with averted aim
the British soldier shot at the sound men; although the latter
rapidly plied their muskets in passing, and some in their
veteran hardihood even dashed across the bridge of Yanzi to
make a counter-attack!   It was a soldier-like but a vain
effort, the night found the British in possession of the bridge;
and though the great body of the French escaped by the road
to Echallar, their baggage was all cut off with many prisoners
by the troops hanging on the rear in pursuit from San
Estevan.

Heavy was the French loss; that of the allies was about a
hundred men, of which sixty-five were British, principally of
the fourth division.   Wellington was justly discontented with
the result.   Neither Longa nor Alten had fulfilled their mission.
The former excused himself as being too feeble to oppose the
mass Soult led down the valley; yet the rocks were so precipitous the French could not have reached him; the resistance
of the Spanish caçadores was Longa's condemnation.   Fatuity
seemed to prevail in many quarters.   If Barceñas had sent his
whole brigade instead of a weak battalion, the small torrent

could not have been forced by D'Erlon; if Longa had been at
the bridge of Yanzi the French must have surrendered, for the
perpendicular rocks on their right forbade even an escape by
dispersion; if Alten, instead of marching down the valley of
Lerins as far as Elgoriaga, had crossed the Santa Cruz mountain by the road used the night of the 28th, he would have
been much earlier at the bridge of Yanzi; and then belike
Longa and Barceñas would also have come down.   Alten's
instructions prescribed Sumbilla and San Estevan as the first
points to head the French; judging them too strong at Sumbilla he marched upon Yanzi; and if he had passed the bridge
there and seized the road to Echallar with one brigade, while
the other plied the flank with fire from the left of the Bidassoa, he would have struck a great blow: it was for that his
soldiers had made such a prodigious exertion.

During the night Soult rallied his divisions about Echallar,
and on the morning of the 2nd occupied the 'Puerto' of that
name.   His left was on the rocks of Zagaramurdi; his right
on the rock of Ivantelly, communicating with the left of Villatte, who was in position on the ridges between Soult and
the head of the great Rhune mountain.   Clausel's three divisions, now reduced to six thousand men, took post on a strong
hill between the 'Puerto' and town of Echallar.   This position
was momentarily adopted to save time, to examine the country,
and to make Wellington discover his views, but the latter
would not suffer the affront.   He had sent Picton and Pakenham to reoccupy the passes of Roncevalles and the Alduides,
—Hill had reached the Col de Maya,—Byng was at Urdax,—
the fourth, seventh, and light divisions remained in hand, and
with these he resolved to fall upon Clausel, whose position was
dangerously advanced.

Combats of Echallar and Ivantelly.—The light division held
the road running from the bridge of Yanzi to Echallar until
relieved by the fourth division, and then marched by Lesaca
to Santa Barbara, thus turning Clausel's right.   The fourth
division marched from Yanzi upon Echallar to attack his front;
the seventh moved from Sumbilla against his left; but Barnes's
brigade, contrary to Wellington's intention, arrived unsupported before the fourth and light divisions were either seen

or felt, and without awaiting the arrival of more troops assailed Clausel's strong position. The fire became vehement, yet neither the steepness of the mountain nor the overshadowing multitude of the enemy, clustered above in support of their skirmishers, could arrest the assailants; and then was seen the astonishing spectacle of fifteen hundred men driving by sheer valour and force of arms six thousand good troops from a position, so rugged that there would have been little to boast of if the numbers had been reversed and the defence made good. The fourth division arrived indeed towards the end of the action, and the French, who had fulfilled their mission as a rear-guard, were worn with fatigue and ill-provided with ammunition, having exhausted all their reserve stores during the retreat: but their inferiority here belongs to the highest part of war. The British soldiers, their natural fierceness stimulated by the remarkable personal daring of their general, Barnes, were excited by success; the French were those who had failed in attack the 28th, had been utterly defeated the 30th, and had suffered so severely the day before about Sumbilla. Such then is the preponderance of moral power. The men who had assailed the terrible rocks above Sauroren with a force and energy that all the valour of the hardiest British veterans scarcely sufficed to repel, were now, only five days afterwards, unable to sustain the shock of one-fourth of their own numbers. And at this very time, eighty British soldiers, the comrades and equals of those who achieved this wonderful exploit, being surprised while plundering, surrendered to some French peasants who, as Wellington truly observed, '*they would under other circumstances have eat up!*' What gross ignorance of human nature then do those declaimers display, who assert that the employing of brute force is the highest qualification of a general!

Clausel thus dispossessed, fell back fighting to a strong ridge beyond the pass of Echallar, having his right covered by the Ivantelly mountain which was strongly occupied. Meanwhile the light division, emerging by Lesaca from the narrow valley of the Bidassoa, ascended the broad heights of Santa Barbara and waited until the operations of the fourth and seventh divisions were far enough advanced to render it

advisable to attack the Ivantelly.   Lifting its peaked head out
of the Santa Barbara heights, it separated them from the
ridges where Clausel was retreating, and as the evening came
on, a thick mist capped the crowning rocks, which contained
a strong French regiment; the British soldiers, still wearied
with their long and terrible march the previous day, had been
for two days without sustenance, and were leaning, weak and
fainting, on their arms when the advancing fire of Barnes's
action about Echallar indicated the necessity of dislodging
the enemy from Ivantelly.   Andrew Barnard instantly led
five companies of his riflemen to the attack, and four companies of the forty-third followed in support.   The misty
cloud had descended, and the riflemen were soon lost to view,
but the sharp clang of their weapons, heard in distinct reply
to the more sonorous rolling musketry of the French, told
what work was going on.   For some time the echoes rendered it doubtful how the action went, but the following companies of the forty-third could find no trace of an enemy
save the killed and wounded: Barnard had fought his way
unaided and without a check to the summit.   His dark-
clothed, swarthy veterans raised their victorious shout from
the highest peak, just as the coming night showed the long
ridges of the mountains beyond, sparkling with the last
musket-flashes from Clausel's troops then retiring in disorder
from Echallar.

This day's fighting cost the British four hundred men, and
Wellington narrowly escaped the enemy's hands.   He had
carried with him towards Echallar half a company of the
forty-third as an escort, and placed a serjeant named Blood,
with a party to watch in front while he examined his maps.
The French being close at hand sent a detachment to cut the
party off; and such was the nature of the ground that their
troops, rushing on at speed, would infallibly have fallen upon
Wellington, if Blood, a young intelligent man, seeing the
danger, had not with surprising activity, leaping rather than
running down the precipitous rocks, given him notice: yet the
French arrived in time to send a volley of shot after him as
he galloped away.

Soult now made D'Erlon occupy the hills about Ainhoa;

Clausel those in advance of Sarre, and he sent Reille with two divisions to St. Jean de Luz, behind Villatte's reserve. Foy, who had after his retreat rashly uncovered St. Jean Pied de Port by descending upon Cambo, was ordered to return and augment his troops with all that he could collect of national guards and detachments.

Wellington had on the 1st directed Graham to move up with pontoons and cross the Bidassoa, but now abandoned this design; the two armies therefore rested quiet in their respective positions, after nine days of continual movement during which they had fought ten serious actions. Of the allies, including the Spaniards, seven thousand three hundred officers and soldiers had been killed wounded or taken, and many were dispersed from fatigue or to plunder. On the French side the loss was terrible, and their disorder rendered the official returns inaccurate. Wellington at first called it twelve thousand, but hearing that the French officers admitted more he raised his estimate to fifteen thousand. The engineer, *Belmas*, in his Journals of Sieges, compiled from official documents by order of the French government, sets down above thirteen thousand. Soult in his despatches at the time, stated fifteen hundred as the loss at Maya, four hundred at Roncevalles, two hundred on the 27th, and eighteen hundred on the 28th, after which he speaks no more of losses by battle. There remains therefore to be added the killed and wounded at the combats of Linzoain on the 26th, the double battles of Sauroren and Buenza on the 30th, the combats of the 31st, and those of the 1st and 2nd of August; finally, four thousand unwounded prisoners. Let this suffice. It is not needful to sound the stream of blood in all its horrid depths.

OBSERVATIONS.

1°. The allies' line of defence was weak. Was it therefore injudiciously adopted? Beaten at Vitoria the French were disorganized, and retreated without artillery or baggage on eccentric lines; Foy by Guipuscoa, Clausel by Zaragoza, Reille by San Estevan, Joseph by Pampeluna. There was no reserve to rally upon, the people fled from the frontier.

Bayonne and St. Jean Pied de Port, if not defenceless, were
certainly in a very neglected state, and the English general
might have undertaken any operation, assumed any position,
offensive or defensive, which seemed good to him. Why then
did he not establish the Anglo-Portuguese beyond the mountains, leaving the Spaniards to blockade the fortresses behind
him? The answer to this question involves the difference
between the practice and the theory of war.

'*The soldiers, instead of preparing food and resting themselves after the battle, dispersed in the night to*
<small>Wellington's
Despatches.</small> *plunder; and were so fatigued that when the rain
came on the next day they were incapable of
marching, and had more stragglers than the beaten enemy.
Eighteen days after the victory twelve thousand five hundred
men, chiefly British, were absent, most of them marauding in
the mountains.*'

Such were the reasons assigned by the English general for
his slack pursuit after the battle of Vitoria; yet he had commanded that army for six years! Was he then deficient in
the first qualification of a general, the art of disciplining and
inspiring troops; or was the English military system defective? It is certain he always exacted the confidence of his
soldiers as a leader; it is not so certain he gained their
affections. The barbarity of the English military code excited
public horror, the inequality of promotion created public
discontent; yet the general complained he had no adequate
power to reward or punish; and he condemned alike the
system and the soldiers it produced. The latter '*were detestable for everything but fighting, and the officers as culpable as
the men.*' The vehemence of these censures is inconsistent
with his celebrated observation, subsequently made, namely,
'that he thought he could go anywhere and do anything
with the army that fought on the Pyrenees; and although it
cannot be denied that his complaints were generally too well
founded, there were thousands of true and noble soldiers, and
zealous worthy officers, who served their country honestly
and merited no reproaches. It is enough that they have
been since neglected, exactly in proportion to their want of
that corrupt aristocratic influence which produced the evils
complained of

2°. When the misconduct of the troops had thus weakened the effect of victory, the question of following Joseph at once into France assumed a new aspect. Wellington's system of warfare had never varied after the battle of Talavera. Rejecting dangerous enterprise, it rested on profound calculation both as to time and resources for accomplishing the gradual liberation of Spain by the Anglo-Portuguese army. Not that he held it impossible to attain that object suddenly—and his battles in India, the passage of the Douro, the advance to Talavera, prove that by nature he was inclined to daring operations,—but such efforts, however glorious, could not be adopted by a commander who feared even the loss of a brigade lest the government he served should put an end to the war. Neither was it suitable to the state of his relations with the Portuguese and Spaniards; their ignorance jealousy and passionate pride, fierce in proportion to their weakness and improvidence, would have enhanced every danger.

3°. No man could have anticipated the extraordinary errors of the French in 1813. Wellington did not expect to cross the Ebro before the end of the campaign, and his battering-train was prepared for the siege of Burgos not for that of Bayonne. A sudden invasion of France, her military reputation considered, was therefore beyond the pale of his methodized system of warfare, which was founded upon political as well as military considerations; and of the most complicated nature, seeing that he had at all times to deal with the personal and factious interests and passions, as well as the great state interests of three nations, two of which abhorred each other. At this moment also the uncertain state of affairs in Germany strongly influenced his views. An armistice which might end in a separate peace excluding England would have brought Napoleon's whole force to the Pyrenees, and Wellington held the military and political proceeding of the coalesced powers cheap. *'I would not move a corporal's guard in reliance upon such a system,'* was the significant phrase he employed to express his contempt.

These considerations justified his caution as to invading France; but there were local military reasons equally cogent.

1°. He could not dispense with a secure harbour, because the fortresses still in possession of the French, namely, Santona, Pancorbo, Pampeluna, and St. Sebastian, interrupted his communications with the interior of Spain.   2°. He had to guard against the union of Suchet and Clausel on his right flank—hence his efforts to cut off the last-named general—hence also the blockade of Pampeluna in preference to siege, and the launching of Mina and the bands on the side of Zaragoza.

4°. After Vitoria the nature of the campaign depended upon Suchet's operations, which were rendered more important by Murray's misconduct.   The allied force on the eastern coast was badly organized; it did not advance from Valencia as we have seen until the 10th, and then only partially and by the coast; whereas Suchet had assembled more than twenty thousand excellent troops on the Ebro as early as the 12th of July.   He might have saved the castle of Zaragoza with its great stores, and then rallying Paris' division, he could have menaced Wellington's flank with twenty-five thousand men exclusive of Clausel's force, and, if that general joined him, with forty thousand.   On the 16th, the day lord William Bentinck quitted Valencia, Suchet might have marched from Zaragoza on Tudela or Sanguessa; and Soult's preparations, originally made to attack on the 23rd instead of the 25th, would have naturally been hastened.   How difficult it would then have been for the allies to maintain themselves beyond the Ebro is evident; much more so to hold a forward position in France.   That Wellington feared an operation of this nature is shown by his instructions to lord William Bentinck and to Mina; and by his keeping Picton and Cole behind the mountains solely to watch Clausel until he regained France, when Cole was permitted to join Byng and Morillo.   It follows that the operations after the battle of Vitoria were well considered and consonant to the general system: their excellence would have been proved if Suchet had seized the advantages within his reach.

5°. A general's capacity is sometimes more taxed to profit from a victory than to gain one.   Wellington, master of all Spain, Catalonia excepted, desired to establish himself solidly in the Pyrenees, lest a separate peace in Germany should enable Napoleon to turn his whole force against the allies. In this expectation, with astonishing exertion of body and mind, he had in three days achieved a rigorous examination of the whole mass of the Western Pyrenees, and concluded, if Pampeluna and San Sebastian fell, that a defensive position, strong as that of Portugal, much stronger than could be found behind the Ebro, might be established. But to invest those places and maintain so difficult a covering line was a greater task than to win the battle of Vitoria. However, the early fall of San Sebastian he expected, because the errors of execution in that siege could not be foreseen; and he counted also on the disorganized state of the French army, on Joseph's want of military capacity, and the moral ascendancy which his own troops had acquired. He could not anticipate the expeditious journey, the sudden arrival of Soult, whose rapid re-organization of the French army and vigorous operations, contrasted with Joseph's abandonment of Spain, illustrated the old Greek saying, that a herd of deer led by a lion are more dangerous than a herd of lions led by a deer.

6°. Soult was little beholden to fortune at the commencement of his movements. Her first contradiction was the bad weather, which breaking up the roads delayed the concentration of his army at St. Jean Pied de Port for two days; and the effect which heavy rain and hard marches have upon the vigour and confidence of soldiers who are going to attack is well known. If he had commenced the 23rd instead of the 25th, the surprise would have been more complete, his army more brisk; and as no conscript battalions would have arrived to delay Reille, that general would have been more ready in his attack; and might possibly have escaped the fog which on the 26th stopped his march along the superior crest of the mountain towards Vellate. On the other hand the allies would have been spared the unsuccessful assault on San Sebastian, and the Col de Maya might have been better furnished with troops. However Soult's combinations were so well knit, that more than one error in execution, more than one accident of fortune, were necessary to baffle him. Had D'Erlon followed his instructions even on the 26th, Hill

would have been shouldered off the valley of Lanz, and there
would have been twenty thousand additional French troops in
the combats of the 27th and 28th. Such failures however
generally attend extensively combined movements, and it is
not certain that D'Erlon could have won the Col de Maya
if all Stewart's forces had been posted here. It would
perhaps have been more strictly within the rules of art, if
D'Erlon had been directed to leave one of his three divisions
to menace the Col de Maya while he marched with the other
two by St. Etienne de Baygorry up the Alduides. This
movement, covered by the national guards who occupied the
mountain of La Houssa, could not have been stopped by
Campbell's Portuguese brigade; and would have dislodged
Hill from the Bastan while it secured a junction with Soult
on the crest of the magistral chain.

7°. The intrepid constancy of Byng and Ross on their
several positions the 25th, the able and clean retreat made by
Cole as far as the heights of Linzoain, gave full effect to the
French errors; and would probably have baffled Soult at an
early period if Picton had comprehended the importance of
his position. Wellington said the concentration of the army
would have been effected on the 27th if that officer and Cole
had not agreed in thinking it impossible to make a stand
behind Linzoain; and surely the necessity of retreating on
that day may be questioned. For if Cole with ten thousand
men maintained the position in front of Altobiscar, Ibañeta,
and Atalosti, Picton might have maintained the more contracted one behind Linzoain and Erro with twenty thousand.
And that number he could have assembled, because Campbell
reached Eugui long before the evening of the 26th; and Wellington had directed O'Donnel to keep three thousand five
hundred of the blockading troops in readiness to act in advance,
of which Picton could not have been ignorant. It was impossible to turn him by the valley of Urroz, that line being too
rugged for the march of an army and not leading directly upon
Pampeluna. The only roads into the Val de Zubiri were by
Erro and Linzoain, lying close together and both leading upon
the village of Zubiri over the ridges which Picton occupied.
The strength of the position was evident from Soult's declin-

ing an attack on the evening of the 26th when Cole only was before him; and to abandon such ground so hastily when the concentration of the army depended upon keeping it, appears therefore an error; aggravated by the neglect of sending timely information to Wellington who did not know of the retreat until the morning of the 27th, and then only from general Long. It might be that Picton's messenger failed, but many should have been sent when a retrograde movement involving the fate of Pampeluna was contemplated.

Note by the Duke of Wellington, MSS.

It has been said Cole was the adviser of this retreat, which, if completed, would have ruined Wellington's campaign. This is incorrect, Picton was not a man to be guided by others. Cole indeed gave him a report, drawn up by colonel Bell, an able topographer, which stated that no position suitable for a very inferior force existed between Zubiri and Pampeluna; and this was true in the sense of the report, which had reference only to a division not to an army. The battle of Sauroren was indeed fought by inferior numbers; but the whole position, including the ridges occupied by Picton and the Spaniards, was only maintained by equal numbers; and if Soult had attacked seriously early on the 27th the position would have been carried. Bell's report influenced Picton, and it was only when his troops had reached Huarte and Villalba that he suddenly resolved on battle; it was a military resolution, vigorous and prompt—and not the less worthy of praise that he so readily adopted Cole's saving proposition to regain the more forward heights above Zabaldica.

Note by General Cole, MSS.

8°. Soult appeared reluctant to attack on the 26th and 27th, yet success depended upon his forestalling the allies at their point of concentration; and it is somewhat inexplicable that on the 28th, having possession of the ridge beyond the Lanz river and plenty of cavalry, he should have known so little of the sixth division's movements. The general conception of his second scheme has been blamed by some of his own countrymen, apparently from ignorance of the facts and because it failed. Crowned with success it would have been cited as a fine illustration of the art of war. To have incurred at once by the two valleys of Zubiri and Lanz, after being reinforced with twenty thousand men, would have given great importance to his repulse on the 28th; his reputation as a general capable of restoring the French affairs would have vanished; and mischief must have accrued, even though he should have effected his retreat safely, which, regard being had to the narrowness of the valleys the position of Hill and Wellington's boldness, was not certain. To abandon the Val de Zubiri and secure that of Lanz; to obtain another and shorter line of retreat by the Doña Maria pass; to crush Hill with superior numbers, gain the Irurzun road, and succour San Sebastian; or failing of that, to secure the union of the whole army and give to his retreat the appearance of an able offensive movement—to combine all these chances by one operation immediately after a severe check was Soult's plan: it was not impracticable and was surely the conception of a great commander.

To succeed however it was essential either to beat Hill off-hand and thus draw Wellington to that side by the way of Marcalain, or so secure the French left that no efforts against it should prevail to the detriment of the offensive movement on the right: neither was effected. An overwhelming force drove Hill indeed from the road of Irurzun but did not crush him, because he fought so strongly and retired with such good order. Meanwhile the French left was completely beaten and the advantage gained on the right was more than nullified. Soult trusted to the remarkable defensive strength of the ground occupied by his left, and had reason to do so, for it was nearly impregnable, but Wellington turned it on both flanks at the same time. Yet neither Picton's advance into the Val de Zubiri on Foy's left, nor Cole's front attack on that general, nor Byng's assault upon the village of Sauroren, would have seriously damaged the French without the sudden and complete success of Inglis beyond the Lanz. The other attacks would indeed have forced the French to retire some-what hastily up the valley of the Lanz, yet they could have held together in mass secure of their junction with Soult. But when the ridges running between them and the right wing of the French army were carried by Inglis, and the

whole of the seventh division was thrown upon their flank and
rear the front attack became decisive. The key of the defence
was on the ridge beyond the Lanz, and instead of two regiments
Clausel should have placed two divisions there.

9°. Wellington's quick perception and vigorous stroke on
the 30th were to be expected from such a consummate commander, yet he was not master of all the bearings of the
French operations; he knew neither the extent of Hill's
danger nor Soult's difficulties; otherwise it is probable he
would have put stronger columns in motion, and at an earlier
hour, towards the pass of Doña Maria on the morning of the
31st. Hill did not commence his march that day until eight
o'clock, and it has been shown, that with the help of the
seventh division he was too weak to hurt the heavy retreating
mass. The faults and accidents which baffled Wellington's
after operations have been sufficiently touched upon in the
narrative; but he halted in the midst of his victorious career
when Soult's army was broken and flying, when Suchet had
retired into Catalonia and all things seemed favourable for
the invasion of France. His motives for this were strong.
He knew the armistice in Germany had been renewed with a
view to peace, and he had therefore reason to expect Soult
would be reinforced. A forward position in France would
have lent his right to the enemy, who, pivoted upon St. Jean
Pied de Port, could operate against his flank. His arrangements for intercourse with his dépôts and hospitals would
have been more difficult and complicated; and as the enemy
possessed all the French and Spanish fortresses commanding
the great roads, his need to gain one at least before the fine
season closed was absolute, if he would not resign his communications with the interior of Spain. Long marches and
frequent combats had fatigued his troops, destroyed their shoes,
and used up their musket ammunition; the loss of men had
been great, especially of British in the second division, where
their proportion to foreign troops was become too small; the
difficulty of re-equipping the troops would have increased on
entering an enemy's state, because the English system did not
make war support war, and his communications would have
been lengthened. Finally France was to be invaded—France

in which every person was a soldier, where the whole population was armed and organized under men, not, as in other
countries inexperienced in war, but who had all served more
or less.   Beyond the Adour he could not advance, and if a
separate peace was made by the northern powers, if any misfortune befel the allies in Catalonia, so as to leave Suchet at
liberty to operate towards Pampeluna—or if Soult, profiting from
the possession of San Jean Pied de Port, should turn the right
flank of the new position, a retreat into Spain would become
necessary; and be dangerous from the hostility and warlike
disposition of the French people directed in a military manner.

10°. These reasons joined to the fact, that a forward position, although offering better communications from right to
left, would have given the enemy greater facilities for operating
against an army which, until the fortresses fell, must hold a
defensive and somewhat extended line, were conclusive as to
the rashness of an invasion; but they do not appear so conclusive as to the necessity of stopping short after the action of
the 2nd of August.   The questions were distinct.   The one
was a great measure involving vast political and military conditions, the other was simply whether he should profit from
the enemy's distress; and in this view the objections above-
mentioned, save the want of shoes the scarcity of ammunition
and the fatigue of the troops, are inapplicable.   But in the
two last particulars the allies were not so badly off as the
enemy, and in the first not so deficient as to cripple the army;
wherefore, if the advantage to be gained was worth the effort
it was an error to halt.

The solution of the problem is to be found in the comparative condition of the armies.   Soult had recovered his reserve,
his cavalry, and artillery; Wellington was reinforced by
Graham's corps, which was more numerous and powerful than
Villatte's reserve.   The new chances then were in favour of the
allies, and the action of the 2nd of August proved that
their opponents could not stand before them; one more victory
would have gone nigh to destroy the French force altogether;
for such was the disorder, that Maucune had on the 2nd only
one thousand men left out of more than five thousand, and on the 6th he had still a thousand
stragglers, besides killed and wounded; Conroux

Soult's
Report,
MSS.

and La Martiniere were scarcely in better plight, and the losses of the other divisions were great. Foy's eight thousand men were cut off from the main body; and the Nivelle, the sources of which were in the allies' power, was behind the French. With their left pressed from the pass of Maya, thier front assailed by the main body, they could hardly have kept together, since more than twenty-one thousand men, exclusive of Foy's troops, were then absent from their colours. As late as the 12th of August, Soult told the minister of war, that he was indeed preparing to assail his enemy again but had not the means of resisting a counter-attack, although he held a different language to his army and to ^{Appendix 17.} the people of the country.

Had Cæsar halted because his soldiers were fatigued, Pharselia would have been but a common battle.

BOOK THE TWENTY-SECOND.

CHAPTER I.

AFTER the combats of Echallar and Ivantelly, Soult adopted a permanent position. His left under D'Erlon, was on the hills of Ainhoa with an advanced guard overhanging Urdax and Zagaramurdi; his centre under Clausel, was in advance of Sarre guarding the issues from Vera and Echallar, and

Soult MSS.
Plan 6,
page 199.

holding the greater Rhune mountain; the right under Reille, lined the lower Bidossoa to the sea— his third division being under Foy at St. Jean Pied de Port. Villatte's reserve was behind the Nivelle near Serres; one cavalry divison was quartered for the sake of forage between the Nive and Nivelle rivers, the other as far back as Dax.

Wellington occupied his old positions from the pass of Roncevalles to the mouth of the Bidassoa, but the disposition of his troops was different. Hill reinforced by Morillo held the Roncevalles and Alduides, having field-works at the former. The third and sixth divisions guarded the Bastan and Col de Maya; the seventh division reinforced with O'Donnel's Spaniards occupied Echallar and Zagaramurdi. The light division held the Santa Barbara heights, with piquets in the town of Vera; the left rested on the Bidassoa, the right on the Ivantelly rock, round which a bridle communication with Echallar was made by the soldiers. Longa was beyond the Bidassoa on the left of the light division; the fourth division was behind him, near Lesaca. The fourth Spanish army under Freyre prolonged the line from Longa to the sea; it crossed the royal causeway, occupied Irun and Fontarabia and guarded the Jaizquibel mountain. The first division was behind Freyre; the fifth division resumed the siege of San

Sebastian, and the blockade of Pampeluna was given to Carlos
d'España.

These dispositions, made with increased means, were more
powerful for defence than the former.   A strong corps under
one general was entrenched at Roncevalles; and in the Bastan,
two British divisions, admonished by Stewart's error, were
more than sufficient to defend the Col de Maya.   The Echallar
mountains were, with the aid of O'Donnel's Spaniards, equally
secure; and the reserves posted near Lesaca supported the left,
now the most important part of the line.   The castles of
Zaragoza and Daroca had fallen, and the Empecinado, directed
upon Alcanitz, maintained the communication between the
Catalan army and Mina; the latter and Duran were near
Jaca, from whence they could retreat by Sanguessa on Pampeluna.   General Paris being thus menaced, retired after a skirmish into France, leaving eight hundred men in Jaca.   Lord
William Bentinck was then before Taragona.   The allies were
thus in direct military communication from the Mediterranean
to the Bay of Biscay, while the French could only communicate
circuitously through France.

Soult did not fear a front attack, but the augmentation of
force at Roncevalles and Maya was disquieting, as menacing
to turn him by the course of the Nive.   Paris was therefore
placed at Oleron to support Foy; the fortresses of St. Jean
Pied de Port and Navareins were armed as a pivot of operations on that side; Bayonne served a like purpose on the other
flank; and a fortified line from the mouth of the Bidassoa, up
to the rocks of Mondarain and the Nive was commenced.
But Wellington, having little to fear from a renewed attack on
the side of Pampeluna, was wholly bent on the siege of St.
Sebastian.   Nor was that a trifling operation, for he was
thwarted in a manner to prove that the English ministers were
no better than the Spanish and Portuguese authorities.   Lord
Melville was at the head of the Admiralty; under him the
navy of England first met with disaster in battle; and his
negligence in giving maritime aid to the operations in Spain
went nigh to fasten a like misfortune on the army.   This,
combined with the cabinet scheme of sending Wellington to
Germany, shows that time had taught the English ministers

nothing as to the Peninsula war; or that elated with the array
of sovereigns against Napoleon they were now careless of a
cause so mixed up with democracy.   That lord Melville, a
man of ordinary capacity, should have been suffered to retard
and endanger the final success of a general, whose sure judgment and extraordinary merit were authenticated by exploits
unparalleled in English warfare, would be incredible if Wellington's correspondence, and that of Mr. Stuart, did not
establish the following facts.

1°. Desertion from the enemy was stopped, chiefly because
the Admiralty refused to let the ships of war carry deserters or
prisoners to England; they were thus heaped up at Lisbon
and maltreated by the Portuguese government, which checked
all desire in the French troops to come over.

2°. When the disputes with America commenced, Mr.
Stuart's efforts to obtain flour for the army were vexatiously
thwarted by the Admiralty; which permitted, if it did not
encourage, the English ships of war to capture American vessels trading under the secret licences.

3°. The refusal of the Admiralty to establish certain cruisers
along the coast caused the loss of many store-ships and merchantmen, to the great detriment of the army before it quitted
Portugal.   Fifteen were taken off Oporto, and one close to the
bar of Lisbon in May.   And afterwards, the
Appendix 14.   Mediterranean packet bearing despatches from
lord William Bentinck was captured, which led to lamentable
consequences; for the papers were not in cipher, and contained
detailed accounts of plots against the French in Italy with the
names of the principal persons engaged.

4°. A like neglect of the coast of Spain caused ships containing money shoes and other indispensable stores to remain
in port, or risk being taken on the passage by cruisers issuing
from Santona, Bayonne, and Bordeaux.   And
Wellington,   while the communications of the allies were thus
MSS.   intercepted, the French coasting vessels supplied
their army and fortresses without difficulty.

5°. After the battle of Vitoria, Wellington was forced to use
French ammunition, though too small for the English muskets,
because the ordnance store-ships which he had ordered from

Lisbon to Santander could not sail for want of convoy. When the troops were in the Pyrenees, a reinforcement of five thousand men was kept at Gibraltar and Lisbon waiting for ships of war; and the transports employed to convey them were thus withdrawn from the service of carrying home wounded men, at a time when the Spanish authorities at Bilbao refused, even for payment, to concede public buildings for hospitals.

6°. When snow was falling on the Pyrenees the soldiers were without proper clothing, because the ships containing their great-coats, though ready to sail in August, were detained at Oporto until November waiting for convoy. When the victories of July were to be turned to profit ere the fitting season for the siege of San Sebastian should pass away, the attack of that fortress was retarded sixteen days, because a battering-train and ammunition, demanded several months before by Wellington, had not yet arrived from England.

7°. During the siege the sea communication with Bayonne was free. 'Anything in the shape of a naval force,' said Wellington, 'would drive away sir George Collier's squadron.' The garrison received reinforcements, artillery, ammunition, and all necessary stores for its defence, sending away the sick and wounded men in empty vessels. The Spanish general blockading Santona complained at the same time that the exertions of his troops were useless, because the French succoured the place by sea when they pleased; and after the battle of Vitoria not less than five vessels laden with stores and provisions, and one transport having British soldiers and clothing on board, were taken by cruisers issuing out of that port. The great advantage of attacking San Sebastian by water as well as by land was foregone for want of naval means; and from the same cause British soldiers were withdrawn from their own service to unload store-ships; the gun-boats employed in the blockade were Spanish vessels manned by Spanish soldiers withdrawn from the army, and the store-boats were navigated by Spanish women!

8°. The coasting trade between Bordeaux and Bayonne being quite free, the French, whose military means of transport had been so crippled by their losses at Vitoria that they could scarcely have collected magazines with land-carriage only, received their supplies by water, and were thus saved trouble and expense and the unpopularity attending forced requisitions.

Between April and August, more than twenty applications and remonstrances were addressed by Wellington to the government upon these points, without producing the slightest attention.   Mr. Croker, under-secretary of the Admiralty, of whose conduct he particularly complained, was permitted to write an offensive official letter to him, while his demands and the dangers to be apprehended from neglecting them were disregarded; and to use his own words, '*since Great Britain had been a naval power a British army had never before been left in such a situation at a most important moment.*'

Nor is it easy to determine whether negligence and incapacity, or a grovelling insensibility to national honour prevailed most in the cabinet, when we find this renowned general complaining, that the government, ignorant even to ridicule of military operations, seemed to know nothing of the nature of the element with which England was surrounded; and lord Melville insensible to the glorious toils of the Peninsula, telling him that his army was the last thing to be attended to!

RENEWED SIEGE OF ST. SEBASTIAN.

[See Plan, page 181.]

Villatte's demonstration against Longa on the 28th of July had caused the ships laden with the battering-train to put to sea, but on the 5th of August the guns were re-landed and the works against the fortress resumed.   On the 8th, a notion having spread that the enemy was mining under the cask redoubt, the engineers seized the occasion to exercise their inexperienced miners by sinking a shaft and driving a gallery; the men soon acquired expertness, but the water rose in the shaft at twelve feet, and the work was discontinued when the gallery had attained eighty feet.   The old trenches were repaired, the heights of San Bartolomeo were strengthened, and the convent of Antigua, built on a rock to the left of those heights, was fortified and armed with two guns to scour the open beach and sweep the bay.   The siege however languished

for want of ammunition; and during this forced inactivity
the garrison received supplies and reinforcements by sea,
repaired their damaged works, made new defences, filled their
magazines, and put sixty-seven pieces of artillery in a condition
to play.   Eight hundred and fifty men had been killed and
wounded since the commencement of the attack in July; but
fresh men came by sea, and more than two thousand six
hundred good soldiers were still present under arms.   And to
evince their confidence, they celebrated the emperor's birth-
day by crowning the castle with a splendid illumination,
encircling it with a fiery legend to his honour in characters so
large as to be distinctly read by the besiegers.

On the 19th, after a delay of sixteen days, the battering-
train arrived from England, and in the night of the 22nd
fifteen heavy pieces were placed in battery, eight at the right
attack seven at the left.   A second battering-train came on
the 23rd, augmenting the number of pieces of various kinds
to a hundred and seventeen, including a large Spanish mortar;
but with characteristic negligence this enormous armament
had been sent out from England with no more shot and shells
than would suffice for one day's consumption!

In the night of the 23rd the batteries on the Chofres were
reinforced with four long pieces and four sixty-eight pound
carronades; the left attack had six additional guns.   Ninety
sappers and miners had come with the train from England,
the seamen under lieutenant O'Reilly were again attached to
the batteries, and part of the field-artillerymen were brought
to the siege.   The Chofre batteries were also enlarged to
contain forty-eight pieces, and two batteries for thirteen pieces
were begun on the heights of Bartolomeo.   These last were to
breach, at seven hundred yards distance, the faces of the left
demi-bastion of the horn-work, that of St. John on the main
front, and the end of the high curtain; for these works, rising
in gradation one above another were in the same line of shot.
The approaches on the isthmus were pushed forward by the
sap, but the old trenches were still imperfect; and before daylight on the 25th the French, coming from the horn-work,
swept the left of the parallel, injured the sap, and made some
prisoners

In the night of the 25th the batteries were all armed on both sides of the Urumea, and on the 26th fifty-seven pieces, opening with a general salvo, continued to play with astounding noise and rapidity until evening. The firing from the Chofre hills destroyed the revêtement of the demi-bastion of St. John, and nearly ruined the towers at the old breach, together with the wall connecting them; but at the isthmus, the batteries although they injured the horn-work made little impression on the main front, from which they were too far distant.

Wellington, present at this attack and discontented with the operation, then ordered a battery for six guns to be constructed amongst some ruined houses on the right of the parallel, three hundred yards from the main front. Two shafts were also sunk with a view to drive galleries for its protection against the enemy's mines; but the sandy soil made this work slow.

Early on the 27th the boats of the squadron, under lieutenant Arbuthnot of the Surveillante, carrying a hundred soldiers of the ninth regiment under captain Cameron, attacked the island of Santa Clara. The troops landed with some difficulty under a heavy fire, but a lodgment was made with the loss of only twenty-eight men and officers, of which eighteen were seamen. In the night the French sallied against the new battery on the isthmus; but as colonel Cameron of the ninth regiment met them on the very edge of the trenches with the bayonet the attempt failed, yet it delayed the arming of the battery. At daybreak the renewed fire of the besiegers was extremely heavy, and the shrapnel shells were supposed to be very destructive; nevertheless the practice with that missile was very uncertain, the bullets frequently flew amongst the guards in the parallel and one struck the field-officer. In the course of the day another sally was commenced, but the enemy being fired upon did not persist. The trenches were now furnished with banquettes and parapets as fast as the quantity of gabions and fascines would permit; yet the work was slow; because the Spanish authorities of Guipuscoa, like those in every other part of Spain, neglected to provide carts to convey the materials from the woods, and this hard labour was performed by Portuguese soldiers: these things however should have been prepared during the blockade.

Wellington visited the works again, and the advanced battery was armed with four guns and opened next morning; but an accident prevented the arrival of one gun, the enemy dismounted another, and only two, instead of six guns as Wellington had designed, smote the demi-bastion of St. John and the end of the high curtain. However the general firing was severe upon the castle and the town-works and the defences were damaged; the French guns were nearly silenced, additional mortars were mounted at the Chofres, making in all sixty-three pieces of which twenty-nine threw shells, and the superiority of the besiegers was established. Now however the Urumea was discovered to be fordable by captain Alexander Macdonald of the artillery, who had waded across in the night, and passed close under the works to the breach. A few minutes would suffice to bring the enemy into the Chofre batteries, and therefore, to save the guns from being spiked their vents were covered at night with iron-plates fastened by chains.

This day the materials and ordnance for a battery of six pieces, to take the defences of the Monte Orgullo in reverse, were sent to the island of Santa Clara; and from the Chofres some guns played on the retaining wall of the horn-work; but with low charges to shake down any mines constructed there without destroying the wall itself, which offered cover for the troops in an assault. The trenches at the isthmus were now wide and good, the sap was pushed close to the horn-work; and the sea-wall, supporting the high road into the town, which had in the first assault lengthened the run and cramped the columns, was broken through to give access to the strand and shorten the approach to the breaches. The crisis was now at hand, and in the night of the 29th a false attack was ordered, to make the enemy spring his mines. This desperate service was executed by lieutenant Macadam of the ninth regiment; the order was sudden and no volunteers were demanded, no rewards offered, no means of excitement resorted to; yet such is the inherent bravery of British soldiers, that seventeen men of the royals, the nearest at hand, immediately leaped forth ready and willing to encounter what seemed certain death. With a rapid pace, all the breaching-batteries playing hotly at the time, they reached the foot of the breach unperceived, and then mounted in extended order shouting and firing; the French were too steady to be imposed upon, their musketry laid the party low, and their commander returned nearly alone to the trenches.

On the 30th the sea flank being opened from the half-bastion of St. John to the most distant of the old breaches, five hundred feet, the Chofre batteries were turned against the castle and the other defences of the Monte Orgullo. The battery on the isthmus, in conjunction with the fire from the Chofres, also demolished the face of the St. John's bastion and the end of the high curtain above it; thus the whole of that quarter was in ruins. The San Bartolomeo batteries then broke the demi-bastion of the horn-work, and Wellington after examining the defences decided to make a lodgment and ordered an assault for the next day at eleven o'clock, when the ebb of tide would leave space between the horn-work and the water. The galleries in front of the advanced battery on the isthmus were now pushed to the sea wall; and three mines were formed with the double view of opening a way for the troops to reach the strand, and rendering useless any subterranean works the enemy might have made in that part. At two o'clock in the morning of the 31st they were sprung and opened three wide passages; these were immediately connected, and a traverse of gabions, six feet high, was run across the mouth of the main trench on the left, to screen the opening from the grape-shot of the castle. Everything was now ready for the assault, but before describing that terrible event it will be fitting to show the exact state of the besieged in defence.

Graham had been before the place for fifty-two days, during thirty of which the attack was suspended. All this time the garrison had laboured incessantly; and though the besiegers' fire appeared to have ruined the defences of the enormous breach in the sea flank it was not so. A perpendicular fall behind of more than twenty feet barred progress; and beyond, amongst the ruins of the burned houses, was a strong counter-wall fifteen feet high, loopholed for musketry and parallel with the breaches, which were also cut off from the sound part of the rampart by traverses at the extremities. The only really practicable road into the town was by the narrow end of the high curtain above the half bastion of St. John.   About the middle of the great breach stood the tower of Los Hornos, still capable of some defence, and beneath it a mine charged with twelve hundred weight of powder.   The streets were all trenched and furnished with traverses to dispute the passage and cover a retreat to the Monte Orgullo; to reach the main breach it was necessary also to form a lodgment in the horn-work, or pass, as in the former assault, under a flanking fire of musketry for two hundred yards: and the first step was close under the sea wall at the salient angle of the covered way, where two mines charged with eight hundred pounds of powder were prepared.

Besides these retrenchments and mines, the French had still some artillery in reserve.   One sixteen-pounder mounted at St. Elmo flanked the left of the breaches on the river face; a twelve and an eight-pounder, preserved in the casemates of the Cavalier, were ready to flank the land face of the half-bastion of St. John; many guns from the Monte   *Belmas.* Orgullo, especially those of the Mirador, could play upon the columns, and there was a four-pounder hidden on the horn-work to be brought into action when the assault commenced.   Neither the resolution of the governor nor the courage of the garrison was abated, but the overwhelming fire of the last few days had reduced the number of fighting men; and Rey who had only two hundred and fifty men in reserve, demanded of Soult whether his brave garrison should be exposed to another assault. 'The army would endeavour to succour him' was the reply, and he abided his fate.

Napoleon's ordinance, which forbade the surrender of a fortress without having stood at least one assault, has been strongly censured by English writers upon slender grounds. The obstinate defences made by French governors in the Peninsula were the results; and to condemn an enemy's system from which we have ourselves suffered will scarcely bring it into disrepute.   The argument runs that the besiegers working by the rules of art must make way into the place and to risk an assault for the sake of military glory or to augment the loss of the enemy, is to sacrifice brave men uselessly; capitulation always followed a certain advance of the besiegers in Louis the Fourteenth's time; and to suppose Napoleon's upstart generals possessed superior courage and sense of military honour to the high-minded nobility of that age was quite inadmissible. It has been rather whimsically added also, that obedience to the emperor's orders might suit a predestinarian Turk but could not be tolerated by a reflecting Christian. From this it would seem, that certain nice distinctions as to extent and manner reconcile human slaughter with Christianity; and the true standard of military honour was fixed by the intriguing depraved and insolent Louis the Fourteenth. It may however be supposed, that as Napoleon's generals far surpassed the cringing courtier commanders of Louis in military daring they possessed greater military virtue. Moreover marshal Villars held, that a governor should never surrender, and when his works were ruined should break through the besiegers. Lord Clive also recommended that an ordinance similar to Napoleon's should be applied to British fortresses in India. Finally Napoleon's ordinance was merely a revival of one issued by Louis himself!

But the whole argument rests on false grounds. To inflict loss on an enemy is the essence of war; and as the bravest men will always be foremost in an assault the loss thus occasioned may be of the utmost importance. To resist when nothing can be gained or saved is an act of barbarous courage which reason spurns at; but Napoleon only demanded a resistance which should make it dangerous for the besiegers to hasten a siege beyond the rules of art,—he would not have a weak governor yield to a simulation of force,—he desired that military honour should rest upon the courage and resources of men rather than upon the strength of walls: in fine he made a practical application of the proverb that necessity is the mother of invention. Granted that a siege conducted with sufficient means must reduce the fortress attacked; still a governor may display his resources of mind. Vauban admits of one assault and several retrenchments after a lodg-

ment is made on the body of the place. Napoleon only
insisted that every effort which courage and genius could
dictate should be exhausted before a surrender, and those
efforts can never be defined or bounded before-hand. Tarifa
is a happy example.

To be consistent, any attack which deviates from the rules
of art must also be denounced as barbarous; yet how seldom
has a general all the necessary means at his disposal. In
Spain not one siege could be conducted by the British army
according to the rules. And there is a manifest weakness in
praising the Spanish defence of Zaragoza, and condemning
Napoleon, because he demanded from regular troops a devo-
tion similar to that displayed by peasants and artisans. What
governor was ever in a more desperate situation than Bizanet
was at Bergen-op-Zoom? General Graham, with a hardihood
and daring which would alone place him amongst the foremost men of enterprise which Europe can boast of, threw
more than two thousand men upon the ramparts of that
almost impregnable fortress. The young soldiers of the garrison, surprised in the night, were dispersed, were flying, the
British had possession of the walls for several hours! yet
some cool and brave officers rallied their men, charged up
the narrow ramps and drove the assailants over the parapets
into the ditch; they who could not at first defend their
works were then able to retake them; and so completely successful and illustrative of the principle was this counter-
attack, that the number of prisoners equalled that of the
garrison. There are no rules to limit energy and genius, and
no man knew better than Napoleon how to call those qualities
forth: he possessed them himself in the utmost perfection and
created them in others.

CHAPTER II.

STORMING OF SAN SEBASTIAN.

To assault the breaches without having destroyed the enemy's defences or established a lodgment on the horn-work was, notwithstanding the increased fire and greater facilities of the besiegers, obviously a repetition of error. And the same generals who had before made their disapproval of such operations public, now more freely dealt out censures, not ill-founded, but very indiscreet, since there is much danger when doubts come down from the commanders to the soldiers. Wellington thought the fifth division had been thus discouraged. He was incensed and demanded fifty volunteers from each of the fifteen regiments composing the first, fourth, and light divisions, *men who could show other troops how to mount a breach.* Such was the phrase employed, and seven hundred and fifty gallant soldiers instantly marched to San Sebastian in answer to the appeal. Colonel Cooke and major Robertson led the guards and Germans of the first division; major Rose commanded the men of the fourth division; colonel Hunt. a daring officer who had already won his promotion at former assaults, was at the head of the fierce rugged veterans of the light division: yet there were good officers and brave soldiers in the fifth division.

It being at first supposed that Wellington designed only a simple lodgment on the great breach, the volunteers and one brigade of the fifth division only were ordered to be ready; but in a council held at night, major Smith maintained that the orders were misunderstood, as no lodgment could be formed unless the high curtain was gained. General Oswald being called to the council was of the same opinion; whereupon the remainder

of the fifth division was brought to the trenches; and general
Bradford having offered the services of his Portuguese brigade,
was told he might ford the Urumea and assail the farthest
breach if he judged it advisable. Leith had now resumed
command of the fifth division, and directed the attack from
the isthmus; but he was extremely offended with the volunteers and would not suffer them to lead the assault; some he
spread along the trenches to keep down the fire of the horn-
work, the remainder were held in reserve with Hay's British
and Sprye's Portuguese brigades of the fifth division; to
Robinson's brigade the assault was confided. It was formed
in two columns, one to attack the old breach between the
towers, the other to storm the bastion of St. John and the end
of the high curtain. The small breach on the extreme right
was left for Bradford's Portuguese, who were on the Chofre
hills; some large boats filled with troops were directed to make
a demonstration against the sea-line of the Monte Orgullo,
and Graham overlooked the whole operations from the right
bank of the river.

Heavily the morning of the 31st broke, a thick fog hid
every object and the besiegers' batteries could not open until
eight o'clock; from that hour however a constant shower of
missiles was poured upon the besieged until eleven, when
Robinson's brigade quitted the trenches, and passing through
the openings in the sea-wall was launched against the
breaches. While the head of this column was still gathering
on the strand, thirty yards from the salient angle of the horn-
work, twelve men under a sergeant, whose heroic death has
not sufficed to preserve his name, running violently forward
leaped upon the covered way with intent to cut the sausage of
the enemy's mines. The French startled by this sudden
assault fired the train prematurely; but though the sergeant and
his followers were all destroyed and the high sea-wall thrown
with a dreadful crash upon the head of the advancing column,
not more than forty men were crushed by the ruins, and the
rush of the troops was scarcely checked. The forlorn hope
had before passed beyond the play of the mine, and now
speeded along the strand amidst a shower of grape and shells,
the leader, lieutenant Macguire of the fourth regiment, con-

spicuous from his long white plume, his fine
Cooke's
Memoirs.
figure and his swiftness, bounding far ahead of
his men in all the pride of youthful strength and
courage; but at the foot of the great breach he fell dead,
and the stormers went sweeping like a dark surge over his
body; many died however with him, and the trickling of
wounded men to the rear was incessant.

This time there was a broad strand left by the retreating
tide, and the sun had dried the rocks; yet they still disturbed
the order and closeness of the formation, and the main breach
was two hundred yards distant. The French, seeing the first
mass pass the horn-work, regardless of its broken bastion,
crowded to the river face and poured their musketry into the
second column as it rushed along a few yards below them;
but the English returned this fire without slackening their
speed. Then the batteries of Monte Orgullo and the St.
Elmo sent down showers of shot and shells, the two pieces on
the Cavalier swept the face of the breach in St. John, the four-
pounder in the horn-work was suddenly mounted on the
broken bastion and poured grape-shot into the rear. Thus
scourged with fire from all sides, the stormers, their array
broken alike by the shot and by the rocks they passed over,
reached their destinations. The first column soon gained
the top of the great breach, but the unexpected gulf below
could only be passed at a few places where meagre parcels of
the burned houses were still attached to the rampart, and the
deadly French muskets, clattering from the loop-holed wall
beyond, strewed the crest of the ruins with dead. In vain the
following multitude, covering the ascent, sought entrance at
every part; to advance was impossible, and slowly sinking
downwards the mass remained stubborn and immoveable on
the lower part of the breach. There they were covered from
the musketry in front; but from isolated points, especially
from Los Hornos under which the great mine was placed, the
French still smote them with small arms, and from Monte
Orgullo came shells and grape without intermission.

At the half bastion of St. John the access to the top of
the high curtain being quite practicable, the efforts to force a
way were more persevering and constant, and the slaughter

was in proportion; for the traverse on the flank was defended by French grenadiers who would not yield; the two pieces on the Cavalier itself swept the front of the opening, and the four-pounder and musketry from the horn-work swept the river face. Some sappers and a working party attached to the assaulting columns endeavoured to form a lodgment; but no artificial materials had been provided, and most of the labourers were killed before they could raise the loose rocky fragments into a cover. During this time the British counter-fire of artillery killed many; and the reserve brigades of the fifth division were pushed on by degrees to feed the attack, until the left wing of the ninth regiment only remained in the trenches. The volunteers also, who had been with difficulty restrained in the trenches, 'calling out to know why they had been brought there if they were not to lead the assault,' these men, whose presence had given such offence to Leith that he would have kept them altogether from the assault, being now let loose went like a whirlwind to the breaches and the crowded masses swarmed up the face of the ruins; but on reaching the crest line, they came down again like a falling wall: crowd after crowd were seen to mount, to totter, to sink; the French fire was unabated, the smoke floated away and the crest of the breach bore no living man!

Graham, standing on the nearest of the Chofre batteries, beheld this frightful destruction with a stern resolution to win at any cost; and he was a man to have put himself at the head of the last company and die sword in hand upon the breach rather than sustain a second defeat; yet neither his confidence nor his resources were yet exhausted. He directed an attempt to be made on the horn-work, and turned all the Chofre batteries and one on the isthmus, that is to say the concentrated fire of fifty heavy pieces upon the high curtain. The shot ranged over the heads of the troops, now gathered at the foot of the breach; and the stream of missiles thus poured along the upper surface broke down the traverses and in its fearful course, shattering all things, strewed the rampart with the mangled limbs of the defenders. Notes by colonel Hunt, MSS. When this flight of bullets first swept over the heads of the soldiers a cry arose from some in-

T 2

experienced people, ' to retire because the batteries were firing
on the stormers;' but the veterans of the light division under
Hunt were not men to be so disturbed; and in the very heat
and fury of the cannonade they effected a solid lodgment in
some ruins of houses actually within the rampart on the right
of the great breach.

For half an hour this horrid tempest smote upon the works
and the houses behind; and when it ceased, the small clatter
of the French muskets showed that the fight was renewed.
At this time also the thirteenth Portuguese regiment, led by
major Snodgrass and followed by a detachment of the twenty-
fourth under colonel Macbean, entered the river from the
Chofres.   The ford was deep, the water rose above the waist,
and when the soldiers reached the middle of the stream, which
was two hundred yards wide, a heavy gun struck the head of
the column with a shower of grape; the havoc was fearful
yet the survivors closed and moved on.   A second discharge
from the same piece tore the ranks from front to rear; still
the regiment moved on; and amidst a confused fire of musketry from the ramparts and of artillery from St. Elmo, from
the castle and from the Mirador, landed on the left bank and
rushed against the third breach.   Macbean's men following
with equal bravery reinforced the great breach eighty yards
to the left of the other, although the line of ruins seemed to
extend the whole way.

Then the fighting became fierce and obstinate again at all
the breaches; but the French musketry still rolled with deadly
effect, the heaps of slain increased, and once more the great
mass of stormers sunk to the foot of the ruins unable to
win—the living sheltered themselves as they could, and the
dead and wounded lay so thickly that hardly could it be
judged whether the hurt or unhurt were the most numerous.

It was now evident the assault must fail unless some accident intervened; for the tide was rising, the reserves all
engaged, and no greater effort could be expected from men
whose courage had been already pushed to the verge of madness.   In this crisis fortune interfered.   A number of powder
barrels, live shells, and combustible materials, which the
French had accumulated behind the traverses for their defence,

caught fire. Soon a bright consuming flame wrapped the whole of the high curtain, a succession of loud explosions were heard, hundreds of the French grenadiers were destroyed, the rest were thrown into confusion; and while the ramparts were still enveloped with suffocating eddies of smoke the British soldiers broke in at the first traverse. The defenders, bewildered by this terrible disaster, yielded for a moment, yet soon rallied and a close desperate struggle took place along the summit of the high curtain; but the fury of the stormers, whose numbers increased every moment, could not be stemmed. The French colours on the Cavalier were torn away by lieutenant Gethin of the eleventh regiment; the horn-work, the land front below the curtain, the loop-holed wall behind the great breach, were all abandoned; the light division soldiers who had already established themselves in the ruins on the French left, penetrated to the streets; and the Portuguese at the small breach, mixed with British who had wandered to that point seeking for an entrance, burst in on their side.

Five hours the dreadful battle had lasted at the walls, and now the stream of war went pouring into the town. The undaunted governor still disputed the victory for a short time with the aid of his barricades; but several hundreds of his men were cut off and taken in the horn-work, and even to effect a retreat behind the line of defences which separated the town from the Monte Orgullo was difficult: however a crowd of his troops, flying from the horn-work along the harbour flank of the town, broke through a body of the British who had reached the vicinity of the fortified convent of Santa Téresa. This post was the only one retained by the French in the town, and it was thought that Monte Orgullo might have been carried, if a general to direct the troops had been at hand; but whether from wounds or accident no officer of that rank entered the place until long after the breach had been won; the battalion chiefs were thus embarrassed for want of orders, and a thunder-storm, coming down from the mountains with unbounded fury immediately after the place was carried, added to the confusion of the fight.

This storm seemed to be a signal from hell for the perpetration of villany which would have ashamed the most ferocious

barbarians of antiquity. At Rodrigo intoxication and plunder
had been the principal object; at Badajos lust and murder
were joined to rapine and drunkenness; but at San Sebastian,
the direst the most revolting cruelty was added to the cata-
logue of crimes,—one atrocity of which a girl of seventeen
was the victim, staggers the mind by its enormous, incredible,
indescribable barbarity. The resolution of the troops to throw
off discipline was quickly made manifest. A British staff-
officer was pursued with a volley of small arms and escaped
with difficulty from men who mistook him for the provost-
marshal of the fifth division; a Portuguese adjutant who
endeavoured to prevent some wickedness was put to death in
the market-place, not with sudden violence from a single
ruffian, but deliberately by a number of English soldiers; and
though many officers exerted themselves to preserve order and
many men were well conducted, the rapine and violence commenced by villains spread; the camp-followers soon crowded
into the place, and the disorder continued until the flames,
following the steps of the plunderer, put an end to his ferocity
by destroying the whole town. Three generals, Leith, Oswald,
and Robinson, had been hurt in the trenches; sir Richard
Fletcher, chief engineer, a brave man who had long served his
country honourably, was killed; colonel Burgoyne, second
engineer, was wounded, and the carnage at the breaches was
appalling. The volunteers, although brought late into the
action had nearly half their number struck down; most of the
regiments of the fifth division suffered in the same proportion,
and the whole loss since the renewal of the siege exceeded two
thousand five hundred men and officers.

When the town was taken the steep and rugged Monte
Orgullo with its citadel remained to be assailed. It presented
four batteries connected with masonry in first line; and from
the extremities, ramps protected by redans led to the Santa
Téresa convent, which offered a salient point of defence. On
the side facing Santa Clara, and behind the Orgullo were some
sea batteries; and if all these works had been of good construction and guarded by fresh troops, the second siege would
have been difficult. But the force of the garrison was shattered
by the recent assault, most of the engineers had been killed,

the governor and many others wounded, five hundred men were sick or hurt, the soldiers fit for duty did not exceed thirteen hundred, and they had four hundred prisoners to guard. The castle was small, the bomb-proofs scarcely sufficed to protect the ammunition and provisions, and only ten guns remained in a condition for service, three of which were on the sea line. There was very little water, and the troops had to lie out on the naked rock exposed to fire or only covered by the asperities of ground: Rey and his brave garrison were however still resolute to fight, and they received nightly by sea small supplies of ammunition.

Wellington arrived the day after the assault. Regular approaches could not be carried up the steep naked rock, he doubted the power of vertical fire, and ordered batteries to be formed on the captured works of the town, intending to breach the enemy's remaining lines of defence and then storm the Orgullo. Meanwhile seeing the Santa Téresa would enable the French to sally by the rampart on the left of the allies, he composed his first line with a few troops strongly barricaded, and placed a supporting body in the market-place with strong reserves on the high curtain and flank ramparts. But from the convent, which was actually in the town, the enemy killed many of the besiegers; and when after several days it was assaulted, they set the lower parts on fire and retired by a communication made from the roof to a ramp on the hill behind. All this time the flames were licking up the houses, and the Orgullo was overwhelmed with a vertical fire of shells.

On the 3rd of September the governor was summoned, but his resolution was not to be shaken, and the vertical fire was therefore continued day and night. The British prisoners suffered as well as the enemy; for the officer com-   Jones.
manding in the castle, irritated by the misery of the garrison, cruelly refused to let the unfortunate captives make trenches to cover themselves; the French also   Bellas.
complain that their wounded and sick men, lying in an empty magazine with a black flag flying, and having the English prisoners in their red uniforms placed around to strengthen the claim of humanity, were fired upon.

Guns for the new batteries were now brought from the

Chofres across the Urumea; at first by night, but the difficulty
of struggling with the water in darkness, induced the transport
by day and within reach of the French batteries, which however did not fire.   The flaming houses impeded the works,
but the ruins furnished cover for marksmen to gall the French,
and the guns on Santa Clara were augmented and worked by
seamen.   With the besieged ammunition was scarce, the
horrible vertical fire subdued their energy, and the besiegers
laboured freely until the 8th; then fifty-nine heavy pieces
opened at once from the island, the isthmus, the horn-work
and the Chofres, and in two hours the Mirador and Queen's
battery were broken, the French fire extinguished, the hill
torn and furrowed in a frightful manner; the bread-ovens
were destroyed, a magazine exploded, and the castle, small and
crowded with men, was overlaid with the descending shells.
Then the governor, proudly bending to fate, surrendered.   On
the 9th this brave man and his heroic garrison, reduced to
one-third of their original number and leaving five hundred
wounded behind them in the hospital, marched out with the
honours of war.   The Spanish flag was hoisted under a salute
of twenty-one guns, and the siege terminated after sixty-three
days open trenches; precisely when the tempestuous season,
then beginning to vex the coast, would have rendered a con-
tinuance of the sea blockade impossible.

OBSERVATIONS.

1°. San Sebastian, a third-rate fortress and in bad condition when first invested, resisted a besieging army possessing
an enormous battering-train for sixty-three days.   This is to
be attributed partly to the errors of the besiegers, principally
to obstructions extraneous to the military operations; and
conspicuous among the last was the misconduct of the Admiralty and general negligence of the government.   The latter
retarded the siege for sixteen days, the former enabled the
garrison to increase its means as the siege proceeded.   The
Spanish failures came next, the authorities would not supply
carts and boats, and even refused the use of their public
buildings for hospitals!   Thus between the sea and the shore,

receiving aid from neither, Wellington had to conduct an operation which more than any other depends for success upon labour and provident care: it was the first time that an important siege was maintained by women's exertions, for the stores of the besiegers were landed from boats rowed by Spanish girls! Soult's advance was but a slight interruption; the want of ammunition would have equally delayed the siege. The measure of the English ministers' negligence is thus obtained—it was more hurtful than the operations of sixty thousand men under a great general.

2°. In the second siege, the approaches on the isthmus were pushed further than in the first attack, and the French fire on the front was more quelled; the openings made in the sea-wall enabled the troops to get out of the trenches more rapidly, and shortened the distance to the breach. These were advantages, but not proportionate to the increase of the besiegers' means, which were sufficient to ruin all the defences, if employed to silence the enemy's fire, according to the rules of art: a lodgment in the horn-work could then have been made with little difficulty, and the breach attacked without much danger.

3°. The faults of the first attack were repeated in the second, and the enemy's resources had increased, because a sea intercourse with France was never cut off; it follows, there was no reasonable chance of success in the assault, nor even to make a lodgment on the breach, for the workmen, being without materials, failed to effect that object. The primary arrangement, the change adopted in the council of war, the option given to Bradford, the remarkable fact, that the simultaneous attack on the horn-work was only thought of when the first efforts against the breach had failed, all prove, that the enemy's defensive means were underrated, and the success exceeded the preparations to obtain it. The place was in fact won by accident. For the explosion of the great mine under Los Hornos, was only prevented by a happy shot which cut the sausage of the train during the fight; and this was followed by the ignition of the French powder-barrels and shells along the high curtain, which alone opened the way into the town. Graham's firmness and perseverance in the

assault, and the judicious usage of his artillery during the
action, were no mean helps to the victory; it was on such
occasions that his prompt genius shone; yet it was nothing
wonderful that heavy guns at short distances, the range
perfectly known, should strike with certainty along a line of
rampart more than twenty-seven feet above the heads of the
troops.   Such practice was to be expected, and Graham's
genius was more evinced by the promptness of the thought
and the trust he put in the valour of his soldiers.   It was
more remarkable that the stormers did not relinquish their
attack when thus exposed to their own guns; for it is a mis-
take to say no mischief occurred; a serjeant of the ninth
regiment was killed close to his commanding officer, and
other casualties also had place.

4°. It is supposed the explosion on the ramparts was
caused by the cannonade from the Chofres; yet a
Captain
Cooke. cool observer, whose account I have adopted
because he was a spectator undisturbed, affirms
that the cannonade ceased before Snodgrass forded the river,
and the great explosion did not happen until half-an-hour
after that event.   That intrepid exploit of the Portuguese
was thought one of the principal causes of success; and an
entrance was certainly made at the small breach by several
soldiers, British and Portuguese, many of the former having
wandered from the great breach and got mixed with the latter,
before the explosion happened on the high curtain.   Whether
those men would have been followed by greater numbers is
doubtful, but the lodgment made by the light division
volunteers within the great breach was solid and could have
been maintained.   The French call the Portu-
Bellas. guese attack a feint.   Graham certainly did not
found much upon it.   He gave Bradford the option to attack
or remain tranquil; and M'Bean actually received counter-
orders when his column was already in the river, but he was
then too far advanced.

5°. When the destruction of San Sebastian became known,
it was used by the anti-British party at Cadiz to excite the
people against England.   The political chief of Guipuscoa
publicly charged Graham with having ' *sacked and burned the*

place because it had formerly traded entirely with France,' his generals were said to have excited the furious soldiers to the horrid work, and his inferior officers to have boasted of it afterwards. A newspaper, edited by an agent of the Spanish government, repeating these accusations called upon the people to avenge the injury upon the British army. The Spanish minister of war demanded explanations. Wellington designating him as the abettor, and even the writer of this and other malignant libels published at Cadiz, addressed a letter of indignant denial and remonstrance to sir Henry Wellesley. 'It was absurd,' he said, 'to suppose the officer of the army would have risked the loss of all their labours and gallantry, by encouraging the dispersion of the men while the enemy still held the castle. To him the town was of the utmost value as a secure place for magazines and hospitals. He had refused to bombard it when advised to do so, as he had previously refused to bombard Ciudad Rodrigo and Badajos, because the injury would fall on the inhabitants and not upon the enemy; yet nothing could have been more easy or less suspicious than this method of destroying the town if he had been so minded. It was the enemy who set fire to the houses, it was part of the defence; the British officers strove to extinguish the flames, some in doing so lost their lives by the French musketry from the castle; and the difficulty of communicating and working through the fire was so great, that he had been on the point of withdrawing the troops altogether. He admitted the plunder, observing, that he knew not whether that or the libels made him most angry; he had taken measures to stop it; but when two-thirds of the officers had been killed or wounded in the action, and when many of the inhabitants taking part with the enemy fired upon the troops, to prevent it was impossible. Moreover he was for several days unable from other circumstances to send fresh men to replace the stormers.

This was a solid reply to the scandalous libels circulated, but the broad facts remained. San Sebastian was a heap of smoking ruins, and atrocities degrading to human nature had been perpetrated by the troops. A detailed statement of these crimes was published and signed by the municipal and

ecclesiastical bodies, the consuls, and principal persons of San
Sebastian, who solemnly affirmed the truth of each case; and
if Spanish testimony here is not to be heeded, four-fifths of the
excesses attributed to the French armies must be effaced as
resting on a like though a weaker foundation. That the town was
fired behind the breaches during the operations, and that it
spread in the tumult following the assault is undoubted; yet
it is not improbable that plunderers increased it; and certainly the great destruction did not befall until long after the
place was in possession of the allies.   I have been assured by
a surgeon, that he lodged the third day after the assault at a
house well furnished, and in a street then untouched by fire
or plunderers, but house and street were afterwards plundered
and burned.   The inhabitants could only have fired upon the
allies the first day, and it might well have been in self-
defence for they were barbarously treated.   The abhorrent
case of the young girl was notorious, so were many others.
Around the piquet fires, where soldiers, as every experienced
officer knows, speak without reserve of their past deeds and
feelings, I have heard the abominable actions mentioned by
the municipality, related with little variation long before that
narrative was published; told however with sorrow for the
sufferers, and indignation against the perpetrators; for these
last were not so numerous as might be supposed from the
extent of the calamities they inflicted.

It is a common but shallow and mischievous notion, that a
villain makes never the worse soldier for an assault, because
the appetite for plunder supplies the place of honour; as ..
the compatibility of vice and bravery rendered the union of
virtue and courage unnecessary in warlike matters.   In all the
host which stormed San Sebastian there was not a man, being
sane, would for plunder only have encountered the danger of
that assault; yet under the spell of discipline all rushed eagerly
to meet it.   Discipline however has its root in patriotism, or
how could armed men be controlled at all?   It would be wise
and not difficult to graft moderation and humanity upon such
a noble stock.   The modern soldier is not necessarily the stern
bloody-handed man the ancient soldier was, there is as much
difference between them as between the sportsman and the

butcher; the ancient warrior, fighting with the sword and reaping his harvest of death when the enemy was in flight became habituated to the act of slaying.   The modern soldier seldom uses his bayonet, sees not his peculiar victim fall, and exults not over mangled limbs as proofs of personal prowess. Hence, preserving his original feelings, his natural abhorrence of murder, he differs not from other men unless often engaged in the assault of towns, where rapacity lust and inebriety, unchecked by the restraints of discipline, are excited by temptation.   It is said no soldier can be restrained after storming a town, and a British soldier least of all because he is brutish and insensible to honour!   Shame on such calumnies!   What makes the British soldier fight as no other soldier ever fights? His pay!   Soldiers of all nations receive pay.   At the period of this assault, a serjeant of the twenty-eighth regiment, named Ball, had been sent with a party *Cadell's Memoirs.* to the coast from Roncevalles, to make purchases for his officers.   He placed the money he was entrusted with, two thousand dollars, in the hands of a commissary, and having secured a receipt persuaded his party to join in the storm : he survived, reclaimed the money, made his purchases and returned to his regiment.   And these are the men, these the spirits, who are called too brutish to work upon except by fear!   it is precisely fear to which they are most insensible.

Undoubtedly if soldiers hear and read that it is impossible to restrain their violence they will not be restrained.   But let the plunder of a town after an assault be expressly made criminal by the articles of war, with a due punishment attached; let it be constantly impressed upon the troops that such conduct is as much opposed to military honour and discipline as it is to morality; let a select body of men receiving higher pay form a part of the army and be charged to follow storming columns, with power to inflict instantaneous punishment, death if it be necessary.   Finally, as reward for extraordinary valour should keep pace with chastisement for crimes committed under such temptation, it would be fitting that money, apportioned to the danger and importance of the service, should be insured to the successful troops and always paid without delay.   This might be taken as ransom from enemies, but if the inhabitants are friends, or too poor, government should furnish the amount. With such regulations the storming of towns would not produce more military disorders than the gaining of battles in the field.

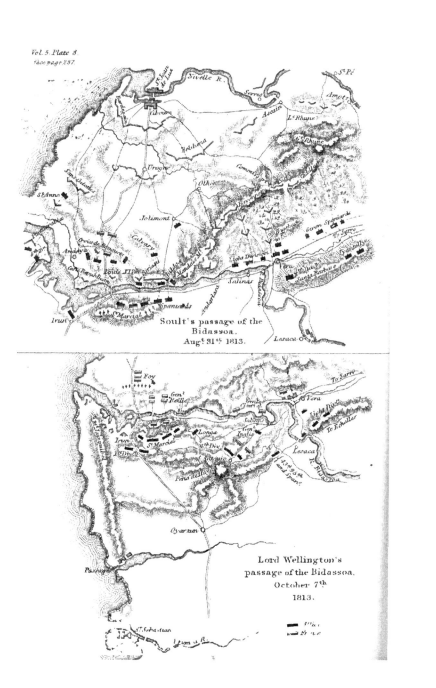

Soult's passage of the
Bidassoa.
Augt 31st 1813.

Lord Wellington's
passage of the Bidassoa.
October 7th
1813.

CHAPTER III.

WHILE San Sebastian was being stormed Soult fought a
battle with the covering force; not willingly nor with much
hope of success; but he was averse to let the place fall without
another effort and thought a bold demeanour would best
hide his real weakness. Guided by the progress of the siege,
which he knew through his sea communication, he awaited
the last moment of action, striving meanwhile to improve his
resources and to revive the confidence of the army and of
the people. Of his dispersed soldiers eight thousand had
rejoined their regiments by the 12th of August, and he was
promised a reinforcement of thirty thousand conscripts; these
last were however yet to be enrolled; and neither the progress of the siege nor the general panic along the frontier,
which recurred with increased violence after the late battles,
would suffer him to remain inactive. He knew his enemy's
superior strength of position, number, and military confidence; but his former efforts had interrupted the attack of
San Sebastian, and another offensive movement would necessarily produce a like effect; wherefore he hoped by repeating
the disturbance, as long as the intercourse by sea enabled him
to reinforce and supply the garrison, to render the siege a
wasting operation. To renew the movement against Pampeluna was most advantageous; but it required fifty thousand
infantry for attack, twenty thousand for observation on the
lower Bidassoa, and he had not such numbers. Subsistence
also was uncertain, because the loss of all the military carriages at Vitoria was still felt; and the resources of the
country were reluctantly yielded by the French people. To
act on the side of St. Jean Pied de Port was therefore impracticable. To attack the allies' centre, at Vera, Echallar, and
the Bastan, was unpromising, seeing that two mountain-

chains were to be forced before the movement could seriously affect Wellington: moreover, the ways being impracticable for artillery, success would lead to no decisive result.

To attack the left of the allies by the great road of Irun remained. Against that quarter he could bring more than forty thousand infantry, but the positions were of perilous strength. The upper Bidassoa was in Wellington's power, because the light division, occupying Vera and the heights of Santa Barbara on the right bank, covered all the bridges. The lower Bidassoa, flowing from Vera with a bend to the left, separated the hostile armies on an extent of nine miles; but from the broken bridge of Behobia in front of Irun, to the sea, the river, broad and tidal, offered no apparent facility for a passage; and between the fords of Biriatu and those of Vera, three miles, there was only the one passage of Andarlassa, two miles below Vera: along this space also, steep craggy mountain ridges without roads, lining the river, forbad any great operations. Thus the points of attack were restricted to Vera, and the fords between Biriatu and the broken bridge of Behobia.

To raise the siege of San Sebastian it was only necessary to force a way to Oyarzun, a small town seven or eight miles beyond the Bidassoa, from thence the assailants could march at once upon Passages and upon the Urumea. The royal road led directly to Oyarzun along the broad valley separating the Peña de Haya from the Jaizquibel mountain. The latter was on the sea-coast, but the Peña de Haya, commonly called the four-crowned mountain, filled with its dependent ridges all the space between Vera, Lesaca, Irun, and Oyarzun. Its staring head bound with a rocky diadem was impassable; but from the bridges of Vera and Lesaca, several roads, one of them not absolutely impracticable for guns, passed over its enormous flanks to Irun at one side, to Oyarzun on the other, falling into the royal road at both places. Soult's first design was to unite Clausel's and D'Erlon's troops, drive the light division from Santa Barbara, and then, using the bridges of Lesaca and Vera, force a passage over the Peña de Haya on the left of its summit, and push the heads of columns towards Oyarzun and the upper Urumea: Reille and Villatte, passing the Bidassoa at Biriatu, were meanwhile to fight their way to Oyarzun by the royal road. He foresaw that Wellington might during this time collect his right wing and seek to envelope the French army, or march upon Bayonne: but he thought daring measures were necessary, and the progress of the besiegers at San Sebastian soon drove him into action.

Soult, MSS.

On the 29th Foy, marching by the road of Lohoussoa, crossed the Nive at Cambo and reached Espelette; leaving behind him six hundred men and the national guards who were very numerous, with orders to watch the roads and valleys leading upon St. Jean Pied de Port. If pressed by superior forces, this corps of observation was to fall back upon that fortress, and it was supported with a brigade of light cavalry stationed at St. Palais. In the night two of D'Erlon's divisions were secretly drawn from Ainhoa, and Foy continued his march through Espelette, by the bridges of Amotz and Serres to San Jean de Luz, from whence the reserve moved forward. Thus in the morning of the 30th two strong French columns of attack were assembled on the lower Bidassoa. One under Clausel, being twenty thousand men with twenty pieces of artillery, was concentrated in the woods behind the Commissari and Bayonette mountains above Vera. The other under Reille, furnished, including Villatte's reserve, only eighteen thousand men; but Foy's division with some light cavalry were in rear ready to augment this column to twenty-five thousand: and there were thirty-six pieces of artillery and two bridge equipages collected near the camp of Urogne on the royal road.

Reille's troops were secreted, partly behind the Croix des Bouquets mountain, partly behind that of Louis XIV. and the lower ridges of the Mandale, near Biriatu. D'Erlon, having Conroux's and Abbé's divisions and twenty pieces of artillery, held the camps in advance of Sarre and Ainhoa. If the allies in his front marched to reinforce their own left on the crowned mountain, he was to vex and retard their movements, avoiding a serious engagement and feeling to his right for Clausel's column—that is to say, Abbé's division, moving from Ainhoa, was to menace Zagaramurdi and the Puerto de Echallar, while

Conroux's division, then in front of Sarre, was to menace the light division, seize the rock of Ivantelly if it was abandoned, and join Clausel if occasion offered. But if the allies assembled a large force to operate offensively by the Nive and Nivelle rivers, D'Erlon, without losing his connexion with the main army, was to concentrate on the slopes descending from the Rhune mountain towards San Pé. If the attack on the lower Bidassoa succeeded he was to join Clausel by Vera, or by the heights of Echallar and the bridge of Lesaca. D'Erlon was also to have been strengthened with the heavy cavalry; but forage could only be obtained for the artillery horses, the light horsemen, six chosen troops of dragoons, and two or three hundred gens-d'armes, which were all assembled on the royal road behind Reille.

Soult designed to attack at daybreak the 30th, but his preparations being incomplete he deferred it until the 31st, and took rigorous precautions to prevent intelligence passing over to the allies' camps. Nevertheless Wellington's emissaries advised him of the movements in the night of the 29th; the augmentation of troops in front of Irun was observed in the morning of the 30th; and in the evening the bridge equipage and the artillery were descried on the royal road beyond the Bidassoa. Thus warned he prepared for battle with little anxiety. For the brigade of English foot-guards, left at Oporto when the campaign commenced, was now come up; most of the marauders and men wounded at Vitoria had rejoined, and three regiments just arrived from England formed a new brigade under lord Aylmer; making the total augmentation of British troops in this quarter little less than five thousand men. His extreme left was on the Jaizquibel. This narrow mountain, seventeen hundred feet high, runs along the coast, abutting at one end upon the Passages harbour, and at the other upon the navigable mouth of the Bidassoa. Offering no mark for attack it was only guarded by a Spanish detachment; but at its foot the small fort of Figueras, commanding the entrance of the river, was garrisoned by seamen from the naval squadron. Fuenterabia, a walled town at the mountain foot, was also occupied, and the low ground between it and Irun was defended by a chain of eight large field redoubts; thus the Jaizquibel was connected with the heights covering the royal road to Oyarzun.

On the right of Irun, between Biriatu and the bridge of Behobia, there was a sudden bend in the river, the concave towards the French, and their positions commanded the passage of the fords below; but opposed to them was the exceedingly stiff ridge, called San Marcial, terminating one of the great flanks of the Pena de Haya. The water flowed round the left of this ridge, confining the road, leading from the bridge of Behobia to Irun, for one mile to the narrow space between its channel and the foot of the height. Irun itself, strongly occupied and defended by a field-work, blocked this way; and it followed that the French, after forcing the passage of the river, must of necessity win San Marcial before their army could use the great road.

Six thousand Spaniards under Freyre were established on the crest of San Marcial, which was strengthened by abbatis and temporary field works. Behind Irun the first British division under Howard was posted, and lord Aylmer's brigade was pushed somewhat in advance to support the left of the Spaniards. The right of San Marcial, falling back from the river, was, although distinct as a position, connected with the Pena de Haya and in some degree exposed to an enemy passing the river above Biriatu; wherefore, Longa's Spaniards were drawn from those slopes of the Pena de Haya which descended towards Vera, to be posted on those descending towards Biriatu:—in that situation he protected the right of San Marcial.

Eighteen thousand fighting men were thus directly opposed to the progress of the enemy. The fourth division, quartered near Lesaca, was still disposable, and a Portuguese brigade was detached from it, to replace Longa on the heights opposite Vera; and to cover the roads leading from the bridge and fords of that place over the flanks of the Pena de Haya. The British brigades were stationed up the mountain, close under the foundry of San Antonio, where they commanded the intersection of the roads coming from Vera and Lesaca, and formed a reserve to the Portuguese brigade, to Longa, and to Freyre, tying the whole together. The Portuguese brigades were how-

ever somewhat exposed, and too weak to guard the enormous
slopes on which they were placed; wherefore Inglis's brigade
of the seventh division came from Echallar to reinforce it:
even then, the flanks of the Pena de Haya being so rough and
vast, the troops seemed sprinkled here and there with little
coherence. Wellington, aware that his positions were too
extensive, had commenced the construction of redoubts on
commanding points of the mountain; and had traced out a
fortified camp on some heights immediately in front of
Oyarzun, which connected the Haya with the Jaizquibel, but
these works were unfinished.

During the night of the 30th, Soult garnished with artillery
all the points commanding the fords of Biriatu, the descent to
the bridge and the banks below, called the Bas de Bebobia.
This was to cover the passage of the fords, and formation
of the bridges, and to stop gun-boats coming up;
Soult. MSS. in which view also he spread Casa Palacio's brigade
of Joseph's Spanish guards along the river to Andaya, fronting
Fuenterabia.

Reille was directed to storm San Marcial, and leave a strong
reserve there in watch for troops coming from Vera or
descending the Pena de Haya; with the rest of his force he
was to drive the allies from ridge to ridge, until he gained
that flank of the great mountain which descends upon Oyarzun.
The royal road being thus opened, Foy's division and the
cavalry and artillery were to cross by bridges to be laid during
the attack on San Marcial; and it was Soult's intention to
retain this last-named ridge and fortify it as a bridge-head with
a view to subsequent operations.

To aid Reille and provide for the concentration of the whole
army at Oyarzun, Clausel was directed to make a simultaneous
attack from Vera; not as at first designed by driving the
allies from Santa Barbara and seizing the bridges; but leaving
one division and his guns above Vera to keep the light division
in check, to cross the river by two fords below and assail that
slope of the Pena de Haya where the Portuguese brigade and
Inglis were posted. Then forcing his way upwards to the
forge of San Antonio, he could aid Reille directly by falling
on the rear of San Marcial, or meet him at Oyarzun by
turning the rocky summit of the Pena de Haya.

Combat of San Marcial.—At daylight on the 1st, Reille, under protection of the French guns, forded the Bidassoa, above Biriatu, with two divisions and two pieces of artillery. He quickly seized a detached ridge of inferior height just under San Marcial, and leaving one brigade there as a reserve, detached another to attack the Spanish left by a slope which descended in that quarter to the river. La Martiniere's division assailed their right at the same time, but the mountain was covered with brushwood and remarkably steep; the French troops preserved no Soult, MSS. order, the supports and skirmishers got mixed in confusion, and when two-thirds of the height were gained the Spaniards charged in columns and drove them headlong down. Meanwhile two bridges were thrown below the fords, and the head of Villatte's reserve passed and renewed the fight more vigorously; one brigade even reached the chapel of San Marcial, and the left of the Spanish line was shaken; but the eighty-fifth regiment advanced from lord Aylmer's brigade to support it, and at that moment Wellington rode up with his staff. The Spaniards cared very little for their own officers; but with that noble instinct which never abandons the poor people of any country, acknowledged real greatness without reference to nation; at his order, with loud shouts they dashed their adversaries down, and with so much violence that many were driven into the river, where some of the pontoon boats coming to their succour were overloaded and sunk. It was several hours before the confused masses could be rallied, or the bridges, which had been broken up to let the boats save the drowning men, be repaired. When this was effected, Soult, who overlooked the action from the summit of the mountain Louis XIV., sent the remainder of Villatte's reserve over the river, and calling up Foy prepared a more formidable attack; and he expected greater success, because the operation on the side of Vera, of which it is time to treat, was now making considerable progress up the Pena de Haya on the allies right.

Combat of Vera.—Clausel had descended the Bayonette and Commissari mountains under cover of a thick fog, but at seven o'clock the weather cleared, and three heavy columns were seen by the troops on Santa Barbara making for the

fords below Vera, in the direction of two hamlets called the
Salinas and the Bario de Lesaca. A fourth division remained
with the guns on the mountain slopes, and the artillery opened
now and then upon the little town of Vera; from which the
piquets of the light division were recalled, with exception of
one post in a fortified house commanding the bridge. At
eight o'clock the enemy's columns began to pass the fords,
covered by the fire of their artillery; yet the first shells
thrown fell into the midst of their own ranks, and the British
troops on Santa Barbara cheered the French battery with a
derisive shout. Their march was however sure, and a battalion of light troops without knapsacks quickly
commenced battle with the Portuguese brigade,
and by their extreme activity and rapid fire forced the latter
to retire up the slopes of the mountain. Inglis
reinforced the line of skirmishers and the whole
of his brigade was soon afterwards engaged; but
Clausel menaced his left flank from the lower
ford, and still forced a way upwards without a check, until
the whole mass disappeared fighting amidst the asperities of the
Pena de la Haya. Inglis lost two hundred and seventy men
and twenty-two officers, and finally halted on a ridge commanding the intersection of the roads leading from Vera and
Lesaca to Irun and Oyarzun. This was somewhat below the
foundry of Antonio, where the fourth division, having now
recovered its Portuguese brigade, was, in conjunction with
Longa's Spaniards, so placed as to support and protect
equally the left of Inglis and the right of Freyre on San
Marcial.

> Soult, MSS.

> Notes by
> general
> Inglis,
> MSS.

From the great height and asperity of the mountain the
fight occupied many hours, and it was past two o'clock ere the
head of Clausel's columns reached this point. The French
troops left in front of Santa Barbara made no movement; and
as Wellington had before directed the light division to aid
Inglis, a wing of the forty-third and three companies of the
riflemen from Kempt's brigade, with three weak Spanish
battalions drawn from O'Donnel's Andalusians at Echallar,
crossed the Bidassoa by the Lesaca bridge. They were to
occupy some lower slopes on the right of Inglis, and cover

another knot of minor communications coming from Lesaca
and Vera; the remainder of Kempt's brigade occupied Lesaca
itself; and thus the connexion between Santa Barbara and the
positions of the fourth division on the Pena de la Haya was
completed.

Clausel seeing these movements, and thinking the allies at
Echallar and Santa Barbara were only awaiting Clausel's
the proper moment to take him in flank and rear Report,
if he engaged further up the mountain, abated MSS
his battle and sent notice to Soult. This opinion was well
founded; Wellington was not a general to let half his army
be paralysed by D'Erlon's divisions. On the 30th, when he
observed Soult's first preparations in front of San Marcial, he
had ordered attacks to be made upon D'Erlon from the Puerto
of Echallar, Zagaramurdi and Maya; Hill was also to show
the heads of columns towards St. Jean Pied de Port. And
on the 31st when the force and direction of Clausel's columns
were known, he directed Giron to sustain the light division on
Santa Barbara, and lord Dalhousie to bring the remainder of
the seventh division by Lesaca to aid Inglis.

Following these orders Giron, who commanded the
Spaniards, O'Donnel being sick, slightly skirmished on the
30th with Conroux's advanced posts in front of Sarre, and
on the 31st at daybreak the whole of the French line was
assailed. That is to say, Giron again fought with Conroux,
feebly as before; but two Portuguese brigades of the sixth
and seventh divisions, directed by lord Dalhousie and general
Colville, drove the French from their camp behind Urdax and
burned it. Abbé who commanded there, being thus pressed,
collected his whole force in front of Ainhoa on an entrenched
position, and repulsed the allies with some loss. Thus five
combats were fought in one day at different points of the
general line; and D'Erlon, who had lost three or four hundred men, seeing a fresh column coming from Maya as if to
turn his left, judged that a great movement against Bayonne
was in progress and sent notice to Soult. He was mistaken.
Wellington only sought by these demonstrations to disturb
the plan of attack. Giron and the seventh division, following
the second orders, then marched towards Lesaca; but as the

fighting at Urdax lasted until mid-day, lord Dalhousie's movement was not completed that evening.

D'Erlon's despatch reached Soult at the time Clausel's report arrived. All his arrangements for a final attack on San Marcial were then completed; but these reports and the ominous cannonade at San Sebastian, plainly heard during the morning, induced him to abandon this object and hold his army ready for a general battle on the Nivelle. In this view he sent Foy, who had not yet crossed the Bidassoa, to Serres behind the Nivelle as a support to D'Erlon, and six troops of dragoons marched to San Pé higher up that river. Clausel was directed to repass the Bidassoa in the night, to leave Maransin upon the Bayonette mountain and the Col de Vera, and march with his other three divisions to join Foy on the heights of Serres.

But Reille's troops were still beyond the Bidassoa and the battle went on sharply; for the Spaniards continually detached men from the ridge, endeavouring to drive the French from the lower positions into the river, until about four o'clock; then their hardihood abating they desired to be relieved; but Wellington, seeing the French attacks were exhausted, thought it a good opportunity to fix the Spanish military spirit, and refused to relieve or to aid them. It would not be just to measure their valour by this fact. The English general blushed while he called upon them to fight, for they had been previously famished by their vile government, and there were no hospitals to receive them when wounded. The battle was however arrested by a tempest which commenced about three o'clock, and raged for several hours with wonderful violence. Huge branches were torn from the trees and whirled through the air like feathers by the howling winds, and the thinnest streams, swelling into torrents, dashed down the mountains rolling innumerable stones along with a frightful clatter. This was the storm which fell at San Sebastian, and amidst its turmoil and under cover of night the French recrossed the Bidassoa.

Clausel's retreat was more unhappy. Having received the order to retire early in the evening when the storm had already put an end to all fighting, he repassed the fords before

dark with two brigades, ordering general Vandermaesen to
follow with the remainder of his divisions.   It would appear
that he expected no difficulty, since he did not take possession of the bridge of Vera, nor of the fortified
house covering it, and occupied himself with sug-   Soult. MSS.
gesting new projects displeasing to Soult.   Meanwhile Vandermaesen's division was endangered; many of his soldiers
attempting to cross were drowned by the rising waters; and
finally, unable to effect a passage at the fords, he marched up
the stream to seize the bridge of Vera.   His advanced guard
surprised a corporal's piquet and rushed over, but it was
driven back by a rifle company posted in the fortified house.
This happened at three o'clock in the morning, and the riflemen defended the passage until daylight, when a second
company and some caçadores came to their aid.   The French
reserve left at Vera, seeing how matters stood, then opened a
fire of guns against the fortified house from a high rock just
above the town; and their skirmishers approached it on the
right bank, while Vandermaesen plied his musketry from the
left bank.   The two rifle captains and many men fell under
this cross fire, and the passage was forced, but Vandermaesen,
urging the attack in person, was killed and more than two
hundred of his soldiers were hurt.

Soult, having heard from Count D'Erlon that offensive
movements on the side of Maya had entirely ceased at twelve
o'clock on the 31st, now contemplated another attack on San
Marcial; but in the course of the day Rey's report of the
assault reached him, and he heard that Hill was in movement
on the side of St. Jean Pied de Port.   San Sebastian was lost,
a fresh attempt to carry off the wasted garrison from the
castle would cost five or six thousand good soldiers, and the
safety of the whole army would be endangered by pushing
headlong amongst the terrible asperities of the crowned
mountain.   Wellington could throw his right wing and centre,
amounting to thirty-five thousand men, upon the French left
during the action; and he would be nearer to Bayonne than
the French right when once the battle was engaged beyond
the lower Bidassoa.   The recent actions had cost three thousand six hundred men; Vandermaesen had been killed,

La Martiniere, Mene, Remond, and Guy were wounded, the first mortally; all the superior officers agreed that a fresh attempt would be most dangerous, and serious losses might draw on an immediate invasion of France before the necessary defensive measures were completed.

Yielding to these reasons, Soult resolved to recover his former positions and remain entirely on the defensive; for which his vast knowledge of war, his foresight, his talent for methodical arrangement and his firmness of character peculiarly fitted him. Twelve battles or combats fought in seven weeks, bore testimony that he had strived hard to regain the offensive for the French army; and willing still to strive if it might be so, he had called upon Suchet to aid him and demanded fresh orders from the emperor; but Suchet helped him not, and Napoleon's answer indicated at once his own difficulties and his reliance upon Soult's capacity and fidelity.

I have given you my confidence, and can add neither to your means nor to your instructions.'

One thousand Anglo-Portuguese and sixteen hundred Spaniards had been killed or wounded, making, with the loss in the assault, above five thousand; yet the siege was not disturbed; the French were powerless against those strong positions. Forty-five thousand French had been poured on to a square of less than five miles, and were repulsed by ten thousand, for that number only of the allies fought. But Soult's battle was only a half measure. Wellington's experience of French warfare, his determined character, coolness, and thorough acquaintance with the principles of his art, left no hope that he would suffer two-thirds of his army to be kept in check by D'Erlon; and accordingly, when that general was menaced, Soult made a counter-movement to deliver battle on more favourable ground. Perhaps his secret hope was to draw his opponent to such a conclusion; but if so, the combat of San Marcial was too dear a price to pay for the chance. If he had really resolved to force a way to San Sebastian, he would have organized his rear so that no serious embarrassment could arise from partial incursions towards Bayonne; he would have concentrated his whole army, and made his attack felt at San Sebastian before a counter-movement could

be felt at Bayonne.   In this view, D'Erlon would have come
in the night of the 30th to Vera, which, without weakening
the reserve opposed to the light division, would have augmented
Clausel by ten thousand men; and on the most important
point, because San Marcial offered no front for the action of
great numbers.

The secret of mountain warfare is, by surprise or the power
of overwhelming numbers to seize such commanding points
as shall force an enemy either to abandon his strong position
or become the assailant to recover the points thus lost.
Now the difficulty of defending the crowned mountain was
evinced by the rapid manner in which Clausel at once gained
the ridges as far as the foundry of San Antonio; with ten
thousand additional men he might have gained a commanding
position on the rear and left flank of San Marcial, and forced
the allies to abandon it.   That Wellington thought himself
weak on the Haya mountain is proved by his calling up the
seventh division from Echallar, and by his orders to the light
division.   Soult's object was to raise the siege, but his plan
involved the risk of having thirty-five thousand allies interposed between him and Bayonne; a more decisive operation
than the raising of the siege; wherefore the enterprise may be
pronounced injudicious.   He admitted indeed   Soult's Cor-
that excited to the enterprise, partly by insinua-   respondence,
tions, whether from the minister of war or his own   MSS.
lieutenants does not appear, partly by a generous repugnance
to abandon the brave garrison, he was too precipitate, acting
contrary to his judgment; but he was probably tempted by
the hope of obtaining at least the camp of San Marcial as a
bridge-head, and thus securing a favourable point for after
combinations.

Wellington having resolved not to invade France at this
time, was unprepared for so great an operation as throwing his
right and centre upon Soult's left; and it is obvious also that
on the 30th he expected only a partial attack at San Marcial.
The order he first gave to assail D'Erlon's position, and the
counter-order for the seventh division to come to Lesaca,
prove this; because the latter was issued after Clausel's
numbers and the direction of his attack were ascertained.

Two Portuguese brigades sent against D'Erlon rendered null
Soult's combinations, and his extreme sensitiveness to their
attacks marks the vice of his own.   Here it may be observed
that the movement of the forty-third the rifle companies and
Spaniards, to secure the right flank of Inglis, was ill-arranged.
Despatched by different roads, without knowing precisely the
point they were to concentrate at, each fell in with the enemy
at different places; the Spaniards got under fire and altered
their route; the forty-third, stumbling on a French division
had to fall back half a mile; it was only by thus feeling the
enemy at different points that the destined position was at
last found, and a disaster was scarcely prevented by the fury
of the tempest.   Those detachments were however finally well
placed to have struck a blow the next morning, because they
were only half an hour's march from the high ground behind
Vandermaesen when he forced the bridge at Vera; the firing
would have served as a guide, and the rest of Kempt's brigade
could also have moved upon the same point from Lesaca; but
it is difficult to seize such occasions in mountain warfare where
so little can be seen of the general state of affairs.

A more obvious advantage was neglected by general Skerrett.
A single company of rifles defended the bridge an hour; and
four brigades of the enemy, crossing in a tumultuous manner
could not have cleared the narrow passage after it was won in
a moment; Wellington's despatch erroneously describes the
French as passing under the fire of great part of Skerrett's
brigade, whereas that officer remained inert on the lower
slopes of Santa Barbara, half a mile distant, and allowed the
enemy to escape.   A large mass of French troops were indeed
on the counter-slopes of the Bayonette mountain, beyond
Vera; but the seventh division, then close to Santa Barbara,
would have prevented any serious disaster if the blow had
failed.   A great opportunity was certainly lost.

CHAPTER IV.

SOULT was so fearful of an attack along the Nive, that his uneasy movements made the allies think he was again preparing for offensive operations: this double misunderstanding did not however last long, and each army resumed its former position. The fall of San Sebastian had given Wellington a new port and point of support, had increased the value of Passages as a dépôt, and let loose many troops for field operations; the armistice in Germany was at an end, Austria had joined the allies, and it seemed therefore certain that he would immediately invade France. The English cabinet had promised the continental sovereigns that it should be so when the French were expelled from Spain, meaning Navarre and Guipuscoa; and the newspaper editors were, as usual, actively deceiving the people of all countries by their dictatorial absurd projects and assumptions. The Bourbon partisans were secretly endeavouring to form a conspiracy in the south; and the duke of Berri desired to join the British army, pretending that twenty thousand Frenchmen, armed and organized, awaited his arrival. All was exultation and extravagance. Wellington however, well understanding the inflated nature of such hopes and promises, while affecting to rebuke the absurdity of the newspapers, took the opportunity to check similar folly in higher places, by observing, '*that if he had done all that was expected he should have been before that period in the moon.*'

With respect to the duke of Berri it was for the sovereigns he said to decide whether the restoration of the Bourbons should form part of their policy, but as yet no fixed line of conduct on that or any other political points was declared. It was for their interest to get rid of Napoleon, and there could be no question of the advantage or propriety of

accepting the aid of a Bourbon party without pledging themselves to dethrone the emperor.   The Bourbons might indeed
decline, in default of such a pledge, to involve their partisans
in rebellion; and he advised them to do so, because Napoleon's power rested, internally upon the most extensive and
expensive system of corruption ever established in any
country; externally upon his military force which was supported almost exclusively by foreign contributions.   Once confined to the limits of France he would be unable to bear the
double expense of his government and army; the reduction
of either would be fatal to him, and the object of the Bourbons thus obtained without risk.   But, if they did not concur
in this reasoning, the allies in the north of Europe must
declare they would dethrone Napoleon before the duke of
Berri should be allowed to join the army; and the British
government must make up its mind upon the question.

   This reasoning put an end to the project, because neither
the English cabinet nor the allied sovereigns were ready to
adopt a decisive open line of policy.   The ministers exulting
at the progress of aristocratic domination, had no thought
save that of wasting England's substance by extravagant subsidies and supplies; these were taken without gratitude by
the continental powers, who held themselves no-ways bound
thereby to uphold the common cause, which each secretly
designed to make available for peculiar interests: moreover
they still trembled before their former conqueror, and none
would pledge themselves to a decided policy.   Wellington
alone moved with a firm composure, the result of profound
and well-understood calculations; yet his mind, naturally so
dispassionate, was strangely clouded at this time by personal
hatred of Napoleon.

   Where is the proof, or even probability, of that great man's
system of government being internally dependent upon '*the
most extensive corruption ever established in any country.*'
The annual expenditure of France was scarcely half that of
England; and Napoleon rejected public loans, which are the
life-blood of state corruption.   He left no debt.   Under him
no man devoured the public substance in idleness merely
because he was of a privileged class; the state servants were

largely paid, but they were made to labour effectually for the state. They did not eat their bread and sleep. His system of public accounts, remarkable for its exactness, simplicity and comprehensiveness, was vitally opposed to public fraud and therefore extremely unfavourable to corruption. Napoleon's power was supported in France by that deep sense of his goodness as a sovereign, and that admiration for his genius which pervaded the poorer and middle classes of the people; by the love they bore him, and still bear for his memory, because he cherished the principles of a just equality. They loved him also for his incessant activity in the public service, his freedom from private vices; and because his public works, wondrous for their number their utility and grandeur, never stood still: under him the poor man never wanted work. To France he gave noble institutions, a comparatively just code of laws, and glory unmatched since the days of the Romans. His *Cadastre*, more extensive and perfect than the Doomsday Book, that monument of the wisdom and greatness of our Norman Conqueror, was alone sufficient to endear him to the nation. Rapidly advancing under his vigorous superintendence, it registered and taught every man the true value and nature of his property, and all its liabilities public or private. It was designed and ably adapted to fix and secure titles to property, to prevent frauds, to abate litigation, to apportion the weight of taxes equally and justly, to repress the insolence of the tax-gatherer without injury to the revenue, and to secure the sacred freedom of the poor man's home. The French *Cadastre*, although not original, would, from its comprehensiveness, have been, when completed, the greatest boon ever conferred upon a civilized nation by a statesman.

To say that the emperor was supported by his soldiers, is to say that he was supported by the people; because the law of conscription, that mighty staff on which France leaned when all Europe attempted to push her down,—the conscription, without which she could never have sustained the dreadful war of antagonist principles entailed upon her by the revolution,—that energetic law, which he did not establish, but which he freed from abuse and rendered great,

national, and endurable, by causing it to strike equally on all
classes,—the conscription made the soldiers the real represen-
tatives of the people. The troops idolized Napoleon, well
they might; and to say their attachment commenced only
when they became soldiers, is to acknowledge that his excellent qualities and greatness of mind turned hatred into devo-
tion the moment he was approached. But Napoleon never
was hated by the people of France; he was their own creation
and they loved him so as never monarch was loved before.
His march from Cannes to Paris, surrounded by hundreds of
thousands of poor men, who were not soldiers, can never be
effaced or even disfigured. For six weeks, at any moment, a
single assassin might by a single shot have acquired the reputation of a tyrannicide; and obtained vast rewards besides
from the trembling monarchs and aristocrats of the earth, who
scrupled not to instigate men to the shameful deed. Many
there were base enough to undertake, none so hardy as to
execute the crime; and Napoleon, guarded by the people of
France, passed unharmed to a throne from whence it required
a million of foreign bayonets to drive him again. From the
throne they drove him, not from the thoughts and hearts of
men. He has been recalled once alive, once dead!

Wellington, having shaken off the weight of the continental
policy, proceeded to consider the question of invading France
simply as a military operation, which might conduce to, or
militate against the security of the Peninsula while Napoleon's
power was weakened by the war in Germany. And such was
his inflexible probity of character, that no secret ambitious
promptings, no facility of gaining personal reputation, diverted
him from this object; he would not evade, when he might
have done so by assenting to the minister's projects for Germany and Italy, the enormous embarrassments and mortifica-
tions still attending his work, though to the surface-seeing
public there appeared none. Austria's accession to the coali-
tion favoured the invasion of France, yet he relied little on the
military skill of the banded sovereigns, and a defeat might at
any moment dissolve their alliance. Napoleon could then
reinforce Soult and drive the allies back upon Spain, where
the French still possessed the fortresses of Santona, Pampe-

luna, Jaca, Venasque, Monzon, Fraga, **Lerida,** Mequinenza, Figueras, Gerona, Hostalrich, Barcelona, Tortoza, Morella, Peniscola, Saguntum and Denia.   In this view lord William Bentinck, misled by false information, had committed a serious error in sending Del Parque to Tudela; because the Ordal disaster and subsequent retreat showed Suchet was strong enough to drive back the Anglo-Sicilians to the Xucar. The affairs of Catalonia were indeed very unpromising, and it was not even certain that the British could remain there.   Lord William, assured of Murat's defection, was again intent upon invading Italy; and the ministers must have leaned to that project; for Wellington now seriously demanded that they should say whether the Anglo-Sicilians were to go or stay in Spain.

Lord William Bentinck had quitted the army, making the seventh change of commanders in fifteen months, which alone accounted for an inefficiency so notorious that the Spanish generals ridiculed its ill success and spoke vauntingly of themselves.   Strenuously did Wellington urge the appointment of some commander who would devote himself to his business, observing that at no period of the war could he have quitted his army, even for a few days, without danger to its interests. But the English ministers' ignorance of everything relating to war was profound, and at this time he was himself being stript of generals.   Graham, Picton, Leith, lord Dalhousie, H. Clinton and Skerrett had gone or were going to England on account of sickness, wounds or private business; Beresford was at Lisbon, where dangerous intrigues to be noticed hereafter menaced the existence of the Portuguese army; Castaños and Giron had been removed by the Spanish regency from their commands; O'Donnel, an able officer but of impracticable temper, being denied the chief command of Elio's, Copons' and Del Parque's troops, also quitted the army under pretext that his old wounds had   Wellington. broken out, and Giron became his successor.   MSS.

But though Catalonia was thus neglected by the ministers Wellington thought it now the most important and inviting theatre of war. The country immediately beyond the Bidassoa, which he was called upon to enter, was sterile; it would be difficult for him to feed his army there in winter; and the twenty-five thousand half-starved Spaniards under him would certainly plunder for subsistence and incense the people of France. Soult's position was strong, his troops still numerous, and his entrenched camp furnished a secure retreat. Bayonne and St. Jean Pied de Port were so placed, that no serious invasion could be made until one or both were taken or blockaded; which in the tempestuous season and while the Admiralty refused to furnish sufficient naval means was scarcely possible; even to get at those fortresses would be a work of time, difficult against Soult alone, impracticable if Suchet came to his support. Towards Catalonia therefore Wellington desired to turn when the frontier of the western Pyrenees should be secured by the fall of Pampeluna; and he would have taken the command there in person if Napoleon's succeeding misfortunes in Germany had not rendered it impossible to reinforce the French armies of Spain. Meanwhile, yielding something to the allied sovereigns, he thought it not amiss to spur public feeling by taking a menacing position within the French territory. This was however no slight military concession to political considerations.

Soult's position was the base of a triangle, Bayonne being the apex, and the great road from Irun and St. Jean Pied de Port the sides. A rugged mass of mountains intervened between the left and centre; but nearly all the valleys and communications, coming from Spain beyond the Nive, united at St. Jean Pied de Port, and were embraced by an entrenched camp which Foy occupied in front of that fortress. He could therefore without aid from Paris, who was at Oleron, bring fifteen thousand men, including national guards, into action, and serious dispositions were necessary to dislodge him; these could not be made secretly, and Soult would have time to aid him and deliver battle on chosen ground. Foy thus held the right bank of the Nive, and could, by the great road leading to Bayonne or by shorter communications through Bidaray, reach the bridge of Cambo, and gain Espelette behind the camps of Ainhoa. From thence, passing the Nivelle by the bridges of Amotz and Serres, he could reach St. Jean de Luz, and it was by this route he moved to the attack of San Marcial,

The allies indeed, marching from the Alduides and the Bastan, could by St. Martin d'Arosa and the Gorospil mountain also reach Bidaray, between Foy's and D'Erlon's positions; but the roads were difficult, the French frequently scoured them, the bridge of Cambo was secured by works and Foy could not be easily cut off.

D'Erlon had an advanced camp at Urdax, and on the Mondarain and Choupera mountains; his main position was a broad ridge behind Ainhoa, the-right covering   Plans 8 & 9, the bridge of Amotz. Beyond that bridge Clausel's   1 p. 287, 363. position extended along a range of strong hills, trending towards Ascain and Serres; and as the Nivelle swept with a curve quite round his rear, his right flank rested on that river also. The redoubts of San Barbe and the camp of Sarre, barring the roads leading from Verra and the Puerto de Echallar, were in advance of his left; the greater Rhune, whose bare rocky head lifted two thousand eight hundred feet above the sea level overtopped all the neighbouring mountains, formed, in conjunction with its dependents the Commissari and Bayonette, a mask for his right. From the Bayonette the line run along the Mandale or Sulcogain mountain; but from thence to the sea the ridges suddenly abated, and there were two lines of defence; the first along the Bidassoa, the second, commencing near St. Jean de Luz, stretched from the heights of Bordegain towards Ascain, having the camps of Urogne and the Sans Culottes in advance. Reille guarded these lines, and the second was connected with Clausel by Villatte who was posted at Ascain. This system of defence was tied to that of St. Jean Pied de Port by the double bridge-head at Cambo, which secured the junction of Foy with the rest of the army.

Diligently the French worked on their entrenchments, yet they were but little advanced when the castle of San Sebastian surrendered, and Wellington yielding to the political pressure then matured a plan for placing himself within the French territory. It was one to prove the idle facility with which the ministers urged measures the nature of which they did not understand; for it involved as dangerous and daring an enterprise as any undertaken by him during the whole war. This was to seize the great Rhune mountain and its dependents, and at the same time force the passage of the lower Bidassoa and establish his left wing in France. The Rhune, Commissari and Bayonette mountains, forming a salient menacing point of great altitude and strength towards the French centre, would thus be brought within his own system, and his communications would be shortened by gaining the road along the river from Irun to Vera. The port of Fuenterabia also would fall, and though bad in winter be of some advantage to a general whose supplies came from the ocean; who had to encounter the perverse opposition of the Spanish authorities; and whose nearest port, Passages, was restricted in its anchorage-ground, hard to make from the sea, and dangerous when full of vessels.

He had designed this operation for the middle of September, immediately after the castle of San Sebastian fell and before the French works acquired strength; but some error retarded the arrival of his pontoons, the weather became bad, and the attack, which depended upon the state of the tides and fords, was of necessity deferred until the 7th of October. Meanwhile, to mislead Soult, ascertain Foy's true position, and strengthen his own right, he brought up part of Del Parque's force to Pampeluna, and sent the Andalusians to Echallar. Mina's troops also gathered about Roncevalles, and Wellington

October.

went there in person the 1st of October. As he passed the Alduides, he caused Campbell to surprise some isolated posts on the rock of Airola, carried off two thousand French sheep from the valleys of

Foy's Report MSS.

Baygorry, and cut off a French scouting detachment. This disquieted Soult. He expected an attack yet could not foresee where. Deceived by false information that Cole had reinforced Hill, he thought the movements of Mina and the Andalusians were to mask an operation

Soult, MSS.

by the Val de Baygorry; the arrival of light cavalry in the Bastan, Wellington's presence at Roncevalles, and the surprise at Airola seemed to confirm this; but the pontoons collected at Oyarzun indicated other objects, and some deserters told him the allies aimed at the great Rhune mountain. However, a French commissary,

taken at St. Sebastian and exchanged after remaining at
Lesaca twelve days, assured him nothing at the British head-
quarters indicated a serious attack, although the officers spoke
of one, and there were movements of troops; this weighed
much with Soult, because the slow march of the pontoons
and the wet weather having delayed the attack, the reports of
the spies and the deserters seemed false.

It was also beyond calculation that Wellington should,
against his military judgment, push his left wing into France
merely to meet the wishes of the allied sovereigns in Germany;
and as the most obvious line for permanent invasion was by
his right and centre, there was no apparent cause for deferring
his operations.   The true reason of the procrastination, namely,
the state of the tides and fords on the lower Bidassoa, was
necessarily hidden; and Soult finally judged that Wellington
only designed to secure his blockade of Pampeluna from interruption, by menacing the French and impeding their entrenchments: nevertheless, as all the deserters and spies came with
the same story, he recommended increased vigilance along the
whole line.   On the 6th he reviewed D'Erlon's divisions at
Ainhoa, and remained that night at Espelette, doubting if any
attack was intended and no way suspecting that it would be
against his right.   For Wellington could not diminish his
force at Roncevalles and the Alduides, lest Foy and Paris,
and the light cavalry under Pierre Soult, should unite at St.
Jean Pied de Port to raise the blockade of Pampeluna; the
troops at Maya menaced the line between the Nive and the
Nivelle; and it was therefore only with his left wing and left
centre, and against the French right that he could act, and
that seemed too dangerous.

Early in October twelve hundred British soldiers arrived
from England; Mina was then in the Ahescoa, on the right
of Hill, who was thus enabled to relieve Campbell's Portuguese
in the Alduides; and the latter marching to Maya replaced
the third division, which, shifting to its left, occupied the
heights above Zagaramurdi to enable the seventh division to
relieve Giron's Andalusians in the Puerto de Echallar.   These
dispositions were made for the attack of the great Rhune and
its dependents, which was arranged in the following manner.

Giron, moving from the Ivantelly, was to assail a lofty ridge or saddle, uniting the Commissari and the great Rhune; one battalion, stealing up the slopes and hollows on his right flank, was to seize the rocky head of the last-named mountain, to

Plan 8, p. 287. place detachments there to watch the roads leading

Order of
Movements,
MSS.

round it from Sarre and Ascain, and thereto descend upon the saddle and menace the rear of the enemy at the Puerto de Vera.   The principal attack was to be made in two columns; but to protect the right and rear against a counter attack from Sarre, Giron was to leave a brigade in the narrow pass leading to Sarre from Vera, between the Ivantelly and the Rhune.

On the left of Giron the light division was to assail the Bayonette mountain and the Puerto de Vera, connecting its right with Giron's left by skirmishers.

Longa, who had resumed his old positions above the Salinas de Lesaca, was to move in two columns across the Bidassoa; one, passing by the ford of Salinas, was to aid the left wing of the light division in its attack on the Bayonette; the other, passing by the bridge of Vera, was to move up the ravine separating the slopes of the Bayonette from the Puerto de Vera, and thus connect the attacks of the light division. During these operations Longa was to send some men over the river at Andarlasa, and seize a telegraph which the French used to communicate between the left and centre of their line.

Behind the light division, Cole was to hold Santa Barbara, pushing forward detachments to secure the commanding points gained by the fighting troops.   The sixth division was to make a demonstration on the right, by Urdax and Zagaramurdi, against D'Erlon's advanced posts.   Thus, without weakening his line between Roncevalles and Echallar, Wellington put nearly twenty thousand men in motion against the Rhune mountain and its dependents; and he had still twenty-four thousand disposable to force the passage of the lower Bidassoa.

From Andarlasa to Biriatu, three miles, there were neither roads nor fords nor bridges; the French, trusting to this difficulty of approach and to their entrenchments on the

craggy slopes of the Mandale, had collected their troops
principally where the Bildox or green mountain and the
entrenched camp of Biriatu overlooked the fords. Against
those points Wellington directed Freyre's Spaniards. They
were to descend from San Marcial, cross the upper fords of
Biriatu, assail the Bildox and Mandale mountains, and turn
the left of that part of the French line which passed behind
the town of Andaya.

Between Biriatu and the sea the advanced points of defence
were the mountain of *Louis XIV.*, the ridge called the *Caffé
Republicain*, and the town of Andaya. Behind these the
Calvaire d'Urogne, the *Croix des Bouquets*, and the camp of
the *Sans Culottes*, served as rallying posts. Against them
were set the first and fifth divisions, and the unattached
brigades of Wilson and lord Aylmer, in all fifteen thousand
men.

The Spanish fishermen had secretly discovered three fords
practicable at low water, between the bridge of Behobia and
the sea, and Wellington decided to pass his columns there; using
the old fords above bridge and these new ones below bridge,
although the tides rose sixteen feet, leaving at ebb heavy
sands not less than half a mile broad; and though his bank
was overlooked from the French hills which were also strong
for defence. But relying on his previous measures he affronted
all these dangers. It appeared so unlikely that a general
having a better line of operations on his right should attempt
to pass the Bidassoa at its mouth, that Soult was completely
deceived; his lieutenants on that side were also negligent. Of
Reille's two divisions one under Boyer was at the camp of
Urogne, and on the morning of the 7th was as usual labouring at the works; Villatte was at Ascain and Serres; Maucune's division five thousand strong was indeed in line, but
unexpectant of an attack; and though the works on the
Mandale were finished and those at Biriatu in a forward
state, from the latter to the sea the entrenchments were
scarcely commenced.

Passage of the Bidassoa.—The night set in heavily. A
sullen thunder-storm, gathering about the craggy crown of
the Pena de Haya, came slowly down its flanks, and towards

morning, rolling over the Bidassoa, fell in its greatest violence
upon the French positions.   During this turmoil, Wellington,
whose pontoons and artillery were close up to Irun, disposed a number of guns and howitzers along the crest of San
Marcial, and his columns attained their respective stations
along the banks of the river.   Freyre's Spaniards, a brigade of
the guards and Wilson's Portuguese, stretching from the
Biriatu fords to that near the broken bridge of Behobia, were
ensconced behind the detached ridge which the French had
first seized in the attack of the 31st.   A second brigade of
guards and the Germans of the first division were concealed
near Irun, at a ford below the bridge of Behobia called the
great Jonco.   The British brigades of the fifth division were
directed to cover themselves behind a large river embankment
opposite Andaya,—Sprye's Portuguese and lord Aylmer's
brigade were posted in the ditch of Fuenterabia.

All the tents were left standing in the camps of the allies,
and the enemy could perceive no change on the morning of
the 7th; but at seven o'clock, the fifth division and lord
Aylmer's brigade, emerging from their concealment, took the
sands in two columns; that on the left pointed against the
French camp of the Sans Culottes, that on the right against
the ridge of Andaya.   No shot was fired until they had
passed the fords of the low-water channel, when a rocket was
sent up from the steeple of Fuenterabia as a signal.   Then
the artillery opened from San Marcial, the troops near Irun,
covered by the fire of a battery, made for the Jonco ford, and
the passage above the bridge also commenced.   From the
crest of San Marcial seven columns could now be seen at once,
moving on a line of five miles; those above bridge plunging
at once into the fiery contest, those below appearing in the
distance like huge sullen snakes winding over the heavy
sands.   The Germans, missing the Jonco ford, got into deep
water, yet quickly recovered the true line; and the French,
completely surprised, permitted even the brigades of the fifth
division to gain the right bank and form their lines before a
hostile musket flashed.

Soult heard the cannonade of San Marcial at Espelette;
and at the same time the sixth division, advancing beyond

Urdax and Zagaramurdi, made a false attack on D'Erlon's positions. A Portuguese brigade under colonel Douglas, being pushed too far, were repulsed with the loss of one hundred and fifty men; the French marshal, having thus detected the true nature of this attack, then hurried to his right, but his camps on the Bidassoa were lost before he arrived. For when the British artillery first opened, Maucune's troops had assembled at their different posts of defence, and the French guns, established principally near the mountain of Louis XIV. and the Caffé Republicain, commenced firing. The alarm spread and Boyer marched from Urogne to support Maucune without waiting for the junction of the working parties; but his brigades moved separately as they could collect, and before the first came into action, Sprye's Portuguese, forming the extreme left of the allies, was menacing the Sans Culottes; thither therefore one of Boyer's regiments was ordered, while the others advanced by the royal road towards the Croix des Bouquets. But Andaya, guarded only by a piquet, was abandoned, and Reille thinking the camp of the Sans Culottes would be lost before Boyer's men could reach it, sent a battalion there from the centre; this weakening his force at the chief point of attack because the British brigades of the fifth division were now advancing from Andaya, and bearing under a sharp fire of artillery and musketry towards the Croix des Bouquets.

By this time the columns of the first division had passed the river, one above bridge preceded by Wilson's Portuguese; one below preceded by Halket's German light troops; who, aided by the fire of the guns on San Marcial, drove back the enemy's advanced posts, won the Caffé Republicain, the mountain of Louis XIV. and drove the French from those heights to the Croix des Bouquets. This was the key of the position, and towards it guns and troops were now hastening from every side; the Germans who had lost many men in the previous attacks were brought to a check, for the heights were strong and Boyer's leading battalions close at hand; but at this moment Cameron arrived with the ninth regiment, and passing through the German skirmishers rushed with great vehemence to the summit of the first height. The

French infantry opened ranks to let the guns retire, and then retreated themselves at full speed to a second ridge somewhat lower but where they could only be approached on a narrow front.   Cameron as quickly threw his men into a single column and bore against this new position, which curving inwards enabled the French to pour a concentrated fire upon his regiment; nor did his violent course seem to dismay them until he was within ten yards, when appalled by the furious shout and charge of the ninth they gave way and the ridges of the Croix des Bouquets were won as far as the royal road. The British regiment lost many men and officers, and during the fight the French artillery and scattered troops coming from different points and rallying on Boyer's battalions, gathered on the ridges to the French left of the road.

Above Biriatu and the Bildox the entrenched camp had been defended with success in front; but Freyre turned it with his right wing, which being opposed only by a single battalion soon won the Mandale mountain, and the French fell back from that quarter to the Calvaire d'Urogne and Jollimont. Reille, beaten at the Croix des Bouquets, and having his flanks turned by the Mandale and along the sea-coast, re-treated in disorder along the royal causeway and the old road of Bayonne.   He passed through the village of Urogne and the British skirmishers entered it in pursuit, but they were beaten out by Boyer's second brigade; and now Soult arriving with part of Villatte's reserve and many guns, restored order, and revived the courage of the troops just as the retreat was degenerating into a flight.

Reille lost eight guns and four hundred men, the allies six hundred, half being Spaniards; so slight and easy had the skill of the general rendered this stupendous operation.   But if Soult, penetrating Wellington's design, had opposed all his troops, amounting with what Villatte could spare to sixteen thousand instead of the five thousand actually engaged, the passage could scarcely have been forced; and a check would have been tantamount to a terrible defeat, because in two hours the returning tide would have come with a swallowing flood upon the rear.

Equally unprepared were the French on the side of Vera, although the struggle there proved more fierce and constant.

Giron had descended from the Invantelly rocks, and Alten from the ridge of St. Barbara at daybreak; the first to the pass leading from Vera to Sarre, the last to the town of Vera, where he was joined by half of Longa's force. The forty-third British, the seventeenth Portuguese, and the first and third battalions of riflemen drew up in column on an open space to the right of Vera; the fifty-second, two battalions of caçadores and a battalion of British riflemen under colonel Colborne, were disposed on the left of Vera. Half of Longa's division was between these columns, the other half, crossing the ford of Salinas, drew up on Colborne's left; the narrow vale of Vera was thus filled with troops ready to ascend the mountains; and Cole, displaying his force to advantage on the heights of Santa Barbara, presented a formidable reserve.

Taupin's division guarded the enormous French positions. His right was on the Bayonette, from whence a single slope descended to a small plain about two parts down the mountain; from this platform three tongues shot into the valley below, each defended by an advanced post; the platform itself was secured by a star redoubt, behind which, half way up the slope, there was a second retrenchment with abbatis. Another large redoubt and an unfinished breast-work on the crest of the Bayonette completed the system.

The Commissari, which is a continuation of the Bayonette towards the great Rhune, was covered by a profound gulf, thickly wooded and defended with skirmishers; between this gulf and another of the same nature the main road, leading from Vera over the Puerto, pierced the centre of the French position. Rugged and ascending with short abrupt turns, this road was blocked at every uncovered point with abbatis and small retrenchments; each obstacle was commanded at half musket shot by small detachments placed on all the projecting parts overlooking the ascent; and a regiment, entrenched above in the Puerto, connected the troops on the crest of the Bayonette and Commissari with those on the saddle ridge against which Giron's attack was directed.

Between Alten's right and Giron's left was an isolated ridge called by the soldiers the *Boar's back*, the summit of which, half a mile long and rounded at each end, was occupied by four French companies. This huge cavalier, thrown as it were into the gulf to cover the Puerto and saddle ridges although of mean height in comparison of the towering ranges behind, was yet so great that the few warning shots fired from the summit by the enemy, reached the allies at its base with that slow singing sound which marks the dying force of a musket-ball. It was essential to take the Boar's back before the general attack commenced, and five companies of British riflemen, supported by the seventeenth Portuguese regiment, were ordered to assail it at the Vera end, while one of Giron's battalions, preceded by a detached company of the forty-third, attacked it on the other.

At four o'clock in the morning Clausel received intelligence

Clausel's Report, MSS. that the Bayonette was to be assaulted that day or the next—at seven o'clock he heard from Conroux, who commanded at Sarre, that Giron's camps were abandoned, but the tents of the seventh division were still standing at the same time musketry was heard on the side of Urdax, a cannonade on the side of Irun, and Taupin reported that the vale of Vera was filled with troops. To this last quarter Clausel hurried. The Spaniards had already driven Conroux's outposts from the gorge leading to Sarre, and a detachment was creeping up towards the unguarded head of the great Rhune; he immediately ordered four regiments of Conroux's division to occupy the summit, the front, and the flanks of that mountain; and he formed a reserve of two other regiments: with these troops he designed to secure the mountain and support Taupin, but ere they could reach their destination that general's fate was decided.

Second Combat at Vera.—[Plan 8.]—At seven o'clock a few cannon-shot from some mountain-guns of which each side had a battery, were followed by the Spanish musketry on the right, and the next moment the Boar's back was simultaneously assailed at both ends. On the Vera side the riflemen ascended to a small pine-wood two-thirds of the way up and there rested; but soon resuming their movement, with a scornful gallantry they swept the French off the top, disdaining to use their rifles beyond a few shots down the reverse side, to show they were masters of the ridge. This was the signal for the general attack. The Portuguese followed the victorious sharpshooters,—the forty-third, preceded by their own skirmishers and the remainder of the riflemen of the right wing, plunged into the rugged pass,—Longa's troops entered the gloomy wooded ravine on the left. Colborne's brigade, moving by narrow paths and throwing out skirmishers, assailed the Bayonette; the fifty-second took the middle tongue, the caçadores and riflemen the two outermost, and all bore with a concentric movement against the star redoubt on the platform above. Longa's second brigade should have skirted the left of this attack, but knowing little of such warfare quietly followed the riflemen.

Soon the open slopes were covered with men and with fire, a mingled sound of shouts and musketry filled the deep hollows between, and the white smoke came curling up above the dark forest trees in their gloomy recesses. The French scattered on the mountain side seemed weak, and Kempt's brigade easily forced all the retrenchments on the main pass; his skirmishers then spread wider, and formed small detachments of support as the depth of the ravine lessened and the slopes melted into the higher ridges. Half way up an open space gave a clear view over the Bayonette and all eyes were turned that way. Longa's right brigade, fighting in the gulf between, seemed labouring and over-matched; but beyond, on the open space in front of the star fort, Colborne's caçadores and riflemen were coming out in small bodies from a forest below the edge of the platform. Their fire was sharp, their pace rapid, and they closed upon the redoubt in mass as if resolved to storm it The fifty-second were not then in sight, and the French seeing only dark clothing thought all were Portuguese and rushed in close order out of the entrenchment, they were numerous and very sudden, the rifle is unequal to the musket and bayonet, and this rough charge sent the scattered assailants back over the rocky edge of the descent With shrill cries the French followed, but just then the fifty-second appeared, partly in line partly in column, and raising their shout rushed forward. The red uniform and full career of this regiment startled the adventurous French; they stopped short, wavered, turned and fled to their entrenchment; the fifty-second entered the works with them, the riflemen and caçadores rallied and passed it on both flanks, and for a few moments everything was hidden by a dense volume of smoke. Soon however the British shout pealed again and the whole mass emerged on the other side, the French flying, until the second entrenchment enabled them to make another stand.

Then with exulting cheers Kempt's brigade made the mountain side ring, and with renewed vigour the men scaled the craggy mountain, fighting their toilsome way to the top of the Puerto. Meanwhile Colborne carried the second entrenchment above the star fort; but he was brought to a check by the works on the crest of the mountain, from whence the French plied their musketry at a great advantage and rolled huge stones down the steep. These works were extensive, well lined with men, and strengthened by a large redoubt on the right; yet their left was already turned by Kempt, and the effects of Wellington's skilful combinations were now felt in another quarter.

Freyre, after carrying the Mandale mountain, had pushed to the road leading from the Bayonette by Jollimont to St. Jean de Luz; this was the line of retreat for Taupin's right wing; but Freyre got there first, and if Longa, instead of following Colborne, had spread out widely on the left a military line would have been completed from Giron to Freyre. Still Taupin's right was cut off on that side, and he was forced to file under fire along the crest of the Bayonette to reach the Puerto de Vera road, where he was joined by his centre: he effected this but lost his battery and three hundred men. These last, apparently the garrison of the large fort on the extreme right of the Bayonette crest, were captured by Colborne in a remarkable manner. Accompanied by only one of his staff and half-a-dozen riflemen, he crossed their march unexpectedly, and with great presence of mind ordered them to lay down their arms; an order which they, thinking themselves entirely cut off, obeyed! And all the French skirmishers in the deep ravine between the two lines of attack were likewise taken; for being feebly pushed by Longa's troops they retreated too slowly, got entangled in the rocks and surrendered to Kempt's brigade. Taupin's right and centre being thus completely beaten fled down the mountain towards Olette pursued by a part of the allies, but they rallied on Villatte, who was in order of battle between Urogne and Ascain. The Bayonette and Commissari, with the Puerto de Vera, were won in this manner after five hours' incessant fighting and toiling up their craggy sides; nevertheless the battle was still maintained by the French on the Rhune.

Giron, after driving Conroux's advanced post out of the gorge leading from Vera to Sarre, had pushed a battalion towards the head of the great Rhune, and placed a reserve in the gorge to cover his rear from any counter-attack. But when the taking of the Boar's back freed his left wing he fought his way up abreast with the British line until near the saddle-ridge, a little to the right of the Puerto. There he was arrested by a strong line of abbatis and the heavy fire of two French regiments. The Spaniards stopped, and though the adventurer Downie, now a Spanish general, encouraged them and they kept their ranks they seemed irresolute and did not advance; but it happened that an officer of the forty-third regiment named Havelock, attached to Alten's staff, had been sent to ascertain Giron's progress, and his fiery temper could not brook the check. Taking off his hat he called upon the Spaniards to follow him, and putting spurs to his horse at one bound cleared the abbatis and went headlong amongst the enemy. Then the soldiers, shouting for *'El chico blanco,'* *'the fair boy,'* so they called him, for he was very young and had light hair, with one shock broke through the French; and this at the very moment when their centre was flying under the fire of Kempt's skirmishers from the Puerto de Vera.

The defeated troops retired by their left along the saddle-ridge to the flanks of the Rhune. Clausel had thus eight regiments concentrated on this great mountain. Two occupied the crest and the rock called the Hermitage; four were on the flanks, descending towards Ascain on one hand, and Sarre on the other; the remaining two occupied a lower and parallel crest behind called the small Rhune. Giron's right wing first dislodged a small body from a detached pile

of crags about musket-shot below the summit, and then
assailed the bald staring rocks of the Hermitage itself; endeavouring at the same time to turn it by the right, but the
attempt was quite defeated; the Hermitage was impregnable;
the French rolled down stones large enough to sweep away a
whole column at once, and the Spaniards resorted to a distant
musketry which lasted until night. Taupin had two generals
and four hundred men killed and wounded, and five hundred
prisoners. The loss of the allies was nearly a thousand, of
which five hundred were Spaniards, and the success was not
complete; for while the French kept possession of the summit
of the Rhune the allies' new position was insecure. The front
and right flank of that mountain were impregnable; but
Wellington observing that the left flank descending towards
Sarre was less inaccessible, concentrated the Spaniards on
that side the 8th; designing a combined attack against the
mountain itself and against the camp of Sarre. The rocks
studding the lower slopes were assailed by the Spaniards, and
detachments of the seventh division descended from the
Puerto de Echallar upon the fort of San Barbe, and other
outworks covering the French camp of Sarre.

The Andalusians then won the rocks and an entrenched
height commanding the camp; for Clausel, alarmed at some
demonstrations now made by the sixth division towards the
bridge of Amotz, thought he should be cut off from his
great camp, and suddenly abandoned not only the slope of the
Rhune, but all his advanced works in the basin below, including the fort of San Barbe. His troops were thus concentrated on the height behind Sarre, still holding with their
right the smaller Rhune, but the consequences of his error
were soon made apparent. Wellington established a strong
body of Spaniards close to the Hermitage; and the French
regiments there, seeing the lower slopes and San Barbe
given up, imagined they also would be cut off and without
orders abandoned their impregnable rocks in the night, retiring
to the smaller Rhune. Next morning some of the seventh
division rashly pushed into the village of Sarre, but were
quickly repulsed and would have lost the camp and works
taken the day before, if the Spaniards had not succoured them.

In the three days' fighting, fourteen hundred French and
sixteen hundred of the allies, one half being Spaniards, were
killed or wounded, but many of the latter were not brought
in until the third day; and several perished miserably where
they fell, it being impossible to discover them in those vast
solitudes: some men also were lost from want of discipline;
for having descended into the French villages they got drunk
and were taken next day by the enemy.   Nor was the
number small of those who plundered in defiance of Wellington's proclamation. He arrested and sent to England
several officers, and renewed his proclamation, saying, if he
had five times as many men he could not venture to invade
France unless marauding was prevented; and it is remarkable
that the French troops, on the same day, acted towards their
own countrymen in the same manner. But Soult also checked
the mischief with a vigorous hand, causing a captain of some
reputation to be shot as an example, for having suffered his
men to plunder a house in Sarre during the action.

These operations had been eminently successful, and the
bravery of troops who assailed and carried such stupendous
positions must be admired.   To them the unfinished state of
the French works was not visible.   Day after day, for more
than a month, entrenchment had risen over entrenchment,
covering the vast slopes of mountains which were scarcely
accessible from their natural steepness and asperity.   This
they could see, yet cared neither for the growing strength of
the works, the height of the mountains, nor the breadth of
the river with its heavy sands and its mighty rushing tide;
all were despised; and while they assailed with confident
valour, the French fought in defence of their dizzy steeps
with less fierceness than, when striving against insurmount-
able obstacles, they attempted to storm the lofty rocks of
Sauroren.   Continual defeat had lowered their spirit, but the
feebleness of the defence on this occasion may be traced to
another cause.   It was a general's not a soldier's battle. Wellington had with overmastering combinations overwhelmed
each point of attack.   Taupin's and Maucune's divisions, each
less than five thousand strong, were separately assailed. the
first by eighteen the second by fifteen thousand men; and at

neither point were Reille and Clausel able to bring their
reserves into action before the positions were won.

Soult complained that he had repeatedly told his lieutenants

Soult, MSS.　　an attack was to be expected, and recommended
extreme vigilance; yet they were quite unprepared, although they heard the noise of the guns and pontoons about Irun on the night of the 5th and again on the
night of the 6th. The passage of the river, he said, had
commenced at seven o'clock, long after daylight; the allies'
masses were then clearly seen forming on the banks, and
there was time for Boyer to arrive before the Croix des
Bouquets was lost. Thus the battle was fought in disorder
with less than five thousand men, instead of with ten thousand
in good order and supported by a part of Villatte's reserve.
To this negligence the generals also added great despondency.
They had so little confidence in the strength of their positions,
that if the allies had pushed vigorously forward before the
marshal's arrival from Espelette, they would have entered St.
Jean de Luz, turned the right of the second position, and
forced the French army back upon the Nive and Adour. This
was true, but the stroke did not belong to Wellington's
system. He could not go beyond the Adour, he doubted
whether he could even maintain his army during the winter
in the position he had already gained; and he was averse to
the experiment while Pampeluna held out and the war in
Germany bore an undecided aspect.

CHAPTER V.

Soult, MSS.

SOULT was apprehensive for some days that Wellington would push his operations further; but when he knew from Foy, and by the numbers assembled on his right, there was no design to attack his left, he resumed his labours on the works covering St. Jean de Luz. He also kept a vigilant watch from his centre, holding his troops in readiness to concentrate towards Sarre; and when he saw the heavy masses in his front disperse by degrees into different camps, he directed Clausel to recover the San Barbe. This work, constructed on a comparatively low ridge, barred issue from the gorge leading from Vera to Sarre; and it defended the narrow ground between the Rhunes and the Nivelle river. Abandoned on the 8th without reason by the French, since it did not naturally belong to the position of the allies, it was now occupied by a Spanish piquet of forty men; some battalions were encamped in a small wood close behind, and many officers and men slept in the fort. On the night of the 12th, three of Conroux's battalions reached the platform on which the fort stood without being perceived and escaladed; the troops behind it went off in confusion at the first alarm, and two hundred soldiers with fifteen officers were made prisoners. The Spaniards made a vigorous effort to recover the fort at daylight, were repulsed, and repeated the attempt with five battalions; Clausel then brought up two guns and a sharp skirmish took place in the wood for several hours, the French endeavouring to regain the whole of their old entrenchments, the Spaniards to recover the fort. Neither succeeded, and San Barbe, too near the enemy's position to be safely held, was resigned with a loss of two hundred men by the French and five hundred by the Spaniards. Soon after this isolated action, a French sloop freighted with stores for Santona attempted to run from St. Jean de Luz, and being chased by three English brigs and cut off from the open sea, her crew, after exchanging a few distant shots with one of the brigs, set her on fire and escaped in their boats to the Adour.

Head-quarters were now fixed in Vera, and the allied army was organized in three grand divisions. The right having Mina and Morillo attached to it was commanded by Hill, and extended from Roncevalles to the Bastan. The centre, occupying Maya, the Echallar, Rhune and Bayonette mountains, was given to Beresford. The left extending from the Mandale mountain to the sea was under sir John Hope. This officer succeeded Graham, who had returned to England. Commanding in chief at Coruña after sir John Moore's death, he was superior in rank to lord Wellington during the early part of the Peninsula war; but when the latter obtained the baton of field-marshal at Vitoria, Hope, with a patriotism and modesty worthy of the pupil of Abercrombie the friend of Moore, offered to serve as second in command; and Wellington joyfully accepted him, saying he was the '*ablest officer in the army.*'

On the right and centre the positions were offensive, but the left was still defensive; and the Bidassoa, impassable at high water below the bridge, was close behind. The ridges were however strong, and powerful batteries established on the right bank; field-works were constructed; and though the fords below Behobia were dangerous for retreat even at low water those above were secure, and there was a pontoon-bridge. The front run along the heights of Croix des Bouquets, facing Urogne and the camp of the Sans Culottes; the reserve was entrenched above Andaya; the right rested on the Mandale, and from that mountain and the Bayonette the allies could flank an attacking army. Soult however looked only to defence. He had not more than seventy-nine thousand old soldiers under arms including officers and artillerymen. His garrisons absorbed thirteen thousand, leaving sixty-six thousand in the field; whereas the allies, counting Mina's and Del Parque's troops, now at Tudela, Pampeluna and the Val de Irati, exceeded one hundred thousand; seventy-three thousand, including officers sergeants and artillerymen, being British and Portuguese. The

Appendix 2,
§ 2. Vol VI

French marshal thought there were more; for exaggerated reports made Del Parque twenty thousand strong, and gave Wellington one hundred and forty thousand combatants. But it was not so, and as good conscripts were joining the French army rapidly, and the national guards of the Pyrenees were many, it was in the number of soldiers rather than of men the English general had the advantage.

Soult's policy was to maintain a strict defensive, under cover of which the spirit of the troops might be revived, the country in rear organized, and the conscripts hardened to war. The loss of the lower Bidassoa had an injurious effect upon the spirit of the frontier departments, and gave encouragement to the secret partisans of the Bourbons, but in a military view it was a relief. For the great development of the mountains bordering the Bidassoa had rendered their defence difficult, the line could always be pierced, and the army suddenly driven beyond the Adour. The position was now more concentrated. The right, under Reille, was on two lines. One across the royal road on the fortified heights of Urogne and the camp of the Sans Culottes; the other in the Plans 8-9, pp. 287-363. entrenched camps of Bourdegain and Belchena, covering St. Jean de Luz and barring the gorges of Olhette and Jollimont. The centre under Clausel, was on the ridges between Ascain and Amotz, holding the smaller Rhune in advance; one division was however retained in the camp of Serres on the right of the Nivelle, overhanging Ascain; to replace it, one of D'Erlon's divisions was on the left of that river, reinforcing Clausel's left above Sarre. Villatte's reserve was about St. Jean de Luz, having the Italian brigade in the camp of Serres. D'Erlon's remaining divisions continued in their old position, the right connected with Clausel's line by the bridge of Amotz; the left held the Choupera and Mondarin mountains bordering on the Nive.

Behind Clausel and D'Erlon Soult had commenced a second chain of entrenched camps, prolonged from the camp of Serres up the right bank of the Nivelle to San Pé; thence by Suraide to the double bridge-head of Cambo on the Nive; and beyond that river to the Ursouia mountain, covering the great road from Bayonne to St. Jean Pied de Port. He called Paris from

Oleron to the defence of the latter fortress and its entrenched camp; and drew Foy down the Nive to Bidarray, half-way between St. Jean Pied de Port and Cambo. Foy thus watched the issues from the Val de Baygorry, and could occupy the Ursouia mountain on the right of the Nive, or, moving by Cambo, reinforce the position on the left of that river.

To complete these immense entrenchments, and between the Nive and the sea they were double, on an opening of sixteen miles, the whole army laboured incessantly; and all the resources of the country in materials or workmen were called out by requisition. This defensive warfare was however justly regarded by Soult as unsuitable to the general state of affairs; the offensive was most consonant to the character of the French soldiers, and also to the exigencies of the time. Experience had indeed shown the impregnable nature of the allies' position, and he was too weak singly to change the theatre of operations; but when he considered how strong the armies appropriated to the Spanish contest were, he thought France would be ill-served if her generals could not resume the offensive successfully. Suchet had proved his power at Ordal. Lord William's successor, of inferior rank and power, having an army unpaid and feeding on salt meat from the ships, and Spanish colleagues unwilling to act cordially or upon a fixed plan, was in no condition to menace the French seriously. And that he was permitted to paralyse fifty or sixty thousand excellent French troops possessing all the strong places of the country, was one of the most singular errors of the war.

Exclusive of national guards and detachments of the line, disposed along the frontier to guard France against marauding excursions, there were available one hundred and seventy thousand men and seventeen thousand horses. One hundred and thirty-eight thousand were present under arms, and thirty thousand conscripts were in march to join them; they held all the fortresses of Valencia and Catalonia, and most of those in Aragon, Navarre and Guipuscoa; and they could all unite behind the Pyrenees for a combined effort. Wellington could not, including the Anglo-Sicilians and the Spaniards on the eastern coast, bring into

Appendix 3, § 2. Vol. VI.

line one hundred and fifty thousand men; he had several sieges
on his hands; and to unite his forces at any point required
skilful dispositions to cover flank marches. Suchet had thirty
thousand disposable men and could make them forty thousand
by relinquishing some unimportant posts; and as his artillery
means were immense, and distributed in all his strong places,
he could furnish himself from almost any point. Ninety
thousand old soldiers and two hundred guns might therefore
have been united on Wellington's flank; thirty thousand conscripts and the frontier national guards would have remained.
These based on the fortresses and camps of Bayonne and of St.
Jean Pied de Port, and on the castles of Jaca and Navarens,
would cover the northern parts while the numerous fortresses
of Catalonia could protect France on the south.

To make this great power bear in a right direction was
Soult's object, but he could never persuade Suchet to adopt
his projects; and that marshal's resistance would appear to
have sprung from personal dislike contracted during Soult's
sojourn near Valencia in 1812. It has been shown how lightly
he abandoned Aragon after quitting Valencia; he did not
indeed then know that Soult commanded and was preparing
his great effort to relieve Pampeluna; but he knew Clausel
and Paris were on the side of Jaca, and that to menace Wellington's flank would palliate the defeat at Vitoria. At Zaragoza he had a large garrison and an immense artillery dépôt;
from thence he could by Jaca have communicated quickly and
surely with Soult; and thus acting in concert they would have
succoured Pampeluna.

Soult had not time to communicate with Suchet. He
quitted Dresden the 4th of July, reached Bayonne the 12th,
and on the 20th he was in march towards St. Jean Pied de
Port; and it was during this rapid journey Suchet abandoned
Valencia. Soult therefore knew nothing of Suchet's plans, of
his forces, of his movements, of his actual positions. However, between the 6th and 16th of August, immediately after
the retreat from Sauroren, he urged Suchet to march upon Zaragoza, open a communication by Jaca, and thus aid the effort
to relieve San Sebastian. As an inducement he stated, that his
recent operations had caused troops actually in march under

Hill towards Catalonia to be recalled; this was an error; his emissaries were deceived by the movements, and counter-movements in pursuit of Clausel after the battle of Vitoria, and by the change in Wellington's plans as to the siege of Pampeluna. No troops were sent towards Catalonia; but it is remarkable that Picton, Hill, Graham and O'Donnel were all mentioned in this correspondence between Soult and Suchet as being actually in Catalonia, or on the march; the three first having been really sounded as to taking the command in that quarter, and the last having demanded it himself.

Suchet treated the proposal as chimerical. His moveable troops did not he said exceed eleven thousand, and a march upon Zaragoza with so few men would be to renew the disaster of Baylen; unless he could fly into France by Venasque where he had a garrison. This extraordinary view of affairs he supported by statements still more extraordinary! *'Hill had joined lord William Bentinck with twenty-four thousand men.'* —*'La Bispal had arrived with fifteen thousand.'*—*'There were more than two hundred thousand men on the lower Ebro.'*— *'The Spanish insurrection was general and strongly organized.'* —*'He had recovered the garrison of Taragona and destroyed the works, and he must revictual Barcelona and then withdraw to the vicinity of Gerona and remain on the defensive!'*

This letter was written the 23rd of August. Lord William had then retreated from the Gaya to the mountains above Hospitalet; the imperial muster-rolls prove that the two armies of Catalonia and Aragon, both under Suchet's command, exceeded sixty-five thousand men, fifty-six thousand being present under arms, thirty thousand were united in the field when he received Soult's letter; there was nothing to prevent him marching by Tortoza except lord William's army, which had just acknowledged by a retreat its inability to cope with him: there was nothing at all to prevent him marching by Lerida. O'Donnel had thrown up his command from bad health, leaving his troops under Giron on the Echallar mountains; Hill was at Roncevalles, and not a man had moved from Wellington's army. Elio and Roche were near Valencia in a starving condition; the Anglo-Sicilians, only fourteen thousand strong including

Appendix 3, § 2. Vol. VI.

Whittingham's division, were on the barren mountains above Hospitalet, where no Spanish army could remain; Del Parque and Sarsfield had gone over the Ebro, Copons had taken refuge in the mountains of Cervera.   In fine not two hundred thousand, but less than thirty-five thousand men, half-organized, ill-fed and scattered from Vich to Vinaros were opposed to Suchet; and their generals had different views and different lines of operations—the Anglo-Sicilians could not abandon the coast, Copons could not abandon the mountains.   Del Parque soon afterwards marched to Navarre, and to use Wellington's phrase there was nothing to prevent Suchet '*tumbling lord William Bentinck back even to the Xucar.*'   The nature of the insurrection which Suchet pretended to dread shall be shown when the political condition of Spain is treated of.

Suchet's errors respecting the allies were easily detected by Soult.   Those touching the French in Catalonia he could not suspect, and acquiesced in the objections to his first plan; but fertile of resource he immediately proposed another, akin to that which he had urged Joseph to adopt in 1812, after the battle of Salamanca; namely, to change the theatre of war. The fortresses in Spain would, he said, inevitably fall before the allies in succession if the French armies remained on the defensive, and the only mode of rendering offensive operations successful was a general concentration of means and unity of action.   The levy of conscripts under an imperial decree issued in August, would furnish, in conjunction with the dépôts of the interior, a reinforcement of forty thousand men; ten thousand would form a sufficient corps of observation about Gerona; and he hoped that by sacrificing some posts Suchet could bring twenty thousand infantry to the field.   He could have produced forty thousand; but Soult, misled by his erroneous statements, assumed only twenty thousand; and he calculated that he could himself bring thirty-five or forty thousand good infantry and all his cavalry, to a given point of junction for the two bodies between Tarbes and Pau.   Fifteen thousand of the remaining conscripts were also to go there; and thus seventy or seventy-five thousand infantry all the cavalry of both armies and one hundred guns, would be suddenly assembled to thread the narrow pass of Jaca and descend

upon Aragon. Once in that kingdom they could attack the
allied troops in Navarre if the latter were dispersed; and if
they were united retire upon Zaragoza, there to fix a solid base
end deliver a general battle upon the new line of operations.
Meanwhile the fifteen thousand unappropriated conscripts
might reinforce twenty or twenty-five thousand old soldiers left
to cover Bayonne.

An army so great and strongly constituted appearing in
Aragon would, Soult argued, necessarily raise the blockades
of Pampeluna, Jaca, Fraga, and Monzon, and it was probable
Tortoza and even Saguntum would be relieved; the great
difficulty was to pass the guns by Jaca; yet he was resolved to
try, even though he should convey them upon trucks to be
made in Paris and sent by post to Pau. He anticipated no
serious inconvenience from the union of the troops in France,
since Suchet had already declared his intention of retiring
towards Gerona; and on the Bayonne side the army to be left
there could dispute the entrenched line between Cambo and
St. Jean de Luz. If driven from thence it could take a
flanking position behind the Nive; the right resting upon the
entrenched camp of Bayonne; the left upon the works at
Cambo and holding communication by the fortified mountain
of Ursouia with St. Jean Pied de Port. There could be little
fear for this secondary force when the great army was once in
Aragon; but what he dreaded was delay, because a fall of
snow, always to be expected after the middle of October, would
entirely close the pass of Jaca.

This proposition, written the 2nd of September immediately after the battle of San Marcial, reached Suchet the 11th,
and was peremptorily rejected. If he withdrew from Catalonia,
discouragement, he said, would spread, desertion would commence and France be immediately invaded by lord William
Bentinck at the head of fifty thousand men. The pass of
Jaca was impracticable and the power of man could not open
it for carriages under a year's labour. His wish was to act on
the defensive, but if an offensive movement was absolutely
necessary he offered a counter project; that is, he would first
make the English in his front re-embark at Taragona, or he
would drive them over the Ebro and then march with one

hundred guns and thirty thousand men by Lerida to the
Gallego river near Zaragoza: Soult's army, coming by Jaca
without guns, might there meet him and the united forces
could then do what was fitting.   But to effect this he required
a reinforcement of conscripts, and to have Paris's division and
the artillerymen and draft horses of Soult's army sent to
Catalonia; he demanded also that two thousand bullocks for
the subsistence of his troops should be provided to meet him
on the Gallego. Then touching upon the difficulties of the
road from Sanguessa to Pampeluna, he declared, that after
forcing Wellington across the Ebro, he would return to
Catalonia to revictual his fortresses and prevent an invasion
of France.   This plan he judged far less dangerous than
Soult's; yet he enlarged upon its difficulties and its dangers if
the combined movements were not exactly executed.   In fine,
he continued, 'The French armies are entangled amongst
rocks, and the emperor should direct a third army upon Spain
to act between the Pyrenees and the Ebro in the centre, while
the army of Spain sixty thousand strong and that of Aragon
thirty thousand strong operate on the flanks. Thus *the reputation of the English army, too easily acquired at Salamanca
and Vitoria, will be abated.'*

  This illiberal remark combined with the defects of his project, proves that the duke of Albufera was far below the duke
of Dalmatia's standard, both in magnanimity and capacity:
the one giving his adversary just praise, thought the force
already supplied by the emperor sufficient to dispute for victory; the other, with an unseemly boast, desired overwhelming numbers.   Soult's letter reached Suchet the day before the
combat of Ordal, and in pursuance of his own plan the latter
should have driven lord William over the Ebro; as he could
well have done, because the Catalan troops had then separated
from the Anglo-Sicilians.   In his former letters he had estimated his enemies at two hundred thousand fighting men and
his own disposable force at eleven thousand, giving that as a
reason why he could not march to Aragon.   Now, forgetful
of his previous objections and estimates, he admitted that he
had thirty thousand disposable troops, and proposed the very
movement which he had rejected as madness when suggested

by Soult. And the futility of his arguments, relative to the general discouragement the desertion and the temptation to an invasion of France if he adopted Soult's plan, is apparent; for these things could only happen on the supposition that he was retreating from weakness; a notion which would, if entertained, have effectually covered the real design until the great movement in advance should change the public opinion.

Soult's plan was surer, better imagined, grander than his; it was less dangerous in the event of failure and more conformable to military principles. Suchet's project involved double lines of operation without any sure communications, and consequently without any certainty of just co-operation; his point of junction was within the enemy's power, and the principal army was to be deprived of its artillery—a failure would have left no resource. But in Soult's project the armies were to be united at a point beyond the enemy's reach, and to operate afterwards in mass with all arms complete, which was conformable to the principles of war. Suchet averred the impracticability of moving the guns by Jaca, yet Soult's counter-opinion claims more respect; Clausel and Paris, who had lately passed with troops through that defile were in his camp; he had made very exact inquiries of the country people, had caused the civil engineers of roads and bridges on the frontiers to examine the route, and from their reports judged the difficulty to be surmountable.

Neither the inconsistency nor the exaggerations of Suchet's statements escaped Soult's observation; but anxious to effect something while Pampeluna still held out and the season permitted operations in the mountains, he frankly accepted the other's modification; and adopted every stipulation save that of sending the artillerymen and horses of his army to Catalonia, which he considered dangerous. The preparations for this great movement were therefore immediately commenced, and Suchet on his part seemed equally earnest although he complained of increasing difficulties; pretending Longa and Morillo had arrived in Catalonia, and that Graham was also in march to that quarter. He also deplored the loss of Fraga from whence the Empecinado had just driven his garrison, as if it were irreparable; but though it commanded a bridge over the Cinca, a river dangerous from its sudden and great floods, he still possessed the bridge of Monzon.

During this correspondence Napoleon remained silent; yet at a later period he expressed discontent at Suchet's inactivity; and indirectly approved of Soult's plans by recommending a movement towards Zaragoza, which Suchet however did not execute. It would appear that having given all the reinforcements he could spare, and full powers to both marshals to act as they judged fitting, he would not, at a distance and while engaged in such vast operations as those he was carrying on at Dresden, decide so important a question. The vigorous execution essential to success was not to be expected if either marshal acted under constraint and against his own opinion: Soult had adopted Suchet's modification, and it would have been unwise to substitute a new plan, which would have probably displeased both commanders. Meanwhile Wellington passed the Bidassoa, and Suchet's project was annulled by the approach of winter and the further operations of the allies.

If the plan of uniting the two armies in Aragon had been happily achieved it would certainly have forced Wellington to repass the Ebro, or fight a great battle with an army less strongly constituted than the French army. If he chose the latter victory would have profited him little, because his enemy, strong in cavalry, could have easily retired on the fortresses of Catalonia. If he received a check he must have gone over the Ebro, perhaps back to Portugal, and the French would have recovered Aragon, Navarre and Valencia. It is not probable however, that such a great operation could have been conducted without being discovered in time by Wellington. It has been already shown, that besides the ordinary spies and modes of gaining intelligence he had secret emissaries amongst Joseph's courtiers, and even amongst French officers of rank; and Soult vainly endeavoured to surprise him the 31st of August when the combinations were only two days old. Suchet's retreat from Catalonia and junction with Soult in France, when Napoleon was pressed in Germany, together with the known difficulty of passing guns by Jaca would indeed have made it appear a movement of retreat and fear;

nevertheless the secret must have been known to more than
one, and the English general had agents who were little
suspected. Soult however could still have returned to his old
positions, and, reinforced by Suchet's troops, repeated his
former attack by the Roncevalles. It might be his secret
design was to involve that marshal in his operations, and that
he was not very eager to adopt his modified plan, which the
approach of the bad season and the menacing position of
Wellington rendered each day less promising. But his own
project, hardy and dangerous for the allies, proved Wellington's
profound acquaintance with his art; for he had entered France
only to please the allied sovereigns, and always watched
closely for Suchet; averring that the true military line of
operations was towards Aragon and Catalonia. Being now
however in France, and the war in Germany having taken a
favourable turn, he resolved to continue operations on the
actual front, awaiting only the

FALL OF PAMPELUNA.

This event was produced by a long blockade, less fertile of
incident than the siege of San Sebastian, yet very honourable
to the firmness of the governor, Cassan. The town, containing fifteen thousand inhabitants, stood on a bold table-land
where a number of valleys opened; and where the great roads
coming from St. Jean Pied de Port, Sanguessa, Tudela, Estella,
Vitoria and Irurzun were concentrated. The northern and
eastern fronts were covered by the Arga, the defences being
only simple walls edging the perpendicular rocky bank of the
river; the other fronts were regularly fortified with ditches
covered way and half-moons. Two unfinished outworks only
were constructed on the south front; but the citadel on the
south-west was a regular pentagon with bomb-proofs and
magazines, vaulted barracks for a thousand men and a complete system of mines.

Pampeluna had been partially blockaded by Mina for eighteen months previous to the battle of Vitoria, and when
Joseph fled there it was badly provisioned. The stragglers
of his army increased the garrison to more than three thou-

sand five hundred men. Many inhabitants went off during
the short interval between the king's arrival and departure,
and Cassan, finding his troops too few for action too many
for the food, abandoned the unfinished outworks, demolished
everything interfering with his defence outside, and commenced other works inside. Moreover, foreseeing the French
army might possibly make a sudden march without guns to
succour the garrison, he prepared a field-train of forty pieces
to meet the occasion. When the blockade was established
his chief object was to obtain provisons, and the 28th and
30th of June he fought actions to cover his foragers; the 1st
of July he burned the suburb of Madalina, beyond the river
Arga, and forced many inhabitants to quit the place before
the blockaders' works were completed. Skirmishes then
occurred almost daily, the French always seeking to gather
grain and vegetables which were ripe and abundant beyond
the walls; the allies seeking to fire the standing corn within
range of the fortress.

On the 14th O'Donnel undertook the blockade, and the
next day the garrison made a successful forage south of the
town; they repeated it on the east beyond the Arga the 19th,
with a sharp engagement of cavalry, during which the infantry carried away a great deal of corn. The 26th the sound
of Soult's artillery reached the place, and Cassan, judging he
was coming to succour Pampeluna, made a sally in the night
by the Roncevalles road; he was driven back, but the next
morning came out again with eleven hundred men and two
guns, overthrew the Spanish outguards, and advanced towards
Villalba at the moment when Picton was falling back with t
third and fourth divisions. Then O'Donnel, as before relat d,
evacuated some of the entrenchments, destroyed ammunition,
spiked guns, and but for the timely arrival of Carlos d'Esp ña
and Picton's stand at Huarte would have abandoned the
blockade altogether.

When the battle on the mountains commenced, the smoke
rose over the intervening heights of Escava and San Miguel,
the French cavalry appeared on the slopes above El Cano,
and the allies' baggage was seen filing along the road of
Irurzun. Cassan thought deliverance sure, and having reaped

much corn during O'Donnel's panic awaited the result.
Soult's bivouac fires could be seen during the night, and in
the morning a fresh sally procured more corn with little loss
of men.   Some deserters from the foreign British corps also
went over with intelligence exaggerated and coloured after
the manner of such men, and the French re-entered the place
elated with hope.   In the evening the sound of conflict
ceased, and the silence of the next day told how the battle
had gone; but Cassan made another sally and again obtained
provisions from the south side.

On the 30th the battle recommenced, and the retreating
fire of the French made sick the spirit of the garrison : nevertheless their indefatigable governor led another sally on the
south side, whence they carried off grain and some ammunition which had been left in one of the abandoned outworks.
Next day Carlos d'España came to resume the blockade
with seven thousand men and maintained it until the middle
of September, when the prince of Anglona's divi-
September.
sion of Del Parque's army relieved the Andalusian portion of the troops, who rejoined their own corps
near Echallar.   The allies' works of contravallation were then
augmented; and when Paris retired into France from Jaca,
part of Mina's troops occupied the valleys leading from the
side of Sanguessa to Pampeluna, and made entrenchments to
bar the escape of the garrison that way.

In October Cassan put his fighting men upon rations of
horse-flesh, four ounces to each with some rice, and he turned
more families out of the town; but this time they were fired
upon by their countrymen and forced to re-enter.

On the 9th of September baron Maucune, who had conducted most of the sallies during the blockade, attacked and
carried some fortified houses on the east side of the place.   He
was assailed by the Spanish cavalry, but he beat them and
pursued the fugitives close to Villalba; whereupon Carlos
d'España advanced with a greater body, and the French were
driven in with the loss of eighty men; yet the Spaniards lost a
far greater number, D'España himself was wounded, and the
garrison obtained some corn which was their principal object.
For the soldiers were now feeding on rats and other disgusting

animals, many seeking for roots beyond the walls were poisoned by eating hemlock in their hunger, and a number deserted. In this state Cassan, designing to break out, made an experimental sally to try the strength of the lines, but after some fighting was driven back with a loss of seventy men and his hope of escape vanished. Yet he still spoke of attempting it, and the public manner in which he increased the mines under the citadel induced Wellington to reinforce the blockade and bring his cavalry into the vicinity.

Scurvy affected the garrison. One thousand men were sick, eight hundred had been wounded, the deaths by battle and disease exceeded four hundred, one hundred and twenty had deserted, and Cassan, moved by the misery around him, proposed to surrender if allowed to retire with six pieces of cannon. Being denied, he offered to yield on condition of not serving for a year and a day, which was also denied; then he broke the negotiation, giving out that he would blow up the works of the fortress and burst through the blockade. To deter him a menacing letter was thrown to his outposts, and Wellington, denouncing his design as contrary to the laws of war, directed Carlos d'España to put him, his officers, non-commissioned officers and a tenth of the soldiers to death when the place should be taken, if any damage were done to the works.

Cassan's object being merely to obtain better terms this order remained dormant, and happily so, for the execution would never have borne the test of public opinion. To destroy the works of Pampeluna and break through the blockading force, as Brennier did at Almeida, would have been a very noble exploit; and a useful one, if Soult's plan of changing the theatre of war by descending into Aragon had been followed. There could therefore be nothing contrary to the laws of war in a resolute action of that nature. On the other hand, if the governor, having no chance whatever of success, made a hopeless attempt the pretence for destroying a great fortress belonging to the Spaniards, thus depriving the allies of the fruits of their long blockade and glorious battles, the conquerors might have justly exercised that severe but undoubted right of war, refusing quarter to an enemy. But Wellington's letter to España involved another question, namely the put-

ting of prisoners to death. For the soldiers could not be
decimated until captured, and their crime would have been
only obedience to orders in a matter of which they dared not
judge; this would have been quite contrary to the usages of
civilized nations; hence, the threat must be considered as a
device to save the works of Pampeluna and avoid the odium
of refusing quarter.

A few days longer the governor and garrison endured their
distress and then capitulated, having defended themselves
more than four months with great constancy. The officers
and soldiers became prisoners of war; the first to keep their
arms and baggage the second their knapsacks, expressly on
the ground that they had treated the inhabitants well during
the investment. This compliment was honourable to both
sides; but there was another article, enforced by España
without being accepted by the garrison, for which it is difficult
to assign any motive save the vindictive ferocity of the
Spanish character: no person of either sex was permitted to
follow the French troops, and women's affections were thus
barbarously brought under the action of the sword.

There was no stronghold now retained by the French in
the north of Spain except Santona. The blockade there had
been tedious, and Wellington, whose sea communications were
interrupted by the privateers from thence, formed a small
British corps under lord Aylmer to attack Laredo which,
on the opposite point of Santona harbour commanded the
anchorage. Accidental circumstances prevented this enterprise and Santona remained in the enemy's possession; but,
with this exception, the contest in the northern parts of Spain
was terminated. It is now fitting to show with what great
political labour Wellington had brought it to this state; and
what contemptible actions and sentiments, what a faithless
alliance, what vile governments his dazzling glory hid from
the sight of the world.

CHAPTER VI.

Political State of Portugal.—In that country national
jealousy, long compressed by fear, had expanded with violence as danger receded, and England's influence declined
in an inverse proportion to her success in removing the
peril of invasion. When Wellington crossed the Ebro the
vile Souza faction became elate; and those members of
government who had supported the British policy while
it sustained them against court intrigues, now sought popularity by an opposite course. Noguera vexatiously resisted
or suspended commercial and financial operations;—principal
Souza wrangled fiercely and insolently at the council-board—
the patriarch fomented ill-will at Lisbon and in
the northern provinces—Forjas, ambitious to com-   Mr. Stuart,
                                                         MSS.
mand the national troops, became the organ of
discontent upon military matters. The return of the prince-
regent, the treaty of commerce, the Oporto company, the
privileges of the British factory merchants, the mode of
paying the subsidy, and the military transport; the convention with Spain relative to the supply of the Portuguese troops
in that country; the recruiting, the organization, the command
of the national army and the honours due to it; all furnished
grounds for factious proceedings, conducted with that ignoble
subtlety which invariably characterized Peninsular politics.
The expenditure of the British army had been immense, the
trade and commerce dependent on it, now removed to the
Spanish ports, enormous: Portugal had lived upon England.
Her internal taxes, carelessly or partially enforced, were
vexatious to the people without being profitable to the government. Nine-tenths of the revenue accrued from duties on
British trade. The sudden cessation of markets and of
employment, the absence of ready money, the loss of profit,

public and private, occasioned by the departure of the army, while the contributions and other exactions remained the same, galled all classes, and the nation was quite ready to shake off the burthen of gratitude.

Emissaries promulgated tales, some true some false, of the disorders perpetrated by the military detachments on the lines of communication, adding that Wellington gave secret orders for this to satisfy his personal hatred of Portugal! Discourses and writings against the British influence abounded in Lisbon and Rio Janeiro, and were re-echoed or surpassed by the London newspapers, whose statements, overflowing of false-hood, could be traced to the Portuguese embassy in that capital. It was asserted that England, designing to retain her power in Portugal, opposed the return of the prince-regent; that the war itself being removed was become wholly a Spanish cause; and it was not for Portugal to levy troops and exhaust her resources, to help a nation whose aggressions she must be called upon sooner or later to resist. Mr. Stuart's diplomatic intercourse, always difficult, became one of con-tinual remonstrance and dispute; his complaints were met with insolence or subterfuge; and illegal violence against the persons and property of British subjects was pushed so far, that Mr. Sloane, an English gentleman upon whom no sus-picion rested, was cast into prison for three months because he had come to Lisbon without a passport. The rights of the English factory were invaded, and the Oporto company, established as its rival in violation of treaty, was openly cherished. Irresponsible and rapacious this pernicious company robbed everybody, and the prince-regent, pro-mising to reform or totally abolish it, ordered a preparatory investigation; but in Mr. Stuart's words, the regency acted no less unfairly by their sovereign than unjustly by their ally.

Especial privileges claimed by the factory merchants were another cause of disquiet. They pretended to exemption from certain taxes and from billets; and that a fixed number of their clerks, domestics and cattle should be exonerated of military service. These pretensions were disputed. The one touching servants and cattle, doubtful at best, had been grossly abused, and that relating to billets unfounded. The taxes were justly resisted, and the merchants offered a voluntary contribution to the same amount. The government rudely refused this offer, seized their property, imprisoned their persons, impressed their cattle to transport supplies that never reached the troops, and made soldiers of their clerks and servants without any intention of reinforcing the army: Mr. Stuart then deducted from the subsidy the amount of the property thus forcibly taken and repaid the sufferers. The regency also commenced a dispute upon the fourth article of the treaty of commerce; and the prince, though he openly ordered it to be executed, secretly permitted count Funchal, his prime minister, to remain in London as ambassador until the disputes arising upon this treaty were arranged : wherefore Funchal, who liked the English capital, took care to interpose many obstacles to a final decision, advising delay under pretence of rendering ultimate concession of value in other negotiations.

When the battle of Vitoria became known, the regency proposed to entreat the return of the prince from the Brazils, hoping thereby to excite the opposition of Mr. Stuart; but when he, contrary to their expectations, approved of the proposal they deferred the execution. The British cabinet, which had long neglected Wellington's suggestions on this head, then pressed the matter at Rio Janeiro, and Funchal, at first averse, now urged it warmly, fearing if the prince remained at the Brazils he must go there. However few of the Portuguese nobles desired the return of the royal family, and when the thing was proposed to the regent he discovered no inclination for the voyage. But the most important subject of discord was the army. The absence of the sovereign and the intrigues at Rio Janeiro virtually rendered the government at Lisbon an oligarchy without a leader, in other words, a government formed for mischief; and it has been sufficiently shown, that Wellington's energy and ability, aided by Mr. Stuart's sagacity and firmness and the influence of England's power and riches, were scarcely able to dry up the evils flowing from this foul source. At the end of 1812 the native military force was for want of sustenance on the point of dissolving.

The strenuous interference of the English general and envoy, seconded by the great exertions of the British officers in the Portuguese service, restored indeed the efficiency of the army, and in the campaign of 1813 the spirit of the troops was surpassing; even the militia-men, deprived of their colours and drafted into the line to punish their bad conduct at Guarda under Trant, nobly regained their standards on the Pyrences. But this state of affairs, acting upon the naturally sanguine temperament and vanity of the Portuguese, created a very exaggerated notion of their military prowess and importance, and withal a morbid sensitiveness to praise or

Mr. Stuart, MSS.

neglect. Picton had thrown some slur upon the conduct of a regiment at Vitoria, and Beresford complained that justice had not been done to their merits. The eulogiums passed in the English parliament and in the despatches upon the conduct of the British and Spanish troops, but not extended to the Portuguese, galled the whole nation; and the remarks and omissions of the London newspapers were as wormwood.

Meanwhile the regency, under pretext of a dispute with Spain relative to a breach of the military convention of supply, neglected the subsistence of the army altogether; and so many obstacles to recruiting were raised, that the dépôts, which ought to have furnished twelve thousand men to replace the losses sustained in the campaign, only contained four thousand without the means of taking the field. This serious matter drew Beresford to Lisbon in October to propose a new regulation, which should disregard the exemptions claimed by the nobles the clergy and the English merchants for their servants and followers. On his arrival Forjas urged the public discontent as to the position of the Portuguese troops. They were, he said, generally incorporated with the British divisions, commanded by British officers, had no distinct recognised existence; their services were unnoticed and the glory of the country suffered—the world at large knew not how many men Portugal furnished for the war. It was known there were Portuguese soldiers as it was known there were Brunswickers and Hanoverians, but as a national army nothing was known of them; their exertions, their courage, only went to swell the general triumph of England, while the

Spaniards, inferior in numbers and far inferior in all military qualities, were flattered, praised, thanked in the public despatches, in the English newspapers, and in the discourses and votes of the British parliament. He proposed therefore to have the Portuguese formed into a distinct army acting under Wellington.

It was objected that the brigades incorporated with the British divisions were fed by the British commissariat, the cost being deducted from the subsidy, and the loss of that advantage the Portuguese could not sustain. Forjas rejoined, that they could feed their own troops cheaper if the subsidy was paid in money, but Beresford referred him to the scanty means of transport; so scanty that the few stores they were then bound to furnish for the unattached brigades depending upon the Portuguese commissariat were not forwarded. Forjas then proposed to withdraw gradually the best brigades from the English divisions, to incorporate them with the unattached brigades and so form an auxiliary corps; the same objection of transport applied however to this matter and it dropped for the moment. The regency then agreed to reduce the legal age of men liable to the conscription for the army; but the islands, which ought to have given three hundred men yearly, were exempt from their control; and the governors, supported by the prince-regent, refused to permit levies and granted asylums to those who wished to avoid the levy in Portugal. In the islands also, the persons so unjustly and cruelly imprisoned in 1810 were still kept in durance, although the regency, yielding to the persevering remonstrances of Stuart and Wellington, had released those at Lisbon.

Soon after this Beresford desired to go to England, and the occasion was seized by Forjas to renew his proposition for a separate army, which he designed to command himself. Silveira's claim to that honour was however supported by the Souzas, to whose faction he belonged; and the only matter in which all agreed was the display of ill-will towards England. Wellington became indignant. The English newspapers, he said, did much mischief by their assertions, but he never suspected they could by their omissions alienate the Portuguese nation and government. The latter complained that their troops were not praised in parliament, nothing could be more different from a debate within the house than the representation of it in the newspapers;—the latter seldom stated an event or transaction as it really occurred, unless when they absolutely copied what was written for them; and even then their observations branched out so far from the text that they appeared absolutely incapable of understanding much less of stating the truth upon any subject. The Portuguese people should therefore be cautious of taking English newspapers as a test of the estimation in which the Portuguese army was held in England, where its character stood high and was rising daily. 'Mr. Forjas is,' said Wellington, 'the ablest man of business I have met with in the Peninsula, it is to be hoped he will not on such grounds have the folly to alter a successful military system. I understand something of the organization and feeding of troops, and I assure him that, separated from the British, the Portuguese army could not keep the field in a good state although their government were to incur ten times the expense under the actual system; and if they are not in a fitting state for the field they can gain no honour, they must suffer dishonour! The vexatious disputes with Spain are increasing daily, and if the omissions or assertions of newspapers are to be the causes of disagreement with the Portuguese *I will quit the Peninsula for ever!'*

This remonstrance being read to the regency, Forjas replied officially.

'The Portuguese government demanded nothing unreasonable. The happy campaign of 1813 was not to make it heedless of sacrifices beyond its means. It had a right to expect greater exertions from Spain, which was more interested than Portugal in the actual operations since the safety of the latter was obtained. Portugal only wanted a solid peace, she did not expect increase of territory; nor any advantage save the consideration and influence which the services and gallantry of her troops would give her amongst European nations, and which, unhappily, she would probably require in her future intercourse with Spain. The English prince-regent, his ministers and his generals, had rendered full justice to her military services in the official reports, but that did not suffice to give them weight in Europe. Official reports did not remove this inconvenience. It was only the public expressions of the English prince and his ministers that could do justice. The Portuguese army was commanded by marshal Beresford, marquis of Campo Mayor. It ought always to be so considered and thanked accordingly for its exploits, with as much form and solemnity by the English parliament and general as was used towards the Spanish army—the more so, that the Portuguese had sacrificed their national pride to the common good, whereas the Spanish pride had retarded the success of the cause and the liberty of Europe. It was necessary also to form good native generals to be of use after the war; but putting that question aside, it was only demanded to have the divisions separated by degrees and given to Portuguese officers: nevertheless such grave objections being advanced they were willing he said to drop the matter altogether.'

The discontent however remained, for the argument had weight, and if any native officers' reputation had been sufficient to make the proceeding plausible, the British officers would have been driven from the Portuguese service, the armies separated, and both ruined. As it was, the regency terminated the discussion from inability to succeed, from fear not from reason. The persons who pretended to the command were Forjas and Silveira. The English officers, who were well-liked by the troops, would not have served under the former and Wellington objected strongly to the latter; having by experience discovered that he was an incapable officer, seeking a base and pernicious popularity by encouraging the views of the soldiers. Beresford then relinquished his intention of going to England, and the justice of the complaint relative to the reputation of the Portuguese army being obvious, the general orders became more marked in favour of the troops. Yet the most effectual check to the project was Mr. Stuart's intimation, that England, bound by no conditions as to the subsidy, had a right to withdraw it altogether.

To have this subsidy in specie and supply their own troops was long the cry of the regency, but finally they gave the matter up. Forjas knew well the administration of Portugal was incapable of supporting an army five hundred miles from its own country; the real object was to shake off the British

influence without losing the subsidy. Neither the regency
nor the prince had any feelings for the honour of the army or
the welfare of the men. The regency, while thus disputing
for command, allowed its subordinates to ruin the only asylum
in Portugal for mutilated soldiers, and turned the helpless
veterans adrift; the prince, while lavishing honours on his
intriguing courtiers, placed those officers whose fidelity and
hard fighting had preserved his throne in Portugal at the
bottom of the list, decorating the menials of the palace with
the same ribands! Honour, justice, humanity, were alike
despised by the ruling men, and Wellington thus expressed
his strong disgust.

' *The British army which I have the honour to command
has met with nothing but ingratitude from the government
and authorities in Portugal for their services; everything that
could be done has been done by the civil authorities lately to
oppress the officers and soldiers on every occasion in which it
has by any accident been in their power. I hope however that
we have seen the last of Portugal!*'

Towards Spain the Portuguese government was not more
friendly, for the Portuguese regency dreaded the democratic
doctrine promulgated in the Cortes; and the leaders of that
assembly were intent to spread those doctrines throughout the
Peninsula. Seven Spanish envoys had succeeded each other
at Lisbon within three years, and the only bond of sympathy
between the governments was hatred of the English who had
saved both: on all other points they differed. The exiled
bishop of Orense, from his asylum in Portugal, excited the
Gallicians against the Cortes so vigorously that his expulsion
from Portugal, or at least his removal from the northern
frontier, was specially demanded by the Spanish minister; a
long and angry discussion followed; yet the bishop was only
civilly requested by the Portuguese government to abstain
from acts disagreeable to the Spanish regency. The latter
demanded him as a delinquent; the Portuguese quoted a
decree of the Cortes which deprived the bishop of his rights
as a Spanish citizen, and denaturalized him: finally he was
removed twenty leagues from the frontier. Nor was the Portuguese government itself quite free from ecclesiastic troubles.

The bishop of Braganza preached doctrines offensive to the patriarch and the government; he was confined, but soon released and an ecclesiastical sentence pronounced against him, which only increased his followers and extended the influence of his doctrines.

Another cause of uneasiness, at a later period, was the return of Ballesteros from his exile at Ceuta. He had been permitted towards the end of 1813, and, as Wellington thought with no good intent, to reside at Fregenal; the Portuguese regency, fearing he would gather discontented persons round him there set agents to watch his proceedings; and under pretence of putting down robbers, established a line of cavalry and called out the militia—thus making it manifest that but a little was wanting to kindle a war between the two countries.

Political state of Spain.—Wellington's victories had put an end to Joseph's intercourse with the French party in Spain, yet those people, not losing hope, formed a strong anti-English party, watching to profit of the disputes between the two factions at Cadiz, which were now rancorous. The serviles, bigoted in religion and politics, had the whole body of the clergy on their side; they were most numerous in the Cortes, and their views generally accorded with the feelings of the people beyond the Isla de Leon, their doctrines being comprised in two sentences—*An absolute king—An intolerant church*. The liberals, supported and instigated by all ardent innovators and the commercial body and populace of Cadiz, had also partisans beyond the Isla; and taking as guides the revolutionary writings of the French philosophers, were hastening onwards to a democracy without regard to ancient usages and without practical ability to carry their theories into execution. There was also a fourth faction in the Cortes, American deputies, who secretly laboured for the independence of the colonies; they sometimes joined the liberals, sometimes the serviles, and often produced anomalous results, because they were numerous enough to turn the scale in favour of the side which they espoused. Jealousy of England was however common to all, and '*Inglesismo*' was used as a term of contempt. Even when Wellington was commencing

the campaign of 1813, the Cortes was with difficulty, and
by threats rather than reason, prevented from passing a
law forbidding foreign troops to enter a Spanish fortress!
Alicant, Tarifa, Cadiz itself had been preserved,—Rodrigo,
Badajos had been retaken by British valour, — English
money had restored their broken walls, replenished their
magazines—English and Portuguese blood still smoked from
their ramparts,—but the men from whose veins that blood
flowed were to be denied entrance at gates they could not
approach without treading on the bones of slaughtered comrades—comrades who had sacrificed their lives to procure for
this sordid ungrateful assembly the power to offer the insult.

To subdue the bishops and clergy, who in Gallicia openly
opposed the abolition of the Inquisition, was of prominent
interest with a section of the liberals called the Jacobins.
They generally ruled the Cortes, because the Americanos
leaned towards their doctrines, and the Anti-English or
French party, desiring dissension, supported the most violent
public men. A fierce and obstinate faction they were, and
they compelled the churchmen to submit for the time; yet not
until the dispute became so serious that Wellington expected
a civil war on his communications, and thought the clergy and
the peasantry would take part with the French. This notion,
which gives his measure for the patriotism of both parties,
proved unfounded, his extreme discontent with the liberal
doctrines somewhat warped his judgment; the people were
less attached to the church than he imagined, the clergy of
Gallicia finding no solid support submitted to the Cortes and
the archbishop of Santiago fled to Portugal.

Deep unmitigated hatred of democracy was indeed the
moving spring of the English Tories' policy. Napoleon was
warred against, not as they pretended because he was a
tyrant and usurper, for he was neither; not because his invasion of Spain was unjust, but because he was the enemy of
aristocratic privileges. The welfare and independence of
the Peninsula were words of no meaning in their state-papers
and speeches; and their anger and mortification were extreme when they found their success against the emperor foster-
ing that democracy they sought to destroy. They were only

prevented by the superior prudence and sagacity of their general from interfering with the internal government of Spain in so arrogant and injudicious a manner, that an open rupture, wherein the Spaniards would have had the appearance of justice, must have ensued. Wellington stifled this folly, he waited to give the blow with effect, and was quite willing to deal it himself; and the conduct of the Cortes and executive government was so injurious to Spain, and to his military operations, so unjust and ungrateful to him personally, that the warmest friends of freedom cannot blame his enmity. Rather should his moderation be admired, when we find his aristocratic hatred of the Spanish constitution exacerbated by a state of affairs thus described by Vegas, a considerable member of the Cortes.

Speaking of the '*Afrancesados*' or French party, more numerous than was supposed and active to increase their numbers, he says, 'The thing which they most enforced and which made most progress was the diminution of the English influence. Amongst the serviles they gained proselytes, by objecting the English religion and constitution which restricted the power of the sovereign. With the liberals, they said the same constitution gave the sovereign too much power; and the Spanish constitution having brought the king's authority under that of the Cortes was an object of jealousy to the English cabinet and aristocracy; who, fearing the example would encourage the reformers of England, were resolved the Spanish constitution should not stand. To the Americans they observed, that Wellington opposed them because he did not help them, and permitted expeditions to be sent from Spain; but to the Europeans who wished to retain the colonies and exclude foreign trade, they represented the English as fomenters and sustainers of the colonial rebellion, because they did not join Spain to put it down. To the honest patriots of all parties they said, that every concession to the English general was an offence against the dignity and independence of the nation. If he was active in the field, he was intent to subjugate Spain rather than defeat the enemy;—if he was careful in preparation, his delay was to enable the French to conquer;—if he was vigorous in urging the government to useful measures, his design was to impose his own laws; if he neglected the Spanish armies he desired they should be beaten;—if he meddled with them usefully, it was to gain the soldiers, turn the army against the country and thus render Spain dependent on England. And these perfidious insinuations flattered the national pride, as proving the Spaniards could do everything for themselves without the aid of foreigners. Nothing could stop the spread of such doctrines but new victories, which would bring the simple honesty and gratitude of the people at large into activity. Those victories came and did indeed stifle the French party in Spain, but many of their views were too well founded to be stifled with their party.

It was hoped the democratic violence of the Cortes would decline under the control of the cardinal Bourbon; but that prince, who was not of true royal blood in the estimation of the Spaniards, because his father had married without the consent of the king, was from age, infirmity, and ignorance, a nullity. The new regency became therefore more the slaves of the Cortes than their predecessors; and the Cadiz newspaper editors, pre-eminent in falsehood and wickedness even amongst their unprincipled European brotherhood, became the champions of the Jacobins and directed the city populace as they pleased. And always the serviles yielded under the dread of personal violence; their own crimes had become their punishment. They had taught the people at the commencement of the contest that murder was patriotism; and now their spirit sunk and quailed, because at every step, to use the terribly significant expression of Wellington, ' *The ghost of Solano was staring them in the face.*'

In support of their crude constitution which they considered as perfect as an emanation from the Deity, the Jacobins sought 1°. To abolish the inquisition, to arrest and punish the Gallician bishops, and to war with the clergy. 2°. To put aside the claim of Carlotta to the regency. 3°. To appoint captain-generals and other officers to suit their factious purposes. 4°. To obtain money for their necessities, without including therein the nourishment of the armies. 5°. To control the elections for a new Cortes, and procure an assembly of their own way of thinking, or prevent its assembling at the legal period in October. In the matter of the bishops they nearly caused a war with Portugal and a civil war with Gallicia. Carlotta's affair was less serious; but her pretensions, wisely opposed by the British authorities while the army was cooped up in Portugal, were, although she was a declared enemy to the English alliance, now rather favoured by sir Henry Wellesley as a mode of checking the spirit of democracy. Wellington held aloof, observing, that if appointed according to the constitution she would not be less a slave to the Cortes than her predecessors, and England would have the discredit of giving power to the 'worst woman in existence.'

To remove the seat of government from the influence of the Cadiz populace was one mode of abating the power of the democratic party; and the yellow fever, coming immediately after the closing of the general Cortes in September, seemed to furnish an opportunity for the English ambassador to effect its removal; for the regency, dreading the epidemic, resolved to proceed to Madrid; telling sir Henry Wellesley, who joyfully hastened to offer pecuniary aid, that to avoid the sickness was their sole motive. Having secretly formed this resolution at night they designed to begin the journey next day; but a disturbance arose in the city; the regents then convoked the extraordinary Cortes, the ministers were called before it, and bending in fear declared with scandalous disregard of truth there was no intention to quit the Isle without consulting the Cortes. Certain deputies were thereupon appointed to inquire if there was any fever, and a few cases being discovered, the deputation, apparently to shield the regents, recommended they should remove to Port St. Mary.

This did not satisfy the assembly. The government was commanded to remain at Cadiz until the new general Cortes should be installed, and a committee was appointed to probe the whole affair; or rather to pacify the populace; who were so offended with the report of the first deputation, that Augustin Arguelles, on presenting it, was hissed from the galleries although the most popular member of the Cortes. The more moderate liberals thus discovered that they were equally with the serviles the slaves of the newspaper writers.

Nevertheless the inherent excellence of freedom, though here presented in such fantastic and ignoble shapes, was involuntarily admitted by Wellington when he declared, that wherever the Cortes and government should fix themselves the press would follow to control, and the people of Seville, Granada, or Madrid would become as bad as the people of Cadiz.

The composition of the new Cortes was an object of hope and fear to all factions; and the result being uncertain, the existing assembly took such measures to prolong its own power, it was thought two Cortes would be established, one at Cadiz the other at Seville, each striving for mastery in the nation. However the new body after many delays was installed at Cadiz in November, and the Jacobins, strong in the violence of the populace, still swayed the assembly and kept the seat of government at Cadiz until the rapid spread of the fever brought a stronger fear into action. Then the resolution to repair to Madrid was adopted, and the sessions in the Isla closed on the 29th of November. Yet not without troubles. For the general belief being that no person could take the sickness twice, and almost every resident family had already suffered from former visitations, the merchants with infamous cupidity declared there was no fever, induced the authorities flagitiously to issue clean bills of health to ships, and endeavoured by intimidation to keep the regency and Cortes in the city. An exact and copious account of these factions and disputes, and of the permanent influence which these discussions of the principles of government this constant collision of opposite doctrines had upon the character of the people, would, if sagaciously traced, form a lesson of the highest interest for nations. But to treat the subject largely would be to write a political history of the Spanish revolution, and it is only the effect upon the military operations which properly appertains to a history of the war. That effect was one of unmitigated evil,—but this did not necessarily spring from the democratic system, since precisely the same mischiefs were to be traced in Portugal, where arbitrary power, called legitimate government, was prevalent. In both cases the people and the soldiers suffered for the crimes of factious politicians.

It has been shown that one Spanish regency contracted an
engagement with Wellington on the faith of which he took the
command of their armies in 1813. Scrupulously adhered to
by him, it was systematically violated by the new rengency
and minister of war, almost as soon as it was concluded.   His
recommendations for promotion after Vitoria were disregarded,
orders were sent direct to the subordinate generals, and
changes were made in the commands and in the destinations
of the troops without his concurrence, and without passing
through him as generalissimo.   Scarcely had he crossed the
Ebro when Castaños, captain-general of Gallicia, Estremadura
and Castille, was disgracefully removed from his government
under pretence of calling him to assist in the council of state :
his nephew, Giron, was at the same time deprived of the Gallician army, although both he and Castaños had been com-
mended for their conduct by Wellington.   Freyre, appointed
captain-general of Castille and Estremadura, succeeded Giron,
and the infamous Lacy replaced Castaños in Gallicia ; chosen,
it was believed, as a fitter tool to work out the measures of the
Jacobins against the clergy in that kingdom : nor was their
sagacity at fault, for Castaños would, according to Wellington,
have turned his arms against the Cortes if an opportunity had
offered.   He and others were now menaced with death, and
the Cortes contemplated an attack upon the tithes, upon the
feudal and royal tenths, and upon the estates of the grandees ;
all except the last very fitting to do if times and circumstances
had been favourable ; but when the nation generally was averse,
and there was an invader in the country to whom the discontented could turn, the attempt was insane.   The clergy were
at open warfare with the government, many generals were
dissatisfied, and menaced the superior civil authorities ; the
soldiers were starving, the people, tired of their miseries,
only desired to get rid of the invaders, and avoid the burthen of supplying the troops of either side.   The English
cabinet, after having gorged Spain with gold and flattery
was totally without influence.   A terrible convulsion was at
hand if the French could have maintained the war with
any vigour in Spain itself ; and the following passages from
Wellington's letters to the ministers, prove, that even he

contemplated a forcible change in the government and constitution.

'If the mob of Cadiz begin to remove heads from shoulders as the newspapers have threatened Castaños, and the assembly seize upon landed property to supply their necessities, I am afraid we must do something more than discountenance them. It is quite impossible such a system can last, and what I regret is that I am the person that maintains it. If I was out of the way there are plenty of generals who would overturn it. Ballesteros positively intended it, and I am much mistaken if O'Donnel and even Castaños, and probably others, are not equally ready. If the king should return he also will overturn the whole fabric if he has any spirit.'—'I wish you would let me know whether if I should find a fair opportunity of striking at the democracy the government would approve of my doing it.' And in another letter he thus seriously treated the question of withdrawing from the contest altogether. 'The government are the best judges of whether they can or ought to withdraw, but Spain cannot be a useful ally, or at all in alliance with England if the republican system is not put down.' Meanwhile he advised the English government and his brother to take no part either for or against the princess of Brazil, and to discountenance the democratical principles and measures of the Cortes; if their opinion was asked regarding the formation of a new regency, to recommend an alteration of that part of the constitution which lodged all power with the Cortes, and to give instead, some authority to the executive government, whether in the hands of king or regent. To fill the latter office one of royal blood, uniting the strongest claims of birth with the best capacity, should he thought be selected; but if capacity was wanting in the royal race, then to choose the Spaniard who was most deserving in the public estimation! Thus necessity teaches privilege to bend before merit.

Spain had at this period but one hundred and sixty thousand men in arms, fifty thousand only being available in the field; and those only because they were paid, clothed and armed, and kept together by the English general. He had proposed an arrangement for the civil and political govern-

ment of the provinces rescued from the French, with a view
to the supply of the armies, but his plan was rejected; and his
repeated representations of the misery the army and the
people endured were unheeded. Certain districts were allotted
for the support of each army; yet, with a jealous fear of military domination, the government refused the captain-generals
the necessary powers to draw forth the resources of the
country, and thus rendered the system a nullity.   Each
branch of administration was conducted by chiefs independent
in their attributes yet too restricted in authority, generally at
variance with one another, and all of them neglectful of their
duty.   The evil effect was thus described by Wellington as
early as August.

'More than half of Spain has been cleared of the enemy
above a year, and the whole of Spain, excepting Catalonia and
a small part of Aragon, since the months of May and June
last. The most abundant harvest has been reaped
in all parts of the country; millions of money   Letter to
spent by the contending armies are circulating   the Spanish
                                                    Minister
everywhere, and yet your armies however weak   of War.
in numbers are literally starving.   The allied British and
Portuguese armies under my command have been subsisted,
particularly latterly, almost exclusively upon the magazines
imported by sea; and I am concerned to inform your excellency, that besides money for the pay of all the armies, which
has been given from the military chest of the British army
and has been received from no other quarter; the British
magazines have supplied quantities of provisions to all the
Spanish armies in order to enable them to remain in the field
at all.   And notwithstanding this assistance I have had the
mortification of seeing the Spanish troops on the outposts,
obliged to plunder the nut and apple-trees for subsistence, and
to know that the Spanish troops employed in the blockade of
Pampeluna and Santona, were starving upon half an allowance
of bread, while the enemy whom they were blockading was
at the same time receiving their full allowance.   The system
then is insufficient to procure supplies for the army, and at
the same time I assure your excellency, it is the most oppressive and injurious to the country that could be devised.   It

A A 2

cannot be pretended the country does not produce means
of maintaining the men necessary for its defence; those means
are undoubtedly superabundant; and the enemy has proved
that armies can be maintained in Spain at the expense of the
Spanish nation, infinitely larger than are necessary for its
defence.' These evils he attributed to the incapacity of the
public servants, and to their overwhelming numbers, that certain sign of an unprosperous state—to the disgraceful negligence and disregard of public duties—and to there being no
power in the country for enforcing the law: the collection of
the revenue cost in several branches seventy and eighty per
cent. No Spanish officers capable of commanding a large
body of troops or keeping it in an efficient state had appeared,
no efficient staff, no system of military administration had been
formed, and no shame for these deficiencies, no exertions to
amend were visible.

From this picture two conclusions are to be drawn, 1°. That
the provinces, thus described as superabounding in resources,
having been for several years occupied by the French armies,
the warfare of the latter could not have been so devastating
and barbarous as it was represented. 2°. That Spain, being
now as helpless as she had been at the beginning and all
through the war, was quite unequal to her own deliverance
either by arms or policy—that it was English valour, English
steel, directed by the genius of an English general, which
rising superior to all obstacles, whether presented by his
own or the Peninsular governments or by the perversity of
national character, worked out her independence. So utterly
inefficient were the Spaniards, that Wellington declared at this
period thirty thousand of their troops could not be trusted to
act separately—they were only useful when mixed in the line
with larger numbers of other nations! And yet all men in
authority, to the lowest alcalde, were as presumptuous as
arrogant and as perverse as ever. Rendered callous to public
misery by the desperate state of affairs, they were reckless of
consequences, and never suffered prudential considerations or
national honour to check the execution of any project.
Repeated failure had rendered the generals insensible to misfortune; and, without any remarkable personal daring, they

were always urgent for battle as if that were a common matter instead of being the great event of war. The government agents were corrupt, and the government itself tyrannical, faithless, mean and equivocating to the lowest degree. In 1812 a Spaniard of known and active patriotism thus commenced an elaborate plan of defence for the provinces. 'Catalonia abhors France as her oppressor, but she abhors still more the despotism which has been carried on in all the branches of her administration since the beginning of the war.' Everything was rotten except the hearts of the poorer people. Even at Cadiz Spanish writers compared the state to a vessel in a hurricane without captain, pilot, compass, chart, sails or rudder, and advised the crew to cry to heaven as their sole resource. But they only blasphemed.

When Wellington, indignant at the systematic breach of his engagement, remonstrated, he was answered that the actual regency did not hold itself bound by the contracts of the former government; no consideration for truth, for they had themselves also accepted the contract, nor of honest policy, nor the usages of civilized states with respect to national faith, had any influence on their conduct. Enraged at this scandalous subterfuge, he was yet conscious how essential it was he should retain his command; and seeing all Spanish generals more or less engaged in political intrigues, none capable of co-operating with him,—conscious also that public opinion in Spain would, better than menaces from the English government, enable him to obtain a counterpoise to the democratic party,—he tendered indeed his resignation if the government engagement was not fulfilled, but at the same time endeavoured with mild argument and reproof to induce reason. He told them however there were limits to his forbearance under injury, and he had been already most unworthily treated even as a gentleman by the Spanish government.

From the world these quarrels were covered by an appearance of the utmost respect and honour. He was made a grandee of the first class, and the estate of Soto de Roma in Grenada, of which the much-maligned miserable Godoy had been despoiled, was settled upon him. He accepted the gift, but, as he had before done with his Portuguese and Spanish pay, transferred the proceeds to the public treasury during the war. The regents however, under pressure of the Jacobins and apparently bearing some personal enmity, though one of them, Ciscar, had been instrumental in procuring him the command of the Spanish army, were now intent to drive him from it; and the excesses committed at San Sebastian served their factious writers as a topic for exciting the people not only to demand his resignation, but to commence a warfare of assassination against the British soldiers. Combining extreme folly with wickedness, they pretended amongst other absurdities that the nobility had offered, if he would change his religion, to make him king of Spain; this tale was eagerly adopted by the English newspapers, and three Spanish grandees thought it necessary to declare that they were not among the nobles who made the proposition. His resignation was accepted in the latter end of September, and he held the command only until the assembling of the new Cortes; but the attempt to render him odious failed even at Cadiz, owing chiefly to the personal ascendancy which all great minds so surely attain over the masses in troubled times. Both the people and the soldiers respected him more than they did their own government; and the Spanish officers had generally yielded as ready obedience to his wishes before he was appointed generalissimo, as they did to his orders when holding that high office. It was this ascendancy which enabled him to maintain the war with such troublesome allies; and yet so little were the English ministers capable of appreciating its importance, that after the battle of Vitoria they proposed as before noticed to remove him from Spain to Germany: his answer was short and modest, but full of wisdom. 'Many might be found to conduct matters as well as I can both here and in Germany; but nobody would enjoy the same advantages here and I should be no better than another in Germany.'

This egregious folly was thus checked, and in December the new Cortes decided that he should retain the command of the armies, and the regency be bound to fulfil its predecessor's engagements. Nevertheless, so deeply had he been offended by the libels relative to San Sebastian, that a private letter to his brother terminated thus:—'*It will rest with the king's government to determine what they will do upon a consideration of all the circumstances of the case, but if I was to decide I would not keep the army in Spain for one hour.*' And to many other persons at different times he expressed his fears and conviction that the cause was lost and that he should fail at last. It was under these and other enormous difficulties he carried on his military operations; it was with an enemy at his back more to be dreaded than the foe in his front that he invaded the south of France. And this is the answer to those French writers who have described him as being at the head of more than two hundred thousand well-furnished soldiers, supported by a well-organized insurrection of the Spanish people, unembarrassed in his movements, and luxuriously rioting in all the resources of the Peninsula and of England.

BOOK THE TWENTY-THIRD.

CHAPTER I.

WAR IN THE SOUTH OF FRANCE.

WHILE Pampeluna held out Soult laboured to complete his works of defence with a view to enter Aragon, pretending to hold this design so late as November; but he must have secretly renounced it before that period, because the snows of an early and severe winter had rendered even the passes of the lower Pyrenees impracticable in October. His political difficulties were not less than Wellington's. All his efforts to draw forth the resources of France were met with apathy or secret hostility, and there was no money in the military chest to answer the common daily expenses. The leading merchants of Bayonne voluntarily provided for the most pressing necessities of the troops; but their means were limited, and he vainly urged the merchants of Bordeaux and Toulouse to follow the patriotic example. It required all his firmness of character to support the crisis; and if the English naval force had intercepted the coasting-vessels between Bordeaux and Bayonne, he must have retired beyond the Adour. As it was, the greatest part of the field-artillery and all the cavalry were sent so far to the rear for forage that they could not be counted a part of the fighting troops; and the infantry, in addition to their immense labours, were forced to carry their own provisions from the navigable points of the rivers to the top of the mountains.

Soult was strongly affected. '*Tell the emperor,*' he wrote to the minister of war, '*tell him when you make your next report that on the very soil of France, this is the situation of the army destined to defend the southern provinces from inva-*

sion; tell him also that the unheard-of contradictions and obstacles I meet with shall not make me fail in my duty.'

On both sides the troops suffered, but the privations of the allies were perhaps greater; for being on higher mountains, more extended, more dependent upon the sea, their distress was in proportion to their distance from the coast. A shorter line had been gained for the supply of the centre, and a bridge, laid down at Andarlassa gave access to the roots of the Bayonette mountain; yet the troops were fed with difficulty, and so scantily, that Wellington reduced the usual stoppage of pay, and invoked the army by its military honour to sustain with firmness the unavoidable pressure. The effect was striking. Murmurs, loud in the camps before, were hushed instantly, although the soldiers knew that some commissaries, leaguing with the speculators upon the coast, secretly loaded the provision mules with condiments and other luxuries to sell on the mountains at enormous profit. Desertion was however great, more than twelve hundred men went over to the enemy in less than four months; and they were all Germans, Englishmen, or Spaniards; for the Portuguese who abandoned their colours invariably went back to their own country.

This difficulty of feeding the Anglo-Portuguese, the extreme distress of the Spaniards, and the certainty that they would plunder in France and so raise the people in arms, together with the uneasy state of the political affairs in the Peninsula, rendered Wellington averse to offensive operations while Napoleon maintained the Elbe. It was impossible to make a formidable and sustained invasion of France with the Anglo-Portuguese alone; and he had neither money nor means of transport to feed the Spaniards, even if policy warranted such a measure; the nature of the country also forbad a decisive victory; and an advance would be attended with the risk of returning to Spain again during the winter when a retreat would be dangerous and dishonouring. On the 20th of October however, a letter from the governor of Pampeluna was intercepted, and lord Fitzroy Somerset, observing the compliment at the beginning was in numerals, ingeniously followed the cue and made out the whole. It announced that the place could not hold out more than a week; and as intelligence of Napoleon's disasters in Germany became known at the same time, Wellington was induced to yield once more to the wishes of the allied sovereigns and the English ministers, who were earnest that he should invade France.

His intent was to attack Soult's entrenched camp on the 29th, thinking Pampeluna would fall before that period; it did not, and in the passes above Roncevalles the troops were knee-deep in snow. His preparations however continued and strict precautions were taken to baffle the enemy's emissaries; yet Soult was informed by deserters of the original design and the cause of the delay! He likewise found on a sergeant-major of artillery, taken the 29th, letters and orders indicating an attack by the bridge of Amotz, between D'Erlon's right and Clausel's left; French peasants also who had passed the outposts said they had been questioned about that bridge and the roads leading to it. Soult therefore augmented his works there, and having thus as he judged provided for its safety, and being in no pain for his right, nor for Clausel's position which was covered by the smaller Rhune, turned his attention towards Foy.

That general was at Bidarray half way between St. Jean Pied de Port and Cambo, having to watch certain roads, leading to the Nive from the high valleys which gave Soult uneasiness for his left. Thinking now the principal attack would be at the Amotz bridge, and not by these roads or St. Jean Pied de Port as he had first supposed and as Wellington had indeed once designed, the French marshal resolved to use Foy's force offensively. In this view he instructed him, if St. Jean Pied de Port should be only slightly attacked, to draw all the troops he could spare from its defence to Bidarray; and when the allies assailed Amotz, to seize the Gorospil mountain and fall upon their right as they descended from the Col de Maya. But if he was himself assailed, he was to call in his detached troops from St. Jean, repass the Nive by the bridge of Bidarray, make the best defence possible behind that river, and open a communication with Pierre Soult and Trielhard, whose divisions of cavalry were at St. Palais and Orthes.

On the 6th, Foy, thinking the Gorospil difficult to pass,

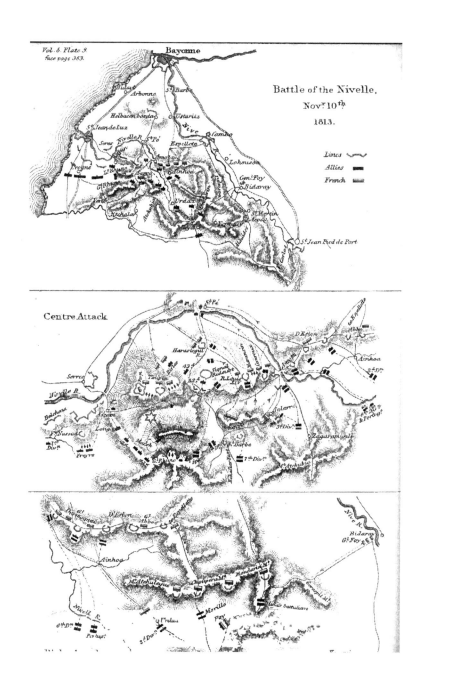

Vol. 8. Plate 9.
face page 363.

Bayonne

Battle of the Nivelle,
Novr 10th
1813.

Lines
Allies
French

Centre Attack

proposed to seize the Col de Yspegui from the side of St. Jean Pied de Port, and so descend into the Bastan. Soult preferred Bidarray as a safer point and more united with the main body of the army; but he gave Foy a discretionary power to march along the left of the Nive upon Itzatzu and Espelette, if he judged it fitting to reinforce D'Erlon's left rather than to attack the enemy. And having thus arranged his defence, he directed the prefect of the lower Pyrenees to post the organized national guards at the issues of all the valleys about St. Jean Pied de Port, but to keep the mass of the people quiet until the allies, penetrating into the country, should at once provoke and offer facilities for an irregular warfare. On the 9th, being still uneasy about the San Martin d'Arosa and Gorospil roads, he brought up his brother's cavalry from St. Palais to the heights above Cambo, and next day the long-expected storm burst.

Allured by some fine weather on the 6th and 7th, Wellington had moved Hill from the Roncevalles to the Bastan with a view to attack Soult, leaving Mina on the position of Alto-biscar and in the Alduides. Orders for the battle, which was to commence the 8th, were issued, but Freyre then declared, that he wanted subsistence, and must withdraw a part of his troops. This was a scheme to obtain provisions from the English magazines, and successful, because the attack could not be made without his aid. Forty thousand rations of flour, with a formal intimation that if he did not co-operate the whole army must retire again into Spain, contented Freyre for the moment; but the extravagant abuses of the Spanish commissariat were plainly exposed when the chief of the staff declared that the flour would only suffice for two days, although there were less than ten thousand soldiers in the field. Spain therefore demanded two rations for every fighting man, and yet her troops were starving! When this difficulty was surmounted heavy rain caused the attack to be again deferred, but on the 10th ninety thousand combatants of all arms, seventy-four thousand being Appendix 2, No. 3. Vol. VI. Anglo-Portuguese, descended to the battle; and with them ninety-five pieces of artillery, all of which were with inconceivable vigour brought into action: in this host however

neither the cavalry, four thousand five hundred strong, nor the
Spaniards blockading Pampeluna are reckoned.   To meet this
power the French had been increased by conscripts, yet many
of those had deserted, and the fighting men did not exceed
seventy-nine thousand, including garrisons.   Six thousand
were cavalry; and as Foy's operations were extraneous to the line of defence, scarcely sixty thousand infantry and artillery were opposed to the allies.

Appendix 3.
Vol. VI.

Wellington seeing the right of Soult's line could not well be
forced, designed to hold it in check while he forced the centre
and left, and pushed down the Nivelle to San Pé.   In this
view, the second and sixth British divisions, Hamilton's Portuguese, Morillo's Spaniards, four of Mina's battalions, and
Grant's brigade of light cavalry, in all twenty-six thousand
men, with nine guns, were collected under Hill in the Bastan
to attack D'Erlon.   The position of Roncevalles was occupied
by the remainder of Mina's troops, supported by the blockading force under Carlos d'España.   The third,
fourth and seventh divisions and Giron's Andalusians, the whole under Beresford, were disposed
about Zagaramurdi, the Puerto de Echallar, and the
lower parts of those slopes of the greater Rhune which descend
upon Sarre.   On the left of this body the light division and
Longa's Spaniards, both under Charles Alten, were disposed
on those slopes of the greater Rhune which led down towards
Ascain.   Victor Alten's light cavalry with three batteries
were placed on the road to Sarre, and six mountain guns
followed Giron and Charles Alten.   Thus thirty-six thousand
fighting men with twenty-four guns were concentrated in this
quarter to attack Clausel.

Wellington's
Order of
Movements,
MSS.

Freyre's Gallicians, nine thousand with six guns, were on
Alten's left, at the fort of Calvary and towards Jollimont;
being held there with design to fall upon any troops which
might come from Serres by the bridge of Ascain, to support
Clausel.   The first and fifth divisions, Wilson's, Bradford's,
and lord Aylmer's brigades of infantry, Vandeleur's light
dragoons and the heavy German cavalry, in all nineteen
thousand men with fifty-four guns, under Hope, opposed
Soult's right wing; and the naval squadron hovered on their
flank to aid the land operations.

On the French side each lieutenant-general had a special position to defend.   D'Erlon's first line rested its left on the fortified rocks of Mondarin, which could not be turned; from thence it run along the Choupera and Atchuleguy mountains, by the forge of Urdax, to the Nivelle.   This range, strongly entrenched, was occupied by one of Abbé's and one of D'Armagnac's brigades, Espelette being behind the former and Ainhoa behind the latter.   Their second line composed of the remaining brigades, was on a broad ridge several miles behind Ainhoa, and its left did not extend beyond the centre of the first line; the right, touching the bridge of Amotz, stretched with a wide flank, because the Nivelle there gave more space : three great redoubts were constructed on this ridge and a fourth had been commenced close to the bridge.

On the right of this second line beyond the Amotz bridge, Clausel's position extended to Ascain, along a range of heights fortified with redoubts, trenches, and abbatis; and as the Nivelle after passing Amotz swept in a curve completely round this range to Ascain, both flanks rested alike upon that river; having communication by the bridges at those places on the right and left, and a retreat by the bridges of San Pé and Harastagui in the rear.   Two of Clausel's divisions, reinforced by one of D'Erlon's under Maransin, were here posted. In front of the left were the redoubts of St. Barbe and Grenadá, covering the camp of Sarre; in front of the right was the smaller Rhune, fortified and occupied by a brigade of Maransin's division; and a new redoubt with abbatis was also commenced to cover the approaches to the bridge of Amotz.

On the right of this line, beyond the bridge of Ascain, Daricau's division, also of Clausel's corps, and San Pol's Italian brigade drawn from Villatte's reserve, held the entrenched camp of Serres and connected Clausel with Villatte, the latter being on a ridge crossing the gorges of Olette and Jollimont. The French right under Reille, strongly fortified on the lower ground and partially covered by inundations, was nearly impregnable.

Soult's weakest point was the opening between the Rhune mountains and the Nivelle.   Gradually narrowing as it approached the bridge of Amotz, this space was the most open, the least fortified; and the Nivelle, fordable above that bridge, could not hamper the allies' movements. A powerful force acting in that direction could pass by D'Erlon's first line, break in upon the right of his second line and upon Clausel's left, and outflank both—and in that view Wellington designed his battle.

Hill, leaving Mina's troops on the Gorospil mountain facing the rocks of Mondarin, moved in the night by the different passes of the Col de Maya; designing that Morillo should menace the French on the Choupera and Atchuleguy mountains while the second division attacked Ainhoa and Urdax. The sixth division and Hamilton's Portuguese were to assault the works covering the bridge of Amotz, either on the right or left bank of the river according to circumstances, and thus twenty-six thousand men were combined against D'Erlon's position from that side. On their left Beresford's corps was assembled. The third division under Colville, descending from Zagaramurdi, was to move against the unfinished redoubts and entrenchments covering the bridge of Amotz on the left bank of the Nivelle; thus turning D'Erlon's right when it was attacked in front by Hill. On the left of the third division, the seventh, descending from the Echallar pass was to storm the Grenada redoubt, and by the village of Sarre to assail Clausel's main position abreast with the attack of the third division. On the left of the seventh, the fourth division, assembling on the lower slopes of the greater Rhune, was to descend upon the San Barbe, and then moving through Sarre also to assail Clausel abreast with the seventh division. On the left of the fourth division, Giron's Andalusians, gathered higher up on the flank of the great Rhune, were to move abreast with the others leaving Sarre on their right; and they were to drive the enemy from the lower slopes of the smaller Rhune and in concert with the rest attack Clausel. In this way Hill's and Beresford's corps, forming a mass of forty thousand infantry, were to be thrust on both sides of the bridge of Amotz between Clausel and D'Erlon.

Charles Alten and Longa, having together eight thousand men, were likewise to attack Clausel on the left of Giron, while Freyre approached the bridge of Ascain. But Alten

could not assail Clausel's right without storming the smaller
Rhune; and that mountain outwork, a hog's-back ridge rising
abruptly out of table-land and parallel with the greater
Rhune, was inaccessible along its front, which was precipitous
and from fifty to two hundred feet high; however, on the
French left the rocks gradually decreased, descending by a
long slope to the valley of Sarre, and about two-thirds of the
way down the thirty-fourth French regiment was placed, with
an advanced post on some isolated crags situated in the
hollow between the two Rhunes.   On the French right the
hog's-back sunk indeed by degrees into the plain or platform
but was there covered by a marsh scarcely passable; hence the
attacking troops had first to move up against the perpendicular rocks in front, and then file to their left under fire,
between the marsh and the lower crags, until they gained an
accessible point, from whence to fight their way along the
narrow ridge of the hog's-back,—the bristles of which were
huge perpendicular crags connected with walls of loose stones,
so as to form small forts or castles communicating with
each other by narrow footways, and rising one above another
until the culminant point was attained.   The table-land
beyond this ridge was extensive, terminating in a very deep
ravine on every side save a narrow space on the French
right of the marsh, where a loose stone wall was constructed,
running perpendicularly from behind the hog's-back and
ending in a star fort overhanging the edge of the ravine.
This rampart and fort and the hog's-back itself were defended
by Barbot's brigade.   The line of retreat was towards a low
narrow neck of land, bridging the deep ravine and linking the
Rhune to Clausel's main position.   At this neck a reserve was
placed, partly to sustain the thirty-fourth French regiment on
the slope of the mountain, partly to protect the neck itself
on the side of Sarre.

Alten collected his troops at midnight on that slope
of the greater Rhune which descended towards Ascain.   The
main body of the light division, turning the marsh by the
left, was to assail the stone wall and overlap the star fort by
the ravine beyond; Longa, stretching still farther on the left,
was to turn the smaller Rhune altogether; and the forty-

third regiment, supported by the seventeenth Portuguese, was
to assail the hog's-back. One battalion of riflemen and
the mountain-guns were left on the summit of the greater
Rhune, with orders to assail the craggy post below and connect Alten's attack with that of Giron; and all these troops
gained their stations so secretly the enemy had no suspicion
of their presence, though the columns were lying within half
musket-shot of the works for several hours. Towards morning, five or six guns fired in a hurried manner from the low
ground near the sea broke the stillness; but on the Rhune
all was quiet and the British troops awaited the rising of the
sun, when three guns fired from the Atchubia mountain were
to give the signal of attack.

BATTLE OF THE NIVELLE.
[Plan 9, page 363.]

Day broke with great splendour, and as the first ray of
light played on the summit of the lofty Atchubia the signal
guns were fired in rapid succession. Then the British leaped
up, and the French, beholding with astonishment their columns
rushing forward from the flank of the great Rhune, run
to the defences with much tumult. They opened a few
pieces which were answered from the top of the greater
Rhune by the mountain artillery, and at the same moment
two companies of the forty-third were detached to cross the
marsh if possible and keep down the fire from the lower part
of the hog's-back; the remainder of the regiment, partly in
line partly in a column of reserve advanced against the high
rocks. From these crags the French shot fast, but the quick
even movement of the British line deceived their aim, and
the soldiers, running forward very swiftly though the ground
was rough, turned suddenly between the rocks and the marsh,
and were immediately joined by the two companies which
had passed that obstacle notwithstanding its depth. Then all
together jumped into the lower works; but the men, exhausted
by their exertions, for they had passed over half a mile of
very difficult ground with a wonderful speed, remained for a
few minutes inactive within half pistol shot of the first stone
castle, from whence came a sharp and biting musketry.

When they recovered breath they arose and with a stern shout commenced the assault. The French as numerous as their assailants had for six weeks been labouring on their well-contrived castles: but strong and valiant in arms must the soldiers have been who stood in that hour before the veterans of the forty-third. One French grenadier officer only dared to sustain the rush. Standing alone on the high wall of the first castle and flinging large stones with both his hands, a noble figure, he fought to the last and fell, while his men, shrinking on each side, sought safety among the rocks on his flanks. Close and confused then was the action, man met man at every turn, but with a rattling musketry, sometimes struggling in the intricate narrow paths, sometimes climbing the loose stone walls, the British soldiers won their desperate way until they had carried the second castle, called by the French the place of arms and the magpie's nest, because of a lofty pillar of rock which rose above it and on which a few marksmen were perched. From these points the defenders were driven into their last castle, which being higher and larger than the others and covered by a natural ditch or cleft in the rocks, fifteen feet deep, was called the Donjon.

There they made a stand, and the assailants, having advanced so far as to look into the rear of the rampart and star-fort on the table-land below, suspended the vehement throng of their attack for a while; partly to gather head for storming the Donjon, partly to fire on the enemy beneath them, who were now warmly engaged with the two battalions of riflemen the Portuguese caçadores and the seventeenth Portuguese. This last regiment was to have followed the forty-third, but seeing how rapidly and surely the latter were carrying the rocks, had moved at once against the traverse on the other side of the marsh; and very soon the French defending the rampart, being thus pressed in front and warned by the direction of the fire that they were turned on the ridge above—seeing also the fifty-second, forming the extreme left of the division, now emerging from the deep ravine beyond the star-fort on the other flank, abandoned their works. Then the forty-third gathering a strong head stormed the Donjon; some leaped

with a shout down the deep cleft in the rock, others turned it
by the narrow paths on each flank, and the enemy abandoned
the loose walls at the moment they were being scaled; thus
in twenty minutes eight hundred old soldiers were hustled out
of this labyrinth—yet not so easily but the victors lost eleven
officers and sixty-seven men.

All the mountain was now cleared of the French, for the
riflemen dropped perpendicularly from the greater Rhune upon
the post of crags in the hollow and seized it with small loss;
but they were ill-seconded by Giron's Andalusians, and hardly
handled by the thirty-fourth French regiment, which obstinately clung to the slope, and covered the flight of the confused crowd rushing down the mountain behind them towards
the connecting neck of land: at that point also, all rallied
and seemed inclined to renew the action, yet after some hesitation continued their retreat. This favourable moment for a
decisive stroke had been looked for by the commander of the
forty-third, but the officer entrusted with the reserve companies of the regiment had thrown them needlessly into the
fight, thus rendering it impossible to collect a body strong
enough to assail such a heavy mass. The contest at the stone
wall and star-fort, shortened by the rapid success on the hog's
back, had not been very severe; Kempt however, always
conspicuous for his valour, was severely wounded; nevertheless he did not quit the field, and soon re-formed his brigade
on the platform he had thus so gallantly won. The fifty-
second, having turned the position by the ravine, was now
approaching the enemy's line of retreat; but Alten, following
his instructions, halted the division partly in the ravine itself
to the left of the neck, partly on the table-land. During the
action Longa got near Ascain in connexion with Freyre, and
in that state, the enemy now and then cannonading, Alten
awaited the progress of the army on his right; for the
columns there had a long way to march and it was essential
to regulate the movements.

The signal-guns from the Atchubia which sent the light
division against the Rhune, had also put the fourth and seventh
divisions in movement against the redoubts of San Barbe
and Grenada, and eighteen guns were instantly placed in bat-

tery against the former. While they poured their stream of
shot the troops advanced with scaling-ladders, and the skirmishers of the fourth division soon got into the rear of the
work; whereupon the French leaped out and fled, and Ross's
battery of horse artillery, galloping to a rising ground in rear
of the Grenada fort, drove them from there also: then the
divisions carried the village of Sarre and the position beyond
it, and advanced to the attack of Clausel's main position.

It was now eight o'clock and from the smaller Rhune a
splendid spectacle of war opened upon the view. On the left
the ships of war slowly sailing to and fro were exchanging
shots with the fort of Socoa; and Hope, menacing all the
French lines in the low ground, sent the sound of a hundred
pieces of artillery bellowing up the rocks, to be answered by
nearly as many from the tops of the mountains. On the
right, the summit of the great Atchubia was just lighted by
the rising sun, and fifty thousand men, rushing down its
enormous slopes with ringing shouts, seemed to chase the
receding shadows into the deep valley. The plains of France
so long overlooked from the towering crags of the Pyrenees
were to be the prize of battle, and the half-famished soldiers
in their fury broke through the iron barrier erected by Soult
as if it were but a screen of reeds.

A space of seven or eight miles contained the principal
action; but the skirts of battle spread wide and in no point
had the combinations failed. Hill, after a long and difficult
night march, had neared the enemy a little before seven
o'clock. Sending Morillo and Mina against the Mondarain
and Atchuleguy rocks, he with the second division brushed
away the French brigade from Urdax and Ainhoa. Then the
sixth division and Hamilton's Portuguese passed the Nivelle
lower down and by the right bank threatened the bridge of
Amotz; thus the Spaniards held Abbé in play on the rocks,
while three Anglo-Portuguese divisions advanced against
D'Erlon's second position. The ground was however so rugged
they could not close before eleven o'clock on the redoubts,
each of which contained five hundred men. They were placed
along the crest of a ridge thickly clothed with bushes, covered
by a deep ravine, and very difficult to attack; but Clinton

turned the ravine with the sixth division on the left, drove
the French from the half-finished works covering the bridge
of Amotz, and wheeling to his right approached the nearest
redoubt, whereupon the garrison abandoned it.   Then Hamilton, passing the ravine on Clinton's right, menaced the next
redoubt, and the second division under Byng, also passing,
stormed the third redoubt.   D'Armagnac now set fire to his
hutted camp and retreated to Helbacen de Borda behind San
Pé, pursued by Clinton.   Abbé's second brigade, on the
French left, was separated from D'Armagnac by a ravine; but
he also after some hesitation retreated towards Espelette and
Cambo, where his other brigade falling back before Morillo,
rejoined him.

It was the progress of the battle on the left of the Nive
that rendered D'Erlon's defence so feeble.   After the fall of
the St. Barbe and Grenada redoubts, Conroux endeavoured to
defend the heights of Sarre; but while the fourth and seventh
divisions and the ninety-fourth regiment, detached from the
third division, carried that point, the third division, being on
their right and less opposed, pushed towards the bridge of
Amotz, forming in conjunction with the sixth division the
small end of the wedge into which Beresford's and Hill's
corps were now thrown.   The French were thus driven from
all their unfinished works covering that bridge on both sides
of the Nivelle, and Conroux's division, spread from Sarre to
Amotz, was broken by superior numbers at every point.   He
indeed vigorously defended the finished works around the
bridge itself but soon fell mortally wounded; then the third
division seizing the bridge, established itself on the heights
between that structure and the redoubt of Louis the XIV.
which was also unfinished.   This happened about eleven
o'clock, and D'Erlon, fearing to be cut off from St. Pé, yielded
as we have seen at once to the attack of the sixth division;
and at the same time Conroux's troops fell back in disorder
from Sarre, closely pursued by the fourth and seventh divisions, which were immediately established on the left of the
third.   Thus the communication between Clausel and D'Erlon
was cut, the left flank of one the right flank of the other
broken, and the direct communication between Hill and Beresford was secured by one and the same blow.

Clausel however still stood firm with Taupin's and Maransin's divisions; and the latter, now complete by the return of Barbot's brigade from the smaller Rhune, occupied the redoubt of Louis XIV., and having eight field-pieces attempted to cover the flight of Conroux's troops. His guns were soon silenced by Ross's horse artillery, the only battery which had surmounted the difficulties of the ground after passing Sarre. The infantry were then assailed, in front by the fourth and seventh divisions, in flank by the third division; the redoubt was stormed, the garrison bayonetted, Conroux's men continued to fly, Maransin's after a stiff combat were cast headlong into the ravines behind their position and he was taken, yet afterwards escaped in the confusion. Giron then came up on the left of the fourth division, somewhat late, and after having abandoned the riflemen on the lower slopes of the smaller Rhune.

On the French side Taupin's troops and a large body of conscripts, forming Clausel's right wing, still remained to fight. Their left rested on a large work called the signal redoubt, which had no artillery but overlooked the whole position; the right was covered by two redoubts overhanging a ravine which separated them from the camp of Serres, and some works in the ravine itself protected the communication by the bridge of Ascain. Behind the signal redoubt, on a ridge crossing the road to San Pé, by which Maransin and Conroux's divisions were now flying in disorder, there was another work called the redoubt of Harastaguia; and Clausel thinking he might still dispute the victory if his reserve division could come to his aid from the camp of Serres, drew the thirty-first regiment from Taupin and posted it in front of this redoubt. His design was to rally Maransin's and Conroux's troops there and so form a new line, the left on the Harastaguia the right on the signal redoubt, into which last he threw six hundred of the eighty-eighth regiment. In this position, having a retreat by the bridge of Ascain, he thought to renew the battle; but his plan failed at the moment of conception, because Taupin could not stand before the light division which was now again in full action.

About half-past nine, Alten, seeing the whole of the columns on his right as far as the eye could reach well

engaged with the enemy, had crossed the low neck of land in
his front. The fifty-second regiment first passed with a very
narrow front under a destructive cannonade and fire of
musketry from entrenchments on the opposite mountain; a
road, coming from Ascain by the ravine, wound up the position, and as the fifty-second pushed their attack along it the
enemy abandoned his entrenchments on each side and forsook
even his crowning works above. This formidable regiment
was followed by the other troops. Taupin, though his division was weak and now diminished by the absence of the
thirty-first regiment, awaited the attack, being supported by
the conscripts drawn up in his rear; but at that time
Longa, having turned the smaller Rhune, approached Ascain
Clausel, MSS. in conjunction with Freyre's troops, and their
skirmishers opened a distant musketry against
the works covering that bridge; panic seized the French, the
Taupin's seventieth regiment abandoned the two redoubts
Report, above, and the conscripts were withdrawn. Clausel
MSS. ordered Taupin to retake the forts, but this
only added to the disorder;—the seventieth regiment disbanded entirely and were not re-assembled until next day.
There remained only four regiments unbroken, the eighty-
eighth which was in the signal redoubt, two under Taupin
in rear of the works on the right, and the thirty-first which
covered the Harastaguia, now the only line of retreat.

. Clausel, anxious to bring off the regiment from the signal
redoubt, ordered Taupin to charge on one side, intending to
do the same himself on the other at the head of the thirty-
first; but the latter was vigorously attacked by the Portuguese
of the seventh division, while the fourth division rapidly
interposed between it and the signal redoubt, which was
moreover turned on its right at musket-shot by the forty-
third and Barnard's riflemen. Wherefore Taupin, instead of
charging was himself charged in front by the riflemen; and
being menaced at the same time in flank by the fourth
division retreated, closely pursued by Barnard until that
intrepid officer fell dangerously wounded. During this
struggle the seventh division broke the thirty-first, and the rout
was complete: the French fled to the different bridges over
the Nivelle and the signal redoubt was left to its fate.

This formidable work barred the way of the light division, but it was of no value to the defence when the forts on its flanks were abandoned. Colborne approached it in front with the fifty-second regiment, Giron menaced it on Colborne's right, Cole was passing to its rear and Kempt's brigade was turning it on the left. Colborne whose military judgment was seldom at fault, halted under the brow of the conical hill on which the work was situated; but some Spaniards making a vaunting though feeble demonstration of attacking it on his right were beaten back, and at that moment a staff-officer, without warrant, for Alten on the spot assured the author of this history he sent no such order, rode up and directed Colborne to advance. It was no moment for remonstrance and covered by the steepness of the hill he reached the flat top forty yards from the work; the rush was then made, but a wide ditch, thirty feet deep, well fraised and palisaded, stopped him short, and the fire of the enemy stretched all the foremost men dead. Colborne, escaping miraculously for he was always at the head and on horseback, immediately led the regiment under cover of the brow to another point, and thinking to take the French unawares made another rush, yet with the same result: at three different places did he rise to the surface in this manner, and each time the French fire swept away the head of his column. Resorting then to persuasion he held out a white handkerchief and summoned the commandant, pointing out to him how his work was surrounded, how hopeless his defence; he yielded, having had only one man killed, whereas on the British side there fell two hundred soldiers of a regiment never surpassed in arms since arms were first borne by men.

During this affair Clausel had crossed the Nivelle in great disorder; Maransin's and Conroux's troops near San Pé, the thirty-first regiment at Harastaguia, Taupin between that place and the bridge of Serres. Pursued by the third and seventh divisions, the skirmishers of the former crossed by Amotz and a bridge above San Pé, and entered the latter place while the French were in the act of passing the river below. It was now past two o'clock, Conroux's troops pushed on to Helbacen de Borda, a fortified position on the road from San

Pé to Bayonne, where they were joined by Taupin and D'Erlon with D'Armagnac's division; but Clausel rallied Maransin's men and took post on some heights immediately above San Pé. Soult who had on the first alarm hurried from St. Jean de Luz to the camp of Serres with all his reserve artillery and spare troops, now menaced the allies' left flank by Ascain. Wellington then halted Cole, Alten and Giron on the reverse slopes of Clausel's original position, facing the camp of Serres; waiting until Clinton, then following D'Armagnac on the right of the Nivelle, was well advanced. When assured of Clinton's progress he crossed the Nivelle with the third and seventh divisions, and drove Maransin from his new position; but with a hard struggle, in which Inglis was wounded and the fifty-first and sixty-eighth regiments handled very roughly. This ended the battle in the centre, for darkness was coming on, and the troops were exhausted, especially the sixth division, which had been marching or fighting for twenty-four hours. However three divisions were then firmly established in rear of Soult's right wing, of whose operations it is time to treat.

In front of Reille's entrenchments were two advanced positions; the camp of the Sans Culottes on his right, the Bons Secours in his centre, covering Urogne. The first was carried early in the morning by the fifth division, which advanced to the inundation covering the heights of Bordegain and Ciboure. The second was taken by Halket's Germans and the guards; and the eighty-fifth regiment, of lord Aylmer's brigade, drove a French battalion out of Urogne. The first division then menaced the camp of Belchena, and the German skirmishers passed a stream covering part of the line; they were however soon driven back by the enemy, whose musketry and cannonade were brisk along the whole front. Freyre, advancing from Jollimont and the Calvaire on the right of the first division, placed eight guns in battery against the Nassau redoubt, constructed on the ridge occupied by Villatte to cover the approaches to Ascain. There he was opposed by his own countrymen under Casa Palacio, who commanded the remains of Joseph's Spanish guards; and during the fight Freyre's skirmishers on the right united as we have seen with Longa.

This false battle was maintained along the whole line until nightfall, with equal loss of men but great advantage to the allies; because it occupied Reille's two divisions and Villatte's reserve, and prevented the troops in the camp of Serres from passing the bridge of Ascain to aid Clausel.   However when he was overpowered and Wellington had entered San Pé, Daricau and the Italian brigade withdrew from Serres and Villatte occupied it; whereupon Freyre and Longa entered the town of Ascain, but Villatte held the camp until Reille had withdrawn into St. Jean de Luz and destroyed all the bridges on the lower Nivelle,—when that was effected the whole retired, and at daybreak reached the heights of Bidart on the road to Bayonne.   During the night the allies halted on the position they had gained in the centre; but the accidental conflagration of a wood completely separated the piquets towards Ascain from the main body, and spreading far and wide over the heath lighted up all the hills, a blazing sign of war to France.

The 11th the army advanced in order of battle.   Hope forded the river above St. Jean de Luz with his infantry and marched on Bidart; Beresford moved by the roads leading upon Arbonne; Hill, communicating by his right with Morillo who was on the rocks of Mondarain, brought his left forward into communication with Beresford, and with his centre took possession of Suraide and Espelette facing Cambo.   The time required to restore the bridges for the artillery at Ciboure and the change of front on the right rendered these movements slow; and gave Soult time to rally his army upon a third line of fortified camps, the right resting on the coast at Bidart, the centre at Helbacen Borda, the left at Ustaritz on the Nive. This front was about eight miles, but the works were only slightly advanced, and Soult, dreading a second battle on so wide a field, drew back his centre and left to Arbonne and Arauntz, broke down the bridges on the Nive at Ustaritz, and at two o'clock a slight skirmish engaged by the allies in the centre closed the day's proceedings.   Next morning the French retired to the ridge of Beyris, their right near Anglet, their left in the entrenched camp of Bayonne.

During this movement a dense fog arrested the allies,

but when the day cleared Hope took post at Bidart on the
left, and Beresford occupied Ahetze, Arbonne, and the hill
of San Barbe, in the centre.   Hill endeavoured to pass
the fords and restore the broken bridges of Ustaritz, and he
also made a demonstration against the works at Cambo; but
the rain which fell heavily in the mountains on the 11th rendered the fords impassable, and both points were defended
successfully by Foy.   That officer's operations had been
isolated.   For though D'Erlon mistrusting the strength of his
own position had in the night of the 9th sent him an order to
move on Espelette from Bidarray, it arrived too late; Foy,
following Soult's previous instructions, drove Mina from
the Gorospil mountain in the morning of the 10th, and
flanking Morillo forced him also back fighting to the Puerto
de Maya.   But then the receding sound and smoke of D'Erlon's
battle caused the French general, who had lost a colonel and
one hundred and fifty men, to retire; he however took much
baggage and a hundred prisoners and continuing his retreat
all night reached Cambo and Ustaritz the 11th, in time to
relieve Abbé's division at those posts, which on the 12th he
defended against Hill.

OBSERVATIONS.

1°. In this battle Soult was driven in a few hours from a
mountain position which he had been fortifying for three
months.   He lost four thousand two hundred and sixty-five
men and officers, including twelve or fourteen hundred prisoners.   One general was killed; all his field-magazines at
St. Jean de Luz and Espelette fell into the hands of the
victors; and fifty-one pieces of artillery were taken, the greater
part having been abandoned in the redoubts of the low country.
The allies had two generals, Kempt and Byng, wounded,
and they lost two thousand six hundred and ninety-four men
and officers.

2°. Soult fared as most generals will, who seek by extensive
lines to supply the want of numbers or of hardiness in the
troops.   Against rude commanders and undisciplined soldiers
lines may avail, seldom against accomplished generals, never
when the assailants are the better soldiers.   Cæsar at Alesia

resisted the Gauls, but his lines served him not at Dyrrachium against Pompey. Crassus failed in Calabria against Spartacus. Marlborough broke through all the French lines in Flanders, and if Wellington succeeded at Torres Vedras it was perhaps because his lines were not attacked. It may be Soult was seduced by that example, for his works were almost as gigantic and upon the same plan; that is to say a river on one flank the ocean on the other, the front on mountains covered with redoubts and partially protected by inundations. But he had only three months to complete his system, his labours were under the gaze of his enemy, and his troops, twice defeated during the execution, were inferior in confidence and numbers to the assailants. Wellington's lines had been laboured for a whole year; Massena only knew of them when they stopped his progress, and his army, inferior in numbers, had been repulsed in the recent battle of Busaco.

3°. This criticism does not apply to entrenched camps within compass around which an active army moves as on a pivot, delivering or avoiding battle according to circumstances; it applies only to those extensive covering lines by which soldiers are taught to consider themselves inferior to their enemies. A general is thus precluded from showing himself at important points and at critical periods; he is unable to encourage his troops or correct errors; and sudden combinations of genius are excluded by the necessity of adhering to the works, while the assailants may menace every point and select where to break through. The defenders seeing the large attacking columns and having no proportionate masses to oppose, become fearful, knowing there must be some weak point which will be the measure of strength for the whole. But the assailants fall on with a heat and vehemence belonging to those who act voluntarily and on the offensive; each mass strives to outdo those on its right and left, and failure is only a repulse; whereas the assailed, having no resource but victory, look to their flanks and are more anxious about their neighbours' fighting than their own

4°. All these disadvantages were illustrated on the Nivelle. D'Erlon attributed his defeat to Conroux's losing the bridge of Amotz, and to that also Maransin traced his discomfiture.

Reports
of French
generals
to Soult,
MSS.

Taupin laid his defeat at Maransin's door, and Clausel ascribed it to want of firmness in the troops; but he also said, if Daricau had come from the camp at Serres to his aid he would have held his ground. Soult thought Clausel had rashly attempted to defend Sarre after the San Barbe and Grenada redoubts were taken, and thus let Conroux be overwhelmed in detail. He should, Soult said, have concentrated his three divisions on the main position, and there covered by the small Rhune should have been victorious; and it was scarcely credible that such entrenchments as Clausel and D'Erlon had to defend should have been carried; —for his part he relied on their strength so confidently, as to think the allies must sacrifice twenty-five thousand men to force them and perhaps fail then. He had been on the right when the battle began, no reports came to him, he could judge of events only by the fire; and when he reached the camp of Serres with his reserve troops and artillery Clausel's works were lost! His arrival had however paralysed the march of three divisions. This was true, yet there seems some foundation for Clausel's complaint, namely, that he had for five hours fought on his main position and during that time no help had come, although the camp of Serres was close at hand, the distance from St. Jean de Luz to that place only four miles and the attack in the low ground evidently a feint. This then was Soult's error. He suffered Hope to hold in play twenty-five thousand men in the low ground, while fifteen thousand under Clausel lost the battle on the hills.

Soult, MSS.

5°. The French army was inferior in numbers and many of the works were unfinished; yet two strong divisions, Daricau's and Foy's, were quite thrown out of the fight; for the slight offensive movement made by the latter produced no effect whatever. Vigorous counter-attacks are no doubt essential to a good defence; and it was in allusion to this that Napoleon, speaking of Joseph's position behind the Ebro in the beginning of the war, said, 'if a river were as broad and rapid as the Danube it would be nothing without secure points for passing to the offensive.' The same maxim affects lines, and Soult applied this principle grandly when he proposed the descent upon Aragon to Suchet; but he conceived it meanly, when he ordered Foy to attack by the Gorospil mountain. That general's numbers were too few, the direction of his march false; one regiment in the battle at the decisive moment, would have been worth three on such a secondary point. Foy's retreat was inevitable if D'Erlon failed, and wanting Foy's aid D'Erlon did fail. What success could Foy obtain? He might have driven Mina over the Col de Maya and through the Bastan; he might have defeated Morillo and perhaps have taken Hill's baggage; yet this would have been little against the allies' success at Amotz, and the deeper he penetrated the more difficult would have been his retreat. The incursion into the Bastan by Yspegui, proposed by him on the 6th, although properly rejected by Soult would have produced greater effects than the one executed by Gorospil on the 10th; for Hill's troops were then in march by brigades through the Alduides, and a sudden attack might have caused a delay of the great battle beyond the 10th; then the heavy rains, which set in the 11th, would have rendered it difficult to attack at all: Soult would thus have had time to complete his works.

6°. It has been advanced as a minor cause of defeat that the French troops were posted in front, whereas they should have been in rear of the redoubts; this, if so, was not by design, for Clausel's report of the action expressly states that Maransin was directed to form in rear and charge when the assailants were between the redoubts and the abbatis. It is however needless to pry closely when the great cause lies broad on the surface—Wellington directed superior numbers with superior skill. The proof will be found in the following analysis, but it must be noted that the conscripts are not included in the French force—they were kept in masses behind and never engaged.

Abbé's division of five thousand old soldiers were paralysed by the operations of Longa and Mina, who at the same time entirely occupied Foy's division—thus six thousand of Wellington's worst soldiers sufficed to employ twelve thousand of Soult's best troops, and meanwhile Hill fell with twenty thousand upon the five thousand under D'Armagnac. The battle was in this manner secured on the right bank of the

Nivelle, while Beresford on the left bank thrust twenty-four thousand against the ten thousand composing Conroux's and Maransin's divisions. Hill and Beresford also in advancing, formed a wedge towards the bridge of Amotz, whereby forty-four thousand men were impelled against the fifteen thousand under D'Armagnac, Conroux, and Maransin; and these last could not even fight together, because part of Conroux's troops were previously defeated near Sarre, and a brigade of Maransin's was beaten on the smaller Rhune before the main attack commenced. Finally, Alten, having eight thousand combatants, first defeated Barbot's brigade on the Rhune and then fell on Taupin who had only three thousand, and the rest of the French army was held in check by Freyre and Hope. Thus more than fifty thousand good and confident troops were suddenly thrown upon eighteen thousand, good men also but dispirited by previous defeats. Against such a thunderbolt there was no defence in the French works. Was it then a simple matter for Wellington so to combine his battle? The mountains on whose huge flanks he gathered his fierce soldiers, the roads he opened, the horrid crags he surmounted, the headlong steeps he descended, the wild regions through which he poured the destructive fire of more than ninety guns, these and the reputation of the French commander furnish the everlasting reply.

And yet he did not compass all that he designed. The French right escaped, because when he passed the Nivelle at San Pé he had only two divisions in hand; the sixth had not come up; three were watching the camp at Serres, and before he could descend in force to the low ground the day closed. The great object of the battle was therefore unattained; and it may be a question, seeing short light and bad roads were not unexpected, whether the principal attack should not have been directed entirely against Clausel. Carlos d'España and the remainder of Mina's battalions could have reinforced Morillo with five thousand men to occupy D'Erlon's attention, and it was not essential to defeat him; for though he attributed his retreat to Clausel's reverse, that general did not complain that D'Erlon's flight endangered his position. This arrangement would have enabled Hill to reinforce

Beresford, and have given Wellington three additional divisions with which to cross the Nivelle before two o'clock Soult's right wing could not then have escaped.

7°. From some oversight the despatches did but scant and tardy justice to the light division. Acting alone, for Longa went off towards Ascain and scarcely fired a shot, that division only four thousand seven hundred strong, first carried the smaller Rhune defended by Barbot, and then beat Taupin from the main position, thus driving superior numbers from the strongest works; and being less than one-sixth of the whole force directed against Clausel, those matchless veterans defeated one-third of his corps. Many brave men they lost, and of two who fell I will speak.

The first, low in rank for he was but a lieutenant, rich in honour for he bore many scars, was young of days—he was only nineteen, and had seen more combats and sieges than he could count years. So slight in person and of such surpassing and delicate beauty that the Spaniards often thought him a girl disguised in man's clothing, he was yet so vigorous, so active, so brave, that the most daring and experienced veterans watched his looks on the field of battle, and, implicitly following where he led, would like children obey his slightest sign in the most difficult situations. His education was incomplete, yet were his natural powers so happy that the keenest and best-furnished intellects shrunk from an encounter of wit; and every thought and aspiration was proud and noble, indicating future greatness if destiny had so willed it. Such was Edward Freer of the forty-third. The night before the battle he had that strange anticipation of coming death so often felt by military men; he was struck with three balls at the first storming of the Rhune rocks, and the sternest soldiers wept even in the middle of the fight when they saw him fall.

On the same day and at the same hour was killed colonel Thomas Lloyd. He likewise had been a long time in the forty-third. Under him Freer had learned the rudiments of his profession; but in the course of the war promotion placed Lloyd at the head of the ninety-fourth, and it was leading that regiment he fell. In him also were combined mental and bodily powers of no ordinary kind. Graceful symmetry, herculean strength, and a countenance frank and majestic, gave the true index of his nature; for his capacity was great and commanding, and his military knowledge extensive both from experience and study. Of his mirth and wit, well known in the army, it only need be said, that he used the latter without offence, yet so as to increase his ascendancy over those with whom he held intercourse; for though gentle he was ambitious, valiant and conscious of fitness for great exploits. And he like Freer was prescient of and predicted his own fall, but with no abatement of courage; for when he received the mortal wound, a most painful one, he would not suffer himself to be moved and remained to watch the battle, making observations upon its changes until death came. It was thus at the age of thirty, that the good the brave the generous Lloyd died. Tributes to his merit have been published by Wellington and by one of his own poor soldiers; by the highest and by the lowest! To their testimony I add mine: let those who served on equal terms with him say whether in aught it has exaggerated his deserts.

The Eventful Life of a Sergeant.

CHAPTER II.

Soult at first designed to leave part of his forces in the entrenched camp of Bayonne, and take a flanking position behind the Nive, half-way between Bayonne and St. Jean Pied de Port; his left secured by the entrenched mountain of Ursouia, his right on the heights above Cambo, the bridge-head of which would give him the power of making offensive movements. He thus hoped to keep his troops together and restore their confidence, while he confined the allies to a small sterile district of France between the river and the sea, and rendered their situation very uneasy during the winter if they did not retire. However he soon modified this plan. The works of the Bayonne camp were not complete and his presence was necessary to urge their progress; the camp on the Ursouia mountain had been neglected, contrary to orders; the bridge-head at Cambo had been only commenced on the right bank, and though complete on the left bank had a bad trace: moreover the Nive in dry weather proved fordable at Ustaritz below Cambo, and at many places above that point. Remaining therefore at Bayonne himself with six divisions and Villatte's reserve, he sent D'Erlon with three divisions to reinforce Foy at Cambo.

Yet neither D'Erlon's divisions nor Soult's whole army would have stopped Wellington, if other circumstances had permitted him to act; for the hardships and privations of the mountains had improved the quality of his troops. Fine air and the absence of drink had confirmed their health, while strict discipline and their own eagerness to enter the fair plains of France spread out before them had excited their military qualities in a wonderful degree. Danger was their sport; and their experienced general, in the vigour of life, was equally impatient for action. Neither the works of the

Bayonne camp nor the barrier of the Nive could have long
withstood the progress of such a fiery host; and if Wellington could have let their strength and fury loose in the
first days succeeding the battle, France would have felt his
conquering footsteps to her centre. But the country at the
foot of the Pyrenees is a deep clay, impassable after rain
except by the royal road near the coast, or that of St. Jean
Pied de Port, both of which were in the power of the French.
On the bye-roads the infantry sunk to the mid leg, the
cavalry above the horses' knees, and even to the saddle-girths
in some places: the artillery could not move at all. Rain
commenced on the 11th, and the mist in the early part of
the 12th gave Soult time to regain his camp and secure the
high road to St. Jean Pied de Port; hence his troops easily
gained their proper posts on the Nive, while his adversary,
fixed in the swamps, could only make the ineffectual demonstration at Ustaritz and Cambo.

Wellington, uneasy for his right flank while the French
commanded the Cambo passage, directed Hill to menace it
again on the 16th. Foy had received orders to preserve the
bridge-head on the right bank in any circumstances, but he
was permitted to abandon the work on the left bank in the
event of a general attack; however, at Hill's approach the
officer in command destroyed all the entrenchments and the
bridge itself; thus doing the allies' work, for their flank
being thereby secured they went into cantonments to avoid
the rain. But bad weather was not the only obstacle to
further operations. On the very day of the battle Freyre's
and Longa's soldiers pillaged Ascain and murdered several
persons; next day all the Spanish troops continued these
excesses in various places; and Mina's battalions, some of
whom were also in a state of mutiny, made a plundering and
murdering incursion from the mountains towards Hellette.
The Portuguese and British soldiers of the left wing had commenced the like outrages : two French persons were killed in
one town. General Pakenham, arriving at the moment, put
the perpetrators to death, thus nipping this wickedness in the
bud at his own risk. Legally he had not that power, but
his generosity, humanity and chivalric spirit, then and always

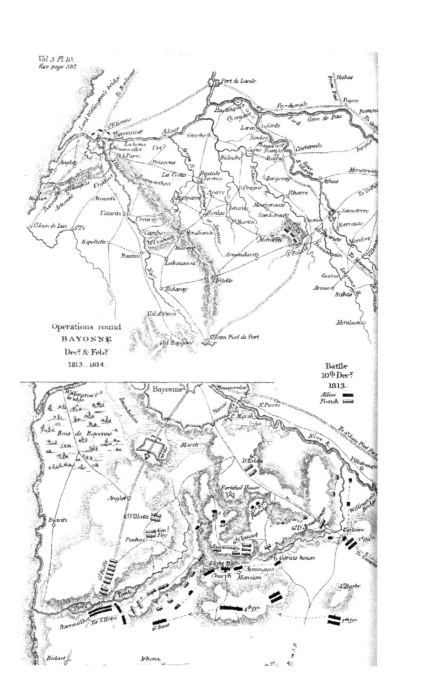

Operations round
BAYONNE
Dec.r & Feb.y
1813 ... 1814.

Battle
10.th Dec.r
1813.

Allies
French

excited the admiration of honourable persons.   He fell afterwards in command at New Orleans, and has been most foully
traduced by American writers.   Pre-eminently distinguished
for detestation of inhumanity and outrage, he has been, with
astounding falsehood, represented as instigating his troops to
the most infamous excesses; but from a people holding millions of their fellow-beings in the most horrible slavery, while
they prate and vaunt of liberty until all men turn with
loathing from the sickening folly, what can be expected?

Terrified by these excesses the French people fled even
from the larger towns.   Wellington quickly relieved them.
On the 12th he put to death all the Spanish marauders he
could take in the act, and then, although expecting a battle,
he with many reproaches, and despite of their leaders' discontent, forced the whole to withdraw into their own country.
Giron's Andalusians were sent to the Bastan, where O'Donnel
resumed the command; Freyre's Gallicians went to the district between Irun and Ernani, Longa over the Ebro; Mina's
insubordinate battalions were disarmed, and Morillo only was
suffered to remain in France.   These decisive proceedings,
marking the lofty character of the man, were not less politic
than resolute; the French people immediately returned, and
finding the strictest discipline preserved and all things paid
for adopted an amicable intercourse with the invaders; but
the loss of so many troops and the bad weather produced
momentary inactivity; head-quarters were suddenly fixed at
St. Jean de Luz, and the troops established in permanent
cantonments.

The left wing, occupying a broad ridge, was placed on both
sides of the great road beyond Bidart, the principal post there
being the mansion-house of the mayor of Biaritz; and the
front was covered by a small stream spreading here and there
into large tanks between which the road was conducted.   The
centre, posted partly on the continuation of this ridge in
front of Arcangues, partly on the hill of San Barbe, extended
by Arrauntz to Ustaritz.   The right was thrown back to face
D'Erlon's position, and stretched by Cambo to Itzassu.   From
this position, which had about six miles of front and eight
miles of flank, strong piquets were pushed forwards, and the

infantry occupied all the villages and towns behind as far
back as Espelette, Suraide, Ainhoa, San Pé, Sarre, and
Ascain.   One regiment of Vandeleur's cavalry remained on
the left, the remainder were sent to Andaya and Urogne;
Victor Alten's horsemen were about San Pé; and the heavy
cavalry remained in Spain.

The establishing o the advanced posts produced several
skirmishes.   On the 18th the generals Wilson and Vandeleur
were wounded.   On the same day Beresford drove the French
from the bridge of Urdains, and maintained his acquisition
next day against a counter attack.   A more serious action
had place the 23rd in front of Arcangues.   This village, held
by the piquets of the light division, was two or three miles in
front of Arbonne where the nearest support was cantoned.
It stood in the centre of a crescent-shaped ridge, and the sen-
tries of both armies were so close that the reliefs and patroles
actually passed each other in their rounds; a surprise was
inevitable if it suited either side to attempt it.   Wellington
visited the post, and the field-officer on duty made known to
him its disadvantages, and the means of remedying them by
taking entire possession of the village, pushing piquets along
the horns of the crescent, and establishing a chain of posts
across the valley between them.   He appeared satisfied with
this project, and two days afterwards the forty-third and some
of the riflemen were employed to effect it, the greatest part of
the division being brought up in support.   The French after a
few shots abandoned Arcangues, Bussussary, and both horns
of the crescent, retiring to a large fortified house situated at
the mouth of the valley.   The matter was thus executed with
the loss of only five men wounded, and the action should have
ceased; but the piquets of the forty-third suddenly received
orders to attack the fortified house, and columns of support
were shown at several points of the semicircle; the French
conceiving they were to be seriously assailed then reinforced
their post; a sharp fight ensued, and the piquets, finally
withdrawn to the ground they had originally gained and
beyond which they should never have been pushed, lost eighty-
eight men and officers, of which eighty were of the forty-third.

Wellington finding that the contracted clayey country he

occupied paralysed all his artillery and his cavalry, that is to say, a hundred guns and nine thousand horsemen, became anxious to pass the Nive; but the rain continued to baffle him, and meanwhile Original Morning States, MSS. Mina, descending again from the Alduides to plunder Baygorry, was beaten by the national guards of that valley. However, early in December the weather amended, forty or fifty pieces of artillery were brought up, and other preparations made to surprise or force the passage of the Nive at Cambo and Usta-ritz; and as this operation led to sanguinary battles it is fit-ting to describe the exact position of the French.

Bayonne being situated at the confluence of the Nive and the Adour rivers commanded the passage of both. It was a weak fortress but derived importance from its position and entrenched camp which could not be easily attacked in front, wherefore Soult kept only six divisions there. His right, composed of Reille's two divisions and Villatte's reserve, touched on the lower Adour, where there was a flotilla of gun-boats; it was covered by a swamp and artificial inundation, through which the royal road led to St. Jean de Luz, and the advanced posts, well entrenched, were pushed along that cause-way beyond Anglet. His left, under Clausel, composed of three divisions, extended from Anglet to the Nive; it was covered partly by the swamp, partly by the fortified house assailed by the light division the 23rd, partly by an inundation spreading below Urdains towards the Nive. Thus entrenched, the fortified outposts may be called the front of battle, the entrenched camp the second line, Bayonne the citadel. The country in front, a deep clay soil, was covered with small woods and farm-houses and very difficult to move in.

Beyond the Nive an entrenched camp, stretching from that river to the upper Adour, was called the front of Mousseroles. This camp was held by D'Erlon with four divisions; but his troops were extended up the right of the Nive to Ustaritz under D'Armagnac, and from thence to Cambo under Foy; while in person he occupied a range of heights two miles in front of the camp, having his right at Villefranque on the Nive, his left at old Moguerre near the Adour. General Paris also came down from St. Jean Pied de Port to Lahoussoa, close under the Ursouia mountain, where he was in connexion with Foy's left by the great road.

The Nive, the Adour, and the Gave de Pau which falls into the Adour many miles above Bayonne, were all navigable; the first as far as Ustaritz, the second to Dax, the third to Peyrehorade, and the large magazines were collected at the two latter places. The French army was however fed with difficulty, and to restrain it from the country beyond the Nive, to intercept communication with St. Jean Pied de Port, to bring the cavalry into activity and to obtain secret intelligence from the interior, were Wellington's inducements to force a passage over the Nive. Yet to place the troops on both sides of a navigable river, where the communication, bad at all times, was subject to entire interruption from rain—to do this in face of an army possessing short communications, good roads, and entrenched camps for retreat, was a delicate and dangerous operation. Orders were however issued for forcing the passage on the 9th. On that day Hope and Original Charles Alten, having the first, fifth and light States, divisions, the unattached brigades of infantry, MSS. Vandeleur's cavalry and twelve guns, in all twenty-four thousand combatants, were to drive back all the French advanced posts between the Nive and the sea. This was partly to examine the course of the lower Adour with a view to subsequent operations; principally to make Soult discover his dispositions on that side, and to keep his troops in check while Beresford and Hill crossed the Nive. To support this double operation, the fourth and seventh divisions were secretly brought up from Ascain and Espelette on the 8th; the latter to the hill of St. Barbe, from whence it detached one brigade to relieve the posts of the third division. There remained the second, third and sixth divisions, Hamilton's Portuguese, and Morillo's Spaniards for the passage. Beresford, leading the third and sixth, six guns and a squadron of cavalry, was to cross at Ustaritz with pontoons; Hill, having the second division, Hamilton's Portuguese, Vivian's and Victor Alten's cavalry and fourteen guns, was to ford the river at Cambo and Larressore: both generals were then to repair the bridges at those points with materials prepared beforehand.

To cover Hill's movement on the right and protect the valley of the Nive from Paris, who might from Lahoussoa penetrate to the rear of the army during the operations, Morillo was to cross at Itzassu.

PASSAGE AND BATTLES OF THE NIVE.

[Plans 10-11; pages 387-405.]

When the passage was commenced Foy's troops were extended from Halzou in front of Larressore to the forts above Cambo, the Ursouia mountain being between his left and Paris, but D'Erlon remained on the heights of Moquerre. At Ustaritz the double bridge was broken, but the connecting island was in the hands of the British, and Beresford laid his pontoons down on the hither stream. At daybreak a beacon on the heights of Cambo gave the signal for attacking, and the troops, supported by a heavy cannonade, immediately forced the passage. The second bridge was then laid, and D'Armagnac was driven back by the sixth division; but the swampy nature of the country between the river and the high road retarded the allies' march, and gave him time to retreat with little loss. At the same time Hill, covered by the fire of artillery, forced the passage in three columns above and below Cambo with slight resistance; yet the fords were so deep that several horsemen were drowned, and the French were also strongly posted, especially at Halzou, where there was a deep mill-race to cross as well as the river.

Foy, seeing by the direction of Beresford's fire, that the retreat was endangered, retired hastily with his left, leaving his right wing under general Berlier at Halzou without orders; hence when general Pringle attacked the latter from Larressore the sixth division had reached the high road between Foy and Berlier; the latter only escaped by cross roads towards Hasparen, and did not rejoin his division until two o'clock in the afternoon. Morillo crossed at Itzassu, and Paris retired to Hellette, where he was joined by a regiment of light cavalry belonging to Pierre Soult who was then on the Bidouse river; Morillo followed him, and in one village near Hellette his troops murdered fifteen peasants, amongst them several women and children.

When Hill had won the passage he placed a brigade of infantry at Urcurray, to cover the bridge of Cambo and support his cavalry, which he despatched to scour the roads towards Lahoussoa, St. Jean Pied de Port, and Hasparen, and to observe Paris and Pierre Soult. With the rest of his troops he marched to the heights of Lormenthoa facing Moguerre and Villefranque, and was there joined by the sixth division, the third remaining to cover the bridge of Ustaritz. It was now one o'clock, and Soult, coming hastily from Bayonne, approved of D'Erlon's dispositions and offered battle. D'Armagnac was in advance at Villefranque and a cannonade and skirmish ensued along the front, but no general attack was made because the deep roads had retarded the rear of Hill's columns. Nevertheless the Portuguese of the sixth division drove D'Armagnac with sharp fighting and after one repulse out of Villefranque, and a brigade of the second division was then established in advance to connect Hill with the troops in Villefranque. Thus three divisions of infantry, wanting the brigade left at Urcurray, hemmed up four French divisions; and as the latter, notwithstanding their superiority of numbers, made no advantage of the broken movements of the allies caused by the deep roads, the passage of the Nive may be judged a surprise.

Wellington had so far overreached his able adversary, yet he had not trusted to this uncertain chance alone. If the French masses had fallen upon the heads of his columns at Lormenthoa while the rear was still labouring in the deep roads, they might have caused some disorder; but they could not have driven either Hill or Beresford over the river again; because the third division was close at hand to reinforce the sixth, and the brigade of the seventh, left at San Barbe, could have followed by the bridge of Ustaritz, thus giving the allies the superiority of numbers. The greatest danger was, that Paris, reinforced by Pierre Soult's cavalry, should have returned and fallen upon Morillo or the brigade left at Urcurray, while Soult, reinforcing D'Erlon with fresh divisions brought from the other side of the Nive, attacked Hill and Beresford in front. It was to prevent this that Hope and Alten, whose operations are now to be related, pressed the enemy on the left bank.

Hope having twelve miles to march from St. Jean de Luz before he could reach the French works put his troops in motion during the night; and about eight o'clock passed between the tanks in front of Barrouilhet with his right, while his left, descending from the platform of Bidart, crossed the valley and moved by the heights of Biaritz. The French outposts retired fighting, and Hope then sweeping on a half circle to his right and being preceded by the fire of his guns and many skirmishers, arrived in front of the entrenched camp about one o'clock. His left rested on the lower Adour, his centre menaced a strong advanced work on the ridge of Beyris beyond Anglet; his right was in communication with Alten, who with a shorter distance to move had halted about Bussussary and Arcangues until Hope's fiery crescent closed on the French camp—then he advanced, but with the exception of a slight skirmish at the fortified house there was no resistance. Three divisions, some cavalry, and the unattached brigades, equal to a fourth division, sufficed therefore to keep six French divisions in check on this side. But when evening closed the allies fell back towards their original positions under heavy rain and with great fatigue to Hope's wing; for even the royal road was knee-deep of mud and his troops were twenty-four hours under arms. The whole day's fighting cost about eight hundred men for each side, the loss of the allies being rather greater on the left bank of the river than on the right.

Wellington's wings were now separated by the Nive, and Soult resolved to fall upon one of them with his whole force united; but he was misled by the prisoners, who told him the third and fourth divisions were at Lormenthoa. This induced him to make his counter-stroke on the other bank of the Nive; the more readily because there he could concentrate his force with less difficulty, and the allies were most extended. The garrison of Bayonne, eight thousand strong, partly troops of the line partly national guards, were to occupy the entrenched camp of Mousserolles; ten gun-boats on the upper Adour were to watch that river as high as the confluence of the Gave de Pau; D'Erlon was to file his four divisions over the bridge of boats between the fortress and Mousserolles, to gain the camp of Marac and take post behind Clausel on

the other side of the Nive. Thus nine divisions of infantry and Villatte's reserve, a brigade of cavalry, and forty guns, in all sixty thousand combatants, including conscripts, were to assail a quarter where
the allies, although stronger by one division than was imagined, had yet only thirty thousand infantry with twenty-four pieces of cannon.

Soult's first design was to burst with his whole army on the table-land of Bussussary and Arcangues, and then to act as circumstances should dictate; and he augured so well of his chances that he desired the minister of war to expect good news for the next day. Indeed the situation of the allies, although better than he knew of, gave him some right to anticipate success; for on no point was there any expectation of this formidable counter-attack. Wellington was on the right of the Nive, preparing to assault the heights where he had seen the French the evening before; Hope's troops, with exception of Wilson's Portuguese now commanded by general Campbell and posted at Barrouilhet, had retired to their cantonments; the first division was at St. Jean de Luz and Ciboure, more than six miles distant from the outposts; the fifth division was between those places and Bidart, and all exceedingly fatigued. The light division had orders to retire from Bussussary to Arbonne, four miles, and part of the second brigade had already marched; but fortunately Kempt, somewhat suspicious of the enemy's movements, kept the first brigade in front until he could see what was going on: he thus saved the position.

The extraordinary difficulty even for single horsemen of moving through the country, the numerous enclosures and copses which denied any distinct view, the recent success in crossing the Nive, and a certain haughty confidence, the sure attendant of a long course of victory, seem to have rendered the English general at this time somewhat negligent of his own security. His army was not disposed as if a battle was expected. The general position, composed of two distinct parts, was indeed strong; the ridge of Barrouilhet could only be attacked along the royal road on a narrow front between the tanks which he had directed to be entrenched; but only

one brigade was there, and a road, opened with difficulty by
the engineers, supplied a bad flank communication with the
light division.   This Barrouilhet ridge was prolonged to the
platform of Bussussary, but in its winding bulged too near the
enemy's works in the centre to be safely occupied in force, and
behind it was a deep valley or basin extending to Arbonne.
On the other side of this basin was the ridge of Arcangues, the
position of battle for the centre; from thence three tongues
of land shot out to the front, and the valleys between them,
as well as their slopes, were covered with copse-woods almost
impenetrable.   The church of Arcangues, a private mansion
and parts of the village, furnished rallying points of defence
for the piquets, which were necessarily numerous because of
the extent of front; and at this time the left-hand tongue was
occupied by the fifty-second regiment, which had also posts in
the great basin separating the Arcangues position from that
of Barrouilhet.   The central tongue was held by the piquets
of the forty-third, with supporting companies placed in succession towards Bussussary, where there was an open common
which must be passed in retreat to reach the church of Arcangues.   The third tongue was guarded partly by the forty-
third partly by the riflemen; but the valley between was not
occupied, and the piquets on the extreme right extended to an
inundation, across a narrow part of which, near the house of
the senator Garrat, there was a bridge: the facility for attack
was there however small.   One brigade of the seventh division
continued this line of posts to the Nive, holding the bridge of
Urdains, the rest of the division was behind San Barbe and
belonged rather to Ustaritz than to this front.   The
fourth division was several miles behind the right of the light
division.

If Soult had, as he first designed, burst with his whole
army upon Bussussary and Arcangues, it would have been
impossible for the light division, scattered as it was over such
an extent of difficult ground, to have stopped him for half an
hour, and there was no support within several miles, no
superior officer to direct the concentration of the different
divisions.   Wellington had indeed ordered all the line to be
entrenched; but the works were commenced on a great scale,

and, as commonly happens when danger does not spur, the
soldiers laboured so carelessly, that beyond a few abbatis the
tracing of some lines and redoubts and the opening of a road
of communication, the ground remained in its natural state.
The French would therefore quickly have gained the broad
open hills beyond Arcangues, and separating the fourth and
seventh from the light division, have cut them off from Hope.
Soult however, in the course of the night, for some unknown
reason changed his project, and at daybreak Reille marched
with Boyer's and Maucune's divisions, Sparre's cavalry, and
from twenty to thirty guns against Hope by the main road.
He was followed by Foy and Villatte, but Clausel assembled
his troops under cover of the ridges near the fortified house in
front of Bussussary, and one of D'Erlon's divisions approached
the bridge of Urdains.

Combat of the 10*th.*—Heavy rain fell in the night, yet the
morning broke fair, and soon after dawn the French infantry
were observed by the piquets of the forty-third to push each
other about as if at gambols, yet lining by degrees the nearest
ditches; a general officer was also seen behind a farm-house
close to the sentinels, and at the same time the heads of columns
could be perceived in the rear. Thus warned, some companies
were thrown on the right into the basin to prevent the enemy
from penetrating that way to the small plain between Bussussary and Arcangues. Kempt was with the piquets, and
immediately placed the reserves of his brigade in the church
and mansion-house of Arcangues; meanwhile the French
breaking forth with loud cries and a rattling musketry, fell at
a running pace upon the piquets of the forty-third both on
the tongue and in the basin; and a cloud of skirmishers
descending on their left penetrated between them and the
fifty-second regiment and sought to turn both: the right
tongue was in like manner assailed and at the same time
the piquets at the bridge near Garrat's house were driven
back.

This assault was so strong and rapid, the enemy so numerous, the ground so extensive, that it would have been impossible to have reached the small plain beyond Bussussary in
time to regain the church of Arcangues if any serious resist-

ance had been attempted; wherefore delivering their fire at pistol-shot distance the piquets fell back in succession, and never were the steadiness and intelligence of veteran soldiers more eminently displayed. For though it was necessary to run at full speed to gain the small plain before the enemy, who was constantly outflanking the line of posts by the basin —though the ways were so deep and narrow that no formation could be preserved, the fire of the French being thick and close and their cries vehement as they rushed on in pursuit—the instant the open ground at Bussussary was attained, the apparently disordered crowd of fugitives turned in good order, defying and deriding the fruitless efforts of their adversaries. The fifty-second, half a mile to the left, though only slightly assailed, fell back also to the main ridge; for though the closeness of the country did not permit colonel Colborne to observe the strength of the enemy, he could see the rapid retreat of the forty-third, and thence judging how serious the affair was, so well did the regiments of the light division understand each other's qualities, withdrew his outposts to secure the main position. And in good time he did so.

On the right-hand tongue the troops were not so fortunate; for whether they delayed their retreat too long, or that the country was more intricate, the enemy moving by the basin, reached Bussussary before the rear arrived, and about a hundred of the forty-third and riflemen were thus intercepted. The French were in a hollow road and careless, never doubting that the officer of the forty-third, ensign Campbell, a youth scarcely eighteen years of age, would surrender; but with a shout he broke sword in hand through them, leaving twenty of the forty-third and thirty of the riflemen with their officers prisoners.

D'Armagnac pushed close up to the little bridge of Urdains, and Clausel assembled his three divisions by degrees at Bussussary keeping up a constant fire of musketry, but the position was safe. The mansion-house on the right, covered by abbatis and not easily accessible, was defended by a rifle battalion and the Portuguese; the church and church-yard were occupied by the forty-third supported with two mountain guns, the front being protected by a declivity of thick copse-

wood, filled with riflemen and only to be turned by narrow
hollow roads leading on each side to the church.   On the left
the fifty-second, supported by the remainder of the division,
spread as far as the great basin separating them from Barrouilhet, towards which some small posts were pushed: but
there was still a great interval between Alten's and Hope's
positions.

Clausel brought up twelve guns to the ridge of Bussussary
and threw shot and shells into the church-yard of Arcangues;
four or five hundred infantry then made a rush forward, but a
heavy fire from the forty-third sent them back over the ridge
where their guns were posted.   The practice of the latter
would have been murderous if this musketry had not made
the French gunners withdraw their pieces a little behind the
ridge, which caused their shot to fly wild and high; Kempt,
thinking the distance too great, was at first inclined to stop
the fire; but the moment it lulled, the French gunners pushed
their pieces forward again and their shells knocked down
eight men in an instant,—when the musketry recommenced
the shells again flew high.   The riflemen in the village and
mansion held the enemy equally at bay, and the action, hottest
where the fifty-second fought, continued all day.   It was not
very severe; but French and English writers, misled perhaps
by an inaccurate phrase in the public despatch, have represented it as a desperate attack by which the light division was
driven into its entrenchments; whereas the piquets only were
forced back, there were no entrenchments save those made at
the moment by the soldiers in the church-yard, and the French
can hardly be said to have seriously attacked.   The real battle
was at Barrouilhet.

There Reille, advancing with two divisions about nine
o'clock, drove back the outposts from Anglet and then fell on
the main position; but moving by a narrow ridge and confined
on each side by the tanks he could only throw two brigades
into action on the main road, and the rain of the preceding
night had rendered all the bye-roads so deep it was mid-day
before the line of battle was filled.   This delay saved the
allies; for the attack was so unexpected, that the first division
and lord Aylmer's brigade were in St. Jean de Luz, Bidart and

Guetary when the fighting commenced; the latter did not reach
the position before eleven o'clock, and the foot-guards did not
arrive until three in the afternoon when the fight was done:
all the troops were exceedingly fatigued, only ten guns could
be brought into play, and from some negligence part of the
infantry were at first without ammunition.   Hope directed
the piquets in person, and resisted the enemy until Campbell's
Portuguese first and then Robinson's British brigades and
Bradford's Portuguese came up.   Meanwhile the French skirmishers spread along the whole valley facing Biaritz, their
principal effort being by the great road and against the platform of Barrouilhet round the mayor's house, where the ground
was so thick of hedges and coppice-wood that a most confused
fight took place.   The assailants cutting ways in the hedges
poured through in smaller or larger bodies as the openings
allowed, and were immediately engaged with the defenders;
at some points they were successful at others beaten back, and
few knew what was going on to the right or left of where
they stood.   By degrees Reille engaged both his divisions, and
some of Villatte's reserve also entered the fight; but then
Aylmer's brigade arrived on the allies' side, which enabled
Greville's brigade of the fifth division, hitherto kept in reserve,
to relieve Robinson, who had lost many men and was dangerously wounded.

   At this time a very notable action was performed by the
ninth regiment under colonel Cameron, who was on the
extreme left of Greville; Robinson was then shifted in
second line towards the right, Bradford at the mayor's house
some distance to the left of the ninth, and the space between
was occupied by a Portuguese battalion.   In front of Greville
was a thick hedge; but immediately opposite the ninth a coppice-
wood was possessed by the enemy, whose skirmishers were
continually gathering in masses and rushing out as if to assail
the line; they were as often driven back, yet the ground was
so broken that nothing could be seen beyond the flanks.
When some time had passed in this manner, Cameron, who
had received no orders, heard a sudden firing along the main
road close to his left, and found that a French regiment,
which must have passed unseen in small bodies through the

Portuguese, between the ninth and the mayor's house, was
Note by
Cameron,
MSS.
rapidly filing into line on his rear. The fourth
regiment was then in close column at a short
distance; its commander, colonel Piper, was
directed by Cameron to face about, march to the rear and
bring up his left shoulder, by which he would infallibly fall
in with the French regiment; but whether Piper misunderstood the order, took a wrong direction, or mistook the
enemy for Portuguese, he passed them, no firing was heard,
the adjutant of the ninth hurried to the rear, and returned
with intelligence that the fourth regiment was not to be seen
and the enemy's line was nearly formed. Cameron, leaving
fifty men to answer the skirmishing fire which now increased
from the copse, immediately faced about and marched in line
against the new enemy under a fire, slow at first but increasing vehemently as the distance lessened; yet when the ninth,
coming close up, sprung forwards to the charge the adverse
line broke and fled to the flanks in the utmost disorder.
Those who made for their own right brushed the left of
Greville's brigade, and even carried off an officer of the royals
in their rush; yet the greatest number were made prisoners,
and Cameron having lost eighty men and officers resumed his
former ground.

The action now subsided for a time, but a third and more
vigorous attack was soon made. The French again passed
the tanks, seized the out-buildings of the mayor's house, and
broke into the coppice-wood in front of it. They were
quickly driven from the out-buildings by the royals; yet the
tumult was great and the coppice was filled with men of all
nations intermixed and fighting in a perilous manner. Robinson's brigade was again very hardly handled, a squadron of
French cavalry, wheeling suddenly round the wood, cut down
many of Campbell's Portuguese; and on the right the colonel
of the eighty-fourth having rashly entered a hollow road
where the French occupied the high banks on each side was
killed with a great number of his men. Sir John Hope,
conspicuous from his gigantic stature and heroic courage, was
seen wherever danger pressed, rallying and encouraging the
troops; at one time he was in the midst of the enemy, his

clothes were pierced with bullets, and he received a severe
wound in the ankle, yet he would not quit the field, and by
his intrepidity restored the battle. The final result was the
repulse of Reille's division; yet Villatte still menaced the
right flank, and Foy, taking possession of the narrow ridge
connecting Bussussary with the platform of Barrouilhet,
threw his skirmishers into the great basin leading to Arbonne,
connected his right with Reille's left and menaced Hope's
flank at Barrouilhet. This was about three o'clock, and
Soult whose columns were now all up was going to renew
the battle, when Clausel reported that a large body of
fresh troops, apparently coming from the other side of the
Nive, was menacing D'Armagnac from the heights above
Urdains. Unable to account for this, and seeing the guards
and Germans moving up fast from St. Jean de Luz and all
the unattached brigades already in line, the French marshal
hesitated, suspended his attack, and ordered D'Erlon, who
had two divisions in reserve, to detach one to the   Soult's MSS.
support of D'Armagnac: before these dispositions
could be completed the night fell.

The fresh troops seen by Clausel were the third, fourth,
sixth and seventh divisions. Wellington discovering at daybreak on the 10th that the French had abandoned the
heights in front of Hill, directed that officer to occupy
them, to push parties close up to the entrenched camp of
Mousseroles, and spread his cavalry up the Adour. The
cannonade on the left bank of the Nive then drew him to
that side, and he made the third and sixth divisions repass
the river; directing Beresford to lay another bridge of communication near Villefranque to shorten the line of movement. When he saw how the battle stood he drew the
seventh division towards the left from the hill of San Barbe,
placed the third division at Urdains, and brought up the
fourth division to an open heathy ridge about a mile behind
Arcangues. From thence Ross's brigade moved into the
basin on the left of Colborne to cover Arbonne; and Cole
prepared to march with his whole division if the enemy
penetrated in force between Hope and Alten. These dispositions were completed about two o'clock, and thus Clausel

was held in check at Bussussary and Soult's renewed attack
on Barrouilhet prevented.

In the battle the Anglo-Portuguese lost more than twelve
hundred killed and wounded, two generals were amongst the
latter, and three hundred men were made prisoners. The
French had one general, Villatte, wounded, and lost two
thousand men; but when the action terminated two regiments of Nassau and one of Frankfort, under colonel Kruse,
came over to the allies.   These men were not deserters.
Their prince had abandoned Napoleon in Germany and sent
secret instructions to his troops to do so likewise; and in
good time, for orders to disarm them reached Soult the next
morning.   The contending generals, one hoping to profit,
the other to prevent mischief, immediately transmitted notice
of the event to Catalonia, where several regiments of the
same nations were serving.   Wellington failed for reasons
to be hereafter mentioned, but Suchet disarmed his Germans
with reluctance, thinking they could be trusted; and the
Nassau troops at Bayonne were perhaps less influenced by
patriotism than by an old quarrel; for when attached to the
army of the centre they had forcibly foraged Soult's district,
and carried off the spoil in defiance of his authority, which
gave rise to bitter disputes at the time.

Combat of the 11th.—In the night of the 10th Reille withdrew from behind the tanks to Pucho; Foy and Villatte
likewise drew back along the connecting ridge towards Bussussary and united with Clausel and D'Erlon.   Thus on the
morning of the 11th the whole French army, with the exception of D'Armagnac who remained in front of Urdains, was
concentrated, for Soult at first expected a counter-attack.   The
French deserters said indeed that Clausel had selected two
thousand grenadiers to assault Arcangues, but the day passed
there with only a slight skirmish.   Not so on the side of Barrouilhet.   A thick fog impeded the view, and Wellington,
desirous to ascertain what the French were about, directed the
ninth regiment at ten o'clock to open a skirmish beyond the
tanks towards Pucho, and to push the action if the French
augmented their force.   Cameron did so, and the fight was
becoming warm when colonel Delancy, a staff-officer, rashly

directed the ninth to enter the village, an error sharply corrected; for the fog cleared up, and Soult, who had twenty-four thousand men at that point, directed a counter-attack so strong and sudden that Cameron was instantly forced to fly, and only saved his regiment with the aid of some Portuguese troops hastily brought up by Hope. The fighting then ceased and Wellington went to the right, leaving orders to reestablish the former outposts on the connecting ridge towards Bussussary.

Hope had taken ground on Soult's right with four regiments when Cameron first attacked, and the French marshal, hitherto undecided, being aroused by these insults, directed Daricau to attack Barrouilhet by the connecting ridge and Boyer to fall on by the main road between the tanks. The allies, expecting no battle, had dispersed to gather fuel, for the weather was wet and cold; the front line was thus composed entirely of Portuguese, and in a moment the French penetrated in all directions. They outflanked the right, passed the tanks and drove the allies back in heaps. However, the ninth regiment plied Boyer's flank with fire, Aylmer's brigade came up, and Soult finally withdrew his troops; yet he retained all his posts of the preceding evening, and continued a galling cannonade until the fall of night. In this fight about six hundred men on each side were killed and wounded, and the fifth division was now so reduced, that it was replaced by the first. Soult then sent Sparre's cavalry over the Nive to check Hill's horsemen.

Combat of the 12*th.*—Heavily the rain fell in the night, and though the morning broke fair neither side seemed inclined to recommence hostilities. The advanced posts were however very close to each other and about ten o'clock they quarrelled. For Soult, observing the fresh regiments of the first division close to his posts, expected an attack and reinforced his front; this movement induced a like error in an English battery, which opened upon the advancing French troops, and in an instant the whole line of posts was engaged. Soult brought up a number of guns, the firing continued without an object for many hours, and three or four hundred men of a side were killed and wounded; but the main body of

Soult, MSS.

D D 2

the French remained quiet on the ridge between Barrouilhet and Bussussary.

As early as the 10th, Wellington had expected Soult would finally fall upon Hill, and had given Beresford orders to carry the sixth division to that general's assistance by the new bridge; and the seventh division by the bridge of Ustaritz, without waiting for further instructions, if Hill was assailed. Now seeing Soult's tenacity at Barrouilhet he drew the seventh division towards Arbonne; but Beresford had made his movement towards the Nive; and this, with the march of the seventh division and some changes in the position of the fourth division, caused Soult to believe the allies were gathering to attack his centre on the morning of the 13th—and it is remarkable that the deserters at this period told him the Spaniards had re-entered France, although orders to that effect were not given until next day. Convinced now that his bolt was shot on the left of the Nive, he placed two divisions and Villatte's reserve in the entrenched camp, and marched with the other seven to Mousseroles intending to fall upon Hill next day.

That general's cavalry scouts were on the Gambouri, and when Sparre's horsemen arrived at Mousseroles on the 12th, Pierre Soult advanced from the Bidouze and, supported by Paris, drove the allies from Hasparen. Colonel Vivian, commanding the English cavalry, ordered major Brotherton to charge across the bridge at this place with the fourteenth dragoons; but the affair was so desperate, that when that officer, so noted for daring, galloped forward, only one brave trooper followed him and was killed. Brotherton was wounded and taken, and lieutenant Southwell, whose horse had fallen on the allies' side of the bridge, was also borne off a prisoner, though Vivian, feeling his order had been rash, made a strong effort to rescue both. Morillo had relieved the British brigade at Urcuray the 11th, but this cavalry movement induced Hill to send it back on the 12th; yet he again recalled it at sunset, for he had descried Soult's columns passing the Nive by the boat-bridge above Bayonne. It was at this time that Wellington, feeling the want of numbers, brought a Gallician division to St. Jean de Luz, and some Andalusians to Itzassu; the

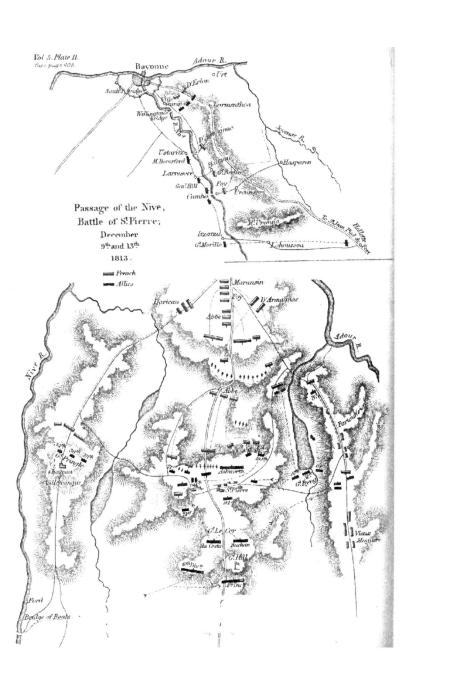

Vol. 5. Plate II.
Face page 408.

Bayonne

Adour R.

Soult's Bridge

D'Erlon.

Urt

Wellington's Bridge

Stranque

Lormenthoa

Nive R.

D'Arraignac

Usturitz

M. Beresford

Heletti

Hasparen

Larresore

G. Bradier

Gen.ᴸ Hill

Foy

Cambo

Urcaray

St. Prandi

To St. Jean Pied de Port

Helette R.

Itzatzu

G. Morillo

Johnussou

Passage of the Nive,
Battle of S.ᵗ Pierre;
December
9.ᵗʰ and 13.ᵗʰ
1813.

French
Allies

Maransin

Horicau

Foy

D'Arnagnac

Abbe

Nive R.

Adour R.

Abbe

Portonfier

Abbe

G.ˡ Pringle

Chateau
Villefranque

Ashworth

G.ˡ Byng

S.ᵗ Pierre

G.ˡ Le Cor

Da Costa

Buchan

Vieux
Mouguere

G.ˡ Hill

6.ᵗʰ Div.

1.ˢᵗ Div.

Ford

Bridge of Boats

former to support Hope, the latter to protect the upper Nive from Paris and Pierre Soult, who could be easily reinforced with the national guards: to prevent plunder he fed them from the British magazines, but they could not arrive in time to aid Hill, whose situation was very critical.

His position of battle was only two miles wide, yet the ground defended by it between the two rivers was nearly four miles. His left, composed of the twenty-eighth, thirty-eighth, and thirty-ninth regiments, under general Pringle, occupied a wooded broken ridge crowned by the chateau of Villefranque and covered the pontoon-bridge, but was separated from the centre by a stream and chain of ponds in a deep marshy valley. The centre was on both sides of the high road near the hamlet of St. Pierre. It occupied a crescent-shaped height, much broken with rocks and close brushwood on the left, but on the right streaked with thick hedges, one of which, a hundred yards in front of the line, was impassable; the seventy-first regiment was on the left, the fiftieth next, the ninety-second on the right. Ashworth's Portuguese were in advance, just beyond St. Pierre, having skirmishers in a small wood to cover their right; twelve guns, under Ross and Tullock, massed in front, looked down the great road; and, half a mile in rear Lecor's Portuguese division and two guns were in reserve. General Byng had the right wing, composed of the third, fifty-seventh, thirty-first and sixty-sixth regiments, the third being on a height running nearly parallel with the Adour, called indifferently the ridge of Partouhiria, or Old Moguerre from a village of that name on the summit. This regiment was pushed in advance to a point where it could only be approached by crossing the lower part of a swampy valley separating Moguerre from the heights of St. Pierre; but the remainder of the brigade was kept by Byng below, where it was well covered by a mill-pond which nearly filled the valley.

One mile in front of St. Pierre was a range of counter-heights belonging to the French, the basin between being broad, open, and commanded in every part by the fire of the allies; and in all parts the country was too heavy and enclosed for cavalry. Nor could the enemy approach in force, except on a narrow front of battle and by the high road, until within cannon-shot, where two narrow lanes branched off to the right and left, and crossing the swampy valleys on each side led, the one to the height where the third regiment was posted, the other to Pringle's position.

In the night of the 12th, rain swelled the Nive and carried away the allies' bridge of communication; thus on the morning of the 13th Hill was completely cut off from the rest of the army. Seven French divisions of infantry, furnishing thirty-five thousand combatants, were approaching him in front; and an eighth under Paris, reinforced with the cavalry of Pierre Soult, menaced him in rear. To meet those in his front he had less than fourteen thousand, and only fourteen guns in position; to oppose Paris there were only four thousand Spaniards with Vivian's cavalry at Urcuray, for the Andalusians had not yet arrived.

Appendix 2, § 4. Vol. VI.

Battle of St. Pierre.—Day broke with a heavy mist, under cover of which Soult formed his order of battle. D'Erlon, having D'Armagnac's, Abbé's, and Daricau's infantry, Sparre's cavalry, and twenty-two guns, marched in front; he was followed by Foy and Maransin; but the remainder of the French were in reserve, for the roads would not allow of any other order. The mist hung heavily, and the French masses, at one moment shrouded in vapour, at another dimly seen or looming sudden and large and dark at different points, appeared like thunder-clouds gathering before the storm. At half-past eight Soult pushed back the British piquets in the centre, the sun burst out at that moment, the sparkling fire of the light troops spread wide in the valley, and crept up the hills on either flank; and the bellowing of forty pieces of artillery shook the banks of the Nive and the Adour. Daricau was directed against Pringle; D'Armagnac taking Old Moguerre as the point of direction, was to force Byng's right; Abbé assailed St. Pierre, where W. Stewart commanded; for Hill had taken his station on a commanding mount in the rear, from whence he could see and direct all the movements of battle.

Abbé, a man noted for vigour, made his attack with great violence, and gained ground so rapidly with his light troops

on the left of Ashworth's Portuguese that Stewart sent the
seventy-first and two guns from St. Pierre to their aid; the
French skirmishers likewise won the small wood on Ashworth's right, and half of the fiftieth was detached to that
quarter.   The wood was thus retaken and the flanks of
Stewart's position secured; but his centre was very much
weakened; the fire of the French artillery was concentrated
against it; and Abbé pushed the attack there with such
a power, that in despite of the musketry on his flanks and
a crashing cannonade in his front he gained the top of the
position; driving back also the remainder of Ashworth's Portuguese and the other half of the fiftieth regiment which had
remained in reserve.

General Barnes who had the ninety-second regiment in
hand behind St. Pierre, immediately brought it on with a
strong counter-attack; whereupon the French skirmishers fell
back on each side leaving two regiments in column to meet
the charge of the ninety-second.   It was rough and pushed
home, the French mass wavered and gave way; but Abbé
replaced it, and Soult, redoubling the heavy play of his guns
from the height he occupied, sent forward a battery of horse
artillery, which galloping into the valley opened its fire close
to the allies with destructive activity.   The cannonade and
musketry now rolled like a prolonged peal of thunder; and
the second French column, regardless of Ross's guns though
they tore the ranks in a horrible manner, advanced so steadily
up the high road that the ninety-second yielding to the
tempest slowly regained its position behind St. Pierre.   The
Portuguese guns limbered up to retire, and the French
skirmishers reached the impenetrable hedge in front of
Ashworth's right.   Barnes, seeing hard fighting only could
save the position, made the Portuguese guns resume their
fire, while the wing of the fiftieth and the caçadores gallantly held the small wood on the right; but he was soon
wounded, most of his and Stewart's staff were hurt, and the
matter seemed desperate; for the light troops, overpowered by
numbers, were all driven in except those in the wood, the
artillerymen were falling at their guns, Ashworth's line
crumbled away rapidly before the musketry and cannonade,

the ground was strewed with the dead in front, and many
wounded were crawling to the rear.

If the French light troops could then have penetrated
through the thick hedge in front of the Portuguese, defeat
would have been inevitable on this point; for the main
column of attack still steadily advanced up the main road;
and a second column launched on its right was already
victorious, because colonel Peacock of the seventy-first had
shamefully withdrawn that gallant regiment out of action
and abandoned the Portuguese. Pringle was indeed fighting
strongly against Daricau's superior numbers on the hill of
Villefranque; but on the extreme right, colonel Bunbury of
the third regiment had also abandoned his strong post to
D'Armagnac, whose leading brigade was thus rapidly turning
Byng's other regiments on that side. And now Foy's and
Maransin's divisions, hitherto retarded by the deep roads,
were coming into line to support Abbé, and at a moment
when the troops opposed to him were deprived of their
reserve. For when Hill beheld the retreat of the third and
seventy-first regiments, descending in haste from his mount he
met and turned the latter back to renew the fight; and then
in person leading one brigade of Le Cor's reserve division to
the same quarter, sent the other against D'Armagnac on the
hill of Old Moguerre: thus at the decisive moment the
French reserve was augmented and that of the allies thrown
as a last resource into action. However the right wing of
the fiftieth and Ashworth's caçadores, both spread as skirmishers, never lost the small wood in front; upholding the
fight there and towards the high road with such unflinching
courage, that the ninety-second regiment had time to re-form
behind the hamlet of St. Pierre. Then its gallant colonel,
Cameron, once more led it down the road with colours flying
and music playing, resolved to give the shock to whatever
stood in the way. At this sight the British skirmishers on
the flanks, suddenly changing from retreat to attack, rushed
forward and drove those of the enemy back on each side;
yet the battle seemed hopeless, for Ashworth was badly
wounded, his line shattered to atoms; and Barnes, who had
not quitted the field for his former hurt was now shot through
the body.

A small force was the ninety-second compared with the heavy mass in its front, and the French soldiers seemed willing enough to close with the bayonet; but an officer at their head suddenly turned his horse, waved his sword, and appeared to order a retreat, for they faced about and retired across the valley to their original position; in good order however and scarcely pursued by the allies, so exhausted were the victors. This retrograde movement, though without panic or disorder, was produced partly by the advance of the ninety-second and the returning rush of the skirmishers, partly by the state of affairs immediately on the right of the French column; where the seventy-first, indignant at their colonel's conduct had returned to the fight with such alacrity, and were so well aided by Le Cor's Portuguese, Hill and Stewart each leading an attack in person, that the hitherto victorious French were overthrown there also just as the ninety-second came with such a brave show down the main road.

Memoir on the battle, by colonel Pringle, R.E.

This double action in the centre being seen from the hill of Villefranque, Daricau, already roughly handled by Pringle, fell back in confusion; and on the right, Buchan's Portuguese, detached by Hill to recover the Old Moguerre ridge, crossed the valley and ascending under a heavy flank fire from Soult's guns rallied the third regiment; in happy time, for D'Armagnac's first brigade, having already passed the flank of Byng's regiments at the mill-pond, was actually in rear of the allies' lines. It was now twelve o'clock, and while the fire of the light troops in the front and the cannonade in the centre continued, the contending generals restored their respective orders of battle. Soult's right had been quite repulsed by Pringle, his left was giving way before Buchan, and the difficult ground forbad his sending immediate succour to either; moreover, in the exigency of the moment he had called down D'Armagnac's reserve to sustain Abbé's retiring columns. However that reserve and Foy's and Maransin's divisions were in hand to renew the fight in the centre, and the allies could not, unsuccoured, have sustained a fresh assault; for their ranks were wasted with fire, nearly all the staff had been killed or wounded, and three generals had quitted the field badly hurt.

In this crisis Hill, seeing Buchan was successfully engaged on the Partouhiria ridge and Byng's regiments masters of their ground in the mill-pond valley, drew the fifty-seventh from the latter place to reinforce his centre. At the same time, the bridge above Villefranque being now restored, the sixth division, which had been marching since daybreak, appeared in order of battle on the mount from whence Hill had descended to rally the seventy-first. It was soon followed by the fourth division, and that by the third division: two brigades of the seventh division were likewise in march. With the first of these troops came Wellington, who had hurried from Barrouilhet when the first sound of the cannon reached him; yet he arrived only to witness the close of the battle: the crisis was past, Hill's glory was complete. Soult, according to the French method, made indeed a demonstration against the centre to cover his new dispositions, but he was easily repulsed, and Buchan drove D'Armagnac headlong off the Partouhiria ridge. The sixth division then appeared behind St. Pierre; and though the French still held the high road and a hillock rising between it and the mill-pond, they were quickly dispossessed; for Wellington now took the offensive with Byng's brigade and with the troops on the high road, where the generals and staff had been so cut down that the aid-de-camp Currie, who carried the order to advance, could find no superior officer to deliver it to and led the attack himself.

Byng found the enemy on the hill stronger than he expected, but the impetus of victory was in full force and he soon planted the colours of the thirty-first on the summit; the allies' front was thus cleared, and two guns of the horse battery sent down early in the fight by Soult were taken. The battle then abated to a skirmish, under cover of which the French endeavoured to carry off their wounded and rally stragglers; but at two o'clock Wellington ordered a general advance, and they retreated fighting, being closely plied with musketry on the side of the Nive until dark. They however maintained their ground on the side of the Adour, and Sparre's cavalry passing out that way joined Pierre Soult. During the action he and Paris had skirmished with Morillo and Vivian at Urcuray, but only thirty men were hurt, and when Soult's failure was known the French generals retired to Bonloc.

Baffled by the unexpected result of the battle, Soult left D'Erlon's three divisions in front of the camp of Mousse-roles, sent two others over the Nive to Marac, and passing the Adour himself during the night with Foy's division, spread it along the right bank of that river as far as the confluence of the Gave de Pau. He had designed to act with great masses, but the restricted nature of the ground had forced him to fight in detail; his loss was certainly three thousand, making a total in the five days' fighting of six thousand, two gene-rals, Villatte and Maucomble, being wounded; the British estimate made the loss much greater, and one French writer raises it to ten thousand, including   La Pene.
probably the Nassau and Frankfort regiments. But the same writer says, the allies lost sixteen thousand; whereas Hill had only three generals and fifteen hundred men killed and wounded, and the whole loss in the five days was five thou-sand and nineteen, five hundred being prisoners; but the generals Hope, Robinson, Barnes, Lecor, and Ashworth were wounded.

OBSERVATIONS.

1°. The French marshal's plan was conceived with genius but the execution was in contrast with the conception. What a difference between the sudden concentration of his whole army on the platforms of Arcangues and Bussussary, from whence he could have fallen with the roll of an avalanche upon any point of the allies' line—what a difference between that and the petty attack of Clausel, which a thousand men of the light division sufficed to arrest at the village and church of Arcangues; yet that was certainly the weak part of the English general's cuirass: the spear pushed home there would have drawn blood. The movements of the third, fourth and seventh divisions were made more with reference to the sup-port of Hill than to sustain an attack from Soult's army; and it is evident that Wellington, trusting to the effect of his victory on the 10th of November, had treated the French more contemptuously than he could have justified by arms

without the aid of fortune.   What induced Soult to alter his
first design has not been made known; but for three hours
after Clausel first attacked the piquets at Arcangues there
were not troops enough to stop three French divisions, much
less a whole army.   And this point being nearer to the
bridge by which D'Erlon passed the Nive, the concentration of
the troops could have been made sooner than at Barrouilhet,
where the want of unity in the attack caused by the difficulty
of the roads ruined the French combinations.

So unexpectant were the allies of an attack, that the battle
at Barrouilhet, which might have been fought by them with
seventeen thousand men, was actually fought by ten thousand;
nor were those brought into action at once; for Robinson's
brigade and Campbell's Portuguese, favoured by the narrow
openings between the tanks, resisted Reille for two hours and
gave time for the rest of the fifth division and Bradford's
brigade to arrive.   But if Foy and Villatte had been able to
assail the flank at the same time by the ridge coming from
Bussussary, the battle would have been won by the French,
although three divisions under Clausel, and two under D'Erlon,
remained hesitating before Urdains and Arcangues, where
their cannonade and skirmishing were the marks and signs of
indecision.

2°. On the 11th the inertness of the French during the
morning may be accounted for by the defection of the German regiments, the necessity of disarming and removing
those that remained, the care of the wounded, and the time
required to re-examine the allies' position and ascertain what
changes had taken place during the night.   The attack in
the afternoon was well judged.   The increase of troops in
Soult's front, and the works constructed at the church of
Arcangues, indicated that no decisive success could be expected
on the left of the Nive, and that the line of attack was to be
changed to the right bank; it was however necessary to
draw Wellington's reserves from the right of the Nive previous
to assailing that quarter, and to be certain they had come;
which could only be done by repeating the attacks at Barrouilhet.   The same cause operated on the 12th; for it was not
until the fourth and seventh divisions were seen by him on

the side of Arbonne that Soult knew his wife had succeeded. Yet again the execution was below the conception. For the bivouac fires on the ridge of Bussussary were extinguished in the evening, and then others were lighted on the side of Mousseroles, thus plainly indicating the march; which was also begun too early, since the leading division was seen by Hill to pass the bridge of boats before sunset.

These were serious errors, yet the French marshal's generalship cannot be thus fairly tested; there are many circumstances to prove, that when he complained to the emperor of contradictions and obstacles, he alluded to military as well as to political and financial difficulties. It is human nature to dislike disturbance of habits; and soldiers are never pleased at first with a general, who introduces and rigorously exacts a system of discipline differing from what they have been accustomed to: its utility must be proved ere it will find favour in their eyes. Now Soult suddenly assumed the command of troops who had been long serving under various generals, and were used to much licence in Spain; and they were, men and officers, uneasy under the austere command of one who from natural character as well as the exigency of the times demanded a ready and exact obedience, and a regularity which habits of a different kind rendered onerous. All the French writers and Soult's own reports furnish proofs that his designs were frequently thwarted or disregarded by his subordinates when circumstances promised impunity. His greatest and ablest military combinations were certainly rendered abortive by the errors of his lieutenants in the first operations to relieve Pampeluna; and their manifest negligence enabled Wellington to force the passage of the Bidassoa. Complaint and recrimination were rife after the defeat on the 10th of November; and on the 19th the bridge-head of Cambo was destroyed contrary to the instructions. These things, joined to the acknowledged jealousy and disputes prevalent amongst the French generals employed in Spain, would indicate that the discrepancy between the conception and execution of the operations in front of Bayonne was not the error of the commander-in-chief: perhaps Joseph's faction, so inimical to Soult, was still powerful in the army.

3°. Wellington has been blamed for putting his troops in a false position; and no doubt he undervalued, it was not the first time, the military genius and resources of his able adversary when he exposed Hill to the action of the 13th. But the passage of the Nive itself, the rapidity with which he moved his divisions from bank to bank, and the confidence with which he relied upon the valour of his troops, so far from justifying the censures which have been passed upon him by French writers, emphatically mark his mastery in the art. The stern justice of sending the Spaniards back into Spain after the battle of the Nivelle is apparent; but the magnanimity of that measure can only be understood by considering his situation at the time. The battle of the Nivelle was delivered on political grounds. Yet of what avail would his gaining it have been if he had remained inclosed as it were in a net between the Nive, the sea, Bayonne, and the Pyronees; unable to open communications with the disaffected in France; and having the beaten army absolutely forbidding him to forage or even to look beyond the river on his right. The invasion of France was not his own operation, it was the project of the English cabinet and the allied sovereigns; both were urging him to complete it, and to pass the Nive and free his flanks was indispensable if he would draw any profit from his victory of the 10th of November. He could not pass it with his whole army unless he resigned the sea-coast and his communications with Spain; and he had to operate with a portion only, which it was desirable to make as strong as possible; yet at that crisis he divested himself of twenty-five thousand Spanish soldiers!

Was this done in ignorance of the military glory awaiting him beyond the spot where he stood!

'*If I had twenty thousand Spaniards paid and fed,*' he wrote to lord Bathurst, '*I should have Bayonne. If I had forty thousand I do not know where I should stop. Now I have both the twenty thousand and the forty thousand, but I have not the means of paying and supplying them, and if they plunder they will ruin all.*'

Requisitions, which the French expected as a part of war, would have enabled him to run this career; but he looked further; he had promised the people protection and his greatness of mind was disclosed in a single sentence. '*I must tell your lordship that our success and everything depend upon our moderation and justice.*' Rather than infringe on either, he sent the Spaniards to the rear and passed the Nive with the British and Portuguese only, thus violating the military rule which forbids a general to disseminate his troops before an enemy in mass. But genius begins where rules end, and a great general always seeks moral power in preference to physical force. Wellington's choice was between a shameful inactivity or a dangerous enterprise. Trusting to the influence of his reputation, to his previous victories, to the ascendancy of his troops in the field, he chose the latter and the result justified his boldness. He surprised the passage of the Nive, laid his bridges, and but for the rain of the night before, which ruined the roads and retarded Hill's march, he would have won the heights of St. Pierre the same day: Soult could not then have withdrawn his divisions from the right bank without being observed. Still it was an error to have the troops on the left bank so unprepared for battle; it was perhaps another error not to have occupied the valley or basin between Hope and Alten; and surely it was negligence not to entrench Hill's position on the 10th, 11th, and 12th. Yet so brave, so hardy, so unconquerable were his soldiers he was successful at every point: and that proves his generalship: Hannibal crossed the Alps and descended upon Italy, not in madness but because he knew himself and his troops.

4°. It is agreed by French and English that the battle of St. Pierre was one of the most desperate of the whole war. Wellington said he had never seen a field so thickly strewn with dead; nor can the vigour of the combatants be well denied where five thousand men were killed or wounded in three hours upon a space of one mile square. How then did it happen, valour being so conspicuous on both sides, that less than fourteen thousand Anglo-Portuguese with four-teen guns, were enabled to withstand thirty-five thousand French with twenty-two guns? The Appendix 2, § 4. Vol. VI. analysis of this fact shows upon what nice calculations and accidents war depends. If Hill had not observed the French passing their bridge on the evening of the 12th, and their bivouac fires in the night, Barnes's brigade, with which he saved the day, would have been at Urcuray and the enemy could not have been stopped. But Soult could only bring his troops into line in succession, so that in fact sixteen thousand French with twenty-two guns actually fought the battle: Foy and Maransin did not engage until after the crisis had passed. On the other hand the proceedings of Peacocke and Bunbury, for which they were deservedly compelled to quit the service, forced Hill to carry his reserve away from the decisive point at that critical period which always occurs in a well-disputed field, and which every great general watches for with the utmost anxiety. This was no error, it was a necessity, and the military qualities of the troops rendered it successful.

5°. The French officer who rode at the head of the second attacking column might be a brave man, doubtless he was; he might be an able man, but he had not the instinct of a general. On his right flank the vigorous counter-attack of the allies was indeed successful, but the battle was to be won in the centre; his column was heavy, undismayed, and only one weak battalion, the ninety-second, was before it; a short exhortation, a decided gesture, a daring example, and it would have overborne the small body in its front; and then Foy, Maransin, and the half of D'Armagnac's division would have followed in the path thus marked out: instead of this, he weighed chances and retreated. How different was the conduct of the British generals, two of whom and nearly all their staff fell at this point, resolute not to yield a step at such a critical period; how desperately did the fiftieth and Portuguese fight to give time for the ninety-second to rally and re-form behind St. Pierre; how gloriously did that regiment come forth again to charge with their colours flying and their national music playing as if going to a review. This was to understand war. The man who in that moment and immediately after a repulse thought of such military pomp was by nature a soldier.

Captain Pringle, R.E.

6°. Hill's employment of his reserve was a fine stroke. He saw that the misconduct of the two colonels would cause

the loss of his position more surely than any direct attack upon
it, and with military decision he descended at once to the
spot, playing the soldier as well as the general, rallying the
seventy-first and leading the reserve himself; trusting meanwhile with a noble and well-placed confidence to the courage
of the ninety-second and the fiftieth to sustain the fight
at St. Pierre.　He knew indeed the sixth division was then
close at hand, and the battle might be fought over again; but
like a thorough soldier he was resolved to win his own fight
with his own troops if he could: and he did so after a manner
that in less eventful times would have rendered him the hero
of a nation.

APPENDIX.

No. I.

The duke of Feltre, minister of war, to the king of Spain.

Paris, le 29 Janvier, 1813.

Sire,—J'ai eu l'honneur d'écrire à V. M. le 4 de ce mois pour lui faire connaître les intentions de l'empereur au sujet des affaires d'Espagne, et la necessité de transporter le quartier général de Madrid à Valladolid. Cette dépêche a été expédiée par duplicate et triplicate, et j'ignore encore si elle est parvenue à V. M. Depuis sa dépêche de Madrid du 4 Decembre je suis privé de ses lettres, et ce long silence me prouve que les communications de Madrid à Vittoria restent constamment *interceptées.* Il est vrai que les opérations du général Caffarelli qui s'est porté avec toutes ses troupes disponibles sur la côte de Biscaye pour dégager Santona fortement menacé par l'ennemi et parcourir la côte, a donné aux bandes de la Castille une facilité entière d'intercepter la route de Burgos à Vittoria. Les dernières nouvelles que je reçois à l'instant de l'armée de Portugal sont du 5 Janvier. A cette époque tout y était tranquille, mais je vois toujours la même difficulté pour communiquer. Cet état de choses rend toujours plus nécessaire de s'occuper très sérieusement et très instamment de balayer les provinces du nord, et de les délivrer enfin de ces bandes qui ont augmentés en forces et en consistance à un point qui exige indispensablement toute notre attention et tous nos efforts. Cette pensée a tellement attiré l'attention de l'empereur que S. M. I. m'a réitéré quatre fois successivement l'ordre exprès de renouveller encore l'expression de ses intentions que j'ai déjà adressée à V. M. par ma lettre du 4 Janvier pour l'engager à revenir à Valladolid, à garder Madrid par une division seulement, et à concentrer ses forces de manière à pouvoir envoyer des troupes de l'armée de Portugal vers le nord, en Navarre, et en Biscaye, afin de délivrer ces provinces, et d'y rétablir la tranquillité. Le général Reille également frappé de l'état des choses dans le nord de l'Espagne a bien compris la nécessité de prendre un parti decisif à cet égard. Il m'a transmis à cette occasion la lettre qu'il a eu l'honneur d'écrire à V. M. le 13 Octobre dernier, et j'ai vu qu'il lui a présenté un tableau frappant et vrai de la situation des affaires qui vient entièrement à l'appui de ma dépêche du 4 courant. Quant à l'occupation de Madrid, l'empereur m'ordonne de mettre sous les yeux de V. M. le danger qu'il y aurait dans l'état actuel des affaires de vouloir occuper cette capitale comme point central, et d'y avoir encore des hôpitaux et établissemens qu'il faudrait abandonner à l'ennemi au premier mouvement prononcé qu'il ferait vers le nord. Cette considération seule doit l'emporter sur toute autre, et je n'y ajouterai que le dernier mot de l'empereur à ce sujet; c'est que toutes les convenances dans la position de l'Europe veulent que V. M. occupe Valladolid, et pacifie le nord. Le premier objet rempli facilitera beaucoup le second, et pour y contribuer par tous les moyens comme pour économiser un tems précieux, et mettre à profit l'inaction des Anglais, je transmets directement aux généraux commandant en chef les armées du nord et de Portugal, les ordres de l'empereur pour que leur exécution ne souffre aucun retard, et que ceux de V. M. pour appuyer et consolider leurs opérations n'éprouvent ni lenteur ni difficulté lorsqu'ils parviendront à ces généraux. Je joins ici copie de mes lettres, sur lesquelles j'ai toujours reservé les ordres que V. M. jugera à-propos de donner pour l'entière exécution de ceux de l'empereur. Ma lettre était terminée lorsqu'un aide-de-camp de M. le maréchal Jourdan est arrivé avec plusieurs dépêches, dont la dernière est du 24 Decembre. J'ai eu soin de les mettre sous les yeux de l'empereur, mais leur contenu ne saurait rien changer aux intentions de S. M. I., et ne peut que confirmer les observations qui se trouvent dans ma lettre. J'aurai l'honneur d'écrire encore à V. M. par le retour de l'officier porteur des dépêches de M. le maréchal Jourdan.

Je suis, avec respect, sire, de votre majesté le très humble et très obéissant serviteur,

Le ministre de la guerre,
Duc de Feltre.

No. II.

The duke of Feltre to the king of Spain.

Sire,—Depuis la lettre que j'ai eu l'honneur d'écrire à votre majesté le 29 Janvier, l'empereur, après avoir pris connoissance des dépêches apportées par l'aide-de-camp de monsieur le maréchal Jourdan, me charge encore de réitérer son intention formelle et déjà deux fois transmise à votre majesté, qu'elle porte son quartier général à Valladolid afin de pouvoir s'occuper efficacement de soumettre et pacifier le nord; par une conséquence nécessaire de ce changement, Madrid ne doit être occupé que par l'extremité de la gauche de manière à ne plus faire partie essentielle de la position générale et à pouvoir être abandonné sans inconvénient, au cas qu'il soit nécessaire de se réunir sur un autre point. Cette nouvelle disposition procure à votre majesté les moyens de faire réfluer des forces considérables dans le nord et jusqu'à l'Arragon pour y détruire les rassemblemens qui existent, occuper en force tous les points importans, interdire l'accès des côtes aux Anglais, et opérer la soumission entière du pays. Il est donc d'une importance extrême pour parvenir à ce bût, de profiter de l'inaction des Anglais, qui permet en ce moment l'emploi de tous nos moyens contre les insurgés et doit amener promptement leur entière destruction, si les opérations entreprises pour cette effet sont conduites avec l'activité, l'energie et la suite qu'elles exigent. Votre majesté a pu se convaincre par la longue et constante interruption des communications autant que par les rapports qui lui sont parvenus de toute l'étendue du mal, et de la nécessité d'y porter remède. On ne peut donc mettre en doute son empressement à remplir les intentions de l'empereur sur ces points importans des changemens, qui ont eu lieu pour le commandement en chef des armées du midi, du nord, et de Portugal, me font espérer que votre majesté n'éprouvera plus de difficultés pour l'exécution de ses ordres et que tout marchera au même bût sans contradiction, et sans obstacle. Ces nouvelles dispositions me dispensent de répondre à différentes observations contenues dans les lettres de votre majesté, et m'engagent à attendre qu'elle me fasse connoître les résultats des changemens ordonnés par l'empereur. Je ne dois pas oublier de prévenir votre majesté d'un ordre que sa majesté impériale m'a chargé de transmettre directement à monsieur le général Reille pour lui faire envoyer une division de son armée en Navarre dont la situation exige impérieusement des secours prompts et efficaces. Cette disposition ne peut contrarier aucune de celles que votre majesté sera dans le cas d'ordonner à l'armée de Portugal pour concourir au même bût et amener la soumission des provinces du nord de l'Espagne.

Je suis, avec respect, Sire, de votre majesté le très humble et très obéissant serviteur,

Le ministre de la guerre,

DUC DE FELTRE.

No. III.

Duke of Feltre to the king of Spain.

Paris, le 12 *Fevrier,* (*No.* 2) 1813.

SIRE,—Par ma lettre de ce jour No. 1, j'ai eu l'honneur de faire connaître à V. M. les intentions de l'empereur sur les opérations à suivre en Espagne. La présente aura pour bût de répondre plus particulièrement à la lettre dont V. M. m'a honoré en date du 8 Janvier, et que j'ai eu soin de mettre sous les yeux de l'empereur. Les plaintes qu'elle contient sur la conduite du maréchal duc de Dalmatie et du général Caffarelli deviennent aujourd'hui sans objet par l'éloignement de ces deux généraux en chef. Je dois cependant prévenir V. M. qu'ayant fait connaître au général Caffarelli qu'on se plaignait à Madrid de ne point recevoir de comptes de l'armée du nord, ce général me répond sous la date du 27 Janvier qu'il a eu l'honneur de rendre à V. M. des compte extrêmement frequens, qu'il lui a envoyé la situation de l'armée et des doubles des rapports qui me sont adressés. Le général Caffarelli ajoute qu'il avait demandé à V. M. d'ordonner que deux divisions de l'armée de Portugal vinrsent appuyer les opérations de l'armée du nord, et il pense que ces lettres se seront croisées avec les dépêches de Madrid parceque les courriers ont éprouvé beaucoup de retard, mais il y a lieu de présumer que tout ce qui a été adressé de l'armée du nord a du parvenir à Madrid avant la fin de Janvier. V. M. réitère dans sa lettre du 8 Janvier ses demandes relativement aux besoins de l'armée. Toutes ont été mises sous les yeux de l'empereur. S. M. I. m'ordonne de répondre au sujet des fonds dont la demande se retrouve dans plusieurs dépêches précédentes que l'argent nécessaire aux armées d'Espagne se serait trouvé dans ces riches et fertiles provinces dévastées par les bandes et par les juntes insurrectionelles, qu'en s'occupant avec l'activité et la viguenr convenables pour rétablir l'ordre et la tranquillité, on y gagnera toutes les ressources qu'elles peuvent encore offrir, et que le tems ramènera dans toute leur étendue. C'est donc un motif de plus pour V. M. d'employer tous les moyens dont elle dispose pour mettre fin à cette guerre interne qui trouble le repos des habitans paisibles, ruine le pays, fatigue nos armées et les prive de tous les avantages qu'elles trouveraient dans l'occupation tranquille de ces belles contrées. L'Arragon et la Navarre aujourd'hui sous les loix de Mina alimentent de leurs productions et de leurs revenus cette lutte désastreuse, il est tems de mettre un terme à cet état de choses et de faire rentrer dans les mains du gouvernement légitime les ressources d'un pays florissant lorsqu'il est paisible, mais qui ne servent aujourd'hui qu'à son détriment.

Je suis, avec respect, Sire, de votre majesté le très humble et très obéissant serviteur,

Le ministre de la guerre,
DUC DE FELTRE.

No. IV.

The duke of Feltre to the king of Spain.

Paris, le 12 Fevrier, 1813.

SIRE,—J'ai eu l'honneur d'écrire trois fois à V. M. dans le courant de Janvier, pour lui transmettre les intentions de l'empereur sur la conduite des affaires en Espagne, et j'ai eu soin de faire expedier toutes mes dépêches au moins par triplicata, tellement que je puis et dois espérer aujourd'hui qu'elles sont parvenues à leur destination. Je reçois en ce moment le dup^ta d'une lettre de V. M. en date du 8 Janvier, dont le primata n'est point arrivé et j'y vois une nouvelle preuve de la difficulté toujours subsistante de communication; les inconveniens de cet état de choses deviennent plus sensibles dans les circonstances actuelles, où il étoit d'une haute importance que les ordres de l'empereur

reçussent une prompte exécution. S. M. I. pénétrée de cette
idée, attend avec une véritable impatience de savoir ce qui s'est
opéré à Madrid, d'après ses instructions, et cette attente, jour-
nellement deçue, lui fait craindre qu'on n'ait perdu un temps précieux, les Anglais étant depuis plus de deux mois dans l'impuissance de rien faire. L'empereur espère du moins que lorsque
V. M. aura eu connaissance du 29ᵐᵉ bulletin, elle aura été frappée
de la nécessité de se mettre promptement en communication
avec la France et de l'assurer par tous les moyens possibles. On
ne peut parvenir à ce but qu'en faisant refluer successivement
les forces dont V. M. peut disposer sur la ligne de communication de Valladolid à Bayonne, et en portant en outre des forces
suffisantes en Navarre et en Aragon pour combattre avec avantage et détruire les bandes qui dévastent ces provinces.

L'armée de Portugal combinée avec celle du nord est bien suf-
fisante pour remplir cet objet tandis que les armées du centre et
du midi, occupant Salamanque et Valladolid, présentent assez de
forces pour tenir les Anglais en échec en attendant les évène-
ments. L'empereur m'ordonne de réitérer à V. M. que l'occupation de *Valladolid* comme quartier général et résidence pour
la personne, est un préliminaire indispensable, à toute operation.
C'est de là qu'il faut diriger sur la route de Burgos et successivement sur tous les points convenables, les forces disponibles qui
doivent renforcer ou seconder l'armée du nord. Madrid et même
Valence ne peuvent être considérés dans ce système que comme
des points à occuper par l'extremité gauche de la ligne, et nulle-
ment comme lieux à maintenir exclusivement par une concentration de forces. Valladolid et Salamanque deviennent aujourd'hui
les points essentiels entre lesquels doivent être réparties des
forces prêtes à prendre l'offensive contre les Anglais et à faire
échouer leurs projets. L'empereur est instruit qu'ils se renforcent en Portugal, et qu'ils paraissent avoir le double projet ou
de pousser en Espagne ou de partir du port de Lisbonne pour
faire une expédition de 25 mille hommes, partie Anglais partie
Espagnols, sur un point quelconque des côtes de France pendant
que la lutte sera engagée dans le nord. Pour empêcher l'exécution de ce plan il faut être toujours en mésure de se porter en
avant et ménacer de marcher sur Lisbonne ou de conquerir le
Portugal. En même tems il faut conserver des communications
aussi sûres que faciles avec la France pour être promptement
instruits de tout ce qui s'y passe, et le seul moyen d'y parvenir
est d'employer le tems ou les Anglais sont dans l'inaction pour
pacifier la Biscaye et la Navarre comme j'ai eu soin de la faire
connaître à V. M. dans mes précédentes. La sollicitude de
l'empereur pour les affaires d'Espagne lui ayant fait réitérer à
plusieurs reprises et reproduire sous toutes les formes ses intentions à cet égard je ne puis achever mieux de les remplir qu'en
récapitulant les idées principales que j'ai eu l'ordre de faire connaître à V. M. Occuper Valladolid et Salamanque, employer
avec la plus grande activité possible tous les moyens de pacifier
la Navarre et l'Aragon, maintenir des communications très

rapides et très sûres avec la France, rester toujours en mesure de prendre l'offensive au besoin, voilà ce que l'empereur me prescrit de faire considérer à V. M. comme instruction générale pour toute la campagne et qui doit faire la base de ses operations. J'ai à peine besoin d'ajouter que si les armées Françaises en Espagne restaient oisives et laissaient les Anglais maîtres de faire des expeditions sur nos côtes, la tranquillité de la France serait compromise et la décadence de nos affaires en Espagne en serait l'infaillible résultat.

Je suis, avec respect, Sire, de votre majesté le très humble et très obéïssant serviteur,

Le ministre de la guerre,
DUC DE FELTRE.

No. V.

The duke of Feltre to the king of Spain.

Paris, le 12 Mars, 1813.

SIRE,—La difficulté toujours subsistante des communications a apporté dans ma correspondance avec V. M. des retards considérables et de longues interruptions dont les résultats ne peuvent être que très préjudiciables au service de l'empereur. Depuis plus de deux mois j'expédie sans cesse et par tous les moyens possibles ordre sur ordre pour faire exécuter les dispositions prescrites par S. M. I., et je n'ai aucune certitude que ces ordres soient parvenus à leur destination. L'empereur extrêmement mécontent de cet état de choses renouvelle sans cesse l'injonction la plus précise de le faire cesser, et j'ignore encore en ce moment si les mouvemens prescrits se préparent ou s'exécutent, mais je vois toujours d'avantage que si des ordres relatifs à cette mesure doivent partir de Madrid cela entrainerait une grande perte de tems. L'empereur en a été frappé. Il devient donc tout-à-fait indispensable de s'écarter un moment de la voie ordinaire et des dispositions par lesquelles tout devroit emaner de V. M. au moins pour ce qui concerne le nord et l'armée de Portugal. Je prends pour cet effet le parti d'adresser directement aux généraux commandant de ces armées les ordres d'exécution qui dans d'autres circonstances devraient leur parvenir de Madrid, et j'ai l'honneur d'adresser ci-joint à V. M. copies des lettres que j'ai écrites au général Reille et au général Clauzel pour déterminer enfin l'arrivée des renforts absolument nécessaires pour soumettre l'Aragon, la Navarre et la Biscaye; les details contenus dans ma lettre au général Clauzel me dispensent de m'étendre davantage sur cet objet important. V. M. y verra surtout qu'en prescrivant l'exécution prompte et entière des ordres de l'empereur j'ai toujours reservé l'exercise de l'autorité supérieure remise entre les mains de V. M. et qu'elle conserve également la direction ultérieure des opérations dès qu'elle pourra les conduire par elle-même.

Toutes mes précédentes dépêches sont d'ailleurs assez précises sur ce point pour ne de laisser pas doute à cet egard.

The duke of Feltre to the king.

Paris, **18 Mars,** 1813.

SIRE,—Parmi les lettres dont V.M. m'a honoré, la plus récente de celles qui me sont parvenues jusqu'à ce jour est du 1 Fevrier, et je vois qu'à cette époque V. M. n'avait point encore reçu celle que j'ai eu l'honneur de lui adresser par ordre de l'empereur le 4 Janvier pour l'engager à transferer son quartier général à Valladolid. Cette disposition a été renouvellée dans toutes mes dépêches postérieures sous les dates de 14, 19 Janvier, 3, 12, 25 Fevrier, 1, 11 et 12 Mars, sans avoir eu jusqu'à present de certitude que mes lettres fussent arrivées à leur destination. Enfin une lettre de M. le duc d'Albufera en date 4 Mars me transmit copie de celle que V. M. lui a adressée le 23 Fevrier pour le prevenir que ma lettre du 4 Janvier est arrivée à Madrid, et qu'on s'y préparait à exécuter les dispositions prescrites par l'empereur. Ainsi c'est de Valence que j'ai reçu la première nouvelle positive à cet égard, et cette circonstance qui dévoile entièrement nôtre situation dans le nord d'Espagne est une nouvelle preuve de l'extrème urgence des mesures prescrites par l'empereur et de tout le mal que d'inexplicables retards ont causé. S. M. I. vient à cette occasion de me réitérer l'injonction de faire sentir à V. M. la fausse direction qu'ont prise les affaires d'Espagne par le peu de soin qu'on a apporté à maintenir les communications avec les frontières. L'empereur est étonné qu'on ait si peu compris à Madrid l'extrème importance de conserver des communications sûres et rapides avec la France. Le defaut constant de nouvelles était un avertissement assez clair et assez positif de l'impuissance où se trouvait l'armée du nord de protéger la route de Madrid à Bayonne. L'état des affaires dans le nord de l'Europe devait plus que jamais faire sentir la nécessité de recevoir des nouvelles de Paris et de prendre enfin des mesures décisives pour ne pas rester si longuement dans un état d'isolement et d'ignorance absolu sur les vues et l'intention de l'empereur. V. M. avoit trois armées à sa disposition pour rétablir les communications avec l'armée du nord, et l'on ne voit pas un mouvement de l'armée de Portugal ou de celle du centre qui soit approprié aux circonstances, tandis que l'inaction des Anglais permettait de profiter de notre supériorité pour chasser les bandes, nettoyer la route, assurer la tranquillité dans le pays. L'empereur m'a ordonné de faire connaître sa façon de penser sur cet objet au général Reille, auquel j'ai adressé directement les ordres de S. M. I. pour les forces qu'il a dû mettre sans retard sous les ordres du général Clauzel ainsi que j'ai eu l'honneur d'en prévenir V. M. par mes lettres du 29 Janvier, 3 Fevrier et 12 Mars. En effet les circonstances rendent cette mesure d'une extrême urgence. L'inaction où l'on est resté pendant l'hiver a encouragé et propagé l'insurrection. Elle s'etend maintenant de la Biscaye, en Catalogne, et l'Aragon exige, pour ainsi dire, le même emploi des forces pour la pacifier, que la Biscaye et la Navarre. Il est donc de la plus haute importance que V.M. etende ses soins sur l'Aragon comme sur les autres provinces du nord de l'Espagne, et les évènemens qui se préparent rendront ce soin toujours plus nécessaire. D'un côté toutes les bandes chassées de la Biscaye et de la Navarre se trouveront bientôt forcées à refluer dans l'Aragon, et d'autre part l'évacuation de Cuenca, par résultat du mouvement général des armées du centre et du midi priverait le général Suchet de toute communication avec V. M. dans un moment où les ennemis se renforcent devant lui d'une manière assez *inquiétante*. Il est donc très important de se procurer une autre ligne de communication avec Valence et cette ligne ne peut s'établir que par l'Aragon. C'est à votre majesté qu'il appartient de donner à cet égard les ordres nécessaires. Il suffira sans doute de lui avoir fait connaître l'état de choses et la position du maréchal Suchet pour lui faire prendre les déterminations que les circonstances rendraient les plus convenables. Il me tarde beaucoup d'apprendre enfin de V. M. elle-même l'exécution des ordres de l'empereur et de pouvoir satisfaire sur ce point la juste impatience de S. M. I.

No. VI.

Joseph O'Donnel to general Donkin.

Malaga, the 6th December, 1812.

DEAR SIR,—The letter you did me the honour to adress to me on the 6th of September has been mislaid all this long time on account of my being separated from the armie since the moment I gave up the command of it, and it was only last night I had the pleasure of receiving it. I feel a great comfort in seingh an officer of your reputation affected so kindly with the sorrows which so unlucky as undeservedly (I believe) fell upon me as a consequence of my shamefull defaite at Castalla. But I beg to be excused if I continue this letter in French. I kno you understand it very well, and I can not explain my toughts so well in English. Je crois, M. le général, que tout militaire, instruit des faits, et à la vue du mal-heureux champ de bataille de Castalla, ou du plan qui le représente, doit faire le même raisonement que vous avez fait, à moins qu'il ne soit épris des petites passions et des prejugés qui ne dominent que trop souvent les hommes. Je crois l'avoir demontré à l'evidence dans mon rapport officiel au gouvernement (que vous devez avoir vu imprimmé) accompagné de la carte des environs et des copies de toutes les ordres que je donnai la veille du combat. J'aurois certainement été vainquer si l'officier qui commandoit les 760 chevaux, avec deux pièces de 8 à mon aile gauche eut obéi mes ordres, on eut seulement tâché de se laisser voir de loin par la cavallerie enemie, qui au nombre de 400 chevaux étoit stationée dans le village de Viar; mais point du tout, cet officier, au lieu de se trouver sur Viar au point du jour de la bataille, pour tenir en échec la cavallerie ennemie, pour la battre s'il en trouvoit une occasion probable, ou pour la suivre en tout cas, et l'empêcher de tomber sur Castalla impunément, comme il lui était très expressément ordonné par des ordres écrites qu'il avoue, cet officier alla se cacher derrière Villena, et quoiqu'il entendit le canon de Castalla, et qu'il fut instruit de la marche des dragons de Viar par la route d'Onil, il resta tranquilement en position de l'autre côté de Villena jusqu'à passé huit heures du matin. Nous étions déjà battus, et trois malheureux bataillons hachés en pièces (quoiqu'ayant repoussé la première charge) quand M. le brigadier Santistevan se mit en marche de Villena pour venir à mon secours. Jugez donc, mons. le général, si j'ay pû empêcher ce désastre. Cependant, le public, qui ne peut juger que par les resultats, se dechaina d'abord contre moi, et je ne m'en plains pas, car cela étoit fort naturel ; c'est un malheur attaché à notre profession, et que les généraux Espagnols doivent resentir sur touts les autres, puisqu'ils font la guerre san resources, et manquant de tout contre un ennemi aguerri qui ne manque de rien ; mais je me plains des *Cortes* de la nation, je me plains de ces pères de la patrie, qui sachant que j'avois demandé moimême à être jugé par un conseille de guerre, ont cependant donné le ton à l'opinion publique se rependant en invectives contre moi, et même contre mon frère le régent, avant de scavoir si je suis en effet coupable. Après un pareille traitement, et dans l'état de misère et de détresse où se trouvent nos armées, ou trouvera t'on de généraux qui veuillent exposer leur honneur, et en accepter le commandement ? Quant à moi je servirai ma patrie par devoir et par inclination jusqu'au dernier soupir, mais je n'accepterai jamais aucun commandement, supposant qu'il me fut offert. Les informations que l'on prend relativement à l'affaire en question ne sont pas encore finies, car tout va doucement chez nous. J'en attends le resultat ici avec l'aveu du gouvernement, et aussitôt que l'on aura prononcé en justice j'irai me présenter comme simple volontaire dans une de nos armées si l'on ne veut pas m'employer dans ma calité de général subalterne. Je vous ay trop ennuyé de mes peines ; c'est que j'en ay le cœur navré, et que votre bonté m'a excité à m'en soulager en vous les racontant. Il me reste encore un espoir flatteur, c'est le jugement de touts mes camarades qui ont vû de près mes dispositions à l'affaire de Castalla, et les efforts que j'avois fait pendant sept mois, luttant toujours contre la detresse et le désordre, pour préparer à la victoire une armée qui étoit tout-à-fait nulle quand je fus obligé a en prendre, malgré moi, le commandement. Je m'estimerai heureux, monsieur le général, de mériter aussi le sufrage d'un officier aussi distingué que vous l'êtes, et je vous prie d'agréer le temoignage du sincère attachement de votre très humble et très obéissant serviteur,

JOSEF O'DONELL.

Monsieur le général Donkin,
&c. &c.

No. VII.

Sir,—I have received your letter of the 12th instant, regarding the conduct of the second Italian regiment, and I entirely concur in all the measures you have adopted, and applaud the decision and firmness of your conduct. I am prepared likewise to approve of whatever you shall determine upon deliberation regarding the future state of the men of the regiment, whether to be formed into a regiment again, or not; or if so formed, whether to be kept as part of the army or sent back to Sicily.

The foreign troops are so much addicted to desertion that they are very unfit for our armies, of which they necessarily form too large a proportion to the native troops. The evil is aggravated by the practice which prevails of enlisting prisoners as well as deserters, and Frenchmen as well as other foreigners, notwithstanding the repeated orders of government upon the subject. The consequence is therefore that a foreign regiment cannot be placed in a situation in which the soldiers can desert from it, that they do not go off in hundreds; and in the Peninsula they convey to the enemy the only intelligence which he can acquire.

With this knowledge I seldom if ever use the foreign British troops of this army on the duty of outposts; and whatever you may determine regarding the second Italian regiment, I recommend the same practice to your consideration.

There is nothing new on this side of the Peninsula. The armies are nearly in the stations which they took up in the end of November.

I have the honour to be, Sir,
Your most obedient servant,
WELLINGTON.

Major-general Campbell,
&c. &c. &c.

No. VIII.

Extract of a letter from the marquis of Wellington to lieutenant-general sir John Murray, dated Freneda, April 6th, 1813.

'In regard to feeding the Spanish troops in Spain, I have invariably set my face against it and have never consented to it or done it, even for a day in any instance. My reasons are, first that it entails upon Great Britain an expense which the country is unable to bear; secondly, that it entails upon the department of the army which undertakes it a detail of business, and a burthen in respect to transport, and other means to which the departments if formed upon any moderate scale must be quite unequal; thirdly, I know from experience that if we don't interfere, the Spanish troops, particularly if paid as yours are, and in limited numbers, will not want food in any part of Spain, whereas the best and most experienced of our departments would not be able to draw from the country resources for them. I have already consented to the formation of a magazine for the use of general Whittingham and general Roche's corps for a certain number of days, if it should be found necessary to give them assistance of this description. I can go no farther, and I earnestly recommend to you if you give assistance at all, to give over a magazine to last a given time, but not to take upon yourself to supply the Spanish troops engaged in operations. If, however, you should notwithstanding this recommendation take upon yourself to give such supplies, I must object, as commander-in-chief of the Spanish army, to your giving more than bread to the troops who receive pay, as that is positively contrary to the regulations and customs of the Spanish army. I recommend to you also to attend with caution to the demands of both general Whittingham and general Roche, and to observe that in proportion as you will comply with their demands, demands will be made upon you by general Elio and others, and you will involve yourself in a scale of expense and difficulty, which will cramp all your operations, and which is quite inconsistent with the views of government on the eastern coast of the Peninsula.'

No. IX.

GENERAL STATE OF THE FRENCH ARMY, APRIL 15, 1812.

EXTRACTED FROM THE IMPERIAL MUSTER-ROLLS.

	Present under arms.		Detached.		Hospital.	Total.	
	Men.	Horses.	Men.	Horses.		Men.	Horses.
Armée du Midi.. ..	55,797	11,014	2,498	700	6,065	64,360	11,714
Centre	19,148	3,993	144	51	624	19,916	4,044
Portugal	56,937	8,108	4,394	2278	7,706	69,037	10,386
Ebre	16,830	1,873	21	6	3,425	20,276	1,879
Arragon	14,786	3,269	2,695	658	1,467	18,948	3,927
Catalogne ..	28,924	1,259	1,163	49	5,540	35,627	1,308
Nord	48,232	7,074	1,309	72	8,677	58,276	7,213
Total	240,654	36,590	12,224	3814	33,504	286,440	40,471
Reserve de Bayonne..	4,038	157	36	35	865	4,939	192
Grand Total	244,692	36,747	12,260	3849	34,369	291,379	40,663
Civic guards attached to the army of the south	6,497	1,655	"	"	258	6,755	1,497
Troupes Espagnols..	33,952	525	"	"	"	33,952	525
Total Espagnols ..	40,449	2,180	"	"	258	40,707	2,022

GENERAL STATE, MAY 15, 1812.

	Present under arms.		Detached.		Hospitals.		Total.	
	Men.	Horses.	Men.	Horses.		Men.	Cavalry.	Artillery.
Armée du Midi ..	56,031	12,101	2,787	660	4,652	63,470	7,311	4,340
Centre ..	17,395	4,208	158	37	766	19,203	3,332	420
Portugal ..	52,618	7,244	9 750	1538	8,332	70,700	4,481	3,448
Arragon ..	27,218	4,768	4,458	605	3,701	35,377	2,976	1,980
Catalogne ..	33,677	1,577	1,844	267	6,009	41,530	1,376	279
Nord	38,771	6,031	2,560	271	7,767	49,098	4,443	1,163
Total ..	225,710	35,929	21,557	3378	31,227	279,378	23,919	11,530
Old Reserve at Bayonne ..	3,894	221	1,642	,,	964	6,500	207	,,
New Reserve at Bayonne ..	2,598	116	3,176	,,	5	5,769	103	,,
General Total ..	232,202	36,266	26,375	3378	32,196	291,647	24,229	11,530

GENERAL STATE OF THE FRENCH ARMIES, MARCH 15, 1813.

	Present under arms.		Detached.		Hospitals.		Total.	
	Men.	Horses.	Men.	Horses.		Men.	Cavalry.	Train.
Armée du Midi ..	36,605	6,602	2060	1617	7,144	45,809	8,650	2,601
Centre ..	16,227	1,966	940	76	2,401	19,568	2,790	451
Portugal ..	34,825	3,654	157	,,	7,731	42,713	6,726	2,140
Arragon ..	36,315	3,852	55	,,	2,442	38,812	6,123	1,799
Catalogne ..	27,323	1,109	110	,,	2,013	29,446	1,884	635
Nord	40,476	1,978	41	,,	8,030	48,547	3,171	830
Reserve de Bayonne	5,877	55	80	,,	634	6,591	78	21
Total ..	197,648	19,216	3443	1693	30,395	231,486	29,422	8,486

The operations and misfortunes of the French prevented any general states being sent home between the 15th of March and the 15th of August, 1813, when a new organization of the armies took place; but the numbers given in the narrative of this history are the result of calculations founded on the comparison of a variety of documents, and are believed to be a very close approximation to the real strength of the armies.

No. X.

ESPECIAL STATE OF THE ARMY OF PORTUGAL, JUNE 15, 1812.

HEAD-QUARTERS, TORDESILLAS.

		Present under arms.		Detached.		Hosp.	Total.		
		Men.	Horses.	Men.	Horses.		Men.	Cav.	Train.
1st Division.. ..	Foy	5,138	,,	319	,,	516	5,973	,,	,,
2nd do.	Clausel ..	7,405	,,	678	,,	613	8,696	,,	,,
3rd do. ..	Ferey ..	5,547	,,	12	,,	926	6,485	,,	,,
4th do.	Sarrut ..	5,056	,,	214	,,	862	6,132	,,	,,
5th do.	Maucune ..	5,269	,,	588	,,	1513	7,370	,,	,,
6th do.	Brennier ..	5,021	,,	124	,,	720	5,865	,,	,,
7th do.	Thomieres	6,352	61	,,	,,	1905	8,257	61	,,
8th do.	Bonnet ..	6,681	139	66	,,	685	7,432	139	,,
Light Cavalry, } 13 escadrons	Curto ..	1,386	1398	1073	324	246	2,705	1722	,,
Dragoons	Boyer ..	1,389	1378	479	358	86	1,954	1736	,,
Artillery ..	..	3,612	2339	513	258	220	4,345	347	2148
Genie ..	..	414	9	67	7	84	565	,,	12
Equipage ..	..	955	1107	51	44	242	1,251	,,	1084
Gen-d'armes et Infirmerie	..	325	75	,,	,,	15	340	54	,,
Total ..		54,550	6506	4184	991	8633	67,370	4059	3244

From these 54,550 men, present under arms, must be deducted the artillery, engineers, equipages, and garrisons, the officers and sergeants, and the losses sustained between the siege of the forts and the battle of Salamanca; the result will be about 42,000 sabres and bayonets in the battle.

Renforcements en marche de l'armée du nord ... 1,370
Do.   de Bayonne...   12,676

Note.—These troops did not join before the battle of Salamanca.

ARTILLERY OF THE ARMY OF PORTUGAL, JUNE 15, 1812.

MATERIEL.

Bouches à feu

Poid et calibre.	Nombre.	
Canon de 12 lbs.	2	
8 do.	20	Total des canons.. 60
4 do.	33	
3 do.	5	
Obusiers de 6 pouces	11	Total des obusiers 14
Ditto de 4 pouces 3 lignes	3	

Total   74

nant de l'armée du nord..   8 { These guns arrived after the battle.
—
82

TOTAL LOSS OF THE ARMY OF PORTUGAL FROM JULY 10 TO AUGUST 10, 1812, INCLUDING THE BATTLE OF SALA-MANCA.

EXTRACTED FROM THE IMPERIAL MUSTER-ROLLS.

	Tués.	Blessés.
Duke de Raguse	,,	1
General Clausel	,,	1
General Bonnet	,,	1
Officiers superieurs .. .. General Ferrey	1	,,
General Thomieres	1	,,
General Desgravier Bertholet	1	,,
General Carrie	,,	1 Prisonnier.
General Menne ..	,,	1
Aide-de-camp du duc de Raguse, Colonel Richemont ..	,,	1
Le Clerc de Montpree ..	1	,,
Darel	,,	1

Total   ..   Tués 4   Blessés 7

Officiers inferieurs et soldats.	Tués ou Pris.	Blessés.	Traineurs.
Officiers	152	232	.,
Soldats	3,867	7,529	645
Grande Total ..	4,029	7,761	435

Officiers et soldats   .. 12,455
Chevaux   1,190
Canons   12
Deux aigles de 101ème Regt. de ligne.

No. XI.

STRENGTH OF THE ANGLO-PORTUGUESE ARMY UNDER LORD VISCOUNT WELLINGTON, ON THE MORNING OF JULY 22, 1812.

EXTRACTED FROM THE ORIGINAL MORNING STATE.

Note.—The numbers are exclusive of officers, sergeants, trumpeters, artillerymen, and staff, showing merely the sabres and bayonets in the field.

British cavalry, one division, present under arms, 3,314 men, 3388 horses.
British infantry, seven divisions   do.   22,067 ,,   ,,   ,,

Total British	25,381
D'Urban's Portuguese cavalry, three regiments, about .. .. .. 1,500 These troops not in the state.	
Portuguese infantry, seven divisions, and two independent brigades .. 16,107	
	17,517
Total Anglo-Portuguese ..	42,898
Carlos d'España's Spanish division, about 3000	
Julian Sanchez' cavalry 500	
	3,500
Sabres and bayonets ..	46,398

NUMBER OF BRITISH, GERMAN, PORTUGUESE, AND SPANISH GUNS AT THE BATTLE OF SALAMANCA.

			Weight of calibre.	No. of guns.
British horse artillery ..	..	..	.. 6 lbs.	18
Foot	do.	.. ..	.. 9 lbs.	12
Do.	do.	.. ..	.. 12 lbs.	12
German	do.	.. ..	.. 9 lbs.	6
Portuguese and British brigaded together ..			.. 24 lb. howitzers	6
				54
One Spanish battery	..	.. ..	..	6
			General total ..	60 pieces

No. XII.

OFFICIAL REPORT OF THE LOSS OF THE ALLIES ON THE TRABANCOS AND GUARENA RIVERS, JULY 18, 1812.

	Officers.	Sergeants.	Rank and file.	Horses.			Men.
British ..	3	3	56	59	Killed ..	..	
	16	7	274	65	Wounded ..	..	
	,,	,,	27	21	Missing ..	..	542
	1	2	21	,,	Killed ..	..	
Portuguese ..	6	3	87	,,	Wounded ..	..	
	,,	,,	27	,,	Missing ..	..	
Total ..	26	15	502	145			

LOSS OF THE ALLIES IN THE BATTLE OF SALAMANCA.

	Officers.	Sergeants.	Rank and file.	Horses.			Men.
British ..	28	24	336	96	Killed ..	..	
	188	136	2400	120	Wounded ..	..	
	..		74	37	Missing ..	..	5224
	13		287	18	Killed ..	..	
Portuguese ..	74		1436	13	Wounded ..	..	
	1		180	7	Missing ..	..	
Total ..	304	207	4713	291			

LOSS OF THE GERMAN CAVALRY ON THE ALMAR STREAM, JULY 23.

Men and Officers.	Horses.	
117	117	117

THE BRITISH LOSS BY INFANTRY DIVISIONS AND CAVALRY BRIGADES.

Cavalry ..	Le Marchant's brigade	lost	Men and officers	105	
	Anson's do.	do.	do.	5	141
	Victor Alten's do.	do.	do.	31	
Infantry..	1st Division General Campbell	do.	do.	69	
	3rd do. General Pakenham	do.	do.	456	
	4th do. General Cole	do.	do.	537	
	5th do. General Leith	do.	do.	464	2386
	6th do. General Clinton	do.	do.	1198	
	7th do. General S. Hope	do.	do.	119	
	Light do. General C. Alten	do.	do.	29	
	Artillery General Framingham	do.	do.	14	
					3027

No. XIII.

STRENGTH OF THE ANGLO-PORTUGUESE ARMY AT VITORIA.

EXTRACTED FROM THE MORNING STATE OF THE 19TH JUNE, 1813.

	Present under arms.	On command.		Total. Present.	On command.
British Cavalry..	7,791	851			
Portuguese do. ..	1,452	225			
Total cavalry	..	..	..	9,243	1073
British infantry	33,658	1771			
Portuguese do. ..	23,905	1038			
Total infantry	..	..	..	57,563	2809
		Sabres and bayonets	..	66,806	3885
	Deduct the 6th division left at Medina de Pomar			6,320	
		Sabres and bayonets	..	60,496	

Spanish Auxiliaries.

Infantry.. ..	Morillo's division	about	3,000	
	Giron's do.	do.	12,000	
	Carlos d'Espagna's do.	do.	3,000	
	Longa's do.	do.	3,300	
Cavalry.. ..	Penne Villemur	do.	1,000	
	Julian Sanchez	do.	1,000	
				23,000
	Grand Total	..	..	83,486

NUMBER OF ANGLO-PORTUGUESE GUNS AT THE BATTLE OF VITORIA.

COLONEL A. DICKSON COMMANDING.

British horse artillery	..	..	.. 9 lbs.	.. ..	.. 45
Do. do.	..	..	.. 6 lbs.	.. ..	.. 30
Do. do.	..	..	.. 5½-inch howitzers	.	15
			Total	..	.. 90

No Spanish guns set down in the return. Number unknown.

No. XIV.

JUSTIFICATORY PIECES.

Lord William Bentinck to sir E. Pellew.

At sea, June 18th, 1813.

SIR,—Y. E. has seen the information I have received of a projected attack upon Sicily by Murat, in conjunction with the Toulon fleet. It seems necessary that the French fleet should leave Toulon, should reach the coast of Naples, embark the men and land them in Sicily, or cover their passage from Calabria or the Bay of Naples, if the intention be, as in the last instance, to transport them to Sicily in the tonnage and small craft of the country.—The most important question is, whether this can be effected by the enemy.—I have no difficulty in saying on my part, that in the present disposition of the Neapolitan army in Sicily, and in the non-existence of any national force, and the imperfect composition of the British force, if half the number intended for this expedition should land in Sicily, the island would be conquered.

(Signed)   W. BENTINCK.

Sir E. Pellew to lord W. Bentinck.

H. M. S. Caledonia, June 19th, 1813.

MY LORD,—I feel it my duty to state to your lordship that in my judgment the Toulon fleet may evade mine without difficulty under a strong N. W. wind to carry them through the passage of the Hieres islands, without the possibility of my interrupting them, and that they may have from twelve to twenty-four hours' start of me in chasing them. When blown off the coast, my look-out ships would certainly bring me such information as would enable me to follow them immediately to the Bay of Naples. Your lordship is most competent to judge whether in the interval of their arrival and my pursuit, the French admiral would be able to embark Murat's army artillery and stores, and land them on the coast of Sicily before I came up with them.—

The facility of communication by telegraph along the whole coast of Toulon would certainly apprize Murat of their sailing at a very short notice, but for my own part, I should entertain very sanguine hopes of overtaking them either in the Bay of Naples or on the coast of Sicily before they could make good their landing.

Lord William Bentinck to lord Wellington.

At sea, June 20th, 1813.

MY LORD,—By the perusal of the accompanying despatch to lord Castlereagh, your lordship will perceive that Murat has opened a negotiation with us, the object of which is friendship with us and hostility to Buonaparte. You will observe in one of the conversations with Murat's agent, that he informed me that Buonaparte had ordered Murat to hold twenty thousand men in readiness for the invasion of Sicily in conjunction with the Toulon fleet. I enclose the copy of a letter I have in consequence addressed to sir E. Pellew, together with his answer, upon the practicability of the Toulon fleet sailing without the knowledge of the blockading fleet. Your lordship will have received my letter of the 21st of May enclosing a copy of my despatch to lord Bathurst, relative to the discontent of the Neapolitan troops in Sicily and the consequent state of weakness if not of danger resulting from it to that island. I stated also that this circumstance had induced me to detain in Sicily the two battalions which had been withdrawn from Spain.

Lord Wellington to lord William Bentinck.

Huarte, July 1st, 1813.

MY LORD,—In answer to your lordship's despatch, I have to observe, that I conceive that the island of Sicily is at present in no danger whatever.

No. XV.

Letter from general Nugent to lord William Bentinck.

Vienna, January 24th, 1812.

MY DEAR LORD WILLIAM,—I hope you have received the letter I wrote to you shortly after my arrival here by a person sent for that purpose. Soon after his departure the affair of La Tour happened, as King mentions in his letter. It required some time before I could judge of the result it would have and the manner it would be considered by the emperor and the government here, and then to settle again the manner of sending officers down to the Mediterranean, for some of those then destined to be sent were implicated. All these circumstances caused the delay of the present which otherwise you would have had much sooner. Another cause of the delay was that I wanted to inform you of the answer which would be given by this house to the speculations that I was commissioned by the prince-regent to propose relative to the archduke. There was no decisive answer given, and the only manner of forming an opinion upon that subject was by observing and getting information of their true intentions. I am now firmly convinced that these are such as we could wish, and that it is only fear of being committed that prevents them to speak in a more positive manner. Their whole conduct proves this, more particularly in La Tour's affair, which has produced no change whatsoever nor led to any discovery of views or connexions. There is even now less difficulty than ever for officers going to the Mediterranean. They get passports from government here without its inquiring or seeming to know the real object. As it can do nothing else but connive, to which this conduct answers, I think a more explicit declaration is not even requisite, and I am convinced that when the thing is once done they will gladly agree. This is likewise King's and Hardenberg's and Johnson's opinion upon the subject, and as such they desire me to express it to you, and to observe that the situation of things here makes the forwarding of the measures you may think expedient in the Mediterranean and the Adriatic the more desirable.

They are here extremely satisfied with the conduct of government in England, and by the accounts we have, the latter is much pleased with the conduct of this country, particularly relative to the affairs of Prussia. These are however not decided yet. But whatever the consequence may be and whatever this country may do for the present, I am convinced that your measures will ultimately contribute much to the result. I am happy to perceive by the last information from England that everything seems to have been settled there by you. The recruiting business of major Burke is going on rapidly. As it was not begun at the time of my departure I can only attribute it to your presence. The letters contain likewise that government is come to the most favourable resolutions relative to the archduke, and I hope the formation of the troops will soon be effectuated. The dispositions of the Adriatic coasts and the Tyrol are as good as can be, but all depends upon establishing a basis and without that all partial exertions would be useless or destructive. At the same time that some regiments would be formed, I think it would be very expedient to form at the same place a Dalmatian or a Croat regiment, particularly as in the present state of things it will be much easier even than the other. The men could be easily recruited in Bosnia, and sent from Durazzo to the place you should appoint. The bearer will give you every information upon the subject, and at all events, I should propose to you to send him immediately back to Durazzo, and, should you adopt the above, to give him the necessary orders and the commission for recruiting and sending the men to the place of formation. No person can be better qualified than he is. He knows the languages, the country, and the character of the people, and understands everything that relates to commercial affairs. As to the place of formation, I think I already proposed Cephalonia to you. Lissa or one of the nearer islands would give too much jealousy in the beginning in those parts, until our capital increases so as to undertake an important enterprise, at all events it is important to form a noyau of the three nations; it is then that we may hope to be joined by the whole of Dalmatia and Croatia after a short time. Major and other officers will shortly proceed to the Mediterranean. They will be directed to Messina where I request you will send orders for them. It would be very useful and saving to provide means for transporting them to that place from Durazzo, and if possible to establish a more frequent and regular intercourse between you and the latter. Johnson who soon sets off from here will in the meantime establish a communication across Bosnia to Durazzo. His presence in those parts will be productive of many good effects. You will find that he is an able active and zealous man, and will certainly be very useful in forwarding your views. I can answer for his being worthy of your full confidence. Should you adopt the proposition relative to the recruiting it would be necessary to put at his disposal the requisite funds.

You will judge by the account the bearer of this will give you whether cloth, &c., can be had at a cheaper rate from this country or where you are, and he will bring back your directions for this object. Allow me to observe that it would be highly useful to have clothes for a considerable number of men prepared beforehand. Many important reasons have prevented me hitherto from proceeding to the Mediterranean as speedily as I wished. I hope however not to be detained much longer, and soon to have removed every obstacle. I think to set off from here in the beginning of March, and request you will be so kind as to provide with the return of the bearer to Durazzo the means of my passage from thence, where I shall come with a feigned name. I hope he will be back there by the time of my arrival. I shall endeavour to hasten my journey, as I have important information in every respect. By that time we shall know the decision relative to the north. King has informed you of the reasons which made an alteration necessary in regard to Frozzi's journey. Part of your object is in fact fulfilled already, and there are agents in Italy &c. As to the other and principal part relative to connexions in the army, and the gaining an exact knowledge of it and of the government in Italy, with other circumstances, I expect soon to have a person of sufficient consequence and ability to execute your instructions, and he will go to Milan &c. as soon as it can be done with safety. His permanent residence in that country seems to be necessary, that he may be able to accomplish fully the object, and as the sum you have assigned for this purpose is sufficient for a considerable time, you can determine whether he is to remain there permanently or not. Frozzi will bring you an exact account of what has been arranged relative to this business, and will himself be a very proper person for communications between you and Italy or this country. He will for that purpose go back to Italy, the obstacle that opposed it hitherto being now no more. I cannot but repeat the importance of giving all possible extent to the arch-duke's establishment, and particularly the raising of as much troops as possible, for all will depend upon having the means of landing. We are then sure of augmenting very speedily, and finding the greatest assistance. The place for beginning cannot be determined on exactly, but there is much to be expected in Dalmatia and Croatia where we could be joined by the inhabitants and troops. The lower part would be best adapted in case we begin with a small force. I shall send and bring officers particularly acquainted with the country and provide every other assistance such as plans, &c., and I think it would be expedient to prevent for the present any enterprise in that country that would alarm them. Since I began my letter a courier has arrived from Paris.

The contingent of the Rhenish confederacy have got orders to be ready for marching. Reinforcements are sending from France to the north and every preparation is making for war. Buonaparte told to Swartzenburg that he would begin in April and all circumstances seem to agree with this. On the other side Russia is very slow in making peace with Turkey. He entirely neglects Prussia, and for this reason it is to be feared that the latter will place his capital with Buonaparte notwithstanding that this cabinet is endeavouring to prevent it. I should be then very much afraid for the conduct of this house, well inclined as the emperor is. Proposals were made by France but no resolution has been taken until it is known how things turn out. The worst is that Romanzow is still in credit with Alexander, which prevents all confidence in other houses and makes Russia adopt half measures. This sketch of the situation will give you some idea of the wavering and uncertain state people are in. There is no calculation to be made as to the conduct of government, nor must we be surprised at anything they may do. On the other side our speculations are not built upon them, but upon the disposition of the people; and whatever may happen I am convinced that this is a good foundation if the measures are taken and the means prepared. A principal object of mine in these parts has been to prepare the measures for the case that it comes here to the very worst. The most important thing is the augmenting in every possible manner the force at your disposition. The accounts we have to-day of your return and the powers I hope you have, give me the best hopes of your overcoming every difficulty. I must here observe that as Johnson's proceedings are entirely subordinate to, and make a part of your plans and operations in general, and that he cannot of course depend upon King, you will be so good as to give him decisive instructions to that purpose, and assign him the means and powers for acting in consequence. I shall combine with him in my passage through Bosnia everything in the hopes that you will approve of this.

Letter from Mr. King to lord William Bentinck.

Vienna, January 24th, 1812.

MY LORD,—I have the honour to acknowledge the receipt of your lordship's letter of the 25th of August, which was delivered to me towards the latter end of October by captain Frozzi, whom I should immediately have furnished with the means of proceeding to Italy for the purpose of carrying your lordship's instructions into effect, had it not appeared to me that the measures which I had taken on my arrival here had already in a great degree anticipated your lordship's intentions. As a confirmation of this, I beg leave to transmit for your lordship's perusal the reports (marked A) of three messengers whom I sent to the north of Italy for the purpose of ascertaining the state of the public mind, particularly in the ci-devant Venetian territories and adjacent districts. These reports confirm in a very satisfactory manner the assurances, which I have received through various other channels, that the inhabitants of those countries are ready and determined to avail themselves of the first opportunity to shake off a yoke which is become insupportable. I have also the honour to transmit to your lordship the copy of a letter from count Montgelas, the minister of foreign affairs in Bavaria, to the commissary-general at Nimpten, from which it appears that the Bavarian government is not altogether ignorant of the intentions of the Swiss and Tyrolese, but I am happy to have it in my power to inform your lordship that the persons who seem to have excited the suspicions of the Bavarian government do not enjoy the confidence of our friends in Switzerland, and have not been made acquainted with their intentions; it is nevertheless indispensably necessary that we should act with the greatest possible caution in the employment of emissaries, lest the French and Bavarian governments should take the alarm and adopt measures which would defeat our projects or at least occasion a premature explosion. On these grounds (having previously consulted with general N. to whom captain Frozzi was particularly addressed and who entirely coincides in my opinion) I think it eligible to send this officer back to Sicily, and I trust that in so doing I shall meet with your lordship's approbation. I beg leave to observe that the only service captain Frozzi could render in Italy at the present moment would be to ascertain the number and distribution of the French forces in this country, but as these undergo continual changes I think it will be sufficient to despatch a confidential agent to your lordship with the latest intelligence from Italy, at a period when the northern war and consequent occupation of the French troops will enable your lordship to derive advantage from such intelligence.

The general opinion is that hostilities will commence between France and Russia in the month of April at which period the preparations of the French government will be completed, and there is little reason to hope that the Russians will avail themselves of the interval, either to annihilate the army of the duchy of Warsaw or to advance to the assistance of the king of Prussia, who will in all probability ally himself with France notwithstanding his former declarations to the contrary. The latest intelligence from Berlin states that count St. Marsan had presented the ultimatum of his government, which demands an unconditional surrender of all the Prussian fortresses, and insists on the military force and resources of Prussia being placed at the disposal of French generals. It is positively asserted that the king is inclined to submit to these humiliating proposals, but nothing has been as yet definitively concluded. I am sorry to inform your lordship that the aspect of affairs in this country is highly discouraging; the injudicious financial measures which count Wallis has thought proper to adopt have rendered it impossible for government to place the army on a respectable footing, and have considerably increased the discontent of the people, who however still retain their characteristic aversion to the French. The government is determined to maintain a strict neutrality during the approaching crisis if possible.

In my former letter I mentioned to your lordship my intention of establishing a person at Durazzo in order to forward messengers &c. &c. and to transmit to me occasionally intelligence of the state of things in the Adriatic. But having received of late repeated assurances of the increasing discontent of the inhabitants of those parts of the coast who have the misfortune to be under the dominion of the French, and of their willingness to make every effort to shake off the yoke, and being aware how important it is at the present moment not to neglect an object of this nature I have desired Mr. Johnson to proceed thither in order to form connexions in Albania, Dalmatia, and to avail himself in every possible manner of the spirit of discontent which has so decidedly manifested itself. Mr. Johnson who has been employed on the continent for some years past as an agent of government, and who has given proofs of his zeal and abilities, will repair to Durazzo, or according to circumstances to some other town in the neighbourhood of the Adriatic, and will there reside as agent of the British government. He will communicate his arrival to your lordship with as little delay as possible.

By the following piece of information, which I have derived from an authentic source, your lordship will perceive that the French and Swedish governments are far from being on friendly terms. An alliance has been proposed by the former to the latter and instantaneously rejected. The terms of the alliance were as follows, viz. 1st, a body of 30,000 Swedes to be placed at the disposal of France; 2nd. 3000 seamen to be furnished to the French marine; and 3rd, a regiment of Swedes to be raised for the service of France as was the case before the French revolution. I transmit this letter to your lordship by captain Steinberg and ensign Ferandi, two officers who have served creditably in the Austrian army. The former has connexions and local knowledge in his native country which may become particularly useful. I fear it will not be in my power to send 50 subaltern officers to Sicily, as your lordship desired. I shall however occasionally despatch some intelligent officers who will I think be extremely useful in the formation of new corps.

No. XVI.

Extracts from the correspondence of sir Henry Wellesley, sir Charles Stuart, and Mr. Vaughan.

Mr. Vaughan to sir Charles Stuart.

'*Cadiz, August 3rd,* 1813.

'The Spanish troops in Catalonia and elsewhere are starving, and the government are feeding them with proclamations to intendants. Since I have known Spain I have never known the seat of government in a worse state. There is a strong feeling against the English and a miserable jacobin party which is violent beyond measure.'

Ditto to Ditto.

'*Chichana, Nov. 2nd,* 1813.

'Never was anything so disgraceful in the annals of the world as the conduct of all the Spanish authorities on the occasion of the sickness breaking out. It is believed that no persons have the sickness twice, and as almost every family in Cadiz has passed the epidemic of the fever the interested merchants would not allow it to be said that the epidemic existed, they have continued to issue clean bills of health to vessels leaving the port in the height of the mortality, and did all they could to intimidate the government and Cortes into remaining amongst them.'

Sir Henry Wellesley to lord Wellington.

'*Sept. 13th,* 1813.

'A curious scene has been passing here lately. The permanent deputation[*] having been appointed, the Cortes closed their session the 14th. There had been for some days reports of the prevalence of the yellow fever which had excited alarm. On the 16th in the evening, I received an official note from the ministers of state apprising me of the intention of the government to proceed to Madrid on the following day, but without assigning any reason for so sudden a resolution. At night I went to the regency, thinking this was an occasion when it would be right to offer them some pecuniary assistance. I found Agar and Ciscar together, the cardinal being ill of the gout. They told me that the prevalence of the disorder was the sole cause of their determination to leave Cadiz; and Ciscar particularly dwelt upon the

---

[*] Called the Extraordinary Cortes.

necessity of removing, saying he had seen the fatal effects of delay at Carthagena. They then told me that there was disturbance in the town, in consequence of which they determined on summoning the extraordinary Cortes. I went from the regency to the Cortes. A motion was made for summoning the ministers to account for the proceedings of the regency. Never was I witness to so disgraceful a scene of lying and prevarication. The ministers insisted that it was not the intention of the regency to leave Cadiz until the Cortes had been consulted, although I had in my pocket the official note announcing their intention to do so, and had been told by Ciscar that the extraordinary Cortes was assembled for no other reason than because there were disturbances in the town.'

Sir Henry Wellesley to lord Wellington.

'*Cadiz, Dec. 10th*, 1813.

'The party for placing the princess at the head of the Spanish regency is gaining strength, and I should not be surprised if that measure were to be adopted soon after our arrival at Madrid, unless a peace and the return of Ferdinand should put an end to all such projects.'

Mr. Stuart to lord Wellington.

'*June 11th*, 1813.

'The repugnancy of the Admiralty to adopt the measures suggested by your lordship at the commencement of the American war for the protection of the coast, has been followed by events which have fully justified your opinion. *Fifteen merchantmen have been taken off Oporto in a fortnight, and a valuable Portuguese homeward-bound merchant ship was captured three days ago close to the bar of Lisbon.*'

No. XVII.

Extract from a manuscript memoir by captain Norton, thirty-fourth regiment.

COMBAT OF MAYA.

'The thirty-ninth regiment, commanded by the hon. col. O'Callaghan, then immediately engaged with the French, and after a severe contest also retired, the fiftieth was next in succession and they also after a gallant stand retired, making way for the ninesecond, which met the advancing French column first with its right wing drawn up in line, and after a most destructive fire and heavy loss on both sides the remnant of the right wing retired, leaving a line of killed and wounded that appeared to have no interval; the French column advanced up to this line and then halted, the killed and wounded of the ninety-second forming a sort of rampart, the left wing then opened its fire on the column, and as I was but a little to the right of the ninety-second I could not help reflecting painfully how many of the wounded of their right wing must have unavoidably suffered from the fire of their comrades. The left wing after doing good service and sustaining a loss equal to the first line retired.'

COMBAT OF RONCEVALLES.

Extracts from general Cole's and Marshal Soult's Official Reports, MSS.

General Cole to lord Wellington.

'*Heights in front of Pampeluna, July 27th,* 1813.
———— 'The enemy having in the course of the night turned those posts, were now perceived moving in very considerable force along the ridge leading to the Puerto de Mendichurri. I therefore proceeded in that direction and found that their advance had nearly reached the road leading from Roncesvalles pass to Los Alduides, from which it is separated by a small wooded valley. Owing to the difficulty of the communications the head of major-general Ross's brigade could not arrive there sooner; the major-general however, with great decision, attacked them with the Brunswick company and three companies of the twentieth, all he had time to form; these actually closed with the enemy and bayonetted several in the ranks. They were however forced to yield to superior numbers, and to retire across the valley; the enemy attempted to follow them, but were repulsed with loss, the remainder of the brigade having come up.'

Marshal Soult to the Minister of War.

'*Linzoin,* 26 *Juilliet,* 1813.
' Leurs pertes ont également été considérables, soit à l'attaque du Lindouz par le général Reille ou le 20ᵐᵉ regiment a été presque détruit à la suite d'une charge à la bayonette executée par un bataillon du 6ᵐᵒ leger, division Foy, soit à l'attaque d'Altobiscar par le général Clauzel.'

Extract from the correspondence of the duke of Dalmatia with the Minister of War.

'*Ascain,* 12 *Août,* 1813.
' Dès à présent V E. voit la situation de l'armée, elle connait ses forces, celles de l'ennemi, et elle se fait sans doute une idée de ses projets, et d'avance elle peut apprécier ce qu'il est en notre pouvoir de faire; je ne charge point le tableau, je dis ma pensée sans détour, et j'avoue que si l'ennemi emploie tous ses moyens, ainsi que probablement il le fera, ceux que nous pourrons en ce moment lui opposer étant de beaucoup inferieurs, nous ne pourrons pas empêcher qu'ils ne fasse beaucoup de mal. Mon devoir est de le dire à V. E. quoique je tienne une autre langage aux troupes et au pays, et que d'ailleurs je ne néglige aucun moyen pour remplir de mon mieux la tache qui m'est imposée.'

No. XVIII.

[This Appendix is referred to at page 180, as No. XIX.]

EXTRACTED FROM THE IMPERIAL MUSTER-ROLLS.

Report of the movements of the army of Aragon during the first fifteen days of September, 1813.

'Le 12ᵉᵐᵉ toute l'armée d'Aragon se réunit à Molino del Rey; une partie de celle de Catalogne et la garnison de Barcelonne se placent à droite à Ollessa et Martorel, pour partir tous ensembles, à 8 heures du soir et se porter la droite par San Sadurni, le reste par la grande route d'Ordal sur Villa Franca, où l'armée Anglaise était rassemblé. Général Harispe rencontre à onze heures du soir une forte avant-garde au Col d'Ordal *dans les anciens retranche-mens.* Un combat des plus vifs s'engagea sous les ordres du général de l'avant-garde Mesclop. Le 7ᵉᵐᵉ et 44ᵉᵐᵉ regⁿˢ mon-trerent une haute valeur, ainsi qu'une partie d'116ᵉᵐᵉ· Les posi-tions sont prises et reprises, et nous restent enfin, couverts de morts et de blessés Anglais. Dans la pursuite le 4ᵉᵐᵉ houssards se saisirent des 4 pièces de cannon Anglais, &c. avec trois ou quatre cents prisonniers, presque tous de la 27ᵉᵐᵉ regⁿ Anglais. La droite ayant rencontré des obstacles et quelques troupes enne-mis à combattre dans les passages, est retarde dans sa marche, et n'arriva pas avec le jour au rendezvous entre L'Ongat et Grénada. Un bataillon de 117ᵉᵐᵉ venant à gauche, par Bejas sur Avionet, rejoint l'armée en position, avec des prisonniers.

'Le maréchal Suchet directe un movement de cavalerie et d'artillerie qui tenaient la tête pour donner le tems à l'infanterie d'entrer en ligne. Les Anglais étaient en bataille sur trois lignes en avant de Villa Franca, ils commencerent aussitôt leur retraite en bon ordre. On les poursuivirent et on les harcelerent, la cavalerie fit plusieurs charges assez vives. Ils opposerent de la resistance, essuyerent des pertes, surtout en cavalerie, precipi-terent leur marche, brulerent un pont et s'éloignerent vers Arbos et Vendrils, laissant plus que 150 hommes pris et beaucoup de morts et de blessés, surtout des houssards de Brunswick. Nôtre avant garde va ce soir à Vendrils et plusieurs centaines de dé-serteurs sont ramassés.'